Glencoe

Oral Interpretation

Bringing Literature to Life Through Perfomance

Glencoe

Oral Interpretation

Bringing Literature to Life Through Perfomance

Teri Gamble • Michael Gamble

 **Glencoe McGraw-Hill**

New York, New York   Columbus, Ohio   Chicago, Illinois   Peoria, Illinois   Woodland Hills, California

CONTENTS

how old do
you
think
he is?

In *Oral Interpretation* you will explore the art of performing literature. As you develop the physical and mental resources necessary for performing literature, you will come to know that analyzing a poem, prose, or drama selection and sharing your interpretation of it with others can be a rewarding experience—both for you and your audience. As you journey into different literary worlds, you will find a unique meeting of yourself and literature through oral interpretation, as well as the realization that you can affect others with your performance.

Oral Interpretation is carefully structured to help you develop oral interpretation skills. In Part One you will focus on how to effectively use your body, voice, and all your senses in the oral interpretation process. In Part Two you will journey into the special worlds of narrative and descriptive prose, drama, and poetry, discovering the varying aspects of those literary genres in performance. In Part Three you will go beyond those worlds to chapters on documentary material as fuel for interpretation, performing literature for children, ensemble or group approaches to interpretation, making connections to another culture's literature, and planning special programs.

Each of the twelve chapters in *Oral Intepretation* contains a number of activities, as well as a wide range of literary selections—cuttings and complete works. The **Performer's Warm-up** exercises will help you loosen up your body, your voice, and your mind to get you into the more physical aspects of interpreting literature. The **Performer's Workshop** activities invite you to practice the various aspects of interpretation, using a wide range of readings. Following these readings, the **Questions** urge you to think about and discuss your experiences with the oral interpretation process and the literary selection at hand. These exercises do get you involved, and they are fun as well as challenging. Approach each of the exercises with an open mind and a willingness to participate. As you move through each chapter, you will find that you can apply what you have learned in one exercise to what you are working on in another.

At the end of each chapter is a section entitled **Performance Applications.** The activities in this section will give you opportunities to synthesize and apply what you have learned throughout the chapter. The **Idea Encore** help you to synthesize the ideas presented in the chapter as an introduction to the exercises that follow. The **Performer's Showcase & Journal** exercises will encourage you to analyze and evaluate your interpretations—your performances—of literary selections through the keeping of a journal or notebook. Using a journal will allow you to chart your personal growth as a performer and your interpretations of literature as you progress through *Oral Interpretation*. These exercises will often ask you to prepare a selection for performance as well. The **Selections for Further Work** following the Performer's Showcase & Journal offer a selection of literary readings with which to practice, or you may find your own piece to interpret for the showcase.

Enjoy the journey as you learn how to make literature come alive through performance!

PART 1

Making Literature Come Alive: The Performer's Resources

Chapter  1

Introducing the Interpretation of Literature: Awakening and Contacting Your Body

Learning Objectives

After completing this chapter, you should be able to

- define "interpretation of literature"
- describe the role the performer plays in interpreting literature
- explain how the interpreter benefits from performing literature
- explain how audience members benefit from literature in performance
- describe how empathy facilitates the interpretation and peformance of texts
- use your body to facilitate both the interpretation and performance of literature

Literature and Interpretation

These two words—*literature* and *interpretation*—are key words in our study of the communicative, expressive, and performance art of oral interpretation. The oral interpreter is an artist whose task is to personally experience and breathe new life into literature. While the author of the literature is a creative artist who chooses to use specific words, sounds, and rhythms and endows these words, sounds, and rhythms with a sense of order or structure, the interpreter is also a creative artist, or more precisely, a re-creative artist who takes what an author has provided and transforms it by translating that human experience into a new artistic product—a text in performance.

Effective interpreters of literature are performers of literature. In fact, interpreters use performances to study texts. Thus, instead of writing papers about what they have read, interpreters share their critical analysis of texts through their performances. As a result, during a performance a part of the interpreter becomes a part of the work. The performance illustrates how the interpreter makes meaning with the text.

As a performer, your challenge is to transform the written words of literature or a text into animated words. As an oral interpreter, your responsibility is to make the words of a text live; your task is to breathe energy into each page of a selected script. How can you meet these responsibilities? How can you make the written words of a literary selection or other text come alive for your audience?

What Is Interpretation?

Oral interpretation is not only a communication art, it is also a performing art. From the performer's perspective, it is the meeting of self and text through performance. From the audience member's perspective, it is the observing, listening to, absorbing, and being touched and engaged by the performance of that text. By first studying and internalizing the language used in both literary and nonliterary works, we process our ideas and feelings and come to understand our relationship to a particular text. By then taking on the voice and body of that text and performing that text, we more fully meet and explore the text—have what might even be called a profound encounter with it—and we ultimately share the understanding or personal vision that results with audience members.

Forms of Interpretation

Interpreters have a virtually unlimited range of material from which to choose. Consequently, today's interpreters need to familiarize themselves with a wide array of texts. A text is any symbolic material that conveys meaning to a viewer or reader. Thus, novels, short stories, poems, plays, essays, diaries, letters, speeches, news and feature articles, interviews, oral histories, personal narratives, advertisements, commercials, songs, billboards, conversations, and graffiti are all texts—all potential resources and fuel for the interpreter.

When interpreting a text, the role of the interpreter is somewhat different from the role of other performers such as actors or public speakers. Interpreters of literature are not actors. Neither are they public speakers. Rather, interpreters merge elements of acting and public speaking into a new and exciting amalgam. Like the actor, the interpreter uses his or her voice and body as tools; like the public speaker, the interpreter stands before an audience. Like the actor, the interpreter projects his or her understanding of a work to the audience; like the public speaker, the interpreter addresses the audience directly. Unlike the actor, however, the interpreter employs an economy of movement and action; and unlike the public speaker, the interpreter does not deliver his or her ideas extemporaneously, but rather delivery is typically tied to the specific words contained in the text being interpreted. While the actor usually plays only one role in each performance, the interpreter may assume a number of different roles. While the public speaker conveys his or her own thoughts and feelings, the interpreter usually conveys the thoughts and feelings of a person other than him- or herself. While the actor usually relies on costumes, makeup, and scenery to create and sustain the illusion of reality for audience members, the interpreter relies on his or her own abilities to spark the imaginations of receivers. While the public speaker communicates his or her own identity when speaking, the oral interpreter usually suggests the character of someone other than him- or herself to receivers. Thus, while they share some things in common with actors and public speakers, interpreters bring unique qualities and characteristics to their task of giving new life to the words of texts.

Preparing to Be an Interpreter: Awakening Your Body

First, think about the characteristics that all living things share. What does it mean to be alive, to be animate? Animate or living organisms are vital, functional, and flexible. Unlike dead organisms, living organisms are always in a state of activity. If you hope to share a literary selection successfully—if you hope to make the words live for your audience—then you should be able to convey the sense of activity or movement that you discover within that selection.

Doing so, however, is not as simple or straightforward as you might think. In order to find and activate movement, you first have to be able to use your whole body to understand and interpret the literature. In other words, you have to embody the literature. This means you must use your body to help you express the experiences literature contains. Keep in mind that using your body will help you to communicate the emotional and intellectual meanings of your work through performance. You can prepare your body for this by helping it be fully aware and elastic. This section will examine some of the techniques you can use in order to ready your body for this effort.

Body Language and Literature in Performance

As a serious interpreter, you will be interested in work done recently in **kinesics,** or body language. Kinesiologists, those who study visible body behavior, regard the entire visible body as potentially communicative. Included under the general category of kinesics are the subcategories of posture and stance, muscle tension and gestures, facial expressions, and eye contact. These modes of behavior have long been recognized as carrying, clarifying, or enhancing meaning in performance situations. Indeed, the body of a performer or interpreter of literature is an essential part of that person's communication resource system. Effective interpreters speak not only with their voices but with their faces, their necks, their shoulders, their torsos, their arms, and their legs as well. Effective interpretations are not simply performances from the neck up. The entire body supports the dynamic experience of reading literature aloud.

How can you prepare your body to explore and communicate literature? Begin with a few body warm-ups. After all, a communicative body is an expressive body, and an expressive body is agile and aware. The following exercise should help you to physically experience, internalize, and perform literature. You should use it to approach a literary selection with your whole being.

PERFORMER'S WARM-UP
The Body Machine

This exercise will help you awaken and loosen the expressive parts of your body. The goal is to discover all the different body parts you can move separately, then in various combinations. As a partner or your instructor calls out a particular body part, begin to move and exercise to the music or beat provided.

A. First, fingers. Move every joint on both hands. Now, shake your wrists. Turn them in circles. Next, band your elbows. How many ways can you move your forearms? Concentrate on your shoulders; swing your arms in circles above your head.

Now, experience silence and stillness. Feel your body at rest. Let your neck stretch upward toward the ceiling. Slowly, let it fall smoothly forward, until the tip of your chin touches your chest. Be careful not to force it. Next, slowly circle your head.

Now concentrate on your face. Exercise your facial muscles. Bat your eyelashes; pretend to chew a huge piece of gum; contort your face. How many masks can you make with your face? Now let your face relax.

Bend at your waist and at your knees. Let yourself sway from side to side. Straighten now and stand on one leg, taking care to keep your balance. Focus on your free leg; bend it at the knee; turn it at your ankle; let your toes wriggle. Now repeat this sequence using your other leg as the free leg. Finally, with both feet on the floor, move your legs together as the beat or music suggests.

B. Let's complicate the exercise a bit. Repeat the above sequence, only this time, after you start to move a body part, try not to let it stop moving. Think of your body as a perpetual-motion machine—a machine that will not stop until it is told to do so.

Move your fingers.
Add your wrists, but keep your fingers moving.
Add your elbows; watch your fingers and wrists move.
Add your shoulders—really swing your arms.
Stretch your neck.
Keep the other parts of your body moving and "start up" your face.
Add your legs, one at a time.
Add your ankles. Are your fingers still moving?
Finally, add your toes.

C. When your partner or instructor claps his or her hands twice, freeze in whatever position you find yourself. At the command "go," start everything moving again, all at once. Be sure to listen carefully to the leader's signals.

Now, on the basis of the experiences you have had in this exercise, answer the following questions.

Questions

1. How does your body feel now?
2. What clues do you have that your body can really work?

The preceding preliminary exercise should serve to awaken your body. Do understand, however, that the goal of this activity is not simply to provide your body with physical stimulation. A flexible and energetic body is your starting point, but it is not your ultimate goal. As a performer you want to be able to harness all the energy your body possesses. You want to make your body's energy work for you.

The Text Is the Conductor

As an interpreter, you want to be able to control your body's energy output effectively and efficiently. The type of energy expenditure you experienced in the preceding exercise was, in fact, quite different from the type of energy expenditures you will experience in performance situations. Why? Because the amount of energy you expend in performing will be directly related to the content of your selection, your space limitations, and your ability to empathize or feel with and for characters in literature. When interpreting a selection, your body is the "machine" and the literature is the "conductor"; in other words, the text fuels your machine—specifically, with the feelings, experiences, and attitudes that are the heart of the selection. In order to share the literature with your audience, your body needs to call on many of its expressive agents for help.

Your instructor will provide you with two envelopes, one labeled "Emotion" and the other labeled "Body Part." Class members will draw a slip of paper from each envelope and attempt to express the named emotion using the named body part.

The following feelings are listed on slips in the Emotion envelope: happiness, sadness, jealousy, pride, sympathy, anger, hope, hatred, greed, scorn. On the slips in the Body Parts envelope are listed the following: left arm, right arm, back, torso, face, whole body.

When it is your turn, name the part of the body on which your fellow students should focus their attention, and they will attempt to identify the emotion you are "physicalizing."

Now, on the basis of your experiences during this exercise, answer these questions:

Questions

1. Which emotions were easiest for you to portray? Which emotions posed a greater challenge to convey?
2. Is it possible for you to isolate one part of your body and allow it to speak?
3. Which parts of your body were more communicative than others? Why?
4. Do you need your whole body to help you communicate or interpret literature?

Physicalizing Metaphors

A metaphor is a figure of speech—an imaginative or unimaginative comparison that suggests that two unlike things resemble each other. For example, when we say that "love is a thorn," we are suggesting that love can be hurtful. When author Virginia Woolf wrote that "Anonymous was a woman," she was suggesting something about the nature of womanhood. With a metaphor, we announce our attitude toward a subject.

When we meet a text, the feelings and emotions we experience are closely linked with the behavior of our bodies. In fact, emotional state or attitude is often described in terms of body parts or body movements. Think about the following metaphors or figures of speech often used in daily conversations to describe behavior:

hair-raising
grit your teeth
pain in the neck
butterflies in your stomach
heart in your throat
white with fear
red with rage
frozen with terror
stiff upper lip
watery knees
under your skin
a cold shoulder
itching to do it
a bleeding heart
a heart of stone
an upstanding person
on your toes
thumbs down
turn your nose up
swallow your tongue

These idiomatic or metaphorical expressions support the fact that your body reflects your emotions or your attitudes. Your body can indicate your moods and your feelings. In fact, as your state of being changes, the parts of your body serve to mirror this difference. A change in posture, gesture, facial expression, or general body tone usually indicates a corresponding change in emotional state.

PERFORMER'S WARM-UP
Body Metaphors

Choose one of the metaphors mentioned above to portray to your class. On the basis of your performance, your fellow students will attempt to determine the expression you are embodying. After you perform and observe others' performances, answer the following questions.

Questions

1. What metaphors were most easily shared with the audience? Why?
2. Which metaphors posed the most difficulty? Why?

PERFORMER'S WARM-UP
Body Walks

Portray one of the following feelings while crossing from the left side to the right side of your classroom: happiness, sadness, jealousy, sympathy, outrage, warmth, coldness, arrogance, timidity. Then answer the following questions.

Questions

1. What happened to your posture as you expressed the particular feeling?
2. What type of path did you map out for yourself?
3. At what rate did you move?
4. How heavy were your steps?
5. What gestures did you use to support the feeling you portrayed?
6. What did your face say?
7. How would you describe the general tone of your body?

Gestures, Posture, Facial Expressions, and Body Tone

The wink of the performer's eye. The tightness in her muscles. The slyness of his smile. The confidence in her posture. The limpness of his body. The eagerness in her face. Each of these nonverbal cues contains clues regarding the attitudes, feelings, and ideas being communicated during an interpretation performance. While we are often unaware of the messages we send with our bodies, performers can afford no such lack of awareness.

As performers of literature, we become part of the message. When we perform, it is no longer just the words that comprise the message we send to our audience. We use a kaleidoscope of bodily cues to help make the text come alive. We might say that during a performance our entire body speaks constantly, revealing to receivers the true meaning of the words we are reading. The goal of the performer is to carefully consider how the actions of the body—gestures, posture, facial expressions, and body tone—can help reinforce the messages communicated through a piece of literature. Let us explore each in turn.

Gestures

Gestures are critical to communication. They are motions of your limbs or body you use to help you express or accentuate an idea. Mood values are inherent in certain gestures. For example, with your arms you can indicate approach or invitation, love or protection, avoidance or anger, jealousy or envy, nervousness or tension, comfort or relaxation. Even the absence of specific gestural signals may serve to enhance your communication effectiveness. Be certain, however, that you neither overuse nor extensively repeat certain gestures, unless your literary script specifically calls for such behavior. The gestures you employ should always reinforce your material; they should grow out of your response to your material. Understand that gestures are not used to call attention to an interpreter; rather, they are used to help an interpreter's audience concentrate on the performance of a piece of literature. Consequently, gestures need to be appropriate to the total effect an interpreter seeks to make.

Observe an ordinary conversation between two people. Notice how they smile; how they jump up and down; how they shake or nod their heads; lift, lower, or shrug their shoulders; manifest excitement or sadness; and in general use their hands, arms, torso, and legs as they interact with each other. They actively participate. As you read a text, you, too, need to actively participate. Part of your job as you read is to consider what a text's words suggest to you about the use of gestures during performance. Your incorporation of an effective gesture can speak volumes to receivers. What movement might you use to express or emphasize the idea being communicated or the emotional response called for? How can you, for example, use hand and arm movements to enrich the text's meaning and convey the emotional tone of the piece?

Posture

When performing, your posture probably serves to reinforce the feeling you choose to portray. **Posture** may be defined as the alignment of your body parts. The way you stand or sit helps to reveal to your audience an emotional or physical state of being. Body posture communicates everything from contentment and confidence to worry and discouragement. Your posture signals your intent to approach and meet the world or your wish to avoid and withdraw from it. Remember, you will add definition to your performance as an interpreter simply by the nature of your posture. The way you hold yourself when sitting or standing is a nonverbal broadcast giving receivers the information they need to assess the text's meaning.

Researchers suggest that the bearing one presents suggests one's position in life. This is supported by television and film offerings which frequently contrast the upright bearing of a wealthy person with the submissive shuffle of a servant or the slumped demeanor of a "nobody." When assuming an inferior role, people often lower their heads. In contrast, when they assume a superior role, they raise their heads. Stooped shoulders can indicate you are heavily burdened or submissive; raised shoulders suggest that you are under a great deal of stress. To Americans, square shoulders suggest strength.

Another aspect of posture is the way you lean, or orient yourself when performing. We usually associate liking and other positive attitudes with leaning forward, not withdrawing. The point is that body posture talks. The messages you send with your posture reflect whether you are feeling content and confident, angry and belligerent, or worried and discouraged.

PERFORMER'S WARM-UP
Posture Poses

Try on various postures and see what you feel like in each. How does each posture affect your emotional state?

First, walk around the room in a stooped posture. Next, walk around the room with your shoulders raised and your head and neck taut. Finally, walk around the room with squared shoulders.

Questions

1. What phrases would you use to describe how you felt when carrying yourself with a stooped posture?
2. What phrases would you use to describe how you felt when exhibiting raised shoulders?
3. Compare and contrast how you felt while displaying a square-shouldered posture with the way you felt when displaying the previous postures.

Facial Expression

Picture this. You play tennis. You suffered a serious injury and had an MRI. You are meeting with your doctor to discuss your treatment and prognosis for a full recovery. You search the doctor's face looking for cues.

Just as you search the faces of the people with whom you interact, so your audience will search your face. In addition to gestures and posture, the face is also rich in communicative potential. The face is the main channel we use to communicate emotion and to analyze the feelings and sentiments of others. We rely on the face to reinforce or contradict what is being spoken. The face broadcasts inner feelings and emotions. Facial expressions help you indicate to others the impact upon you that certain experiences or feelings have.

Truly remarkable qualities of the human face are its mobility and its elasticity. If used effectively, your **face-work** can provide a direct physical counterpart to the actions, feelings, or emotions expressed in your selection. For example, if you raise your eyebrows, what emotion are you showing? Surprise is probably most common, but fear is also expressed by raised eyebrows. The brows help convey other emotions as well. Move your brows into as many configurations as you can. With each movement, analyze your emotional response, and you'll have a feel for what the brows can communicate. Your forehead also helps convey both physical and emotional state. A furrowed brow, for example, suggests tension, worry, or deep thought.

Your eyes also add to your expressiveness. We have a number of expressions that speak to the communicative power of the eyes: "shifty eyes," "the look of love," and "the evil eye" are just a few. A downward glance can suggest modesty. Staring may suggest coldness; wide eyes may suggest wonder, naiveté, or fright. Excessive blinking may suggest nervousness or insecurity.

Like the eyes, the lower facial area also communicates. For example, some faces lack a smile and have a neutral expression. Others display a frown, a snarl, or different kinds of smiles. What is important is that you work to match your facial expressions to the meanings inherent in the text you are interpreting.

Body Tone

Your general **body tone**—your overall degree of body tension or relaxation—should also be affected by the nature of your selection and by your performance goals. Your body might be compared to a rubber band. Sometimes nerves are stretched, causing muscles to tense and tighten, veins to constrict, blood pressure to rise, and the heart to race. At other times nerves are eased, so muscles relax, veins dilate, joints become more flexible, head and neck rest comfortably on the shoulders, and swallowing becomes easier. An interpreter needs to realize that body tension and relaxation are not separate, unrelated states. They are, in fact, opposite points on a continuum. The body can be stretched taut and the body can be at ease. It is important, however, to know how to discover and manifest the amount of body tension appropriate to a reading. With this in mind, during rehearsal periods you should experiment with various degrees of movement, continuing to make adjustments during the course of a single selection, passage, sentence, or phrase.

At this point, we want to emphasize that your body is not simply a collection of parts working independently. Instead, it works as a synchronized whole. Though it is helpful for our purposes to examine it part by part as we consider the body's communication potential, bear in mind it is the movements of the entire body that help to interpret literature and to enrich a performance.

Before you try to apply what you have learned about body expressiveness to specific literary selections, try the following exercises.

PERFORMER'S WARM-UP
Texture Movement

You are walking in space. What happens to your body? You are slogging through sticky taffy. How do your movement capabilities change? Now you are slipping on a floor slick with grease. How will you adapt your movements to this slithery situation? Finally, your sneakers are sinking into foam rubber. How does your body react?

PERFORMER'S WARM-UP
Move to the Music

Your instructor will play some musical selections that vary in rhythm, volume, and tone. Working alone or with a group, react with your body to each of the pieces of music. Then answer the following questions.

Questions

1. How did the selection make you feel?
2. How did you choose to move to it?
3. Did your way of moving change during the course of a single selection? Why?

Your physical responses probably changed in the first exercise as the texture of the atmosphere changed and in the second exercise as the tempo and tone of the music changed. In effect, you reacted to the **moods** or "feeling-tones" ingrained in each of the atmospheric textures and musical compositions.

Like the atmosphere and like music, literature also affects your whole body. You can use your whole body to respond to the mood changes of a literary selection. Tuning into music is enjoyable and fulfilling, and so is tuning into literature.

PERFORMER'S WORKSHOP
Miming the Text I

Either your instructor or a student will read Lawrence Ferlinghetti's "Constantly Risking Absurdity" aloud. This selection depends on the suggestion of movement for its effect. As the poem is read aloud, class members should mime the movements it suggests.

"Constantly Risking Absurdity"
Lawrence Ferlinghetti

Constantly risking absurdity and death
whenever he performs
above the heads
of his audience

Gestures, Posture, Facial Expressions, and Body Tone

the poet like an acrobat
                climbs on rime
                        to a high wire of his own making
and balancing on eyebeams
                above a sea of faces
        paces his way
                to the other side of day
performing entrechats
                and sleight-of-foot tricks
and other high theatrics
                and all without mistaking
        any thing
                for what it may not be

        For he's the super realist
                        who must perforce perceive
        taut truth
                        before the taking of each stance or step
in his supposed advance
                        toward that still higher perch
where Beauty stands and waits
                        with gravity
                                to start her death-defying leap

        And he
                a little charley chaplin man
                        who may or may not catch
                her fair eternal form
                        spreadeagled in the empty air
                of existence

Questions

1. What kinds of movements did you use to reinforce the ideas in the piece?
2. How did the amount or kind of movement you mimed change as the reader progressed?
3. How did the action of your own body help you to appreciate the poem?

Continue to experiment with body movements by performing the following short segment from "Shiloh" by Bobbie Ann Mason.

"Shiloh"

Bobbie Ann Mason

Leroy Moffitt's wife, Norma Jean, is working on her pectorals. She lifts three-pound dumbbells to warm up, then progresses to a twenty-pound barbell. Standing with her legs apart, she reminds Leroy of Wonder Woman.

"I'd give anything if I could just get these muscles to where they're real hard," says Norma Jean. "Feel this arm. It's not as hard as the other one."

"That's 'cause you're right-handed," says Leroy, dodging as she swings the barbell in an arc.

"Do you think so?"

"Sure."

Questions

1. What should the interpreter do to suggest the use of barbells?
2. What actions can the interpreter use to differentiate between difficult and effortless movements?

The Mind-Body Connection

The mind and the body work together. Our physical responses make our mental and emotional reactions vivid and intense. Our thoughts affect us, and the effects of our ruminations are visible. We externalize what we feel internally. In this way, the mind and the body are inextricably linked.

Relax and close your mind to your immediate surroundings and all of your daily concerns. This is your chance to let your mind and your body rest—

to let them ease into contentment. Feel your toes and your legs relax; let your arms go limp; breathe deeply.

Now, think about feeling pain. Think of pain as an extension of the sense of touch. Concentrate on the particular set of circumstances that originally caused you to experience intense physical pain. Recall the conditions that made you feel the pain. Was it a fire? Was it an illness? A wound? Get in touch with the pain once again. Let your body react to the discomfort you are reexperiencing. Respond with your face, your back, your muscles. Close your eyes and let your entire body process this pain.

Questions

1. What type of pain did you imagine?
2. What happened to your body as in your mind you re-created this pain? Be as specific as possible in describing the physical sensations you just experienced. For example, how did the calves of your legs feel? What did you do with your arms? How was your muscle tone affected?
3. Why do you think you needed to use your body in order to really "remember" your pain?

By developing a sense memory you can use it later. Once you have experienced it and recall that experience, you can re-create it in your imagination and externalize it through performance. Interpreters are often called upon to re-create an impression, feeling, or experience in order to share it with audience members during performance. Sharing these images involves the externalization or projection of the experience; this process is also referred to as **sensory showing.** During this process the feelings in your mind are reconstructed and projected or made physical, visible, and audible for audience members.

The exercises that follow give you the opportunity to externalize your understanding of what you have learned to this point. As you approach them, try to participate physically in the words of the printed page. Feel the words—don't just see them. If you succeed in doing this, you and your receivers will both develop a more complete understanding of the texts you share.

PERFORMER'S WORKSHOP
Building on Experience

Read aloud to a group the following passage from "Flight" by John Steinbeck. In this passage Pepe is suffering from a wound that has become grossly infected. He has no choice but to treat it himself.

When the dawn came, Pepe pulled himself up. His eyes were sane again. He drew his great puffed arm in front of him and looked at the angry wound. The black line ran up from his wrist to his armpit. Automatically he reached in his pocket for his big black knife, but it was not there. His eyes searched the ground. He picked up a sharp blade of stone and scraped at the wound, sawed at the proud flesh and then squeezed the green juice out in big drops. Instantly he threw back his head and whined like a dog. His whole right side shuddered at the pain, but the pain cleared his head.

Questions

1. What happened to your muscle tension as you read?
2. What happened to the muscle tone of your audience?
3. How, if at all, did your posture change? Did your audience reflect or react to this change?
4. What gestures did you use to reinforce meaning? What did these gestures communicate to the audience?

PERFORMER'S WORKSHOP
Eye-Openers

A. Your instructor or a partner will lead you in the next "eye-opening" exercise. First, close your eyes and relax as you clear your mind of all extraneous thoughts. When you open your eyes, "see" an imaginary caterpillar clinging to the palm of your left hand. Study the caterpillar. What does it look like? How does it feel to have a caterpillar crawling on your palm? Watch the caterpillar crawl off your hand and close your eyes again.

B. Open your eyes. This time, notice that a butterfly has just landed on your hand. Examine the patterns and colors of its wings. Touch it gently with your free hand. Watch it as it flies away. Use your face to reflect your feelings. Close your eyes again.

C. Now you are enclosed in a very small space from which you cannot escape. You try, but you cannot raise your hands or your head more than six inches. As you lie flat on your back, you begin to have trouble breathing. How else is your body responding to being confined? Process the experience through each of your nerve centers.

The following passage builds on the prior sensory-revealing experiences. It focuses on a nightmarish situation in which the speaker wakes to find that he has been buried in a sealed coffin. Read aloud the excerpt from "The Premature Burial" by Edgar Allan Poe.

from "The Premature Burial"
Edgar Allan Poe

I remained without motion . . . I could not summon courage to move. I dared not make the effort which was to satisfy me of my fate—and yet there was something at my heart which whispered to me it was true. Despair—such as no other species of wretchedness ever calls into being—despair alone urged me, after long irresolution, to uplift the heavy lids of my eyes. I uplifted them. It was dark—all dark. I knew that the fit was over. I knew that the crisis of my disorder had long passed. I knew that I had now fully recovered the use of my visual faculties—and yet it was dark—all dark—the intense and utter raylessness of the Night that endureth for evermore.

I endeavored to shriek; and my lips and my parched tongue moved convulsively together in the attempt—but no voice issued from the cavernous lungs, which, oppressed as if by the weight of some incumbent mountain, gasped and palpitated, with the heart, at every elaborate and struggling inspiration.

The movement of the jaws, in this effort to cry aloud, showed me that they were bound up, as is usual with the dead. I felt, too, that I lay upon some hard substance; and by something similar my sides were, also, closely compressed. So far, I had not ventured to stir any of my limbs—but now I violently threw up my arms, which had been lying at length with the wrists crossed. They struck a solid wooden substance, which extended above my person at an elevation of not more than six inches from my face. I could no longer doubt that I reposed within a coffin at last. . . .

As this awful conviction forced itself, thus, into the innermost chambers of my soul, I once again struggled to cry aloud. And in this second endeavor I succeeded. A long, wild, and continuous shriek, or yell, of agony resounded through the realms of the subterrene Night.

Questions

1. How can your body help you to experience this selection imaginatively?
2. Is it necessary to lie down in order to present this passage effectively?
3. What body movements can you use instead of lying down?

Your body helps you to sense all the experiences described in a selection of literature. It helps you to feel yourself move into a selection or to project yourself imaginatively into the world of the selection. In other words, your body helps you to feel with or **empathize** with the persons and the things that inhabit the piece of literature you wish to interpret. It helps you to relate actively to the thoughts, emotions, and attitudes described. It also helps you to share these same thoughts, emotions, and attitudes with your audience.

Empathy: Understanding and Sharing Feelings

Empathy means the ability to project yourself intellectually and emotionally into the experiences of another, so that you actually experience the feelings, thoughts, responses, and attitudes of that person. It comes from the Greek word *empatheia*, which is a combination of *en* (meaning "in" or "into") and *pathos* (meaning "feeling"). It is this "feeling into," this imaginative projecting and identification, that is at the core of the interpreter's art. It is also a part of our daily lives.

Think of a situation during which you felt you had engaged in empathy. What feelings did you share? Why did you think you empathized? For empathy to have occurred, you need to have understood and shared another's feelings. You need to have established an emotional connection. When this happens you even share physiological responses. You may share smiles, tears, and pain. For example, have you ever sat watching a movie as one character yelled at another character and you felt your body tense in response? Have you sat at a baseball game and strained with the batter in an effort to hit that home run? Have you sat with a friend who has just suffered a loss and, as you feel with this person, bent your body as if to envelop his or her grief? If you have done any of these, then you have been fully engaged by another's experience. In effect, you have become an integral participant in that experience—you have "felt into" the experience of that person and duplicated what he or she felt.

With your performance, you can help your receivers accomplish the same kind of empathic exchange. You can identify completely with and embody the feelings of the speaker or characters in a selection. Your performance can enable audience members to "feel into" the text you are sharing. They will then transmit that feeling back to you. In effect, empathy works for the interpreter in three separate stages: from the literature to the interpreter; from the interpreter to the audience; from the audience back to the interpreter.

As you read, you relate to a text actively. When this activity is transferred to your receivers, they will probably unconsciously imitate your physical movement. Just as you tend to smile when you see a baby smile at his or her mother, to look up when you notice other people looking up, to clench your fists when one boxer punches another boxer, to stretch your neck when number nineteen aims for the basket, to mimic your friend's facial expression when telling a joke or relating a sad tale, and to imitate a monkey's movements as you watch it swing in a cage at the zoo, so your audience tends to respond physically to your performance. The audience will imitate your muscle tone and unconsciously mimic your facial expressions. If your performance is successful, you will find that your audience will duplicate the tensions, the emotions, and the general behavioral cues or motor adjustments that you externalize for them. They then will send back to you an empathic response that completes the cycle.

Thus, empathy functions to guide your audience's responses to you. There is, consequently, a give-and-take relationship established between your selection, yourself, and your audience. Your entire body mirrors your thoughts and feelings, and your audience mirrors you. You promote your audience's reaction, and they feed it back to you.

Chapter 1 Performance Applications

IDEA ENCORE

Interpretation is a communicative and expressive performance art. The interpreter is both a critic and a performer, a public presenter and an actor. The task of the interpreter is to take the words and images of a text and transform them into an animated work—that is, a text in performance.

You may have begun your study of interpretation with the understanding that this course would require you to analyze literature and read it aloud. Now that you have had the opportunity to work your way through this chapter, you should realize that this course is far more than a course in reading literature aloud or analyzing texts. Instead, it is a course in how to become part of a text and how to make the words and images of a text come alive for an audience.

Interpreters today choose the materials for their performances from a wide array of traditional and nontraditional texts. To perform a text the interpreter relies on both voice and body to convey meaning. By harnessing his or her kinesic resources, the interpreter is able to incorporate those gestures, postures, facial expressions, and movements to support interpretive performances. In effect, the performer's mind and body work together. The performer also uses his or her body to develop the empathy needed to enter the world developed in a text, and then re-create it during performance.

PERFORMER'S SHOWCASE & JOURNAL
The Body and Performance

It is now time to use the following end-of-chapter selections or other selections of your or your instructor's choosing to illustrate what you have learned about your body's expressive qualities. As you prepare to perform, assess the degree of body tension, gesture, and movement that each passage requires. Remember to let your muscles respond completely as you perform or interpret each piece of literature. For each selection, be prepared to answer the following questions in your performer's journal. The journal is a notebook in which you keep performer's notes—understandings you gain as a result of experiencing, analyzing, and interpreting a text.

Questions

1. How did you use your body to reinforce the emotional and intellectual content of the material?
2. At which points in the selection did your muscle tone change? Why?

SELECTIONS FOR FURTHER WORK

In this excerpt from Ernest Hemingway's *The Old Man and the Sea*, we meet Santiago, an elderly man who has spent his life waging a constant tug-of-war with the sea.

 The Old Man and the Sea

Ernest Hemingway

When the old man saw him coming he knew that this was a shark that had no fear at all and would do exactly what he wished. He prepared the harpoon and made the rope fast while he watched the shark come on. The rope was short as it lacked what he had cut away to lash the fish.

The old man's head was clear and good now and he was full of resolution but he had little hope. It was too good to last, he thought. He took one look at the great fish as he watched the shark close in. It might as well have been a dream, he thought. I cannot keep him from hitting me but maybe I can get him. Dentuso, he thought. Bad luck to your mother.

The shark closed fast astern and when he hit the fish the old man saw his mouth open and his strange eyes and the clicking chop of the teeth as he drove forward in the meat just above the tail. The shark's head was out of water and his back was coming out and the old man could hear the noise of skin and flesh ripping on the big fish when he rammed the harpoon down onto the shark's head at a spot where the line between his eyes intersected with the line that ran straight back from his nose. There were no such lines. There was only the heavy sharp blue head and the big eyes and the clicking, thrusting all-swallowing jaws. But that was the location of the brain and the old man hit it. He hit it with his blood mushed hands driving a good harpoon with all his strength. He hit it without hope but with resolution and complete malignancy.

The shark swung over and the old man saw his eye was not alive and then he swung over once again, wrapping himself in two loops of the rope. The old man knew that he was dead but the shark would not accept it. Then, on his back with his tail lashing and his jaws clicking, the shark plowed over the water as a speed-boat does. The water was white where his tail beat it and three-quarters of his body was clear above the water when the rope came taut, shivered, and then snapped. The shark lay quietly for a little while on the surface and the old man watched him. Then he went down very slowly.

In her powerful selection "For My People," African American poet Margaret Walker recounts the long struggle for freedom experienced by her people, calls for peace among humans, and asks that strength and healing lead the way into the future.

"For My People"
Margaret Walker

For my people everywhere singing their slave songs repeatedly:
    their dirges and their ditties and their blues and jubilees,
    praying their prayers nightly to an unknown god, bending
    their knees humbly to an unseen power;

For my people lending their strength to the years, to the gone years and the now years and the maybe years, washing ironing cooking scrubbing sewing mending hoeing plowing digging planting pruning patching dragging along never gaining never reaping never knowing and never understanding;

For my playmates in the clay and dust and sand of Alabama backyards playing baptizing and preaching and doctor and jail and soldier and school and mama and cooking and playhouse and concert and store and hair and Miss Choomby and company;

For the cramped bewildered years we went to school to learn to know the reasons why and the answers to and the people who and the places where and the days when, in memory of the bitter hours when we discovered we were black and poor and small and different and nobody cared and nobody wondered and nobody understood;

For the boys and girls who grew in spite of these things to be man and woman, to laugh and dance and sing and play and drink their wine and religion and success, to marry their playmates and bear children and then die of consumption and anemia and lynching;

For my people thronging 47th Street in Chicago and Lenox Avenue in New York and Rampart Street in New Orleans, lost disinherited dispossessed and happy people filling the cabarets and taverns and other people's pockets needing bread and shoes and milk and land and money and something—something all our own;

For my people walking blindly spreading joy, losing time being lazy, sleeping when hungry, shouting when burdened, drinking when hopeless, tied, and shackled and tangled among ourselves by the unseen creatures who tower over us omnisciently and laugh;

For my people blundering and groping and floundering in the dark of churches and schools and clubs and societies, associations and councils and committees and conventions, distressed and disturbed and deceived and devoured by money-hungry glory-craving leeches, preyed on by facile force of state and fad and novelty, by false prophet and holy believer;

For my people standing staring trying to fashion a better way from confusion, from hypocrisy and misunderstanding, trying to fashion a world that will hold all the people, all the faces, all the adams and eves and their countless generations;

Let a new earth rise. Let another world be born. Let a bloody
peace be written in the sky. Let a second generation full of
courage issue forth; let a people loving freedom come to
growth. Let a beauty full of healing and a strength of final
clenching be the pulsing in our spirits and our blood. Let the
martial songs be written, let the dirges disappear. Let a race
of men now rise and take control.

John Steinbeck took a commonplace situation that most of us would over-
look and described it in a way that is unforgettable. In this excerpt from his
novel *The Grapes of Wrath*—a work that explores Oklahoma and its people in
the 1930s during the Great Depression—Steinbeck describes the trials of a turtle who desires simply to cross the road.

The Grapes of Wrath

John Steinbeck

The sun lay on the grass and warmed it, and in the shade under the
grass the insects moved, ants and ant lions to set traps for them,
grasshoppers to jump into the air and flick their yellow wings for a
second, sow bugs like little armadillos, plodding restlessly on many tender
feet. And over the grass at the roadside a land turtle crawled, turning aside
for nothing, dragging his high-domed shell over the grass, not really walking, but boosting and dragging his shell along. The barley beards slid off his
shell, and the clover burrs fell on him and rolled to the ground. His horny
beak was partly open, and his fierce/humorous eyes, under brows like fingernails, stared straight ahead. He came over the grass leaving a beaten
trail behind him, and the hill, which was the highway embankment,
reared up ahead of him. For a moment he stopped, his head held high. He
blinked and looked up and down. At last he started to climb the embankment. Front clawed feet reached forward but did not touch. The hind feet
kicked his shell along, and it scraped on the grass, and on the gravel. As
the embankment grew steeper and steeper, the more frantic were the
efforts of the land turtle. Pushing hind legs strained and slipped, boosting
the shell along, and the horny head protruded as far as the neck could
stretch. Little by little the shell slid up the embankment until at last a
parapet cut straight across its line of march, the shoulder of the road, a
concrete wall four inches high. As though they worked independently the
hind legs pushed the shell against the wall. The head upraised and peered
over the wall to the broad smooth plain of cement. Now the hands, braced
on top of the wall, strained and lifted, and the shell came slowly up and
rested its front end on the wall. For a moment the turtle rested. A red ant

was crushed between body and legs. And one head of wild oats was clamped into the shell by a front leg. For a long moment the turtle lay still, and then the neck crept out and the old humorous frowning eyes looked about and the legs and tail came out. The back legs went to work, straining like elephant legs, and the shell tipped to an angle so that the front legs could not reach the level cement plain. But higher and higher the hind legs boosted it, until at last the center of balance was reached, the front tipped down, the front legs scratched at the pavement, and it was up. But the head of wild oats was held by its stem around the front legs.

Now the going was easy, and all the legs worked, and the shell boosted along, waggling from side to side. A sedan driven by a forty-year-old woman approached. She saw the turtle and swung to the right, off the highway, the wheels screamed and a cloud of dust boiled up. Two wheels lifted for a moment and then settled. The car skidded back onto the road, and went on, but more slowly. The turtle had jerked into its shell, but now it hurried on, for the highway was burning hot.

And now a light truck approached, and as it came near, the driver saw the turtle and swerved to hit it. His front wheel struck the edge of the shell, flipped the turtle like a tiddly-wink, spun it like a coin, and rolled it off the highway. The truck went back to its course along the right side. Lying on its back, the turtle was tight in its shell for a long time. But at last its legs waved in the air, reaching for something to pull it over. Its front foot caught a piece of quartz and little by little the shell pulled over and flopped upright. The wild oat head fell out and three of the spearhead seeds stuck in the ground. And as the turtle crawled on down the embankment, its shell dragged dirt over the seeds. The turtle entered a dust road and jerked itself along, drawing a wavy shallow trench in the dust with its shell. The old humorous eyes looked ahead, and the horny beak opened a little. His yellow toe nails slipped a fraction in the dust.

In this poem a daughter speaks to her mother. Let your body reflect the movement and emotion you feel as you read this poem aloud.

"My Mother Pieced Quilts"
Teresa Palomo Acosta

They were just meant as covers
in winter
as weapons
against pounding January winds

but it was just that every morning I awoke to these
October ripened canvases
passed my hand across their cloth faces
and began to wonder how you pieced
all these together
these strips of gentle communion cotton and
flannel nightgowns
wedding organdies
dime store velvets

how you shaped patterns square and oblong and round
positioned
balanced
then cemented them
with your thread
a steel needle
a thimble

how the thread darted in and out
galloping along the frayed edges, tucking them in
as you did us at night
oh how you stretched and turned and re-arranged
your michigan spring faded curtain pieces
my father's santa fe work shirt
the sunnier denims, the tweeds of fall

in the evening you sat at your canvas
—our cracked linoleum floor the drawing board
me lounging on your arm
and you staking out the plan:
whether to put the lilac purple of easter against the
red plaid of winter-going
into-spring
whether to mix a yellow with blue and white and
paint the
corpus christi noon when my father held your

hand
whether to shape a five-point star from the
somber black silk you wore to grandmother's
funeral

you were the river current
carrying the roaring notes
forming them into pictures of a little boy reclining
a swallow flying
you were the caravan master at the reins
driving your threaded needle artillery across the
mosaic cloth bridges
delivering yourself in separate testimonies.

oh mother you plunged me sobbing and laughing
into our past
into the river crossing at five
into the spinach fields
into the plainview cotton rows
into the tuberculosis wards
into braids and muslin dresses
sewn hard and taut to withstand the thrashings of
twenty-five years

stretched out they lay
armed/ready/shouting/celebrating

knotted with love
the quilts sing on

The river Sumpul separates Salvador from Honduras. On May 14, 1980, six hundred men, women, and children were fleeing the Salvadoran army and trying desperately to get into Honduras. When they reached the river they thought that they had found safety. As they crossed the river, however, the Honduran army arrived, and all of the peasants were slaughtered as gunfire from both armies rained down on them.

José Alejandro Romero, a Salvadoran emigrant now living in New England, wrote this poem, "Sumpul," to protest against repression and barbarism.

"Sumpul"

José Alejandro Romero

The afternoon has fallen into black dust,
and from the dust emerges death.
In the red river we swam, desperate to live.
We splashed in its waters and then,
bruised, we were floated by them.
From the river the massacred body arose.
Sumpul drowned in blood,
Sumpul deafened by the shots,
river turned red,
river swollen with anguish,
witnessing river, your hidden heart
containing the anonymous screams of martyrs—
of children, tender shoots,
of mothers, fruiting trees
and old ones ancient oaks.
Facing you is Yankee torture,
murderous sounds and the growl of the dog,
splattering this universe with shrapnel,
splitting open pregnant stars,
slashing the face of the peasant.
Beast, take note:
the worker's face will carry this scar.

River,
We seek your water made holy by force,
and with it anoint our arms,
with reddened eyes.
In a single, slaughtered droplet we watch
the sun, its hopeful yellow;
in its yellow is a future,
a victory, a triumph, a people.
In your winding current

We seek the wide and war-injured reflection of the people
confronting a vast machine;
their last words cursing despotism
their words like weapons, their body a shield,
their ideals, pure light.

I want to respond to the screams of the people,
to fixed eyes shooting off hatred,
to hoist your spirit in the fighting flag of guns.
I salute you with each shot aimed at the enemy
I swear to remember you in our future land,
and in the sky brimming with stars,
and in the first maize field of winter,
and in the waters of every river where I live.

Chapter 2

Discovering and Developing Your Voice

Learning Objectives

After completing this chapter, you should be able to

- explain how paralinguistics affects the meaning of messages
- discuss the role intelligibility, rate, pitch, volume, force, and quality play in performance
- provide examples of how you use your voice as a tool in the interpretation of texts

Your task as an oral interpreter is challenging. You are asked to share with your audience all the experiences that exist within a piece of literature or text, and you are expected to accomplish this using only the literature or text and your mind, body, and voice as tools. Indeed, your job of interpreter is not a simple one.

Consider the four resources available to you—the text or selection, your mind, your body, and your voice. While you may decide to use costumes, music, and props at times to supplement these resources, your mind, body, voice, and text are the primary tools upon which you will rely. With these, you transform written words into performed words. In effect, these four resources form the framework of an interpreter's performing system. Each component is related to and is interdependent with the other components in the system; a change in one component of the performing system should call forth corresponding changes in all other parts of the system.

Chapter 2 will focus on the vocal component of the interpreter's performing system. It is very important that you realize, however, that this aspect of interpreter behavior is isolated for purposes of examination only. In a performance situation, the interpreter's voice never functions alone; rather, it functions in relation to each of the three remaining elements. It is only by the successful interaction of selection, mind, body, and voice that literature will be fully revealed or communicated to an audience.

Levels of Meaning in Texts

First of all, you need to realize that every text has two levels of meaning associated with it: its report or **content level** and its command or **relationship level.** It is the relationship level that concerns you as an interpreter, because it is this level that helps to define the actual meaning of a word, phrase, or passage. The relationship level helps you decide how to interpret the literal content, because as an interpreter you are concerned not only with the dictionary meaning of words but also with the ways these words sound when read aloud. Thus, it remains for you to restore the vocal cues the words "lost" when the literature was transferred from the writer's mind to the written page.

The spoken word is rarely, if ever, neutral. It is, in fact, always affected by **paralinguistic,** or vocal, factors. Among these paralinguistic factors are speech intelligibility, time, volume and force, pitch, and vocal quality. Effective interpreters are able to use these basic elements of paralanguage to help them communicate both the emotional and intellectual meanings of their selections. In other words, trained readers know how to use vocal qualities to help their audiences appreciate and understand the content and mood-tones of their literature. Their voices are adaptable and tensile, responding totally to the literature.

How can you as an interpreter acquire this sought-after vocal flexibility and agility? First you need to be willing to unleash your voice—to play with it freely.

The Importance of Vocal Warm-Ups

Preparation for performance is central to this book. This book is your performance laboratory. Body and voice need to work together in performance. Just as you learned to use your body as a tool in the last chapter, so you need to learn to use your voice as a tool. In effect, you need to learn how to let the words of others live through your voice.

The warm-up exercises that follow are designed to prepare you to use your voice to advantage whenever you perform a text—any text. They will help you learn what to do with your voice in order to become another person or to speak on stage the words of another person. During these warm-ups you will have the chance to "play" your voice. In the process, you will discover the full range of its possibilities. You will also test your voice by using it to facilitate your response to a text. You will experiment with different readings in an effort to identify which feels right and works best. Once you have done this, you will find yourself in better position to choose the voice that best supports the interpretation of a text and present that voice in performance.

PERFORMER'S WARM-UP
Freeing the Voice

A. Open your mouth wide and yawn. Try it again and really get into that yawn, stretching your arms and legs as an extension of it.

Questions

1. What happens in the back of your mouth as you yawn?
2. What happens to your eyes?

B. This time, yawn with your mouth closed. Keeping your lips together, try to attain an open feeling in the back of your mouth.

Questions

1. How do you feel now?
2. What has happened to the muscles in your throat and neck?

C. Now, sitting up straight in your chair, place your hand on your stomach, inhale through your nose, drop your jaw as you did in the open-mouth yawn, and use your stomach muscles or diaphragm to push the sound "Ha" up from within you. Try this several times; aim to create a full, resonant, unstrained tone.

Questions

1. When you inhale through your nose, what happens to the hand resting on your stomach?
2. What happens to the tone of your voice?

D. Again, attain the open feeling of the yawn at the back of your throat and emit a "Ha," as you did in the preceding portion of this exercise. Now speed up the production of these sounds until they gradually form a full-bodied, resonant laugh.

Questions

1. What did your laugh sound like?
2. How did it differ from your normal laugh?

Now that your voice is partially freed, try channeling its effectiveness in new directions. Try this.

PERFORMER'S WARM-UP
Voice Orchestras

A. The class divides into five vocal sections. Each section corresponds to an instrument section in an orchestra: violins, clarinets, drums, tubas, and trumpets. The following themes are given to instrument groups to perform vocally, as members pantomime playing their instruments:

Violins: n

        n   n

          n

Clarinets: th

      th

         th

            th

Drums: broo-oom boom boom

Trumpets: tatatata ta ta

Tubas: ump pa omp pa omp pa pa

The instructor or a student acts as the orchestra conductor. He or she warms up each instrument of the orchestra. When the rehearsal is over, the conductor mounts an imaginary platform, raises his or her arms, and leads the group in performing the musical piece. The group must be alert to the conductor's signals as the instrument sections of the orchestra are faded out, emphasized, or faded in at his or her will.

B. Next, the class divides into new musical teams. Each team's goal is to become a specific type of musical combo. You can use only your voices and bodies as tools—words are not allowed. For example, you might choose to become a rock group, a jazz combo, a classical chamber group, or a sound-effects studio. Do not be limited by these suggestions; conduct your own voice-combo explorations. When each group has prepared its musical presentation, it will perform for the class. Then, as a group, discuss answers to the following questions:

Questions

1. What type of combo did your group choose to create?
2. How did you use your voices and bodies to create this combo?
3. What expressive qualities did you discover in your own voice?

Playing Your Voice

Learning to "play" your voice is akin to learning to play an instrument. In order to develop vocal skill, artistry, and dexterity, you have to practice using your voice as you would practice the piano, the tuba, the violin, or the guitar. Like their musician relatives, interpreters are orchestrators. Instead of orchestrating a musical score, however, interpreters orchestrate a written script. Musical cues are replaced with paralinguistic or vocal cues. Now that your voice is warmed up, let us examine more closely some of these paralinguistic factors.

Speech Intelligibility

It is essential that you are able to communicate accurately your author's words to your audience. To do so, you must form the sounds of your script with *precision* and *control*. Just as musicians are careful not to play the note A when the note E is called for, so interpreters must be certain they play only the sounds their authors supply. If interpreters slur their words when they should not be slurred or mix their sounds when they should not be mixed, then their performances are liable to be called sloppy or lazy, rather than clean and precise. Thus, interpreters need to work to develop distinct and accurate speech.

Inflection

Vocal inflection—the upward and downward movement of the voice within or between words—is also an important speech characteristic. For example, we usually signal a question with a rising inflection and a statement with a falling inflection. We can suggest different meanings for the same word by using different inflections. The sentence "I love you" can be said to suggest real affection or just the opposite. The word *okay* can be uttered with an upward inflection as if one were asking if something is okay, or it can be said adamantly as if there were an exclamation point after it. When inflection is flat or unvarying—in other words, when one's speaking key does not change—speech becomes repetitive and monotonous. A lack of inflection leads to a lack of expressiveness and a decrease in the perceived vitality of the speaker.

PERFORMER'S WORKSHOP
Sound Combinations

To refine and improve the way you form sounds and enunciate words, pay careful attention to the sound combinations in the following poem. In his book *Through the Looking Glass*, Lewis Carroll provides this delightful poem of nonsense words. How can you use your voice to give meaning to Carroll's "Jabberwocky"?

"Jabberwocky"
Lewis Carroll

'Twas brillig, and the slithy toves
    Did gyre and gimble in the wabe;
All mimsy were the borogoves,
    And the mome raths outgrabe.

"Beware the Jabberwock, my son!
    The jaws that bite, the claws that catch!
Beware the Jubjub bird, and shun
    The frumious Bandersnatch!"

He took his vorpal sword in hand;
    Long time the manxome foe he sought—
So rested he by the Tumtum tree,
    And stood awhile in thought.

And, as in uffish thought he stood,
    The Jabberwock, with eyes of flame,
Came whiffling through the tulgey wood,
    And burbled as it came!

One, two! One, two! And through and through
    The vorpal blade went snicker-snack!
He left it dead, and with its head
    He went galumphing back.

"And hast thou slain the Jabberwock?
    Come to my arms, my beamish boy!
O frabjous day! Callooh, Callay!"
    He chortled in his joy.

'Twas brillig, and the slithy toves
    Did gyre and gimble in the wabe;
All mimsy were the borogoves,
    And the mome raths outgrabe.

Questions

1. How do the sounds within the poem affect its sense?
2. How did your vocal reading add definition to the nonsense words?

Besides transferring the sounds of their selections accurately, interpreters should also add clarity to a work by varying the way they play the sounds within it. In doing so, interpreters share the hidden meanings of a piece of literature. You can use each of the vocal attributes we will examine to help you reveal to your audience the thoughts and feelings contained in your selection.

Time

We all have a **habitual rate** of speaking, and this rate helps characterize each of us as individuals. Although your normal speaking rate may be comfortable for you, as a performer you need to recognize that your usual speaking tempo may not match or be in accord with the speaking tempo called for by the literature. In other words, you should be certain that your reading rate fits the sense of your selection.

You need to be aware of another matter as well: your reading rate should vary as the mood or the created atmosphere of your material varies. Consequently, when approaching a literary selection, your first task is to analyze that selection's emotional and intellectual content, then to find a rate of speaking appropriate to it.

PERFORMER'S WORKSHOP
Tempo Tips

Read the following selections. What is the dominant tempo of each selection? That is, does it seem to be rapid or slow, a saunter or a jog? Where in each selection is it appropriate for you to vary your reading rate? Why?

In this first selection, the poet José Juan Tablada offers descriptions of four different creatures. Use your voice and body to reflect each of the distinct "images" so that your audience can complete the pictures you present.

"Images"
José Juan Tablada

Although he never stirs from home
the tortoise, like a load of furniture,
jolts down the path.

The tiny monkey looks at me . . .
He would like to tell me something
that escapes his mind!

Lumps of mud, the toads
along the shady path
hop . . .

The dragonfly strives patiently
to fasten its transparent cross
to the bare and trembling bough.

A child's vision of old age matures during this next poem by Frances Cornford. Let your speaking tempo slow when the mood changes.

"Childhood"
Frances Cornford

I used to think that grown-up people chose
To have stiff backs and wrinkles round their nose,
And veins like small fat snakes on either hand,

On purpose to be grand.

Till through the banisters I watched one day

My great-aunt Etty's friend who was going away,

And how her onyx beads had come unstrung.

I saw her grope to find them as they rolled;

And then I knew that she was helplessly old,

As I was helplessly young.

As the speaker in this cutting from Edgar Allan Poe's famous tale lies strapped down, he observes a razor-sharp pendulum descending slowly. Using tempo, indicate your lack of concern in the first paragraph and your anger at the rats in the second paragraph; then allow your tempo to increase further as you realize what is about to happen.

 ## "The Pit and the Pendulum"

Edgar Allan Poe

Looking upward, I surveyed the ceiling of my prison. It was some thirty or forty feet overhead, and constructed much as the side walls. In one of its panels a very singular figure riveted my whole attention. It was the painted figure of Time as he is commonly represented, save that, in lieu of a scythe, he held what, at a casual glance, I supposed to be the pictured image of a huge pendulum such as we see on antique clocks. There was something in the appearance of this machine which caused me to regard it more attentively. While I gazed directly upward at it (for its position was immediately over my own) I fancied that I saw it in motion. In an instant afterward the fancy was confirmed. Its sweep was brief, and of course slow. I watched it for some minutes, somewhat in fear, but more in wonder. Wearied at length with observing its dull movement, I turned my eyes upon the other objects in the cell.

A slight noise attracted my notice, and, looking to the floor, I saw several enormous rats traversing it. They had issued from the well, which lay just within view to my right. Even then, while I gazed, they came up in troops, hurriedly, with ravenous eyes, allured by the scent of the meat. From this it required much effort and attention to scare them away.

It might have been half an hour, perhaps even an hour (for I could take but imperfect note of time) before I again cast my eyes upward. What I saw confounded and amazed me. The sweep of the pendulum had increased in extent by nearly a yard. As a natural consequence, its velocity was also much greater. But what mainly disturbed me was the idea that it had perceptibly descended. I now observed—with what horror it is needless to say—that its nether extremity was formed of a crescent of glittering steel, about a foot in length from horn to horn; the horns upward, and the under edge evidently as keen as that of a razor. Like a razor also, it seemed massy and heavy, tapering from the edge into a solid and broad structure above. It was appended to a weighty rod of brass, and the whole hissed as it swung through the air.

I could no longer doubt the doom prepared for me. . . .

Questions

1. Where and how did you alter your tempo during these pieces?
2. What kinds of changes in tone and atmosphere were suggested by each of your vocal alterations?

Words and Tempo

Usually, the heavier the content of a selection, the slower the interpreter's tempo; the lighter the content, the quicker the interpreter's pace. However, this is not a hard-set rule. For example, a rapid or a slow tempo may be used to create an atmosphere of suspense or a sense of fear. Practiced performers of literature use occasional changes in speaking rates to enhance the moods they are working to create. Often, interpreters find that a selection is characterized by a poetic beat, but they also discover that within that established beat there are fluctuations. You need to be sensitive to such fluctuations, matching your tempo to the beat of the literature. In addition, keep in mind that just as you can stretch or compress the tempo of a selection to enhance its meaning, so you can also stretch or compress a selection's key words to enhance their meaning.

In many ways, your rate reflects the pulse of the words you speak. It typically quickens to communicate agitation, excitement, and happiness, and it falls to convey seriousness, serenity, or sadness. The emotional content of the material guides you in selecting the appropriate tempo.

PERFORMER'S WORKSHOP
Word-Work

As you read Walter de la Mare's poem "Silver," ask yourself if the piece is serious and contemplative or light and fun. Ask yourself if it is filled with contempt or grief, or excitement and action. Your answers should guide you in adjusting your normal rate to match the emotional requirements called for in the literature.

"Silver"
Walter de la Mare

Slowly, silently, now the moon
Walks the night in her silver shoon;
This way, and that, she peers, and sees
Silver fruit upon silver trees;
One by one the casements catch
Her beams beneath the silvery thatch;
Couched in his kennel, like a log,
With paws of silver sleeps the dog;
From their shadowy cote the white breasts peep
Of doves in a silver-feathered sleep;
A harvest mouse goes scampering by,
With silver claws, and silver eye;
And moveless fish in the water gleam,
By silver reeds in a silver stream.

Questions

1. Which words in the passage do you believe reinforce or add to the emotional impact of the selection?
2. How can you use your vocal rate to communicate this? For example, at what rate would you read words such as "Slowly, silently"? Would your reading rate change for "A harvest mouse goes scampering by"?

Word Flavors

Have you ever considered that key words in a literary selection can have flavor values? As you read, should you savor a particular word or only taste it? Should you prolong the vowels to slow the tempo down, or should you only touch the consonants to increase speed? Never neglect to consider the flavor of a key word—flavor adds power to your interpretation.

Words that help to create or sustain a mood are rarely, if ever, neutral in taste. Therefore, to emphasize this, you will want to vary the sound duration of certain words within your passage. For example, the consonants *p, b, t,* and *d* are plosives, relatively short sounds that virtually explode from our lips. In comparison, the consonants *m, n, ng,* and *l* are continuants, relatively long sounds. The interpreter uses duration for emphasis. When we stress a word, we may extend the length of its sound. By doing this, we also suggest the word's emotional qualities and importance to receivers.

Pauses

In addition to duration, another useful instrument of time is the **pause**—an absence of sound that can emphasize or reinforce important ideas and feelings in your selection. A pause gives you extra time to transmit a particular experience to your audience, and it gives your audience extra time to process and appreciate the experience. In reading aloud you can emphasize the important ideas or feeling of a selection by pausing either before or after, or both before and after, a key word or group of words. In this way you can more efficiently create for an audience a mood of suspense or surprise, a mood of fear or exhilaration.

Pauses should not be randomly placed; rather, they should be carefully and thoughtfully planned. A *planned pause* is alive with meaning; it allows your audience to hear what is not actually said. A *random pause,* on the other hand, may detract from and destroy—rather than sustain—the emotional content of the work. Consequently, interpreters need to focus on varying the length of their pauses. They need to insure that the silent seconds of their performances are effectively placed and in accord with the meaning of their selection.

PERFORMER'S WORKSHOP
To Pause or Not . . .

A. In this passage from Shakespeare's *King Lear,* Lear rages against the elements he feels are conspiring against him. As you read the passage, pause only at the end of lines.

 King Lear

William Shakespeare

> Blow, winds, and crack your cheeks! Rage! Blow!
> You cataracts and hurricanoes, spout
> Till you have drenched our steeples, drowned the cocks!
> You sulphurous and thought-executing fires,
> Vaunt-couriers to oak cleaving thunderbolts,
> Singe my white head! And thou, all-shaking thunder,
> Smite flat the thick rotundity o' the world!

B. Now read the passage again, pausing this time for meaning.

Questions

1. How did the meaning of the selection change during your second reading of it?
2. How did pausing help to clarify the content?

PERFORMER'S WORKSHOP
Place the Pause

Most of the written punctuation in the following selection has been removed for the purpose of this exercise. It is your task to determine where to place the pauses in the passage. Remember, a pause is one very specific type of oral punctuation. Mark a single slash line / in your passage to indicate a short silence and a double slash line // to indicate silence of a somewhat longer duration.

In the following portion from the poem "When Lilacs Last in the Dooryard Bloom'd," Walt Whitman describes the coffin of Abraham Lincoln as it is taken to its burial place.

 "When Lilacs Last in the Dooryard Bloom'd"
Walt Whitman

Coffin that passes through lanes and streets
Through day and night with the great cloud darkening the land
With the pomp of the inloop'd flags with the cities draped in
    black
With the show of the States themselves as of crape-veil'd women
    standing
With processions long and winding and the flambeaus of the
    night
With the countless torches lit with the silent sea of faces and the
    unbared heads
With the waiting depot the arriving coffin and the sombre faces
With dirges through the night with the thousand voices rising
    strong and solemn
With all the mournful voices of the dirges pour'd around the
    coffin
The dim-lit churches and the shuddering organs—where amid
    these you journey

With the tolling tolling bells' perpetual clang

Here, coffin that slowly passes

I give you my sprig of lilac.

Questions

1. What aspects of your material helped you to determine your pauses?
2. How did pausing help your audience understand?
3. How does the meaning of the selection change as the placement of pauses changes?

Volume and Force

Volume refers to an interpreter's degree of loudness as he or she reads the words of a selection; **force** refers to the intensity, emphasis, or weight that he or she gives the words of the selection. Determining the appropriate degree of volume or the appropriate amount of force is not easy. In order to make the proper decisions, an interpreter must be able to "touch" the words of the literature. After "touching" the literature, an interpreter will be in a better position to determine which words in the passage are warm words, calling for an outward and open expression style, and which words in the passage are cool words, requiring a gentle or restrained expression style.

For example, we would probably use a gentle volume level and a restrained amount of force when we read, "Slowly and silently the funeral process wound by," which contains cool words. In contrast, when reading, "Ring the alarum-bell:—murder and treason!" which contains warm words, we would probably use greater volume and force. Different texts call on the interpreter to exhibit different kinds of touch. The choices are as varied as the kinds of emotion we experience.

In addition, interpreters want to be able to determine which words in their selections should be spotlighted and given emphasis and which words should remain subordinate in their impact. Test your own talent for this with the following exercise.

PERFORMER'S WARM-UP
Touching Meaning

Read the following sentences, emphasizing the boldface word in each one. How do different vocal emphases influence the meaning given to the message?

He's giving this package to Morris.
He's **giving** this package to Morris.
He's giving **this** package to Morris.
He's giving this **package** to Morris.
He's giving this package **to** Morris.
He's giving this package to **Morris.**

Clearly, your vocal emphasis serves to influence the way a sentence or phrase is perceived. As an interpreter, you need to be certain that a change in either force or volume will work to complement your literature and that your motivation for making such changes is inherent in the sense of your selection.

PERFORMER'S WORKSHOP
Touching Literature

Read Nikki Giovanni's "Knoxville, Tennessee." Where in the poem would you increase or decrease your volume as you read aloud? Why? On which words would your touch be heaviest? Which words would receive the lightest touch? Why?

"Knoxville, Tennessee"
Nikki Giovanni

I always like summer
best
you can eat fresh corn
from daddy's garden
and okra
and greens
and cabbage
and lots of
barbecue
and buttermilk
and homemade ice-cream
at the church picnic
and listen to
gospel music

outside

at the church

homecoming

and go to the mountains with

your grandmother

and go barefooted

and be warm

all the time

not only when you go to bed

and sleep

Pitch in Performance

Pitch refers to the highness or lowness of an individual's voice—that is, its place on the musical scale, or its frequency level. An effective voice has an extensive pitch range and is consequently capable of expressing a large variety of tones. Your *habitual pitch* is the pitch level you use most frequently when speaking. Your *optimum* or *ideal pitch* is the range within which your voice operates with the greatest ease, that is, the best or most favorable one for speaking. Habitual and optimum pitch may not be the same. If your optimum and habitual pitches diverge, your vocal flexibility and responsiveness may be limited.

In order to identify your optimum pitch, sing a vowel from the lowest to the highest notes you can reach without straining. Locate those notes on a piano. Then find the midpoint between those two notes. Your optimum pitch is approximately two notes below the midpoint.

Previous readings should have helped demonstrate to you your pitch range—the pitch tones you are able to produce that lie either above or below your habitual pitch level. In terms of scale range, your pitch may be high, medium, or low. A skilled interpreter uses his or her voice to produce varied degrees of high or low tones and thereby suggest shades of meaning. How successful you are in varying your pitch determines your expressiveness. In performance situations your pitch should be controlled by the intellectual and emotional content of your selection. Focus on your variation in pitch as you try the following exercises.

PERFORMER'S WORKSHOP
All That Jazz

In "Jazz Fantasia," Carl Sandburg has given us a poem designed to reflect an improvised jazz concert. It is almost an early version of today's rap music. As you read the poem, use your voice to reflect the sounds of the various instruments. Experiment with a variety of pitches and work to find a beat that holds the poem together.

"Jazz Fantasia"
Carl Sandburg

Drum on your drums, batter on your banjoes, sob on
　　your long cool winding saxophones,
Go to it, O jazzmen!
Sling your knuckles on the bottoms of the happy tin pans;
Let your trombones ooze, and go hush-a-hush-a-hush
　　on the slippery sand paper.
Moan like an autumn wind high in the lonesome tree-tops;
Cry like a racing car slipping away from a motorcycle cop!
Bang, bang, you jazzmen! Bang all together, drums,
　　traps, banjoes, horns, tin-cans!
Make two people fight on the top of a stairway and scratch
　　each other's eyes in a clinch tumbling down the stairs.
Can the rough stuff!
Now a Mississippi steamboat pushes up the night river,
　　with a hoo-hoo-hoo,
And the green lanterns calling to the high soft stars;
A red moon rides on the humps of the low river hills;
Go to it, O jazzmen!

Questions

1. Where did you employ a relatively low pitch? Why? Where did your pitch rise?
2. How did pitch variation enhance the meaning of the poem?

PERFORMER'S WORKSHOP
Pitch Practice

Read the following brief text, "Young and Old" by Charles Kingsley, aloud. Pay careful attention to the contrasting ideas expressed in each verse. Use pitch variations to highlight these changes in thought and feeling. In this poem we see that age can alter a person's view of life. Can you reflect this perceptual change with a corresponding change in pitch?

 "Young and Old"
Charles Kingsley

When all the world is young, lad,
    And all the trees are green;
And every goose a swan, lad,
    And every lass a queen;
Then hey for boot and horse, lad,
    And round the world away;
Young blood must have its course, lad,
    And every dog his day.

When all the world is old, lad,
    And all the trees are brown;
And all the sport is stale, lad,
    And all the wheels run down;
Creep home, and take your place there,
    The spent and maimed among:
God grant you find one face there,
    You loved when all was young.

Questions

1. What clues did you find in the text that helped you ensure that your pitch level was appropriate?
2. In what ways did you vary your pitch as you attempted to bring forth the meaning?

Vocal Quality

Just as different rates, different vocal tones, and different degrees of volume help an interpreter suggest certain attitudes or emotions to an audience, so do different vocal qualities. Of course, people have different vocal qualities as well. In fact, many stars and media personalities have quite distinctive and recognizable qualities. Try this.

PERFORMER'S WARM-UP
Voice Typing

Recall the voices of some famous people. They may include some of the following entertainers:

Eddie Murphy
Jennifer Lopez
Whoopi Goldberg
James Earl Jones
Fran Drescher
Dennis Miller

Can't you almost hear them right now?

Your instructor may decide to have you listen to tapes of some famous or familiar voices gathered at random. After you listen to them, try your hand at re-creating their voices or the voices of other famous people. How successful are you? Offer a "great impersonator" award for the class member who can most closely re-create the vocal quality of a celebrity or noted person.

Timbre

Most of us have a distinctive vocal quality or **timbre.** Vocal quality yields clues regarding a speaker's health, emotions, and sociocultural circumstances. In effect, the distinctive sound of an individual's voice varies according to his or her age, health, mood, and attitude.

Your role as an interpreter is like that of a radio announcer or an actor, in that you can develop different vocal qualities to reflect a wide range of communicative purposes. The announcer calling a baseball game uses a voice different from the one a reporter might use at a presidential press conference. An actor playing the part of a mobster would use a different voice altogether to play a suave society person. Your voice, too, should be used to mirror to your audience the nature and contents of various scripts. Like performers, interpreters need to work at adopting vocal qualities to suit or enhance their selected materials.

What vocal qualities can an interpreter choose to help him or her perform literature? A breathy vocal quality can suggest anything from a confidential manner or a seductive demeanor to fear and horror. A hoarse or throaty timbre can suggest roughness, crudity, or brusqueness. A shrill or hypernasal vocal quality, often used to create a character who habitually whines or nags, has also been used to suggest stupidity or a lack of breeding. A hollow or barrel-sounding voice is characterized by its use of rich, round tones; interpreters may use it to suggest remoteness, dignity, power, or even morbidity. They may use a tremulous voice, shaking with uncertainty, pain, or old age. The list of vocal qualities interpreters may use to help them share selections of literature with an audience is practically endless. A broad voice, a passionate voice, a falsetto voice—even a normal, conversational voice—can be useful.

Increase your understanding of vocal quality by considering the following exercise.

PERFORMER'S WORKSHOP
Pick a Voice

Read the following selections. What type of vocal quality would you use when performing each of the passages? Why?

Explore ways to create the voices of three witches in this opening scene from Shakespeare's play *Macbeth*. You may want to experiment with the entire class chanting the "Double, double, toil and trouble . . ." refrain.

Macbeth
William Shakespeare

FIRST WITCH: Round about the cauldron go;
   In the poison'd entrails throw;
   Toad, that under cold stone
   Days and nights has thirty-one
   Swelt'red venom sleeping got,
   Boil thou first i' th' charmed pot.
ALL: Double, double, toil and trouble;
   Fire burn, and cauldron bubble.
SECOND WITCH: Fillet of a fenny snake,
   In the cauldron boil and bake;
   Eye of newt and toe of frog,
   Wool of bat and tongue of dog,
   Adder's fork and blind-worm's sting,
   Lizard's leg and howlet's wing,
   For a charm of pow'rful trouble,
   Like a hell-broth boil and bubble.
ALL: Double, double, toil and trouble;
   Fire burn, and cauldron bubble.
THIRD WITCH: Scale of dragon, tooth of wolf,
   Witch's mummy, maw and gulf
   Of the ravin'd salt-sea shark,
   Root of hemlock digg'd i' th' dark,

Liver of blaspheming Jew,
Gall of goat, and slips of yew
Sliver'd in the moon's eclipse,
Nose of Turk and Tartar's lips,
Finger of birth-strangled babe
Ditch-deliver'd by a drab,
Make the gruel thick and slab.
Add thereto a tiger's chawdron,
For th' ingredience of our cau'dron
ALL: Double, double, toil and trouble;
Fire burn, and cauldron bubble.

Did you ever walk along the sandy shore and collect shells? This cutting from the story "Abalone, Abalone, Abalone" by the Japanese American writer Toshio Mori reflects the simple charm and beauty of the inside of a highly polished shell.

from "Abalone, Abalone, Abalone"
Toshio Mori

Before Mr. Abe went away I used to see him quite often at his nursery. He was a carnation grower just as I am one today. At noontime I used to go to his front porch and look at his collection of abalone shells.

They were lined up side by side against the side of his house on the front porch. I was curious as to why he bothered to collect them. It was a lot of bother polishing them. I had often seen him sit for hours on Sundays and noon hours polishing each one of the shells with the greatest of care. Of course I knew these abalone shells were pretty. When the sun strikes the insides of these shells it is something beautiful to behold. But I could not understand why he continued collecting them when the front porch was practically full.

He used to watch for me every noon hour. When I appeared he would look out of his room and bellow, "Hello, young man!"

"Hello, Abe-san," I said. "I came to see the abalone shells."

Then he came out of the house and we sat on the front porch. But he did not tell me why he collected these shells. I think I have asked him dozens of times but each time he closed his mouth and refused to answer.

"Are you going to pass this collection of abalone shells on to your children?" I said.

"No," he said. "I want my children to collect for themselves. I wouldn't give it to them."

"Why?" I said. "When you die?"

Mr. Abe shook his head. "No. Not even when I die," he said. "I couldn't give the children what I see in these shells. The children must go out for themselves and find their own shells."

"Why, I thought this collecting hobby of abalone shells was a simple affair," I said.

"It is simple. Very simple," he said. But he would not tell me further.

For several years I went steadily to his front porch and looked at the beautiful shells. His collection was getting larger and larger. Mr. Abe sat and talked to me and on each occasion his hands were busy polishing shells.

"So you are still curious?" he said.

"Yes," I said.

One day while I was hauling the old soil from the benches and replacing it with new soil I found an abalone shell half buried in the dust between the benches. So I stopped working. I dropped my wheelbarrow and went to the faucet and washed the abalone shell with soap and water. I had a hard time taking the grime off the surface.

After forty minutes of cleaning and polishing the old shell it became interesting. I began polishing both the outside and the inside of the shell. I found after many minutes of polishing I could not do very much with the exterior side. It had scabs of the sea which would not come off by scrubbing and the surface itself was rough and hard. And in the crevices the grime stuck so that even with a needle it did not become clean.

But on the other side, the inside of the shell, the more I polished the more lustre I found. It had me going. There were colors which I had not seen in the abalone shells before or anywhere else. The different hues, running berserk in all directions, coming together in harmony. I guess I could say they were not unlike a rainbow which men once symbolized. As soon as I thought of this I thought of Mr. Abe.

I remember running to his place, looking for him. "Abe-san!" I said when I found him. "I know why you are collecting the abalone shells!"

He was watering the carnation plants in the greenhouse. He stopped watering and came over to where I stood. He looked me over closely for awhile and then his face beamed.

"All right," he said. "Do not say anything. Nothing, mind you. When you have found the reason why you must collect and preserve them, you do not have to say anything more."

"I want you to see it, Abe-san," I said.

"All right. Tonight," he said. "Where did you find it?"

"In my old greenhouse, half buried in the dust," I said.

He chuckled. "That is pretty far from the ocean," he said, "but pretty close to you."

At each noon hour I carried my abalone shell and went over to Mr. Abe's front porch. While I waited for his appearance I kept myself busy polishing the inside of the shell with a rag.

One day I said, "Abe-san, now I have three shells."

"Good!" he said. "Keep it up!"

"I have to keep them all," I said. "They are very much alike and very much different."

"Well! Well!" he said and smiled.

That was the last I saw of Abe-san. Before the month was over he sold his nursery and went back to Japan. He brought his collection along and thereafter I had no one to talk to at the noon hour. This was before I discovered the fourth abalone shell, and I should like to see Abe-san someday and watch his eyes roll as he studies me whose face is now akin to the collectors of shells or otherwise.

Questions

1. How did you use vocal quality to try and suggest the mood and feeling associated with a character?
2. How did your empathic responses influence your use of vocal quality?

Remember to be cautious in your creation of voices. Never impose a specific vocal quality on a selection; rather, explore the selection in order to discover the vocal quality appropriate to it—one that works to enhance its intellectual and emotional meaning.

Chapter ② Performance Applications

IDEA ENCORE

Chapter 2 explored how the interpreter can harness his or her voice to transform written words into animated words that support the performance of a text. To that end, we examined the various vocal tools you possess, and we focused on how you can use each in creating an interpretive performance.

Among the vocal or paralinguistic cues that you, the performer, must be sensitive to are speech intelligibility, time (rate), volume, pitch, and vocal quality. By learning to vary these elements appropriately so that they enhance a text's meaning, you become better able to communicate not only the intellectual meaning of a selection but its emotional meaning as well.

It is through working to free the expressiveness of the voice and practicing playing the voice that the interpreter develops the skill and vocal flexibility needed to share both the overt and hidden meaning of texts with audiences.

PERFORMER'S SHOWCASE & JOURNAL
Voice Vigorizers

Now try to put together what you have learned about a performer's voice by working on the following materials. Read the following end-of-chapter selections. For each, note in your performer's journal how using the paralingual or vocal qualities presented in this chapter can help you to share meaning with an audience. Choose a selection to showcase what you have learned about voice.

SELECTIONS FOR FURTHER WORK

In Pat Mora's poem "Immigrants," the poet reveals her attitude toward immigrants. How can you convey this attitude with your voice? To what extent, if any, does your attitude toward immigrants affect your own reading of the poem?

"Immigrants"
Pat Mora

> wrap their babies in the American flag,
> feed them mashed hot dogs and apple pie,
> name them Bill and Daisy,
> buy them blonde dolls that blink
> blue eyes or a football and tiny cleats
> before the baby can even walk,
> speak to them in thick English,
>   hallo, babee, hallo.
> whisper in Spanish or Polish
> when the babies sleep, whisper
> in a dark parent bed, that dark
> parent fear, "Will they like

our boy, our girl, our fine american
boy, our fine american girl?"

In "Incident," Countee Cullen shows us how a single word can alter our perceptions. Work to let your voice reflect this change.

"Incident"
Countee Cullen

Once riding in old Baltimore,
    Heart-filled, head-filled with glee,
I saw a Baltimorean
    Keep looking straight at me.

Now I was eight and very small,
    And he was no whit bigger,
And so I smiled, but he poked out
    His tongue, and called me, "Nigger."

I saw the whole of Baltimore
    From May until December;
Of all the things that happened there
    That's all that I remember.

Theodore Roethke also creates a child's-eye view of the world in his poem
"Child on Top of a Greenhouse." How can you use vocal quality to suggest the
child's state of mind?

"Child on Top of a Greenhouse"
Theodore Roethke

The wind billowing out the seat of my britches,
My feet crackling splinters of glass and dried putty,
The half-grown chrysanthemums staring up like accusers,
Up through the streaked glass, flashing with sunlight,
A few white clouds all rushing eastward,
A line of elms plunging and tossing like horses,
And everyone, everyone pointing up and shouting!

In this cutting from a Poe story, the speaker is just completing the construction of a wall that will become the living tomb of Lord Fortunato.

 "The Cask of Amontillado"
Edgar Allan Poe

I had scarcely laid the first tier of masonry when I discovered that the intoxication of Fortunato had in a great measure worn off. The earliest indication I had of this was a low moaning cry from the depth of the recess. It was not the cry of a drunken man. There was then a long and obstinate silence. I laid the second tier, and the third, and the fourth; and then I heard the furious vibrations of the chain. The noise lasted for several minutes, during which, that I might hearken to it with the more satisfaction, I ceased my labors and sat down upon the bones. When at last the clanking subsided, I resumed the trowel, and finished without interruption the fifth, the sixth, and the seventh tier. The wall was now nearly upon a level with my breast. I again paused, and holding the flambeaux over the masonwork, threw a few feeble rays upon the figure within.

A succession of loud and shrill screams, bursting suddenly from the throat of the chained form, seemed to thrust me violently back. For a brief moment I hesitated. . . . I reapproached the wall; I replied to the yells of him who clamored. I reechoed, I aided, I surpassed them in volume and in strength. I did this, and the clamorer grew still.

It was now midnight, and my task was drawing to a close. I had completed the eighth, the ninth, and the tenth tier. I had finished a portion of the last and the eleventh; there remained but a single stone to be fitted and plastered in. I struggled with its weight; I placed it partially in its destined position. But now there came from out the niche a low laugh that erected the hairs upon my head. It was succeeded by a sad voice, which I had difficulty in recognizing as that of the noble Fortunato. The voice said

"Ha! ha! ha!—he! he! he!—a very good joke indeed—an excellent jest. We will have many a rich laugh about it at the palazzo—he! he! he!—over our wine—he! he! he!"

"The Amontillado!" I said.

"He! he! he!—he! he! he!—yes, the Amontillado. But is it not getting late? Will not they be awaiting us at the palazzo, the Lady Fortunato and the rest? Let us be gone."

"Yes," I said, "let us be gone."

"For the love of God, Montresor!"

"Yes," I said, "for the love of God!"

Chapter 3

Training Your Sense Memory for Oral Interpretation

Learning Objectives

After completing this chapter, you should be able to

- explain "sense memory"
- use sense memory
- rely on sense memory to enrich the performance of various texts

What is **sense memory?** Consciousness? Alertness? Perceptiveness? Yes, yes, and yes. Your senses help you to understand life's mysteries and secrets. Your sensory awareness allows things to affect you and encourages you to respond to stimuli. Your sense memory enables you to feel.

In Chapter 3, as a performer of literature you will come to your senses. You will explore ways to enlarge and extend your sense memory antennae. You will be asked to process and draw on everything you discover in your store of sensory experience, which will continually serve you as a sense memory resource center. As an interpreter you will use your senses to help you experience the literature you hope to share with your audience; you will also use them to make the literature live for your audience.

Coming to Your Senses

Your senses operate much like the theatrical or movie spotlight that highlights various areas of a darkened stage or screen. The senses, like the spotlight, focus only on specific aspects of an event at any given moment.

Your Perceptual Spotlight

An interpreter must be certain that his or her perceptual spotlight is "clean"—not soiled or colored by preconceptions. The spotlight must also be sufficiently wide in scope, rather than local or narrow. In other words, you must be open to the wide variety of stimuli an author provides.

Eventually, your concentration as an interpreter will be focused on the imaginary worlds and the imaginary people in literature. To respond effectively to literature, you must be able to respond sensitively to life, having developed your own sensory apparatus and sense memory. You have to be able to bring sights, sounds, tastes, smells, feelings, movements, and other sensations present in literature to your audience through your interpretation. If you are to develop the power to elicit imagined sensory perceptions in your audience, you need first to evoke sensory perceptions in yourself.

How can you refine your senses and sense memory to better respond to and perform literature? The Performer Warm-Ups in this chapter will help you focus on cultivating each of your senses for controlled use in the performance of literature. The different senses to be explored are grouped into "departments": auditory, visual, olfactory (smell), gustatory (taste), touch, and kinesthetic (movement).

Experiencing Sound

Interpreters need to be sensitive to sound and the interplay of different sounds. They need to be able to internalize and transmit auditory cues. They need to hear an image and be able to translate it from an auditory impression into an auditory expression. Instead of just saying "I heard the child's piercing scream," the interpreter actually tries to hear the scream (the impression) and to re-create it internally so that she or he can share it with audience members. By re-creating auditory responses, the interpreter helps receivers imagine what the auditory cue was like.

PERFORMER'S WARM-UP
Listen to Your World

A. Listen to the world around you for one minute. Become aware of all the different sounds that "live" and "die" in your immediate world. Compare the sounds you focused on with the sounds that were noticed by your fellow students. How were the sounds similar? How were they different?

B. Listen again, choosing one specific sound on which to focus. Close your eyes and immerse yourself in the private world of this particular sound. Then turn to a partner and take turns telling each other a story involving your specific sound. For example, if you listened to rain falling, you might create an imaginary tale involving puddle jumping.

C. You are stretched out on a sandy beach, sending a Frisbee sailing at the park, or lazing by a smoky camp fire. Work with your group to create a sound collage, representative of all the auditory stimuli you might hear at your specific summer site. Be imaginative—lapping or splashing water is not the only sound you will hear. What other sounds are typical of your summer place? Weave them into your group's sound collage.

D. Working with your group, perform your created sound collage for the other groups. Let them attempt to identify your summer site and the specific sounds associated with it.

Questions

1. What sounds were clearly identifiable? Why was this so?
2. What sounds required the most audience effort to identify? Why?
3. How could your group make its sound collage even more effective?

PERFORMER'S WORKSHOP
Sound into Meaning

Before you read the following poem, try to imagine a world without sound. "Mutterings Over the Crib of a Deaf Child," by James Wright, describes a parent pondering over the problems that will beset an infant who was born deaf. Will the adult pity the child or find ways for the child to live life to the fullest, even with this disability? Try to re-create your image of a soundless world as you read the poem.

 "Mutterings Over the Crib of a Deaf Child"

James Wright

"How will he hear the bell at school
Arrange the broken afternoon,
And know to run across the cool
Grasses where the starlings cry,
Or understand the day is gone?"

Well, someone lifting cautious brows
Will take the measure of the clock.
And he will see the birchen boughs
Outside the sagging dark from the sky,
And the shade crawling upon the rock.

"And how will he know to rise at morning?
His mother has other sons to waken,
She has the stove she must build to burning
Before the coals of night-time die,
And he never stirs when he is shaken."

I take it the air affects the skin,
And you remember when you were young,
Sometimes you could feel the dawn begin
And the fire would call you, by and by,
Out of the bed and bring you along.

"Well, good enough. To serve his needs
All kinds of arrangements can be made.
But what will you do if his finger bleeds?
Or a bobwhite whistles invisibly
And flutes like an angle off in the shade?"

He will learn pain. And, as for the bird,
It is always darkening when that comes out.
I will putter as though I had not heard,
And lift him into my arms and sing
Whether he hears my song or not.

Questions

1. What sounds did you attempt to re-create for your audience?
2. How does this poem help demonstrate that we can "listen" with more than our ears?

Sight

Just as hearing is not the same as listening, looking is not the same as seeing. For receivers to imagine the visual dimensions of a piece of literature, the interpreter must be able to see them in his or her mind's eye, and with his or her voice and body imbue them with substance. Instead of saying, "The dog leaped into his arms," you see the image in your mind first, then project an imaginary dog into the line of vision of your receivers as you re-create that impression for them. This next warm-up should help you master this skill.

PERFORMER'S WARM-UP
Visual Cues

A. Bring to class an object from nature, such as a rock or a flower, place it on your desk, and observe it carefully. Examine it from different angles; note its numerous characteristics and qualities. List them. After fifteen minutes, trade objects with a classmate nearby and repeat the above process. Compare your lists.

Questions

1. How were your observation lists similar?
2. In what ways did they differ?

B. Your instructor will divide the class into small groups. Each group will choose to visit an imagined environment, such as a zoo or a toy shop. Members of each group should re-create or pantomime some of the sights that might be seen in the respective environments. Other groups will guess what those sights are. They may suggest additional sights that the group might re-create.

Questions

1. What did you have to do in order to "see" the imagined environment?
2. What performances were most effective? Why?

PERFORMER'S WORKSHOP
Sight-Sense

Prepare to read the following poem, Walt Whitman's "A Noiseless Patient Spider," aloud. Before you read it, ask yourself what the spider looks like as it goes about its task. Pretend you are a spider and move as the poem suggests.

"A Noiseless Patient Spider"
Walt Whitman

A noiseless patient spider,
I mark'd where on a little promontory it stood isolated,
Mark'd how to explore the vacant vast surrounding,
It launch'd forth filament, filament, filament, out of itself,
Ever unreeling them, ever tirelessly speeding them.

And you O my soul where you stand,
Surrounded, detached, in measureless oceans of space,
Ceaselessly musing, venturing, throwing, seeking the spheres to connect them,
Till the bridge you will need be form'd, till the ductile anchor hold,
Till the gossamer thread you fling catch somewhere, O my soul.

Questions

1. What do you envision a soul looks like?
2. How can you re-create the vision of this poem for an audience?

Smell

Our olfactory sense, or sense of smell, also plays a part in oral interpretation. Since our sense of smell affects whether our perceptions of experience are positive or negative, the interpreter needs to provide the necessary approach or avoidance cues. Though the interpreter's point of concentration will rarely be placed exclusively on the sense of smell, smell is a part of the text's environment, and the interpreter's skill in evoking olfactory responses in receivers can be a vital part of his or her performance.

PERFORMER'S WARM-UP
Olfactory Experiences

Think of a place you have visited—a bakery, a musty attic, the circus—that had a specific aroma you can recall. Without naming the place, describe for the class the distinctive scents that might be found in this remembered environment. Give only one smell clue at a time and let the class guess the place you are describing.

Questions

1. What type of clue did you find worked most effectively?
2. What happened to each performer's body and facial expressions as he or she delivered the clues?
3. How did the audience members react to each of the clues?

PERFORMER'S WORKSHOP
It's Olfactory

Perform this cutting from Thomas Wolfe's *The Hills Beyond.* Prior to reading it, highlight each olfactory image it contains.

 The Hills Beyond

Thomas Wolfe

A waft of air, warm, chocolate-laden, filled his nostrils. He tried to pass the white front of the little eight-foot shop; he paused, struggling with conscience; he could not go on. It was the little candy shop run by old Crocker and his wife. And Grover could not pass.

"Old stingy Crockers!" he thought scornfully. "I'll not go there any more. But"—as the maddening fragrance of rich cooking chocolate touched him once again—"I'll just look in the window and see what they've got." He paused a moment, looking with his dark and quiet eyes into the window of the little candy shop. The window, spotlessly clean, was filled with trays of fresh-made candy. His eyes rested on a tray of chocolate drops. Unconsciously he licked his lips. Put one of them upon your tongue and it just melted there, like honeydew. And then the trays full of rich homemade fudge. He gazed longingly at the deep body of the chocolate fudge, reflectively at maple walnut, more critically, yet with longing, at the mints, the nougatines, and all the other dainties.

Questions

1. How did identifying the olfactory images simplify your task?
2. What did you do with your voice and body to facilitate the transference of these olfactory cues to your receivers?

Taste

Since we are multichannel communicators, we also receive and respond to gustatory, or taste, messages. Taste, smell, and our other senses work together. In fact, our sense of smell or sight often stimulates or turns off our desire to taste something. Taste is personally based. We have different preferences for food textures and tastes. When we interpret and perform literature, we need to physicalize taste—to show receivers the sensations that a particular taste evokes in us.

PERFORMER'S WARM-UP
Physicalizing Taste

A. Members of your class will be divided into teams, seated before a table, and blindfolded. Your instructor will present each team with a series of foods they will be asked to sample and then identify.
B. Think of a food such as cotton candy, peanut butter, pizza, or even a lemon. Write the name of this food on a slip of paper and drop it on a tray your instructor provides for this exercise. When your instructor calls on you, come to the front of the room, pick an entry from the tray, and pantomime eating this food for the rest of the class. The class will attempt to guess what you are eating.

Questions

1. What happened to the inside of your mouth as you ate this food?
2. What did it do to your eyes? Your forehead? Your neck? Your fingers?
3. Did your sense of smell operate together with your sense of taste? How could you tell?

PERFORMER'S WORKSHOP
Tasting Literature

Now read and "taste" the following two poems. Which poem has a sweet taste? Which has a bitter taste? How can your readings reinforce these different flavors?

When was the last time you raided the refrigerator or the cookie jar? How much did you enjoy eating what you found? Let your audience know how very much the speaker in William Carlos Williams's poem "This Is Just to Say" enjoyed the plums he found in the ice box.

"This Is Just to Say"
William Carlos Williams

I have eaten
the plums
that were in
the ice box

and which
you were probably
saving
for breakfast

Forgive me
they were delicious
so sweet
and so cold

Questions

1. What roles do physicalization and vocalization play in interpreting and performing this poem?
2. Show how the speaker might have looked when eating the plums.

What have you eaten lately that is really bitter? Can you recall that taste? Is it difficult to continue eating something bitter? Let your audience feel the surreal mood and taste bitterness as you read Stephen Crane's "In the Desert."

"In the Desert"
Stephen Crane

In the desert
I saw a creature, naked, bestial,
Who, squatting upon the ground,
Held his heart in his hands,
And ate of it.
I said, "Is it good, friend?"
"It is bitter—bitter," he answered;
"But I like it
"Because it is bitter,
"And because it is my heart."

Questions

1. How do you envision the creature sitting as he eats his heart?
2. How would you portray the creature?
3. What facial expressions can you imagine the creature making as he swallows a piece of his own heart?

Touch

Our sense of touch, both tactile and thermal, is involved in many of our most meaningful contacts with other people and our environment. We use touch for different purposes: to communicate affect or attitude, to facilitate affiliation, and to demonstrate power or exert control. Through touch we investigate our environment, sense its warmth or coldness, and establish many of our closest relationships.

Our touching behavior is governed by a set of norms. When these norms are violated—when we touch what we should not touch, or when we engage in too much or too little touching—we and others may experience discomfort. Touch helps us maintain both our physiological and psychological well being. It serves a therapeutic function that begins with birth. Infants wither emotionally and physically when not touched and thrive when picked up and held. Clearly, touch has message value and should be carefully considered by the oral interpreter.

PERFORMER'S WARM-UP
The Communicative Touch

Choose a partner for this exercise. One of you is blindfolded and led on a silent five-minute sensory journey by your partner. The goal of the journey is to allow the blindfolded partner to touch various items in your immediate environment, such as the desktop, the wall, the windowpane, a pencil, fabric samples, cold water, and warm water. Remember, neither of you is to speak during the touch tour.

After five minutes, you and your partner trade roles—the leader is blindfolded and the blindfolded partner becomes the leader. After five more minutes of a silent touch tour, the blindfolded one should remove the blindfold. Each of you will then travel the touch-sense trail alone. Try to reexamine carefully the items you just experienced.

Questions

1. When blindfolded, which items could you identify most easily? Which items were difficult to name?
2. How did you react to the "cool" items? The "warm" ones?
3. What did you learn from this exercise about your sense of touch?

PERFORMER'S WARM-UP
Mood Magic

Were you ever in a particular mood that could be represented with a color? We sometimes talk about feeling "blue" or experiencing "white-hot" anger.

Think of a number of emotions that might be associated with different colors. Or, alternately, write a list of colors and think of moods that might go with them.

Questions

1. Which colors lend themselves readily to expressing moods or experiences? Why? Which colors are more difficult to connect with?
2. How might you use color to represent an experience or a time in your life?
3. How could you convey a sense of color to an audience? What words, gestures, and tone of voice would you use?

Movement

We are a unified organism. We respond to experience kinesthetically, not just with our five senses or intellectually. **Kinesthesia** is the sensory experience of physical actions. Our kinesthetic sense tells us whether to relax or tense; it tells us what bodily movements support the content of a text or the personality of a speaker. Our sense of kinesthesia and our physical expressiveness also help us involve audience members in the moving, changing world of a text. If, for example, we feel sadness in the pit of our stomachs or express happiness with a smile, then we have succeeded in using our bodily sensations to communicate meaning.

PERFORMER'S WARM-UP
Kinesthetic Experiences

A. Listen to one member of your group squeak a piece of chalk or fingernails across the blackboard.

Questions

1. Did you hear the chalk or nails just with your ears?
2. What other parts of your body heard the squeak? How do you know?
3. What happened to your facial muscles as you experienced the sound? What happened to your shoulders? Your stomach? Your legs?

B. Now imagine that, on a dark night, you are standing alone waiting for a bus. The street is absolutely deserted and is not well lit. Suddenly you hear a shrill scream behind you.

Questions

1. Describe the scream as you just heard it in your mind's ear.
2. Describe how your body reacted to this imagined stimulus. Did you tense? Did you relax? What happened to your eyebrows? Your mouth? Your back? Your fingers?

3. How might you perform a piece of literature in order to elicit similar responses from an audience?

C. Your instructor may wish to use a drum to pace this section of the exercise. Imagine yourself taking a leisurely walk on a quiet night. Now you increase your pace to a jog; suddenly, you discover you are being chased by a car. You dart back and forth across a narrow alley to avoid being hit. You see a small gate at the end of the alley and you sprint for it. You are safe!

Questions

1. How did your body respond differently as the situation changed? What happened to your eyes? Your lips? Your knees? Your rate of breathing?
2. How did your sensory responses affect your overall muscle tone?

PERFORMER'S WORKSHOP
Kinesthesia

Read the following passage from *Incidents in the Life of a Slave Girl.* In this cutting from her narrative, Harriet A. Jacobs tells of going into hiding to escape being abused by a master during the time of slavery in the United States. Remember to allow your kinesthetic sense to demonstrate your internalization of the text.

 ### *Incidents in the Life of a Slave Girl*
Harriet A. Jacobs

A small shed had been added to my grandmother's house years ago. Some boards were laid across the joists at the top, and between these boards and the roof was a very small garret, never occupied by any thing but rats and mice. It was a pent roof, covered with nothing but shingles, according to the southern custom for such buildings. The garret was only nine feet long and seven wide. The highest part was three feet high, and sloped down abruptly to the loose board floor. There was no admission for either light or air. My uncle Phillip, who was a carpenter, had very skillfully made a concealed trap-door, which communicated with the storeroom. He had been doing this while I was waiting in the swamp. The storeroom opened upon a piazza. To this hole I was conveyed as soon as I entered the house. The air was stifling; the darkness total. A bed had been spread on the floor. I could sleep quite comfortably on one side; but the slope was so sudden that I could not turn on the other without hitting the roof. The rats and mice ran over my bed; but I was weary, and I slept such sleep as the wretched may, when a tempest has passed over them. Morning came. I knew it only by the noises I heard; for in my small den day and night were all the same. I suffered for air even more than for light. But I was not comfortless. I heard the voices of my children. There was joy and there was sadness in the sound. It made my tears flow. How I longed to speak to them! I was eager to look on their faces; but there was no hole, no crack, through which I could peep. This continued darkness was oppressive. It seemed horrible to sit or lie in a cramped position day after day, without one gleam of light. Yet I would have chosen this, rather than my lot as a slave, though white people considered it an easy one; and it was so compared with the fate of others. I was never cruelly overworked; I was never lacerated with the whip from head to foot; I was never so beaten and bruised that I could not turn from one side to the other; I never had my heel-strings cut to prevent my running away; I was never chained to a log and forced to drag it about, while I toiled in the fields from morning till night; I was never branded with hot iron, or torn by bloodhounds. On the contrary, I had always been kindly treated, and tenderly cared for, until I came into the hands of Dr. Flint. I had never wished for freedom till then. But though my life in slavery was comparatively devoid of hardships, God pity the woman who is compelled to lead such a life!

Questions

1. How can your kinesthetic sense help you to successfully perform this selection for an audience?
2. At what points in the passage will your muscle tone change?
3. At what point will your state of physical tension be greatest?

Work your kinesthetic responses to this segment from "The Highwayman" by Alfred Noyes.

 "The Highwayman"
Alfred Noyes

> The wind was a torrent of darkness among the gusty trees,
> The moon was a ghostly galleon tossed upon cloudy seas,
> The road was a ribbon of moonlight over the purple moor,
> And the highwayman came riding—
> Riding—riding—
> The highwayman came riding, up to the old inn-door.

Questions

1. Where does your muscle tone change in this passage?
2. Where is the tension the greatest?

Feelings are universal—everyone has them. An interpretative performer uses methods to help audience members feel and understand literature in ways they could not simply by reading the piece themselves. An interpretative performer must be an expert on feelings and the descriptive words that convey them. The following exercise will help you to refine your descriptive talents.

PERFORMER'S WARM-UP
Descriptions

A. As a group, select one of the following images: clouds, fire, rain, a flower, a car, softball, football, hockey.
B. Working individually, visualize the chosen image. Write down as many descriptive words as you can think of to help paint a verbal picture.
C. Next, work with a team to devise a more extensive list of words to describe the chosen image. For example, if you had chosen "clouds," you might describe them as open, fluid, feathery, fleecy, threatening, light, magical, gloomy, ominous, rainbowlike, shadowy, and nebulous.
D. Now perform the description aloud. Each member of the team should select specific words to read. Working together, communicate the various meanings of your image through your performance.

Questions

1. How did the various images held by individuals in your group merge during the actual reading?
2. How did sense-memory skills help you communicate your assigned descriptive words to your audience?
3. Given another opportunity, in what ways would you like to change your performance?

IDEA ENCORE

Chapter 3 focused on the role sense memory plays in the interpretation and performance of texts. In this chapter, you explored ways to enlarge and extend your sensory capabilities so that you can identify and recall the sense memories needed to evoke sensory perceptions in audience members during a performance.

By concentrating on experiences that let sensory experiences come to the surface and by working consciously to enrich your auditory, visual, olfactory, gustatory, thermal, tactile, and kinesthetic acuities, you empower yourself to more readily feel and understand a text, and you harness your ability to use sense memories habitually during preparation and performance.

PERFORMER'S SHOWCASE & JOURNAL
Senses Census

The following selections give you the opportunity to apply and demonstrate what you have learned about sense memory. After you read the selections, record in your journal how you plan to use sense memory to help you interpret the literature.

SELECTIONS FOR FURTHER WORK

In the first selection, the Japanese American author Mitsuye Yamada speaks of immigrating to the United States to join her husband.

"Marriage Was a Foreign Country"
Mitsuye Yamada

I come to be here
because
they say I must
follow my husband

so I come.

My grandmother cried:
you are not cripple
why
to America?

When we land the boat full
of new brides
lean over railing
with wrinkled glossy pictures
they hold inside hand
like this
so excited
down there a dock full of men
they do same thing
hold pictures
look up and down
like this
they find faces to
match pictures.

Your father I see him on the dock
he come to Japan to marry
and leave me
I was not a picture bride
I only was afraid.

In the second selection, an excerpt from Alex Haley's Pulitzer Prize-winning work *Roots*, Kunta Kinte has been captured and placed on a slave ship bound from Africa for America. He and hundreds of other men are living in a stinking, filthy compartment of the ship.

from *Roots*

Alex Haley

The stinging bites, then the itching of the body lice, steadily grew worse. In the filth, the lice as well as the fleas had multiplied by the thousands until they swarmed all over the hold. They were worst wherever the body crevices held any hair. Kunta's armpits, and around his foot, felt as if they were on fire, and his free hand scratched steadily wherever his shackled hand couldn't reach.

He kept having thoughts of springing up and running away; then, a moment later, his eyes would fill with tears of frustration, anger would rise in him, and he would fight it all back down until he felt again some kind of calm. The worst thing was that he couldn't move anywhere; he felt he wanted to bite through his chains. He decided that he must keep himself focused upon something, anything to occupy his mind or his hands, or else he would go mad—as some men in the hold seemed to have done already, judging from the things they cried out.

By lying very still and listening to the breathing sounds of the men on either side of him, Kunta had long since learned to tell when either of them was asleep or awake. He concentrated now upon hearing farther away from him. With more and more practice at listening intently to repeated sounds, he discovered that his ears after a while could discern their location almost exactly; it was a peculiar sensation, almost as if his ears were serving for eyes. Now and then, among the groans and curses that filled the darkness, he heard the thump of a man's head against the planks he lay on. And there was another odd and monotonous noise. It would stop at intervals, then resume after a while; it sounded as if two pieces of metal were being rubbed hard together, and after hearing more of it Kunta figured that someone was trying to wear the links of his chains apart. Kunta often heard, too, brief exclamations and janglings of chains as two men furiously fought, jerking their shackles against each other's ankles and wrists.

Kunta had lost track of time. The urine, vomit, and feces that reeked everywhere around him had spread into a slick paste covering the hard planking of the long shelves on which they lay. Just when he had begun to think he couldn't stand it any more, eight toubob came down the hatchway, cursing loudly. Instead of the routine food container, they carried what seemed to be some kind of long-handled hoes and four large tubs. And Kunta noticed with astonishment that they were not wearing any clothes at all.

PART 2

Exploring Literary Worlds

Chapter 4

The Interpretation
of Descriptive Prose

Learning Objectives

After completing this chapter, you should be able to

- define descriptive prose
- define and distinguish between different types of imagery
- use both primary and secondary sense appeals to enrich performance
- discuss how character descriptions and setting guide the performer in interpreting literature

In Chapter 4 we will focus on descriptive prose—the type of prose that uses literary close-ups to present a detailed picture of someone or something. Reflecting careful and deliberate thought, descriptive prose envelops and surrounds the action of a story. It functions to slow or suspend time as the speaker stops to study or scrutinize the intricacies of a subject.

The Power of Description

As an interpreter, you use your senses as a kind of "open sesame" to literature. In order to share a literary world with an audience, you must communicate the experience that resides within the literary selection, conveying its full meaning by embodying its emotional qualities. Only by using all your senses will you be able to empathize with and to re-create the fictional world an author has created with carefully selected words.

An important part of an author's fictional world is presented through descriptive prose. Description introduces characters and setting; it creates suspense or sustains a mood; it gives a picture of something essential to a piece of literature. Descriptive prose awakens our senses. By exploring the sensory qualities of people, places, things, or events, it calls on us to respond physically and emotionally.

PERFORMER'S WORKSHOP
Refreshing the Senses

Read the following excerpt from *Johnny Got His Gun* by Dalton Trumbo. This passage describes Joe, a human being whom war has turned into a living vegetable.

from *Johnny Got His Gun*
Dalton Trumbo

He began to resent the question itself and the way they asked it and the ignorance that lay behind it. Who did they think they were and what did they think he wanted that they could give him? Did they think he would ask for an ice-cream cone?

. . . Maybe they thought he would ask for a change of diet. The coffee you've been pouring into my tube lately needs a little more sugar; it tastes bitter to my intestines so add a half teaspoonful of sugar and stir it well please. . . .

They should know what he wanted . . . and they should know they couldn't give it to him. He wanted eyes to see with. Two eyes to see sunlight and moonlight and blue mountains and tall trees and little ants and houses that people live in and flowers opening in the morning and snow on the ground and streams running and trains coming and going and people walking and a puppy dog playing with an old shoe worrying it and growling at it and backing away from it and frowning and wiggling its bottom and taking the shoe very seriously. He wanted a nose so he could smell rain and burning wood and cooking food and the faint perfume that stays in the air after a girl has passed by. He wanted a mouth so he could eat and talk and laugh and taste and kiss. He wanted arms and legs so that he could work and walk and be like a man like a living thing.

Questions

1. Using what you've learned in Chapter 3, how can you relate to Joe's feelings?
2. How could you convey the ideas expressed in the above passage so that the audience would relate to Joe's situation?

PERFORMER'S WORKSHOP
Meeting Descriptive Prose

Imagine having the same dream night after night. In that dream you see your father, whom you have not seen in years—not since he was imprisoned in a concentration camp. Then one day you are told that he is alive in a hospital—but that his mind has been destroyed. This is what faces Karen Clement, a character in *Exodus* by Leon Uris.

Read the following passage and pay attention to the word-pictures the author creates.

 from ***Exodus***

Leon Uris

The doctor led them down a corridor and stopped before a door. A nurse unlocked it. He held the door open.

Karen walked into a cell-like room. The room held a chair, a stand and a bed. She looked around for a moment and then she stiffened. A man was sitting on the floor in a corner. He was barefooted and uncombed. He sat with his back against the wall and his arms around his knees and stared blankly at the opposite wall.

Karen took a step toward him. He was stubble-bearded and his face was scarred. Suddenly the pounding within Karen's heart eased. This is all a mistake, she thought . . . this man is a stranger . . . he is not my father . . . he cannot be. It is a mistake! A mistake! She was filled with the urge to turn around and scream out . . . *you see, you were wrong. He is not John Clement, he is not my father. My father is still alive somewhere and looking for me.* Karen stood before the man on the floor to assure herself. She stared into the crazed eyes. It had been so long . . . so very long, she could not remember. But the man she had dreamed about meeting again was not this man.

There was a fireplace and the smell of pipe tobacco. There was a big moppy dog. His name was Maximillian. A baby cried in the next room. "Miriam, see to Hans. I am reading a story for my girl and I cannot be disturbed."

Karen Hansen Clement slowly knelt before the hulk of mindless flesh.

Grandma's house in Bonn always smelled of newly baked cookies. She baked all week getting ready for the family on Sunday.

The insane man continued to stare at the opposite wall as though he were alone in the room.

Look how funny the monkeys are in the Cologne Zoo! Cologne has the most wonderful zoo. When will it be carnival time again?

She studied the man from his bare feet to his scarred forehead. Nothing . . . nothing she saw was like her father. . . .

"Jew! Jew! Jew!" the crowd screamed as she ran into her house with the blood pouring down her face. "There, there, Karen don't you cry. Daddy won't let them hurt you."

Karen reached out and touched the man's cheek. "Daddy?" she said. The man did not move or react.

There was a train and lots of children around and they were talking of going to Denmark but she was tired. "Goodby, Daddy," Karen had said. "Here, you take my dolly. He will watch after you." She stood on the platform of the train and watched her Daddy on the platform as he grew smaller and smaller.

"Daddy! Daddy!" Karen cried. "It's Karen, Daddy! I'm your girl. I'm all grown up now, Daddy. Don't you remember me?"

The doctor held Kitty in the doorway as she shook from head to foot. "Let me help her, please," Kitty cried.

"Let it be done," he said.

And Karen was filled with remembering—"Yes! Yes! He is my father! He is my father!"

"Daddy!" she screamed and threw her arms around him. "Please talk to me. Please say something to me. I beg you . . . beg you!"

The man who was once the living human person of Johann Clement blinked his eyes. A sudden expression of curiosity came over his face as he became aware of a person clutching at him. He held the expression for a tense moment as though he were trying, in his own way, to allow something to penetrate the blackness—and then, his look lapsed back into lifelessness.

"Daddy!" she screamed. "Daddy! Daddy!"

And her voice echoed in the empty room and down the long corridor— "Daddy!"

The strong arms of the doctor pried her loose, and she was gently dragged from the room. The door was closed and locked and Johann Clement was gone from her—forever. The girl sobbed in anguish and crumpled into Kitty's arms. "He didn't even know me! Oh, my God . . . God . . . why doesn't he know me? Tell me, God . . . tell me!"

Questions

1. What types of feelings did the preceding passage evoke in you?
2. Can you point to specific phrases in the passage that you find particularly effective?
3. Why do you believe these phrases affect you as they do?

Describing Character and Setting

The descriptions of a character's physique or body shape, clothes or general style of dress, and attitude or general affective mood are written to influence and to determine response. As Sherlock Holmes said: "By a man's fingernails, by his coat sleeve, by his boots, by his trouser-knees, by the callosities of his forefinger and thumb, by his expression, by his shirtcuffs—by each of these things a man's calling is plainly revealed. That all united should fail to enlighten the competent inquirer in any case is almost inconceivable." An interpreter must learn to be a "competent inquirer"—to look for clues in the text that reveal character and to think of ways to convey that character to an audience.

An author uses descriptions of setting or environment in much the same way. Just as the details of character assist a reader in arriving at an effective interpretation, so the description of a city, a town, a home, a room, or an object may also be used to further refine a reader's perception. After all, the environments in which people find themselves frequently contribute directly to the nature and outcome of their communications with others. In other words, an author may use the location of a character and the objects that surround him or her to influence, either subtly or overtly, the character's attitudes and communicative behavior.

The following exercises will illustrate how authors use description to establish who the characters are and what they are like, as well as to establish the environment or setting of the selection.

PERFORMER'S WORKSHOP
Character Descriptions

What do the following descriptions tell you about each of the characters in them?

In the first passage from "All Gold Canyon," Jack London focuses on the face of a man in order to establish his personality traits for the reader.

 ### "All Gold Canyon"
Jack London

He was a sandy-complexioned man in whose face geniality and humor seemed the salient characteristics. It was a mobile face, quick-changing to inward mood and thought. Thinking was in him a visible process. Ideas chased across his face like wind flows across the surface of a lake. His hair, sparse and unkempt of growth, was as indeterminate and colorless as his complexion. It would seem that all the color of his frame had gone into his eyes, for they were startlingly blue. Also, they were laughing and merry eyes, within them much of the naiveté and wonder of the child; and yet in an unassertive way, they contained much of calm self-reliance and strength of purpose founded upon self-experience and experience of the world.

Charles Dickens gives us a description of his character Scrooge in this excerpt from his famous tale *A Christmas Carol.*

A Christmas Carol
Charles Dickens

Oh! but he was a tight-fisted hand at the grindstone, Scrooge! a squeezing, wrenching, grasping, scraping, clutching, covetous old sinner! Hard and sharp as flint, from which no steel had ever struck out generous fire; secret, and self-contained, and solitary as an oyster. The cold within him froze his old features, nipped his pointed nose, shriveled his cheek, stiffened his gait; made his eyes red, his thin lips blue; and spoke out shrewdly in his grating voice. A frosty rime was on his head, and on his eyebrows, and his wiry chin. He carried his own low temperature about with him; he iced his office in the dog-days, and didn't thaw it one degree at Christmas.

External heat and cold had little influence on Scrooge. No warmth could warm, no wintry weather chill him. No wind that blew was bitterer

Describing Character and Setting **81**

than he, no falling snow was more intent upon its purpose, no pelting rain less open to entreaty. Foul weather didn't know where to have him. The heaviest rain, and snow, and hail, and sleet, could boast of the advantage over him in only one respect. They often "came down" handsomely, and Scrooge never did.

Nobody ever stopped him in the street to say, with gladsome looks, "My dear Scrooge, how are you? when will you come to see me?" No beggars implored him to bestow a trifle, no children asked him what it was o'clock, no man or woman ever once in all his life inquired the way to such and such a place, of Scrooge. Even the blindmen's dogs appeared to know him; and when they saw him coming on, would tug their owners into doorways and up courts; and then would wag their tails as though they said, "No eye at all is better than an evil eye, dark master!"

Questions

1. How do the physical appearances and personalities of the characters in each cutting differ from each other?
2. What type of physical stance would you, as interpreter, assume when portraying these characters?
3. What mood-tones would you work to reinforce?

PERFORMER'S WORKSHOP
Environmental Descriptions

Analyze the way environment is used by John L'Heureux and Isak Dinesen in the following passages from their works "Fox and Swan" and "Sorrow-Acre."

 "Fox and Swan"

John L'Heureux

It seemed the cold would never let up. For over a week the temperature had been below freezing and for most of that time it had hovered around zero. Francis hated cold weather, his long stringy body responding to it with unmanly shivers. Nor could he afford the winter coat he needed.

Christ, will it never end, he asked himself, and he pulled his scarf tighter. It was a long striped scarf worn like a college student's—outside the jacket, hanging down in front and in back—even though he knew he was too old for that sort of thing.

"Sorrow-Acre"
Isak Dinesen

The low, undulating Danish landscape was silent and serene, mysteriously wide-awake in the hour before sunrise. There was not a cloud in the pale sky, not a shadow along the dim, pearly fields, hills and woods. The mist was lifting from the valleys and hollows, the air was cool, the grass and the foliage dripping wet with morning-dew. Unwatched by the eyes of man, and undisturbed by his activity, the country breathed a timeless life, to which language was inadequate.

All the same, a human race had lived on this land for a thousand years, had been formed by its soil and weather, and had marked it with its thoughts, so that now no one could tell where the existence of the one ceased and the other began. The thin grey line of a road, winding across the plain and up and down hills was the fixed materialization of human longing, and of the human notion that it is better to be in one place than in another.

A child of the country would read this open landscape like a book. The irregular mosaic of meadows and cornlands was a picture in timid green and yellow, of the people's struggle for its daily bread; the centuries had taught it to plough and sow in this way. On a distant hill the immovable wings of a windmill, in a small blue cross against the sky, delineated a later stage in the career of bread. The blurred outline of thatched roofs—a low, brown growth of the earth—where the huts of the village thronged together, told the history, from his cradle to his grave, of the peasant, the creature nearest to the soil and dependent on it, prospering in a fertile year and dying in years of drought and pests.

Questions

1. How can you as interpreter help your audience to envision these environments?
2. What physical and vocal responses can you use to suggest the feelings associated with each environment?

As we have seen, description fills in the qualities of a person, a place, an object, or even an event in terms of the senses; it tells how something looks, sounds, smells, tastes, feels, or moves.

The Role of Imagery in Descriptive Prose

One of the chief characteristics of descriptive prose is its reliance on **imagery**. An image is simply a group of words that affects your senses so as to elicit an internal and external response from you. As they appeal to your senses, images place a picture in your mind.

As an interpreter, you need to be aware that the effectiveness of imagery—and, consequently, of description—depends upon four things:

- the writer's ability to describe a sensory experience
- the reader's ability to process the sensory experience by making associations from his or her own experience
- the interpreter's ability to embody the sensory experience described in the literature
- the performer's ability to share the literature in a way that enlivens and communicates the emotional experience to the audience

Thus, descriptive cues or images help you enter the literature—they sharpen your perception of the created world and the created characters. Description transforms the skeleton or plot of a tale into something that seems to live and breathe. As an interpreter, you can use the enrichment that description brings to literature to enhance your performance of it.

The interpreter and performer of literature needs to be able to detail completely the way a descriptive passage appeals to the senses, pointing to and identifying each type of image a selection contains. There are six basic image categories with which an interpreter of literature should be familiar. These six image categories correspond to the six senses explored in the preceding chapter.

Types of Images

We can classify images into several categories. Images that appeal primarily to the sense of sight are *visual images* ("future days strung together like pearls in a rosary"—Mary E. Wilkins Freeman); to the sense of hearing are *auditory images* ("the loud, iron, clanking of the lift machinery"—John Cheever); to the sense of taste are *gustatory images* ("the acrid, metallic taste of gunfire"—Alberto Moravia); and to the sense of smell are *olfactory images* ("The room was heavy with the rich odor of mellowing pears"—Thomas Wolfe). The sense of touch is appealed to in either tactile or thermal imagery. *Tactile imagery* evokes a sensation of physical contact ("the ache of marriage throbs in the teeth"—Denise Levertov), while *thermal imagery* refers to the feeling of cold or of heat ("The blueblack cold of early morning"—Robert Hayden).

In addition to the images that appeal to the five traditional senses, an interpreter is also concerned with images of motion which are designed to appeal to his or her motor sense (for example, a thought "bumping like a helium balloon at the ceiling of the brain"—Sandra Cisneros). These images are classified as *kinetic* in nature if they describe a large overt action of the muscles: "John ran and then he jumped." The images are *kinesthetic* in nature if they refer to degrees of muscular tension or relaxation: "John sat down nervously while Kevin smiled smugly." Consider some imagery examples from literature.

PERFORMER'S WORKSHOP
Imagery

What are the predominant sensory responses evoked by each of the descriptions in the following cuttings? Carefully note them in your performer's journal and describe how they affect you.

 The Red Badge of Courage
Stephen Crane

The youth tried to observe everything. He did not use care to avoid trees and branches, and his forgotten feet were constantly knocking against stones or getting entangled in briers. He was aware that these battalions with their commotions were woven red and startling into the gentle fabric of softened greens and browns. It looked to be a wrong place for a battlefield.

The skirmishers in advance fascinated him. Their shots into thickets and at distant and prominent trees spoke to him of tragedies—hidden, mysterious, solemn.

Once the line encountered the body of a dead soldier. He lay upon his back staring at the sky. He was dressed in an awkward suit of yellowish brown. The youth could see that the soles of his shoes had been worn to the thinness of writing paper, and from a great rent in one the dead foot projected piteously. And it was as if fate had betrayed the soldier. In death it exposed to his enemies that poverty which in life he had perhaps concealed from his friends.

 "The Lesson"
Toni Cade Bambara

Back in the days when everyone was old and stupid or young and foolish and me and Sugar were the only ones just right, this lady moved on our block with nappy hair and proper speech and no makeup. And quite naturally we laughed at her, laughed the way we did at the junk man who went about his business like he was some big-time president and his sorry horse his secretary. And we kinda hated her, too, hated the way we did the winos who cluttered up our parks . . . and stank up our hallways and stairs so you couldn't halfway play hide-and-seek without a gas mask. Miss Moore was her name. The only woman on the block with no first name. And she was black, cept for her feet, which were fish-white and spooky. And she was always planning these boring things for us to do, us being my cousin, mostly, who lived on the block cause we all moved North the same time and to the same apartment then spread out gradual to breathe. And our parents would yank our heads into some kinda shape and crisp up our clothes so we'd be presentable for travel with Miss Moore, who always looked like she was going to church, though she never did. Which is just one of the things the grownups talked about when they talked behind her back like a dog.

 ## *Look Homeward, Angel*

Thomas Wolfe

Dusk came. The huge bulk of the hills was foggily emergent. Small smoky lights went up in the hillside shacks. The train crawled dizzily across high trestles spanning ghostly hawsers of water. Far up, far down, plumed with wisps of smoke, toy cabins stuck to bank and gulch and hillside. The train toiled sinuously up among gouged red cuts with slow labor. As darkness came, Oliver descended at the little town of Old Stockade where the rails ended. The last great wall of the hills lay stark above him. As he left the dreary little station and stared into the greasy lamplight of a country store, Oliver felt that he was crawling, like a great beast, into the circle of those enormous hills to die.

Questions

1. How can you physically and vocally embody the sensory appeals in these selections?
2. Why do sensory responses help make the literature live for your audience?

From your reading, you may have realized already that images do not usually reside solely in one sensory class or category. There is virtually no such thing as a purely auditory image, a purely visual image, and so on. An image nearly always stimulates more than one sense. While its emphasis may be in one area, the image will almost always contain secondary sense appeals as well. Identifying both the primary (dominant) and the secondary (subdominant) sense appeals that reside in an image is a critical skill for an interpreter, who must always be a thorough sensory tracker. How are your tracking skills? Try the following exercise.

PERFORMER'S WORKSHOP
The Sense Search Game

The class should divide into a number of teams. Each team is to find and classify all the images contained in one of the following passages. Groups should note both primary and secondary sense appeals.

After your group has completed its sense search, select one member to perform the passage for the rest of the class. Those who do not perform are to serve as their chosen performer's "training team," helping him or her to rehearse the passage, and being certain to communicate which images are being sent clearly and which images need further work or clarification. After the rehearsal period, your group's representative will perform the passage for the remaining class members, who will also have a chance to evaluate the clarity and effectiveness of the re-created images. (You may wish to use this group rehearsal method at various points during the course. Performance exercises throughout this book may be easily adapted to include this type of preparation approach.)

 "The Hopeland"

K. Kam

I try to imagine my mother as a young girl, small and frail with a quiet heart, shiny black hair cropped to prevent her from indulging in hours of vanity before the mirror. I laugh when she tells me some pranksters in her village filled a large vat with dung and lit a fire under it, boiling the smelly contents until they exploded.

But the funny stories are always followed by somber ones that will not let me forget the horrors my parents must have endured. I hear only bits and pieces. My mother tells of drunken soldiers banging on the doors of houses nearby, dragging out screaming girls and raping them in the night. She watched an angry crowd of villagers haul a traitor to the top of a hill, where they hanged him for selling secrets to the enemy. There were the victims forced to kneel on broken glass and the hunted ones who chose suicide. During land raids, she stared mutely as soldiers smashed windows and shot down old women barricading doorways with their bodies to protect young ones inside. During one onslaught, she hid underneath the bed as a soldier entered her house and held a bayonet to her mother's throat.

I am disturbed, yet intrigued. I listen to the stories, casting the characters and writing the script, but my mental exercise is only a game. My parents' China still eludes me.

"Miss Thompson"

W. Somerset Maugham

He scratched his mosquito bites. He felt very short-tempered. When the rain stopped and the sun shone, it was like a hothouse, seething, humid, sultry, breathless, and you had a strange feeling that everything was growing with savage violence. The natives, blithe and childlike by reputation, seemed then, with their tattooing and their dyed hair, to have something sinister in their appearance; and when they pattered along at your heels with their naked feet you looked back instinctively. You felt they might at any moment come behind you swiftly and thrust a long knife between your shoulder blades. You could not tell what dark thoughts lurked behind their wide-set eyes. They had a little the look of ancient Egyptians painted on a temple wall, and there was about them the terror of what is immeasurably old.

Autobiography

Mark Twain

I spent some part of every year at the farm until I was twelve or thirteen years old. The life which I led there with my cousins was full of charm, and so is the memory of it yet. I can call back the solemn twilight and mystery of the deep woods, the earthy smells, the faint odors of the wild flowers, the sheen of rainwashed foliage, the rattling clapper of drops when the wind shook the trees, the far-off hammering of woodpeckers and the muffled drumming of wood pheasants in the remoteness of the forest, the snapshot glimpses of disturbed wild creatures scurrying through the grass—I can call it all back and make it as real as it ever was, and as blessed. I can call back the prairie, and its loneliness and peace, and a vast hawk hanging motionless in the sky, with his wings spread wide and the blue of the vault showing through the fringe of their end feathers. I can see the woods in their autumn dress, the oaks purple, the hickories washed with gold, the maples and the sumacs luminous with crimson fires, and I can hear the rustle made by the fallen leaves as we plowed through them. I can see the blue clusters of wild grapes hanging among the foliage of the saplings, and I remember the taste of them and the smell. I know how the wild blackberries looked, and how they tasted, and the same with the pawpaws, the hazelnuts, and the persimmons; and I can feel the thumping rain, upon my head, of hickory nuts and walnuts when we were out in the frosty dawn to scramble for them with the pigs, and the gusts of wind loosed them and sent them down. I know the stain of blackberries, and how pretty it is, and I know the stain of walnut hulls, and how little it minds soap and water, also what grudged experience it had of either of them. I know the taste of maple sap, and when to gather it, and how to arrange the troughs and the delivery tubes, and how to boil down the juice, and how to hook the sugar after it is made, also how much better hooked sugar tastes than any that is honestly come by, let bigots say what they will. I know how a prize watermelon looks when it is sunning its fat rotundity among pumpkin vines and "simblins"; I know how to tell when it is ripe without "plugging" it; I know how inviting it looks when it is cooling itself in a tub of water under the bed, waiting; I know how it looks when it lies on the table in the sheltered great floor space between house and kitchen, and the children gathered for the sacrifice and their mouths watering; I know the crackling sound it makes when the carving knife enters its end, and I can see the split fly along in front of the blade as the knife cleaves its way to the other end; I can see its halves fall apart and display the rich red meat and the black seeds, and the heart standing up, a luxury fit for the elect; I know how a boy looks behind a yard-long slice of that melon, and I know how he feels; for I have been there. I know the taste of the watermelon which has been honestly come by, and I know the taste of the watermelon which has been acquired by art. Both taste good, but the experienced know which tastes best.

This type of sensory-search experience should evoke certain emotional or empathic responses in you—responses that are essential if you hope to communicate word pictures effectively. Emotional responses help you create a meaningful reflection of a literary world. When you have fully processed the images of your selection, you are ready to re-create the literature physically and vocally, to interpret and perform the literature so that others may appreciate it.

IDEA ENCORE

Chapter 4 built on the work completed in Chapter 3. It explored descriptive prose and the techniques necessary to effectively perform it. Descriptive prose is the kind of prose that contains close-ups, that is, detailed pictures of someone, someplace, or something. Most usually, description is used to introduce the characters and the setting of a selection. Description relies on imagery for its effect and impact. The six kinds of images of concern to the interpreter are visual, auditory, gustatory, olfactory, tactile/thermal, and kinetic/kinesthetic. After considering character, environment or setting, and imagery, you should improve your ability to re-create the world of a text for an audience.

The interpretive performer's job is to analyze how description is used in a selection, identify how it appeals to the senses, and decide what he or she needs to do in order to help the audience respond appropriately to the descriptive passages during a performance.

PERFORMER'S SHOWCASE & JOURNAL
Performing Descriptive Prose

Choose a four- to five-minute passage of descriptive prose to perform in class. Your selection may include some dialogue, but it should be predominantly descriptive in nature. Because of the time limits, you may have to do some thoughtful cutting of the selection; however, be sure the lines you eliminate do not disturb the flow of the passage. Your deletions should not distort the picture your author has tried to create.

You may select your reading from the end-of-chapter selections in this text or from literature you find on your own. Try to ensure that the piece you select is worthy of your time and study. Will its content appeal to and hold your audience's attention? Will the material provide you with a performance challenge, broadening your reading abilities?

When rehearsing and performing your selection, keep in mind your sensory education experiences. Work to fully capture and internalize the sensory qualities of the person, place, action, or object described. This is essential if you hope to communicate the word pictures, the mood, and the tone of the passage to your audience. Also, write a few sentences that will serve both to introduce your literature to the class and to help your audience to empathize. Finally, as you rehearse, use all your senses to appreciate and fully understand what you hope to convey to your audience.

After you have chosen your selection, write your responses to the following questions in your journal.

1. Why did you choose this selection? What about it appeals to you?
2. What is being described in the literature?
3. What is the speaker's attitude in the passage?
4. What types of sense images did the author use? Discuss how the imagery contributed to the development of mood.
5. What emotional values may be stimulated by an interpretation of your selection?
6. What would you like to impel your audience to imagine, feel, remember, or know about your selection?

SELECTIONS FOR FURTHER WORK

The following selection from Joyce Carol Oates's "Heat" is full of sense images. While reading, think of how you would convey the picture that Oates draws with words.

 "Heat"

Joyce Carol Oates

It was midsummer, the heat rippling above the macadam roads, cicadas screaming out of the trees, and the sky like pewter, glaring.

The days were the same day, like the shallow mud-brown river moving always in the same direction but so slow you couldn't see it. Except for Sunday: church in the morning, then the fat Sunday newspaper, the color comics, and newsprint on your fingers.

Rhea and Rhoda Kunkel went flying on their rusted old bicycles, down the long hill toward the railroad yard, Whipple's Ice, the scrubby pastureland where dairy cows grazed. They'd stolen six dollars from their own grandmother who loved them. They were eleven years old; they were identical twins; they basked in their power.

Rhea and Rhoda Kunkel: it was always Rhea-and-Rhoda, never Rhoda-and-Rhea, I couldn't say why. You just wouldn't say the names that way. Not even the teachers at school would say them that way.

We went to see them in the funeral parlor where they were waked; we were made to. The twins in twin caskets, white, smooth, gleaming, perfect as plastic, with white satin lining puckered like the inside of a fancy candy box. And the waxy white lilies, the smell of talcum powder and perfume. The room was crowded; there was only one way in and out.

Rhea and Rhoda were the same girl; they'd wanted it that way. Only looking from one to the other could you see they were two.

This excerpt from Edgar Allan Poe's "The Telltale Heart" has a certain urgency and edge. How would you read it to make the narrator's madness evident?

 ## "The Tell-Tale Heart"
Edgar Allan Poe

True!—nervous—very, very dreadfully nervous I had been and am! but why *will* you say that I am mad? The disease had sharpened my senses—not destroyed—not dulled them. Above all was the sense of hearing acute. I heard all things in the heaven and in the earth. I heard many things in hell. How, then, am I mad? Hearken! and observe how healthily—how calmly I can tell you the whole story.

It is impossible to say how first the idea entered my brain; but once conceived, it haunted me day and night. Object there was none. Passion there was none. I loved the old man. He had never wronged me. He had never given me insult. For his gold I had no desire. I think it was his eye! yes, it was this! He had the eye of a vulture—a pale blue eye, with a film over it. Whenever it fell upon me, my blood ran cold; and so by degrees—very gradually—I made up my mind to take the life of the old man, and thus rid myself of the eye forever.

Now this is the point. You fancy me mad. Madmen know nothing. But you should have seen *me.* You should have seen how wisely I proceeded—with what caution—with what foresight—with what dissimulation I went to work!

I was never kinder to the old man than during the whole week before I killed him. And every night, about midnight, I turned the latch of his door and opened it—oh, so gently! And then, when I had made an opening sufficient for my head, I put in a dark lantern, all closed, closed, so that no light shone out, and then I thrust in my head. Oh, you would have laughed to see how cunningly I thrust it in! I moved it slowly—very, very slowly, so that I might not disturb the old man's sleep. It took me an hour to place my whole head within the opening so far that I could see him as he lay upon his bed. Ha!—would a madman have been so wise as this? And then, when my head was well in the room, I undid the lantern cautiously—oh, so cautiously—cautiously (for the hinges creaked)—I undid it just so much that a single thin ray fell upon the vulture eye. And this I did for seven long nights—every night just at midnight—but I found the eye always closed; and so it was impossible to do the work; for it was not the old man who vexed me, but his Evil Eye. And every morning, when the day broke, I went boldly into the chamber, and spoke courageously to him, calling him by name in a hearty tone, and inquiring how he had passed the night. So you see he would have been a very profound old man, indeed, to suspect that every night, just at twelve, I looked in upon him while he slept.

Upon the eighth night I was more than usually cautious in opening the door. A watch's minute hand moves more quickly than did mine. Never before that night had I *felt* that extent of my own powers—of my sagacity. I could scarcely contain my feelings of triumph. To think that there I was, opening the door, little by little, and he not even to dream of my secret deeds or thoughts. I fairly chuckled at the idea; and perhaps he heard me; for he moved on the bed suddenly, as if startled. Now you may think that I drew back—but no. His room was as black as pitch with the thick darkness (for the shutters were close fastened, through fear of robbers), and so I knew that he could not see the opening of the door, and I kept pushing it on steadily, steadily.

I had my head in, and was about to open the lantern, when my thumb slipped upon the tin fastening, and the old man sprang up in bed, crying out—"Who's there?"

I kept quite still and said nothing. For a whole hour I did not move a muscle, and in the meantime I did not hear him lie down. He was still sitting up in the bed listening;—just as I have done, night after night, harkening to the death watches in the wall.

Presently I heard a slight groan, and I knew it was the groan of mortal terror. It was not a groan of pain or of grief—oh no!—it was the low stifled sound that arises from the bottom of the soul when overcharged with awe. I knew the sound well. Many a night, just at midnight, when all the world slept, it has welled up from my own bosom, deepening, with its dreadful echo the terrors that distracted me. I say I knew it well. I knew what the old man felt, and pitied him, although I chuckled at heart. I knew that he had been lying awake ever since the first slight noise, when he had turned in the bed. His fears had been ever since growing upon him. He had been trying to fancy them causeless, but could not. He had been saying to himself—"It is nothing but the wind in the chimney—it is only a mouse crossing the floor," or "it is merely a cricket which has made a single chirp." Yes, he had been trying to comfort himself with these suppositions: but he had found all in vain. *All in vain;* because Death, in approaching him, had stalked with his black shadow before him, and enveloped the victim. And it was the mournful influence of the unperceived shadow that caused him to feel—although he neither saw nor heard—to *feel* the presence of my head within the room.

When I had waited a long time, very patiently, without hearing him lie down, I resolved to open a little—a very, very little crevice in the lantern. So I opened it—you cannot imagine how stealthily, stealthily—until, at length, a simple dim ray, like the thread of the spider, shot from out the crevice and fell full upon the vulture eye.

It was open—wide, wide open—and I grew furious as I gazed upon it. I saw it with perfect distinctness—all dull blue, with a hideous veil over it that chilled the very marrow in my bones; but I could see nothing else of the old man's face or person: for I had directed the ray as if by instinct, precisely upon the damned spot.

And I have not told you that what you mistake for madness is but over-acuteness of the senses?—now, I say, there came to my ears a low, dull, quick sound, such as a watch makes when enveloped in cotton. I knew *that* sound well too. It was the beating of the old man's heart. It increased my fury, as the beating of a drum stimulates the soldier into courage.

But even yet I refrained and kept still. I scarcely breathed. I held the lantern motionless. I tried how steadily I could maintain the ray upon the eye. Meantime the hellish tattoo of the heart increased. It grew quicker and quicker, and louder and louder every instant. The old man's terror *must* have been extreme! It grew louder, I say louder every moment!—do you mark me well? I have told you that I am nervous: so I am. And now at the dead hour of the night, amid the dreadful silence of that old house, so strange a noise as this excited me to uncontrollable terror. Yet, for some minutes longer I refrained and stood still. But the beating grew louder, louder! I thought the heart must burst. And now a new anxiety seized me—the sound would be heard by a neighbor! The old man's hour had come! With a loud yell, I threw open the lantern and leaped into the room. He shrieked once—once only. In an instant I dragged him to the floor, and pulled the heavy bed over him. I then smiled gaily, to find the deed so far done. But for many minutes, the heart beat on with a muffled sound. This, however, did not vex me; it would not be heard through the wall. At length it ceased. The old man was dead. I removed the bed and examined the corpse. Yes, he was stone, stone dead. I placed my hand upon the heart and held it there many minutes. There was no pulsation. He was stone dead. His eye would trouble me no more.

In this passage from "Death in the Woods," Sherwood Anderson describes old people in a rural community.

from "Death in the Woods"
Sherwood Anderson

She was an old woman and lived on a farm near the town in which I lived. All country and small-town people have seen such old women, but no one knows much about them. Such an old woman comes into town driving an old worn-out horse or she comes afoot carrying a basket. She may own a few hens and have eggs to sell. She brings them in a basket and takes them to a grocer. There she trades them in. She gets some salt pork and some beans. Then she gets a pound or two of sugar and some flour.

Afterward she goes to the butcher's and asks for some dog meat. She may spend ten or fifteen cents, but when she does she asks for something. In my day the butchers gave liver to anyone who wanted to carry it away. In our family we were always having it. Once one of my brothers got a whole cow's liver at the slaughter-house near the fair-grounds. We had it until we were sick of it. It never cost a cent. I have hated the thought of it ever since.

The old farm woman got some liver and a soup bone. She never visited with anyone, and as soon as she got what she wanted she lit out for home. It made quite a load for such an old body. No one gave her a lift. People drive right down a road and never notice an old woman like that.

There was such an old woman used to come into town past our house one summer and fall when I was sick with what was called inflammatory rheumatism. She went home later carrying a heavy pack on her back. Two or three large gaunt-looking dogs followed at her heels.

The old woman was nothing special. She was one of the nameless ones that hardly anyone knows, but she got into my thoughts. I have just suddenly now, after all these years, remembered her and what happened. It is a story. Her name was, I think, Grimes, and she lived with her husband and son in a small unpainted house on the bank of a small creek four miles from town.

The husband and son were a tough lot. Although the son was but twenty-one, he had already served a term in jail. It was whispered about that the woman's husband stole horses and ran them off to some other county. Now and then, when a horse turned up missing, the man had also disappeared. No one ever caught him. Once, when I was loafing at Tom Whitehead's livery barn, the man came there and sat on the bench in front. Two or three other men were there, but no one spoke to him. He sat for a few minutes and then got up and went away. When he was leaving he turned around and stared at the men. There was a look of defiance in his eyes. "Well, I have tried to be friendly. You don't want to talk to me. It has been so wherever I have gone in this town. If, some day, one of your fine horses turns up missing, well then what?" He did not say anything actually. "I'd like to bust one of you on the jaw," was about what his eyes said. I remember how the look in his eyes made me shiver.

The old man belonged to a family that had had money once. His name was Grimes, Jake Grimes. It all comes back clearly now. His father, John Grimes, had owned a sawmill when the country was new and had made money. Then he got to drinking and running after women. When he died, there wasn't much left.

Life for some of our senior citizens is less rewarding than it should be. In this passage by the New Zealand–born short-story writer Katherine Mansfield, we get a picture of the elderly Miss Brill.

"Miss Brill"
Katherine Mansfield

Although it was so brilliantly fine—the blue sky powdered with gold and great spots of light like white wine splashed over the Jardins Publiques—Miss Brill was glad that she had decided on her fur. The air was motionless, but when you opened your mouth there was just a faint chill, like a chill from a glass of iced water before you sip, and now and again a leaf came drifting—from nowhere, from the sky. Miss Brill put up her hand and touched her fur. Dear little thing! It was nice to feel it again. She had taken it out of its box that afternoon, shaken out the moth-powder, given it a good brush, and rubbed the life back into the dim little eyes. "What has been happening to me?" said the sad little eyes. Oh, how sweet it was to see them snap at her again from the red eiderdown! . . . But the nose, which was of some black composition, wasn't at all firm. It must have had a knock, somehow. Never mind—a little dab of black sealing-wax when the time came—when it was absolutely necessary. . . . Little rogue! Yes, she really felt like that about it. Little rogue biting its tail just by her left ear. She could have taken it off and laid it on her lap and stroked it. She felt a tingling in her hands and arms, but that came from walking, she supposed. . . . Only two people shared her "special" seat: a fine old man in a velvet coat, his hands clasped over a huge carved walking-stick, and a big old woman, sitting upright, with a roll of knitting on her embroidered apron. This was disappointing, for Miss Brill always looked forward to the conversation. She had become really quite expert, she thought, at listening as though she didn't listen, at sitting in other people's lives just for a minute while they talked round her. . . .

The old people sat on the bench, still as statues. Never mind, there was always the crowd to watch. To and fro, in front of the flower-beds and the band rotunda, the couples and groups paraded, stopped to talk, to greet, to buy a handful of flowers from the old beggar who had his tray fixed to the railings. Little children ran among them, swooping and laughing; little boys with big white silk bows under their chins, little girls, little French dolls, dressed up in velvet and lace. And sometimes a tiny staggerer came suddenly rocking into the open from under the trees, stopped, stared, as suddenly sat down "flop" until its small high-stepping mother, like a young hen, rushed scolding to its rescue. Other people sat on the benches and green chairs, but they were nearly always the same, Sunday after Sunday, and—Miss Brill had often noticed—there was something funny about nearly all of them. They were odd, silent, nearly all old, and from the way they stared they looked as though they'd just come from dark little rooms or even—even cupboards! . . .

On her way home she usually bought a slice of honeycake at the baker's. It was her Sunday treat. Sometimes there was an almond in her slice, sometimes not. It made a great difference. If there was an almond it was like carrying home a tiny present—a surprise—something that might very well not have been there. She hurried on the almond Sundays and struck the match for the kettle in quite a dashing way.

But today she passed the baker's by, climbed the stairs, went into the little dark room—her room like a cupboard—and sat down on the red eiderdown. She sat there for a long time. The box that the fur came out of was on the bed. She unclasped the necklet quickly, quickly, without looking, laid it inside. But when she put the lid on she thought she heard something crying.

Joyce Carol Oates is one of America's most prolific writers. In this passage from *I Lock the Door upon Myself*, she combines calm descriptive prose with a surprise ending.

from *I Lock the Door upon Myself*
Joyce Carol Oates

. . . there on the river, the Chautauqua, in a sepia sun, the rowboat bucking the choppy waves with a look almost of gaiety, defiance. And in the boat the couple: the man, rowing, a black man, the woman a white woman whose face is too distant to be seen. The man is rowing the boat downstream in a slightly jagged course yet with energy, purpose, the oars like blades rising and dropping and rising and again dropping, sinking into the water only to emerge again dripping and impatient; the woman is facing him, close, their knees touching, or so it appears from shore . . . the woman sits straight, ramrod straight, in a posture of extreme attentiveness to the man's and the boat's every move. With one hand she clutches the lurching side of the boat to steady herself, the other hand is shut into a fist, white-knuckled, immobile, in her lab.

. . . past Milburn, past Flemingville, past Shaheen, and then they begin to be seen, to be remarked upon . . . but only when they are a mile above Tintern Falls do people begin to shout in warning and now even the cries of birds at the river's edge lift sharp and piercing with warning. Then about a half-mile above Tintern the rowboat is taken by the swift-flowing current as by a giant hand and now it would require the black man's most strenuous and desperate exertions to steer it from its course yet he lifts the oars and rests them calmly in place as the woman sits continuing to watch him closely, possibly smiling, are the two of them smiling?—talking together?—hearing nothing of the shouts from shore and nothing of the increasing roar of the falls ahead, the sixty-foot drop on the other side of the bridge and the churning white water beyond. . . .

Chapter 5

The Interpretation of Narrative Prose

Learning Objectives

After reading this chapter, you should be able to

- define and distinguish narrative prose from descriptive prose
- describe the narrator's role
- define point of view and distinguish between first-person and third-person points of view
- explain and demonstrate the differences between omniscient, limited omniscient, and objective narrators
- describe and demonstrate character placement
- present an oral interpretation of narrative prose

Oral Interpretation as Storytelling

In Chapter 5, you will turn your attention to **narrative prose**—prose that tells a story. When you react to narrative prose, among the first aspects you notice are the story's actions and events, or "the what's it about." The plot, the sequence of events that occur in the story, creates the narrative's structure. In most traditional narratives, the plot structure resembles something like this:

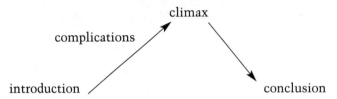

In the narrative's *introduction,* we find out who or what characters the action concerns and where the action takes place. Next, a series of *complications* unfold; these may be small or large, comic or serious. The complications are often revealed through *dialogue.* Eventually, the story reaches a *climax*—the point of greatest tension or the turning point. From this point, the story unfolds to its *conclusion,* which reveals the effects of the climactic action or decision.

PERFORMER'S WARM-UP
Character Craft

Choose an animal to portray. Try to assume all the physical and vocal characteristics of your animal. Consider the following questions: What is your animal's attitude toward life? Is it fearful? Lazy? Aggressive? Restless? Bored? Proud? Jaunty? Why does your animal act the way it does? Think carefully about your answers to these questions.

Now, assuming the physical and vocal characteristics of your animal, interact with one other animal near you. As you do so, ask yourself the following questions: What type of animal are you interacting with? How can you tell? Why do you react the way you do to this animal? What happens to your animal's dominant characteristics when you are relating to another animal character?

Still in character, widen your circle of animal contacts to include at least two additional animals. As you relate to and make contact with the other animals, allow yourself to become more and more human. Begin to straighten up, assuming the posture of a human, but retain your animal's dominant characteristics and traits as you gradually change.

Questions

1. What happened as you started to relate to the other animals in your group?
2. Were you able to interact meaningfully with each other? Why or why not?
3. What was said? What action occurred? Did a *story* begin to evolve?

In order to prepare to interpret narrative prose, try the following exercise. It introduces you to fables, a kind of narrative prose which teach an explicit lesson and usually feature animals who can talk and, in general, act just as rationally or irrationally as we do.

PERFORMER'S WORKSHOP
Fable Frolics

Read the following fable, "The Owl Who Was God" by James Thurber. As you are reading, answer the following questions:

1. What is happening in the story? (the plot)
2. Where and when is it happening? (the setting)
3. To whom is it happening? (the characters)
4. Why is it happening? (the motivation)
5. How is it happening? (the author's attitude)
6. Who is telling what is happening? From what perspective or point of view does he or she speak? (speaker or narrator)

Your instructor will either divide the class into small groups or select one demonstration group to act out Thurber's story. As you prepare, you may want to consider the following questions: At what point should your action begin? Where should it end?

Next, improvise each incident or scene. Remember, you must try to assume all the attributes of your assigned character in the fable. After a brief rehearsal, perform your version of "The Owl Who Was God" for the rest of the class.

"The Owl Who Was God"
James Thurber

Once upon a starless midnight there was an owl who sat on the branch of an oak tree. Two ground moles tried to slip quietly by, unnoticed. "You!" said the owl. "Who?" they quavered in fear and astonishment, for they could not believe it was possible for anyone to see them in that thick darkness. "You two!" said the owl. The moles hurried away and told the other creatures of the field and forest that the owl was the greatest and wisest of all animals because he could see in the dark and because he could answer any question. "I'll see about that," said a secretary bird, and he called on the owl one night when it was again very dark. "How many claws am I holding up?" said the secretary bird. "Two," said the owl, and that was right. "Can you give me another expression for 'that is to say,' or 'namely'?" asked the secretary bird. "To wit," said the owl. "Why does a lover call on his love?" asked the secretary bird. "To woo," said the owl.

The secretary bird hastened back to the other creatures and reported that the owl was indeed the greatest and wisest animal in the world because he could see in the dark and because he could answer any question. "Can he see in the daytime too?" asked the red fox. "Yes," echoed a dormouse and a French poodle. "Can he see in the daytime too?" All the other creatures laughed loudly at this silly question, and they set upon the red fox and his friends and drove them out of the region. Then they sent a messenger to the owl and asked him to be their leader.

When the owl appeared among the animals it was high noon and the sun was shining brightly. He walked very slowly, which gave him an appearance of great dignity, and he peered about him with large, staring eyes, which gave him an air of tremendous importance. "He's God!" screamed a Plymouth Rock hen. And others took up the cry. "He's God!" So they followed him wherever he went and when he began to bump into things, they began to bump into things too. Finally, he came to a concrete highway and he started up the middle of it and all the other creatures followed him. Presently a hawk, who was acting as outrider, observed a truck coming toward them at fifty miles an hour, and he reported to the secretary bird and the secretary bird reported to the owl. "There's danger ahead," said the secretary bird. "To wit?" said the owl. The secretary bird told him. "Aren't you afraid?" he asked. "Who?" said the owl calmly, for he could not see the truck. "He's God!" cried all the creatures again, and they were still crying "He's God!" when the truck hit them and ran them down. Some of the animals were merely injured, but most of them, including the owl, were killed.

Moral: You can fool too many of the people too much of the time.

Questions

1. What similarities do you note between the fable and your first animal improvisations?
2. What additional elements does the Thurber fable include that your initial improvisational skits did not?

Thurber's fable is an example of narrative prose. Let's examine more closely the characteristics of this particular prose form. Narrative prose tells a story and involves action or experience. It evokes a special world—the world of literature. It is to this literary world that you, as a performer of literature, must be able to respond.

The World of Narrative Prose

The world in your mind must merge with the world of the text. What creative processes can you use to allow this to happen? You can begin by building on the experiences you have already had with descriptive prose. Use the setting, the time, and the character pictures to help you tell your author's tale. With these elements, you create the appropriate mood or atmosphere. Narrative prose involves a greater number of elements than does descriptive prose, however, and you should become familiar with them. Whether a simple fable, a short story, a portion of a complex novel, or a historical account, narrative prose involves a number of elements including setting, plot, and character. Let's examine them further.

The **setting** of a narrative is the time and place where the story occurs. The *exterior setting* includes the social, political, and economic background to the story. The *interior setting* includes those aspects of setting that reside inside the minds and hearts of the characters.

The **plot** of a narrative holds the story together. As stated earlier, the plot is the answer to the question of what happens in the story. Like setting, the plot includes both *external actions* (actions we can see and hear) and *internal actions* (events that occur inside the characters).

A narrative is peopled with **characters** whose lives unfold before us. If we are to stay interested in the narrative, we have to find the characters interesting in some way. Characters can interest us for different reasons. Some interest us because they are like us, some because they live in an intriguing place or time, some by being glamorous or having a unique sense of style, and others by being evil. Some narratives contain characters who do not remain static but change— these are *dynamic characters*.

The Narrator

The **narrator** is the person who tells what happens in a story. This person establishes the point of view or perspective from which the story is detailed. Like tour guides, narrators lead you skillfully through a world of the author's choosing. The narrator's angle of vision, decided by the author, determines the details the author chooses to include and how these details are used within the story. It is always the narrator—the voice or person telling the story—who determines the way the story is revealed.

PERFORMER'S WARM-UP
Room Tour

A. You will have three minutes to guide your classmates through a room that lives in your imagination. It can be a room you have actually experienced or one you invent. Your goal is to make that room visible to the other members of your class. You may not use any props to do this, but you may walk around as you describe the various qualities of the room that lives in your mind.

B. Now change your perspective. Pretend you are extremely nearsighted. How does this modify your view of the room? What would you notice if you looked at the room through the eyes of a farsighted person? Through the eyes of a very short person? A giant? A busybody? An interior decorator? Do the things you notice or describe change depending on who you are? How? Why?

In the preceding "Warm-Up" exercise, you were asked to adopt different perspectives. Each perspective you adopted determined both the organization and your perception of the world around you. Actually, each time you changed your angle of vision, you became a somewhat different narrator. As interpreters, remember it is always the "I" behind the eye that is in control.

The "I" Behind the Eye

Let's examine more fully the forms of control that may be exerted by various types of narrative voices. A narrator may function as a *character* in the story. He or she may be a main character who is intimately involved in the action or an outsider or minor character who simply views and reports on the occurrences in the story. In either case, this particular type of narrator would use the personal pronoun *I* as the story is told, and we can recognize him or her by the presence of such phrases as "I saw" or "I heard." If the narrator uses *I*, the story is considered to be told from the *first-person point of view.*

PERFORMER'S WORKSHOP
First-Person Point of View

The following version of Aesop's fable "Slow but Sure" is told from the first-person point of view.

"Slow but Sure"

based on the fable by Aesop

One day I noticed a tortoise resting in the middle of the road. I tapped him on the shell to get his attention. "Anyone home in there?" I inquired. The tortoise tentatively stuck his head out of his shell and stared me up and down. Then he slowly drew his head back in to its natural resting place. I knew that I was far superior to that lazy tortoise, so I could not allow him to simply retreat; instead, I started an argument with him. "Bet I could run the pants off you in a race," I interjected. "Why that old shell is just too heavy for you to bear." I was quite sure that I had duly insulted his ego, and I was right, for he ever so tentatively stuck his head out again. I knew he would hear me out.

"Well, there you are," I said rather innocently as I looked him in the eye. "What do you say, is it a race?"

"I meet your challenge, sir," he said. I knew, however, that he would never measure up to it. He was much too hesitant.

We set a time and a place for the race. After a few laps I knew I could afford to give the slowpoke a break, so I laid down to take a nap. I must have overslept, however, because the next thing I heard was the voice of the tortoise gleefully calling from the finish line, "I won! I won!" He was darn smug about it, too.

Moral: He who rests assured on his laurels is often overtaken by a plodder.

Questions

1. Who is the narrator in this fable?
2. How does the point of view affect how you react to the narrator and other characters?

Third-Person Point of View

A story may also be recounted by various third-person points of view. The narrator may be **omniscient**—in telling the story, he or she may be able to move from one character's mind to another's. Such narrators have complete access to the motivations, thoughts, and feelings of all the characters. They are free to introduce information to the reader when and where they choose.

A third-person narrator also may possess what is termed **limited omniscience.** This type of narrator closely identifies with only one character, and that particular character is known as the narrator's sentient center. The narrator journeys with, or resides within, that character, following him or her throughout the story and restricting the reader to that character's range of knowledge and angle of vision solely. Notice that a third-person narrator usually includes some passages of interior speech or indirect discourse. In this way the reader is allowed to move into the character's mind and hear his or her unspoken thoughts.

An author may also endow the narrator with an **objective** rather than a sub-jective point of view. Such a narrator lets the characters speak for themselves through dialogue or direct discourse. In this case, the narrator does not overtly tell us whether he or she approves or disapproves of a character's actions or thoughts.

PERFORMER'S WORKSHOP
Third-Person Point of View

Following are three more versions of Aesop's fable "Slow but Sure." Read each version and determine which kind of third-person narrator (omnis-cient, limited omniscient, or objective) presents the story. Then answer the questions that follow.

A.

A tortoise awoke one afternoon after being tapped on the shell by a hare. "Anyone home in there?" The tortoise tentatively stuck his head out of his shell and stared at the hare standing before him. He gazed at him a while but then he slowly drew his head back in to its natural resting place. The hare, however, was quite eager to prove that he was superior to his fel-low creature, so he started an argument with him. "Bet I could run the pants off you in a race," he chortled. "Why that old shell of yours is just too heavy for you to bear."

The hare, full of pride, grinned contentedly. He was quite sure that the tortoise would not dare meet his challenge. The tortoise, however, ever so tentatively stuck his head out again. "I think I'll just hear him out," he thought to himself.

"Well, there you are," said the cocky hare, as he looked the tortoise in the eye. "What do you say, is it a race?"

The tortoise looked the hare up and down. "I know his kind," he thought. And he said, "I meet your challenge, sir."

So a time and place for the race was agreed. The hare began the race, but had such confidence in his natural fleetness that he did not trouble about it, and instead lay down by the roadside and went to sleep. "I'll just rest for a while and easily overtake Mr. Slowpoke in a few minutes," he ration-alized. He was quite unaware of what was about to happen to him; he was too busy snoring.

The tortoise, acutely conscious of its slow movements, simply plodded along continuously until it passed the still napping hare and won the race.

B.

A tortoise was awakened one afternoon by a hare who tapped him on his shell. The tortoise stuck his head out of his shell, looked at the hare, and then drew his head back in to its natural resting place. The hare, however, did not give up his attempt to communicate with the tortoise. "Bet I could run the pants off you in a race," he said. "Why that old shell of yours is just too heavy for you to bear." The tortoise stuck his head out of his shell again.

"Well, there you are," said the hare as he looked the tortoise in the eye. "What do you say, is it a race?"

The tortoise looked the hare up and down. "I meet your challenge, sir," he said.

So a time and place for the race was agreed.

The hare began the race, but soon after lay down by the roadside to rest. The tortoise, however, persevered and crossed the finish line first. "I won, I won," he called back to the napping hare.

C.

A tortoise awoke one afternoon after being tapped on the shell by a hare. "Anyone home in there?" he heard the hare ask. The tortoise tentatively stuck his head out of his shell and stared at the hare standing before him. Then he slowly drew his head back in to its natural resting place.

"Bet I could run the pants off you in a race," he heard the hare cry. "Why that old shell of yours is just too heavy for you to bear." The tortoise saw the hare grin much too contentedly. Ever so tentatively he stuck his head out again. "I think I'll just hear him out," he thought to himself.

"Well, there you are," said the hare. "What do you say, is it a race?"

The tortoise looked the hare up and down. "I know his kind," he thought. And he said, "I'll meet your challenge, sir."

So a time and place for the race was agreed.

The hare started the race, but soon lay down by the roadside and went to sleep.

The tortoise, acutely conscious of its slow movements, simply plodded along continuously until he passed the still napping hare and won the race. "I won! I won!" he declared with evident satisfaction.

Questions

1. Which kind of third-person narrator presented each version of the fable? How can you tell?
2. What difference does point of view make to your response to the fable? Which ideas or details are emphasized in one version and not in another?
3. How might you prepare differently if you are performing the hare's first-person version versus one of the third-person versions?

In order to solidify your understanding of the narrative point of view, imagine you are flying in an airplane that suddenly experiences engine difficulty. The plane must make an emergency landing, and you escape from the crash unscathed. Now, how would you tell your friends about your close call? You would probably use the first-person point of view—you were directly involved in the events that occurred. On the other hand, if you were waiting at the airport and a close friend was in that airplane when it experienced difficulty, you might tell the story from the point of view of a third person with limited omniscience. Your friend would serve as your sentient center.

If you were at the airport gathering research for a report to be given in class and suddenly heard news that a plane was about to crash-land, which angle of vision might you adopt in relating the story? If you acted as a newspaper reporter, you would present your story from the objective point of view. You would become an omniscient narrator only if you wished to hover inside the mind of each panicky occupant in the cabin, to share the desperate determination of the pilot, and to pace up and down the aisles with each fearful flight attendant. It is only with this point of view that you would be in a position to see and report on the true feelings, experiences, and behavior of all persons involved in the incident.

PERFORMER'S WORKSHOP
Determining the Point of View

A. Check your understanding by selecting a recent news item such as a sports story or national or local event. Work individually or with others to tell the story from two of the following points of view.

> first person
> omniscient third person
> limited omniscient third person
> objective third person

B. Select two or three literary texts and identify the type of narrative perspective found in each. (You may use selections from this book or ones of your choosing.) How does the author of each piece use point of view to enhance the story? How would changing the point of view affect your response to the story?

Shifting Point of View

It is not unusual to find modern writers shifting their point of view during the course of a single story. For example, in one scene in Virginia Woolf's novel *Mrs. Dalloway*, the point of view shifts from one character to another and another as they encounter each other in a park. As an interpreter, you need to recognize such shifts in perspective and develop ways to make them clear and meaningful for your audience.

Determine where and why the author Bernard Malamud shifts his point of view in the following excerpt from "My Son the Murderer."

 "My Son the Murderer"

Bernard Malamud

The father got his hat and coat and left the house. He ran for a while, running then walking, until he saw Harry on the other side of the street. He followed him a half block behind.

He followed Harry to Coney Island Avenue and was in time to see him board a trolleybus going toward the Island. Leo had to wait for the next bus. He thought of taking a taxi and following the bus, but no taxi came by. The next bus came by fifteen minutes later and he took it all the way to the Island. It was February and Coney Island was cold and deserted. There were few cars on Surf Avenue and few people on the streets. It looked like snow. Leo walked on the boardwalk, amid snow flurries, looking for his son. The grey sunless beaches were empty. The hot-dog stands, shooting galleries, and bathhouses were shuttered up. The gunmetal ocean, moving like melted lead, looked freezing. There was a wind off the water and it worked its way into his clothes so that he shivered as he walked. The wind white-capped the leaden waves and the slow surf broke on the deserted beaches with a quiet roar.

He walked in the blow almost to Sea Gate, searching for his son, and then walked back. On his way toward Brighton he saw a man on the beach standing in the foaming surf. Leo went down the boardwalk stairs and onto the ribbed-sand beach. The man on the shore was Harry, standing in water up to his ankles.

Leo ran to his son. Harry, it was my mistake, excuse me. I'm sorry I opened your letter.

Harry did not turn. He stayed in the water, his eyes on the leaden waves.

Harry, I'm frightened. Tell me what's the matter. My son, have mercy on me.

It's not my kind of world, Harry thought. It fills me with terror.

He said nothing.

A blast of wind lifted his father's hat off his head and carried it away over the beach. It looked as if it were going to land in the surf but then the wind blew it toward the boardwalk, rolling like a wheel along the ground. Leo chased after his hat. He chased it one way, then another, then toward the water. The wind blew the hat against his legs and he caught it. He pulled the freezing hat down tight on his head until it bent his ears. By now he was crying. Breathless, he wiped his eyes with icy fingers and returned to his son at the edge of the water.

He is a lonely man. This is the type he is, Leo thought. He will always be lonely.

My son who became a lonely man.

Harry, what can I say to you? All I can say to you is who says life is easy? Since when? It wasn't for me and it isn't for you. It's life, what more can I say? But if a person don't want to live what can he do if he's dead? If he doesn't want to live, maybe he deserves to die.

Come home, Harry, he said. It's cold here. You'll catch a cold with your feet in the water.

Harry stood motionless and after a while his father left. As he was leaving, the wind plucked his hat off his head and sent it rolling along the sand.

My father stands in the hallway. I catch him reading my letter. He follows me at a distance in the street. We meet at the edge of the water. He is running after his hat.

My son stands with his feet in the ocean.

Questions

1. Why do you believe the author chose to narrate this story using shifting points of view?
2. How do the shifts in point of view help us learn more about the characters?
3. How do they shape what we know and feel about the narrative's events?

When an author shifts point of view, we learn about the perceptions of different characters. Though the point of view is still limited, it gives us the opportunity to see the story unfold from more than one character's perspective. It gives us more than one side of the story.

The Gender of Narration

Does it matter if the author of a book is a female and the narrator a male, or if the author of a book is a male and the narrator a female? What is the relationship between writer and narrator? Currently, we are witnessing an increased interest in cross-gender narration—that is, male writers speaking in the voice of a female character, and vice versa. If the author is one sex and the narrator another, does the gender gap make it harder for the receiver to suspend disbelief?

First-person intimacy, when combined with cross-gender narration, poses challenges for oral interpreters of both sexes. Should you interpret such a work, ask yourself these questions:

1. Does the narrator's voice have gender qualities? How can I make this clear to an audience?
2. Do male and female narrators speak differently? How can I distinguish this for an audience?

Interpreters do have the luxury of taking on both male and female personae. It is just as difficult to give voice to a woman as to a man, no matter what your own gender. To speak credibly as a performer in any voice takes work.

Why Is the Narrator So Important?

Why is it important for a performer of literature to understand the role the narrator plays in a story? As oral readers, you must use this information to help you know when to adjust your tone, attitude, and degree of openness. Only by making adaptations will a performance be truly effective.

As a performer, you should think of yourself as similar to a movie or video camera. You have the ability psychologically and physically to back up and look at a scene from a distance, or to move in for a close-up of one particular individual or event. You can view a scene through the eyes of a single character. Or, like a camera, you can juxtapose two images and allow your audience to attain the subjective vision of a number of characters. If you think of your job as interpreter as being like a camera, you will not allow yourself to become static; instead, you will move smoothly and efficiently through the varied incidents and narrative perspectives of your story, adjusting your focus as needed and drawing your audience's attention to the key aspects of the text.

Narrative Prose Presentation Techniques

As an interpreter, you sometimes speak directly to your audience as if you were the narrator, while at other times you allow this narrator to disappear for a while and permit your audience to hear the story's characters speak. Adapting your perspective in a manner such as this is a crucial aspect of performance. There are other techniques you will need to master as well. You should be able to communicate those portions of your selection that are predominantly *scene*—that is, those primarily written in dialogue form. The units of the story that are treated as scene give you the greatest opportunity to suggest and delineate the characters in the story. Unless both you and your audience are aware of the type of people involved in the action of your story, the material will not come alive fully.

What should you, as interpretative performer, consider when deciding how to play a character? What methods or strategies do you think you could use to help suggest the qualities of the people who reside in the imaginary world of your selection? Let's examine some techniques that you can use to re-create a character. Begin by seeking to build in your mind an *image* of each character you have to interpret. Try this now.

PERFORMER'S WORKSHOP
Image Building

Read the following literary excerpts, concentrating on the character pictures that emerge. Then demonstrate your feel for each of the described characters by responding to the prompts that follow. Work on only one character sketch at a time.

 ### "The God-Seeker"
Sinclair Lewis

The reverend Mr. Chippler, who had organized the revival which would wind up this afternoon, was a leaping little man, fuller of friendliness, optimism, go, zip, imagination, ingenuity, cheeriness and oratory than the nobler and slower animals. In joy over his camp meeting, he was jammed with exuberant wrath at sinners, this bountiful June morning. His text was from Job: "For the arrows of the Almighty are within me, the poison whereof drinketh up my spirit: the terrors of God do set themselves in array against me."

What I so greatly feared, happened! Miss Whiteside, the dean of our college, withheld my diploma. When I came to her office, and asked her why she did not pass me, she said that she could not recommend me as a teacher because of my personal appearance.

She told me that my skin looked oily, my hair unkempt, and my fingernails sadly neglected. She told me that I was utterly unmindful of the little niceties of the well-groomed lady. She pointed out that my collar did not set evenly, my belt was awry, and there was a lack of freshness in my dress. And she ended with: "Soap and water are cheap. Anyone can be clean."

In those four years while I was under her supervision, I was always timid and diffident. I shrank and trembled when I had to come near her. When I had to say something to her, I mumbled and stuttered, and grew red and white in the face with fear.

Every time I had to come to the dean's office for a private conference, I prepared for the ordeal of her cold scrutiny, as a patient prepares for a surgical operation. I watched her gimlet eyes searching for a stray pin, for a spot on my dress, for my unpolished shoes, for my uncared-for fingernails, as one strapped on the operating table watches the surgeon approaching with his tray of sterilized knives.

She never looked into my eyes. She never perceived that I had a soul. She did not see how I longed for beauty and cleanliness. How I strained and struggled to lift myself from the dead toil and exhaustion that weighed me down. She could see nothing in people like me, except the dirt and the stains on the outside.

But this last time, when she threatened to withhold my diploma because of my appearance, this last time when she reminded me that "Soap and water are cheap. Anyone can be clean," this last time, something burst within me.

I felt the suppressed wrath of all the unwashed of the earth break loose within me. My eyes blazed fire. I didn't care for myself, nor the dean, nor the whole laundered world. I had suffered the cruelty of their cleanliness and the tyranny of their culture to the breaking point. I was too frenzied to know what I said or did. But I saw clean, immaculate, spotless Miss Whiteside shrivel and tremble and cower before me, as I had shriveled and trembled and cowered before her for so many years.

Why did she give me my diploma? Was it pity? Or can it be that in my outburst of fury, at the climax of indignities that I had suffered, the barriers broke, and she saw into the world below from where I came?

from "Slipping Beauty"
Jerome Weidman

He was a little man with an untidy beard and a prominent paunch that seemed startlingly out of place because of his emaciated appearance. Winter and summer he wore a battered cap, a leather vest, and a look of indifferent resignation, well seasoned with disgust, that gave no hint of the almost violent loquacity he could attain without even a moment of preparation. In a world of trucks and automobiles he drove a flat, open wagon behind a huge, drooping horse. And although his seltzer bottles came in neatly cased boxes of ten, he preferred to carry them by their spouts, five in each hand, like clusters of grapes, and take his chances on opening doors with shoulder shoves and kicks.

Questions

1. Draw a line graph that represents your feel for the character's way of moving. For example, do you perceive this particular character as tense? Does he or she have sudden spurts of activity? If so, your graph might look something like this:

   On the other hand, if you see your character as graceful and fluid, the graph you draw might resemble this one:

   Also, draw a line graph that represents your feel for your own way of moving. How does your own graph differ from that of your character?

2. Move across the room as you believe your personal graph directs you to move. Then move as you believe your character's graph directs. What movement adaptation must you make to embody the character?
3. Create a mood simile to represent the character you are describing. How would you complete the following sentence: "This character is like a. . . ." Try to determine what you associate with this specific character. For example, if he or she is a particularly dull individual, you might say the character reminds you of mashed potatoes without salt. What does the character make you feel or make you want to do?
4. Now, put an imaginary mask on your face. This mask should symbolically represent your view of your character's face and attitude toward life. Can you allow your face to help you experience this?
5. Stand as your character would stand; walk as you imagine your character would walk. Are you allowing yourself to see your character with your arms and legs as well as with your eyes?

6. Use the sounds of the alphabet to suggest the tone of voice, speaking rate, and vocal quality you perceive your character has. How does your voice sound?

These exercises should be part of your rehearsal repertoire for any character you perform. If you use them, they will allow you to share in the physical and mental world of various fictional characters. The exercises will enable you to know the character you are interpreting with your whole being, rather than with only your mind.

Revealing Characters to Audiences

Having clarified the image of a particular character for yourself while rehearsing, how will you reveal this character to your audience during performance? First, you can use all the emotional and intellectual information you gained during your rehearsal sessions. Use visible action to suggest your character's traits or moods. Indicate speech habits by changing your own voice pattern. Use muscle memory to convey your character's degree of tension or relaxation.

Keep in mind that many times an oral interpreter will be called on to assume more than one character during a single presentation. Thus, another technique might also prove useful to you, one termed **character placement.** It is certainly a convention about which all beginning interpreters should be aware. The following passage and diagram will help explain this tool.

PERFORMER'S WORKSHOP
Using Character Placement I

Read the following excerpt from Eudora Welty's story "A Visit of Charity." Then study the character placement diagram below.

 "A Visit of Charity"

Eudora Welty

Marian stood enclosed by a bed, a washstand and a chair; the tiny room had altogether too much furniture. Everything smelled wet—even the bare floor. She held onto the back of the chair, which was wicker and felt soft and damp. Her heart beat more and more slowly, her hands got colder and colder, and she could not hear whether the old women were saying anything or not. She could not see them very clearly. How dark it was! The window shade was down, and the only door was shut. Marian looked at the ceiling. . . . It was like being caught in a robber's cave, just before one was murdered.

"Did you come to be our little girl for a while?" the first robber asked.

Then something was snatched from Marian's hand—the little potted plant.

"Flowers!" screamed the old woman. She stood holding the pot in an undecided way. "Pretty flowers," she added.

Then the old woman in bed cleared her throat and spoke. "They are not pretty," she said, still without looking around, but very distinctly.

Marian suddenly pitched against the chair and sat down in it.

"Pretty flowers," the first woman insisted. "Pretty—pretty . . ."

Marian wished she had the little pot back for just a moment—she had forgotten to look at the plant herself before giving it away. What did it look like?

"Stinkweeds," said the other old woman sharply.

Now study the character placement diagram below:

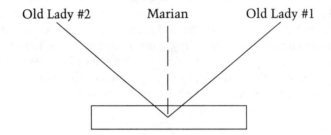

The diagram demonstrates how the interpreter can use placement to create the illusion that more than one speaker is involved in the performed reading. When re-creating a selection in which more than one character speaks, the interpreter simply establishes his or her eye focus for each character at a specific position on the back wall of the performing area.

For example, whenever Old Lady #1 speaks, the interpreter's angle of address would be along the line labeled #1; when the speaker looks along this position, he or she is Old Lady #1 and no one else. Likewise, when Old Lady #2 converses, the interpreter's angle of address would now move along the line labeled #2. Similar adaptations would be made for each additional character. The interpreter must concentrate on keeping the essential locations of each character clear, but at the same time he or she must be careful not to exaggerate the shift in eye focus in moving from one character to another.

Questions

1. Why do you think this performer placed Marian between the two old women?
2. How would rearranging the characters' locations affect the performance of this selection? Which arrangement do you think would work best?

Using character placement, you will make it clear which character is speaking, thus helping your audience to differentiate one character from another. The audience will learn to expect a character to direct his or her words to a specifically defined area. Even more significant, however, is that in choosing a concentrated location, you can imagine the character whom you are addressing at that moment.

Though this technique is not particularly difficult to employ, do not underestimate the need to practice and master it. Be careful not to overemphasize your changes in eye focus: avoid a "tennis match." Overly wide visual placement, as shown in the diagram below, will contribute to a back-and-forth effect. Try to be natural in your eye shifts. For best results, combine this strategy with those discussed previously to bring characters to life for your audience.

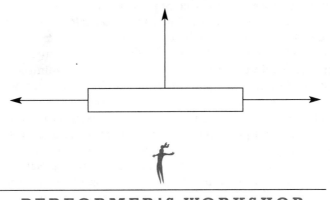

PERFORMER'S WORKSHOP
Using Character Placement II

Concentrating on character placement only, prepare to read one or more of the versions of "Slow but Sure" presented earlier in this chapter.

Questions

1. What does your character-placement diagram look like?
2. In what ways does your approach differ from others created by your classmates?

IDEA ENCORE

The focus of Chapter 5 was on narrative prose—the kind of prose used to reveal the story's plot. Most narratives contain an introduction, one or more complications, a climax, and a conclusion.

One important aspect of narrative prose is the narrator's point of view. The narrator is the story's teller. The narrator's angle of vision or perspective affects the story's telling. Thus, the interpreter needs to be able to determine and communicate the "I" that is in control of the story. Narrators may exhibit a first-person point of view, an omniscient point of view, a limited omniscient point of view, an objective point of view, or a shifting point of view. They also may be gendered.

While it is the interpretive performer's responsibility to determine the role that the narrator plays in the story and then to communicate that role to audience members using specific performance presentation techniques, it is also the interpretive performer's task to define character placement through the use of focal points. In order to accomplish this, the interpretive performer must learn about the characters so that he or she knows them as completely as possible.

PERFORMER'S SHOWCASE & JOURNAL
Putting It All Together

Choose a selection of narrative prose to interpret before the class. Either select one of those provided at the end of this chapter or find one on your own. Carefully rehearse your material, combining all the techniques you have learned thus far. Focus on the literature and prepare to give a really fine performance.

As you prepare your performance, write a brief analysis of your selection and interpretation of it as part of your Performer's Journal. Cover these questions:

1. Why did you choose this particular piece of literature? Why do you think it will appeal to your audience? Why is it worth your preparation time and effort?

2. What type of narrator is involved? What are the dominant ideas and actions within your selection?

3. What types of characters are included in your passage? How do the characters relate to each other?

4. What kind of posture will you assume? How and where will you stand? Draw a character-placement diagram for your performance.

5. Describe the physical sensations you experienced during your rehearsal period. How can you use your body to help you express the literature?

6. As a result of your performance, what would you like your audience to feel, know, or imagine?

SELECTIONS FOR FURTHER WORK

Meeting new people socially is sometimes difficult. In "The Waltz," Dorothy Parker showed that the dance can add to the difficulties.

from "The Waltz"
Dorothy Parker

*W*hy, thank you so much. I'd adore to.

I don't want to dance with him. I don't want to dance with anybody. And even if I did, it wouldn't be him. . . . Just think, not a quarter of an hour ago, here I was sitting, feeling so sorry for the poor girl he was dancing with. And now I'm going to be the poor girl. . . .

And I had to go and tell him that I'd adore to dance with him. I cannot understand why I wasn't struck dead. Yes, and being struck dead would look like a day in the country, compared to struggling out a dance with this boy. But what could I do? Everyone else at the table had got up to dance, except him and me. There I was, trapped. Trapped like a rat in a trap.

What can you say, when a man asks you to dance with him? . . . Oh, yes, do let's dance together—it's so nice to meet a man who isn't a scaredy-cat about catching my beriberi. No. There was nothing for me to do, but say I'd adore to. . . .

Why, I think it's more of a waltz, really. Isn't it? We might just listen to the music a second. Shall we? Oh yes, it's a waltz. Mind? Why, I'm simply thrilled. I'd love to waltz with you.

I'd love to waltz with you. I'd love to waltz with you. I'd love to have my tonsils out, I'd love to be in a midnight fire at sea. Well, it's too late now. We're getting under way. Oh. Oh, dear. Oh, dear, dear, dear. Oh, this is even worse than I thought it would be. I suppose that's the one dependable law of life—everything is always worse than you thought it was going to be. Oh, if I had any real grasp of what this dance would be like, I'd have held out for sitting it out. Well, it will probably amount to the same thing in the end. We'll be sitting it out on the floor in a minute if he keeps this up. . . .

Why can't we stay in one place just long enough to get acclimated? It's this constant rush, rush, rush, that's the curse of American life. That's the reason that we're all of us so—OW! For heaven's sake don't kick, you idiot, this is only the second down. Oh, my shin. My poor shin that I've had ever since I was a little girl!

Oh, no, no, no. Goodness no. It didn't hurt the least little bit. And anyway it was my fault. Really it was. Truly. Well, you're just being sweet, to say that. It really was all my fault.

I wonder what I'd better do—kill him this instant, with my naked hands, or wait and let him drop in his traces. Maybe it's best not to make a scene. . . .

Maybe he didn't do it maliciously. Maybe it's just his way of showing his high spirits. I suppose I ought to be glad that one of us is having such a good time. I suppose I ought to think myself lucky if he brings me back alive. . . .

Yes, it's lovely, isn't it? It's simply lovely. It's the loveliest waltz. Isn't it. Oh, I think it's lovely, too.

OW! Get off my instep, you hulking peasant! What do you think I am, anyway—a gangplank? OW!

No, of course it didn't hurt. Why, it didn't a bit. Honestly. And it was my fault. You see that little step of yours—well, it's perfectly lovely, but it's just a tiny bit tricky to follow at first. Oh, did you work it up yourself? You really did! Well, aren't you amazing! Oh, now I think I've got it. Oh, I think it's lovely. I was watching you do it when you were dancing before. It's awfully effective when you look at it.

It's awfully effective when you look at it. I bet I'm awfully effective when you look at me. My hair is hanging along my cheeks, my skirt is swaddled about me, I can feel the cold damp of my brow. I must look like something out of the "Fall of the House of Usher." Is that orchestra never going to stop playing? Or must this obscene travesty of a dance go on until hell burns out?

Oh, they're going to play another encore. Oh, goody. Oh, that's lovely. Tired? I should say I'm not tired. I'd like to go on like this forever.

I should say I'm not tired. I'm dead, that's all I am. . . . I wonder why I didn't tell him I was tired. I wonder why I didn't suggest going back to the table. . . .

Still, if we were back at the table, I'd probably have to talk to him. Look at him—what could you say to a thing like that! Did you go to the circus this year, what's your favorite kind of ice cream, how do you spell cat? I guess I'm as well off here. As well off as if I were in a cement mixer in full action.

I'm past feeling now. The only way I can tell when he steps on me is that I can hear the splintering of bones. And all the events of my life are passing before my eyes. There was a time I was in a hurricane in the West Indies, there was the day I got my head cut open in the taxi smash, there was the night the drunken lady threw a bronze ash tray at her own true love and got me instead, there was that summer that the sailboat kept capsizing. Ah, what an easy, peaceful time was mine, until I fell in with Swifty, here. . . . I think my mind is beginning to wander. It almost seems to me as if the orchestra were stopping. It couldn't be, of course; it could never be. . . .

Oh, they've stopped, the mean things. They're not going to play any more. Oh, darn. Oh, do you think they would? Do you really think so, if you gave them twenty dollars? Oh, that would be lovely. And look, do tell them to play this same thing. I'd simply adore to go on waltzing.

Is it ever appropriate to fabricate a story? In Corey Ford's "Snake Dance," Jerry thinks that he must do just that.

"Snake Dance"

Corey Ford

"Hello. That you, Mom? . . . Oh, I'm sorry, operator, I thought I was connected with . . . No, I'm trying to get long distance . . . What? Centerville, Ohio, ring five. I told that other operator . . . What? . . . I am holding it."

He fished nervously in his pocket for a pack of cigarettes, pulled one cigarette out of the pack with his thumb and forefinger, and stuck it swiftly between his lips. He glanced at his watch and scowled. The game had been over for half an hour. The snake dance would be coming down the street this way any minute now. With his free hand he tore a match from the paper safe, and propped the telephone receiver for a moment between shoulder and ear while he struck the match on the flap. As he put the match to the tip of the cigarette, a thin voice rasped vaguely inside the receiver, and he whipped out the match.

"Hello. Mom? . . . Oh, I'm sorry," he mumbled. "How much?" He took a handful of silver from his pocket and began to drop the coins into the slot of the pay telephone. He could hear someone speaking above the echoing reverberations inside the phone.

"What? Oh, Mom? Hello, Mom. This is Jerry. I say, this is—Can you hear me now? . . . Sure, I can hear you fine . . . Sure, I'm all right. I'm fine. And you? . . . That's fine.

"Mom"—and his voice seemed to falter for a fraction of a second. Then: "How is he? Is there any change?"

There was a tiny silence.

"Oh." His voice was a little duller when he spoke again. "I see. Yeh. This afternoon, eh? And that other specialist, he said the same thing? Um-hummm . . . Oh, sure, sure. No, of course, Mom, there's nothing to worry about. No, I'm not worried; I only just called to find out if there was any change, that was all. . . . Did they say he could ever—I mean, can he move his arms any yet?" He gulped. "Well, that doesn't mean anything, really . . . No, of course, all those things take time. Sure, a year, maybe less . . . What?"

He took a second cigarette out of his pocket and thrust it between his lips nervously. He lit it from the stub of the first one and ground out the stub beneath his heel.

"What money? Oh, you mean I sent you last week? Now, Mom," impatiently, "I told you all about that already in the letter, didn't I? . . . Sure it's a scholarship. I got it for playing football. And so naturally I didn't need all that money you and Pop had been saving up for me to go to college, and so I just thought maybe with Pop being laid up now for a while and all . . .

"Where? Why right here." He frowned. "No, this isn't exactly a dormitory; it's—I live here in the fraternity house, you see. Sure I'm in a fraternity. It's the one Pop wanted me to join, too, tell him . . . No, honest, Mom, it doesn't cost me a cent for my room. It's on account of my football."

He opened the folding door a little. He thought he could hear the band in the distance.

"Who, me? Homesick? Not so you'd notice it." He laughed. "I'm having the time of my life here. Everybody's so swell. I know practically everybody here at Dover already. They even call me by my first name. Say, if you don't think I'm sitting pretty, you ought to see my fraternity house here." He gazed out through the glass door of the phone booth.

"Every night the fellows sit around and we . . . go down to Semple's for a milk shake . . . No, that's only the drugstore . . . No." He smiled slowly. "I promised you I wouldn't drink, Mom."

In the distance now he could hear the sound of the band approaching.

"Well, Mom, I gotta hang up now. The gang'll be here in a minute. We're having a celebration after the game today. We played Alvord—took 'em sixteen to nothing. . . . Sure I did, the whole game; you oughta seen me in there. I made two touchdowns. Everybody's going down to Semple's after the game, and I gotta be ready, because of course they'll all want me to be there too. Can you hear the band now?"

It was growing louder, and the eager voices in the snake dance could be heard above the brasses, chanting the score of the game in time with the band.

"Now, listen, Mom. One other thing before they get here. Mom, see, I'm going to be sending you about ten or twelve dollars or so each week from now on until Pop is better. . . . No, Mom. Heck, I got plenty. Sure they always fix you up with a soft job if you're a good enough player. The alumni do it. . . . Here they are now. Hear them?"

The band had halted outside. Someone led a cheer.

"That's for me, Mom. . . . Sure. Didn't I practically win the game for them today? Hear that?" He kicked open the door of the phone booth.

He held the receiver toward the open door of the phone booth. They were calling, "Jerry! Hey Jerry, hang up on that babe!"

"Hear that, Mom? Now goodby. And look, by the way, if you should ever happen to see Helen," he added carelessly, "tell her I couldn't ask her up to the freshman dance like I planned, but with the football season and my scholarship and all—tell her, Mom. She—she didn't answer my last letter. O.K. Mom. Tell Pop everything's O.K., see? Now don't worry. . . . Bye."

He replaced the receiver slowly on the hook and stared at the mouthpiece a moment. As he opened the door and stepped out of the booth, he could see his reflection for a moment in the tall mirror behind the soda fountain—the familiar white cap, the white jacket with "Semple's" stitched in red letters on the pocket. The crowd was lined along the soda fountain, shouting, "Jerry!" "Milk shake, Jerry!"

A driver's test is a stressful experience under the best of circumstances. Angelica Gibbs shows us a situation in which bigotry makes it impossible.

"The Test"

Angelica Gibbs

On the afternoon Marian took her second driver's test, Mrs. Ericson went with her. "It's probably better to have someone a little older with you," Mrs. Ericson said as Marian slipped into the driver's seat beside her. "Perhaps the last time your Cousin Bill made you nervous, talking too much on the way."

"Yes, Ma'am," Marian said in her soft unaccented voice. "They probably do like it better if a white person shows up with you."

"Oh, I don't think it's that," Mrs. Ericson began, and subsided after a glance at the girl's set profile. Marian drove the car slowly through the shady streets. It was one of the first hot days in June, and when they reached the boulevard they found it crowded with cars headed for the beaches.

"Do you want me to drive?" Mrs. Ericson asked. "I'll be glad to if you're feeling jumpy." Marian shook her head. Mrs. Ericson watched her dark, competent hands and wondered for the thousandth time how the house had ever managed to get along without her, or how she had lived through those earlier years when her household had been presided over by a series of slatternly white girls who had considered housework demeaning and the care of children an added insult. "You drive beautifully, Marian," she said. "Now don't think of the last time. Anybody would slide on a steep hill on a wet day like that."

"It takes four mistakes to flunk you," Marian said. "I don't remember doing all the things the inspector marked down on my blank."

"People say that they only want you to slip them a little something," Mrs. Ericson said doubtfully.

"No," Marian said. "That would only make it worse, Mrs. Ericson, I know."

The car turned right, at a traffic signal, into a side road and slid up to the curb at the rear of a short line of parked cars. The inspectors had not arrived yet.

"You have the papers?" Mrs. Ericson asked. Marian took them out of her bag: her learner's permit, the car registration, her birth certificate. They settled down to the dreary business of waiting.

"It will be marvelous to have someone dependable to drive the children to school every day," Mrs. Ericson said.

Marian looked up from the list of driving requirements she had been studying. "It'll make things simpler at the house, won't it?" she asked.

"Oh, Marian," Mrs. Ericson exclaimed, "if I could only pay you half of what you're worth!"

"Now, Mrs. Ericson," Marian said firmly. They looked at each other and smiled with affection.

Two cars with official insignia on their doors stopped across the street. The inspectors leaped out, very brisk and military in their neat uniforms. Marian's hands tightened on the wheel. "There's the one who flunked me last time," she whispered, pointing to a stocky, self-important man who had begun to shout directions at the driver at the head of the line. "Oh, Mrs. Ericson."

"Now Marian," Mrs. Ericson said. They smiled at each other again, rather weakly. The inspector who finally reached their car was not the stocky one, but a genial, middle-aged man who grinned broadly as he thumbed over their papers. Mrs. Ericson started to get out of the car. "Don't you want to come along?" the inspector asked. "Mandy and I don't mind company."

Mrs. Ericson was bewildered for a moment. "No," she said, and stepped to the curb. "I might make Marian self-conscious. She's a fine driver, Inspector."

"Sure thing," the inspector said, winking at Mrs. Ericson. He slid into the seat beside Marian. "Turn right at the corner, Mandy Lou."

From the curb, Mrs. Ericson watched the car move smoothly up the street.

The inspector made notations in a small black book. "Age?" he inquired presently, as they drove along.

"Twenty-seven."

He looked at Marian out of the corner of his eye. "Old enough to have quite a flock of pickaninnies, eh?"

Marian did not answer.

"Left at this corner," the inspector said, "and park between that truck and the green Buick."

The cars were very close together, but Marian squeezed in between them without too much maneuvering. "Driven before, Mandy Lou?" the inspector asked.

"Yes, sir. I had a license for three years in Pennsylvania."

"Why do you want to drive a car?"

"My employer needs me to take her children to and from school."

"Sure you don't really want to sneak out nights to meet some young blood?" the inspector asked. He laughed as Marian shook her head.

"Let's see you take a left at the corner and then turn around in the middle of the next block," the inspector said. He began to whistle "Swanee River." "Make you homesick?" he asked.

Marian put out her hand, swung around neatly in the street, and headed back in the direction from which they had come. "No," she said. "I was born in Scranton, Pennsylvania."

The inspector feigned astonishment. "You-all ain't Southern?" he said. "Well dog my cats if I didn't think you-all came from down yondah."

"No, sir," Marian said.

"Turn onto Main Street and let's see how you-all does in heavier traffic."

They followed a line of cars along Main Street for several blocks until they came in sight of a concrete bridge which arched high over the railroad tracks.

"Read that sign at the end of the bridge," the inspector said.

"Proceed with caution. Dangerous in slippery weather," Marian said.

"You-all sho can read fine," the inspector exclaimed. "Where'd you learn to do that, Mandy?"

"I got my college degree last year," Marian said. Her voice was not quite steady.

As the car crept up the slope of the bridge the inspector burst out laughing. He laughed so hard he could scarcely give his next direction. "Stop here," he said, wiping his eyes, "then start 'er up again. Mandy got her degree, did she? Dog my cats!"

Marian pulled up beside the curb. She put the car in neutral, pulled on the emergency, waited a moment, and then put the car into gear again. Her face was set. As she released the brake her foot slipped off the clutch pedal and the engine stalled.

"Now, Mistress Mandy," the inspector said, "remember your degree."

"Damn you!" Marian cried. She started the car with a jerk.

The inspector lost his joviality in an instant. "Return to the starting place, please," he said, and made four very black crosses at random in the squares on Marian's application blank.

Mrs. Ericson was waiting at the curb where they had left her. As Marian stopped the car, the inspector jumped out and brushed past her, his face purple. "What happened?" Mrs. Ericson asked, looking after him with alarm.

Marian stared down at the wheel and her lip trembled.

"Oh, Marian, again?" Mrs. Ericson said.

Marian nodded. "In sort of a different way," she said, and slid over to the right-hand side of the car.

War is painful. In "The Sniper," a story written in 1925, Irish writer Liam O'Flaherty narrates a story that could and does still happen every day.

"The Sniper"
Liam O'Flaherty

The long June twilight faded into night. Dublin lay enveloped in darkness but for the dim light of the moon that shone through fleecy clouds, casting a pale light as of approaching dawn over the dark waters of the Liffey. Around the beleaguered Four Courts the heavy guns roared. Here and there through the city, machine guns and rifles broke the silence of the night, spasmodically, like dogs barking on lone farms. Republicans and Free Staters were waging civil war.

On a rooftop near O'Connell Bridge, a Republican sniper lay watching. Beside him lay his rifle and over his shoulders were slung a pair of field glasses. His face was the face of a student, thin and ascetic, but his eyes had the cold gleam of the fanatic. They were deep and thoughtful, the eyes of a man who is used to looking at death.

He was eating a sandwich hungrily. He had eaten nothing since morning. He had been too excited to eat. He finished the sandwich, and, taking a flask of whisky from his pocket, he took a short draught. Then he returned the flask to his pocket. He paused for a moment, considering whether he should risk a smoke. It was dangerous. The flash might be seen in the darkness, and there were enemies watching. He decided to take the risk.

Placing a cigarette between his lips, he struck a match, inhaled the smoke hurriedly and put out the light. Almost immediately, a bullet flattened itself against the parapet of the roof. The sniper took another whiff and put out the cigarette. Then he swore softly and crawled away to the left.

Cautiously he raised himself and peered over the parapet. There was a flash and a bullet whizzed over his head. He dropped immediately. He had seen the flash. It came from the opposite side of the street.

He rolled over the roof to a chimney stack in the rear, and slowly drew himself up behind it, until his eyes were level with the top of the parapet. There was nothing to be seen—just the dim outline of the opposite housetop against the blue sky. His enemy was under cover.

Just then an armored car came across the bridge and advanced slowly up the street. It stopped on the opposite side of the street, fifty yards ahead. The sniper could hear the dull panting of the motor. His heart beat faster. It was an enemy car. He wanted to fire, but he knew it was useless. His bullets would never pierce the steel that covered the gray monster.

Then round the corner of a side street came an old woman, her head covered by a tattered shawl. She began to talk to the man in the turret of the car. She was pointing to the roof where the sniper lay. An informer.

The turret opened. A man's head and shoulder appeared, looking toward the sniper. The sniper raised his rifle and fired. The head fell heavily on the turret wall. The woman darted toward the side street. The sniper fired again. The woman whirled round and fell with a shriek into the gutter.

Suddenly from the opposite roof a shot rang out and the sniper dropped his rifle with a curse. The rifle clattered to the roof. The sniper thought the noise would wake the dead. He stopped to pick the rifle up. He couldn't lift it. His forearm was dead. "I'm hit," he muttered.

Dropping flat onto the roof, he crawled back to the parapet. With his left hand he felt the injured right forearm. The blood was oozing through the sleeve of his coat. There was no pain—just a deadened sensation, as if the arm had been cut off.

Quickly he drew his knife from his pocket, opened it on the breastwork of the parapet, and ripped open the sleeve. There was a small hole where the bullet had entered. On the other side there was no hole. The bullet had lodged in the bone. It must have fractured it. He bent the arm below the wound. The arm bent back easily. He ground his teeth to overcome the pain.

Then taking out his field dressing, he ripped open the packet with his knife. He broke the neck of the iodine bottle and let the bitter fluid drip into the wound. A paroxysm of pain swept through him. He placed the cotton wadding over the wound and wrapped the dressing over it. He tied the ends with his teeth.

Then he lay still against the parapet, and, closing his eyes, he made an effort of will to overcome the pain.

In the street beneath all was still. The armored car had retired speedily over the bridge, with the machine gunner's head hanging lifeless over the turret. The woman's corpse lay still in the gutter.

The sniper lay for a long time nursing his wounded arm and planning escape. Morning must not find him wounded on the roof. The enemy on the opposite roof covered his escape. He must kill that enemy and he could not use his rifle. He had only a revolver to do it. Then he thought of a plan.

Taking off his cap, he placed it over the muzzle of his rifle. Then he pushed the rifle slowly upward over the parapet, until the cap was visible from the opposite side of the street. Almost immediately there was a report, and a bullet pierced the center of the cap. The sniper slanted the rifle forward. The cap slipped down into the street. Then catching the rifle in the middle, the sniper dropped his left hand over the roof and let it hang lifelessly. After a few minutes he let the rifle drop to the street. Then he sank to the roof, dragging his arm with him.

Crawling quickly to the left, he peered up at the corner of the roof. His ruse had succeeded. The other sniper, seeing the cap and rifle fall, thought that he had killed his man. He was now standing before a row of chimney pots, looking across, with his head clearly silhouetted against the western sky.

The Republican sniper smiled and lifted his revolver above the edge of the parapet. The distance was about fifty yards—a hard shot in the dim light, and his right arm was paining him like a thousand devils. He took a steady aim. His hand trembled with eagerness. Pressing his lips together, he took a deep breath through his nostrils and fired. He was almost deafened with the report and his arm shook with the recoil.

Then when the smoke cleared he peered across and uttered a cry of joy. His enemy had been hit. He was reeling over the parapet in his death agony. He struggled to keep his feet, but he was slowly falling forward, as if in a dream. The rifle fell from his grasp, hit the parapet, fell over, bounded off the pole of a barber's shop beneath and then clattered on the pavement.

Then the dying man on the roof crumpled up and fell forward. The body turned over and over in space and hit the ground with a thud. Then it lay still.

The sniper looked at his enemy falling and he shuddered. The lust of battle died in him. He became bitten by remorse. The sweat stood out in beads on his forehead. Weakened by his wound and the long summer day of fasting and watching on the roof, he revolted from the sight of the shattered mass of his dead enemy. His teeth chattered, he began to gibber to himself, cursing the war, cursing everybody.

He looked at the smoking revolver in his hand, and with an oath he hurled it to the roof at his feet. The revolver went off with the concussion and the bullet whizzed past the sniper's head. He was frightened back to his senses by the shock. His nerves steadied. The cloud of fear scattered from his mind and he laughed.

Taking the whisky flask from his pocket, he emptied it at a draught. He felt reckless under the influence of the spirit. He decided to leave the roof now and look for his company commander to report. Everywhere around was quiet. There was not much danger in going through the streets. He picked up his revolver and put it in his pocket. Then he crawled down through the skylight to the house underneath.

When the sniper reached the laneway on the street level, he felt a sudden curiosity as to the identity of the enemy sniper whom he had killed. He decided that he was a good shot, whoever he was. He wondered did he know him? Perhaps he had been in his own company before the split in the army. He decided to risk going over to have a look at him. He peered around the corner to O'Connell Street. In the upper part of the street there was heavy firing, but around here all was quiet. The sniper darted across the street. A machine gun tore up the ground around him with a hail of bullets, but he escaped. He threw himself face downward beside the corpse. The machine gun stopped.

Then the sniper turned over the dead body and looked into his brother's face.

In *Growing Up*, Pulitzer Prize-winner Russell Baker reflects on his mother's aging process and how it affected him as an adult.

from *Growing Up*
Russell Baker

At the age of eighty my mother had her last bad fall, and after that her mind wandered free through time. Some days she went to weddings and funerals that had taken place half a century earlier. On others she presided over family dinners cooked on Sunday afternoons for children who were now gray with age. Through all this she lay in bed but moved across time, traveling among the dead decades with a speed and ease beyond the gift of physical science.

"Where's Russell?" she asked one day when I came to visit at the nursing home.

"I'm Russell," I said.

She gazed at this improbably overgrown figure out of an inconceivable future and promptly dismissed it.

"Russell's only this big," she said, holding her hand, palm down, two feet from the floor. That day she was a young country wife with chickens in the backyard and a view of hazy blue Virginia mountains behind the apple orchard, and I was a stranger old enough to be her father.

Early one morning she phoned me in New York. "Are you coming to my funeral today?" she asked.

It was an awkward question with which to be awakened. "What are you talking about, for God's sake?" was the best reply I could manage.

"I'm being buried today," she declared briskly, as though announcing an important social event.

"I'll phone you back," I said and hung up, and when I did phone back she was all right, although she wasn't all right, of course, and we all knew she wasn't.

She had always been a small woman—short, light-boned, delicately structured—but now, under the white hospital sheet, she was becoming tiny. I thought of a doll with huge, fierce eyes. There had always been a fierceness in her. It showed in that angry, challenging thrust of the chin when she issued an opinion, and a great one she had always been for issuing opinions.

"I tell people exactly what's on my mind," she had been fond of boasting. "I tell them what I think, whether they like it or not." Often they had not liked it. She could be sarcastic to people in whom she detected evidence of the ignoramus or the fool.

"It's not always good policy to tell people exactly what's on your mind," I used to caution her.

"If they don't like it, that's too bad," was her customary reply, "because that's the way I am."

And so she was. A formidable woman. Determined to speak her mind, determined to have her way, determined to bend those who opposed her. In that time when I had known her best, my mother had hurled herself at life with chin thrust forward, eyes blazing, and an energy that made her seem always on the run.

Chapter 6

The Interpretation of Drama

Learning Objectives

After finishing this chapter you should be able to

- identify the similarities and differences between drama and prose
- discuss plot and its components: exposition, conflict, characters, setting, and time
- identify the protagonist and antagonist of a play
- distinguish between the various periods and styles of theatre: Greek, Roman, Medieval, Elizabethan, Realistic, and Absurdist

This chapter focuses on the interpretation of drama. Your class will be transformed into a series of drama workshops exploring the nature of dramatic literature and the unique challenges this art form presents to the interpretative performer.

Like the other forms of literature we have explored thus far, dramatic literature also functions to exhibit human nature and the human experience. Reading plays allows you to learn about people—to listen to and to watch them as they go about the business of being human. The plays that succeed reveal something about the human predicament; successful plays widen our understanding and appreciation of the way human beings interact, the way they affect each other psychologically, and the way they cope with the external and internal forces that affect them.

The Relationship between Drama and Prose

Drama is a literary cousin of narrative prose. Like narrative prose, a dramatic work includes the elements of *plot* (a series of incidents), *setting* (a location), *time* (a point in past, present, or future history), and *characters* (individuals to people the literary world). Consequently, much of what you learned while studying narrative prose may also be applied here.

Drama, however, distinguishes itself from narrative prose in a number of significant ways. In prose, narration tells us what we can't see. The narrator takes us into the thoughts of the characters, explains what motivates the story's actions, and, thereby, gives us the information we need to follow the action. In contrast to narrative prose, in a play, the narrator is not usually the central speaker. The characters are the central players.

Interpreting a play requires a greater imaginative effort than interpreting a story. Whereas the writer of a story tells it, the writer of a play presents it. The dramatist, unlike the prose writer, does not use much description or exposition. Neither does she or he alternate between scene, summary, and description. Except for the author's brief stage directions, drama is written almost exclusively in scenes. Thus, the dialogue of the play is the prime carrier of its message. Also, in contrast to prose works which tend to be based on actions in the past, plays are usually written in the present tense as if the action were occurring right now.

PERFORMER'S WARM-UP
All the World's a Stage

Create a basic story line on which you can improvise dialogue. As a group, perform your spontaneous dramatization for your classmates.

The elements you used in your improvisations are the same elements a writer uses to create a play. In this chapter you will look more closely at some of those elements.

PERFORMER'S WORKSHOP
Drama Versus Prose

In order to enhance your understanding of the similarities and differences between drama and prose, compare and contrast the following two versions of *One Flew Over the Cuckoo's Nest*. One version is in narrative form, written by Ken Kesey; the other version is in play form, adapted from Kesey's novel by Dale Wasserman. In each version we are given a look at life inside a particular mental institution.

 ## *One Flew Over the Cuckoo's Nest*
Ken Kesey

I'm the last one. Still strapped in the chair in the corner. McMurphy stops when he gets to me and hooks his thumbs in his pockets again and leans back to laugh, like he sees something funnier about me than about anybody else. All of a sudden I was scared he was laughing because he knew the way I was sitting there with my knees pulled up and my arms wrapped around them, staring straight ahead as though I couldn't hear a thing, was all an act.

"Hooeee," he said, "look what we got here."

I remember all this part real clear. I remember the way he closed one eye and tipped his head back and looked down across that healing wine-colored scar on his nose, laughing at me. I thought at first that he was laughing because of how funny it looked, an Indian's face and black, oily Indian's hair on somebody like me. I thought maybe he was laughing at how weak I looked. But then's when I remember thinking that he was laughing because he wasn't fooled for one minute by my deaf-and-dumb act; it didn't make any difference how cagey the act was, he was onto me and was laughing and winking to let me know it.

"What's your story, Big Chief? You look like Sittin' Bull on a sitdown strike." He looked over to the Acutes to see if they might laugh about his joke; when they just sniggered he looked back to me and winked again. "What's your name, Chief?"

Billy Bibbit called across the room. "His n-n-name is Bromden. Chief Bromden. Everybody calls him Chief Buh-Broom, though, because the aides have him sweeping a l-large part of the time. There's not m-much else he can do, I guess. He's deaf." Billy put his chin in his hands. "If I was d-d-deaf"—he sighed—"I would kill myself."

McMurphy kept looking at me. "He gets his growth, he'll be pretty good-sized, won't he? I wonder how tall he is."

"I think somebody m-m-measured him once at s-six feet seven; but even if he is big, he's scared of his own sh-sh-shadow. Just a bi-big deaf Indian."

"When I saw him sittin' here I thought he looked some Indian. But Bromden ain't an Indian name. What tribe is he?"

"I don't know," Billy said. "He was here wh-when I c-came."

"I have information from the doctor," Harding said, "that he is only half Indian, a Columbia Indian, I believe. That's a defunct Columbia Gorge tribe. The doctor said his father was the tribal leader, hence this fellow's title, 'Chief.' As to the 'Bromden' part of the name, I'm afraid my knowledge in Indian lore doesn't cover that."

McMurphy leaned his head down near mine where I had to look at him. "Is that right? You deef, Chief?"

"He's de-de-deef and dumb."

McMurphy puckered his lips and looked at my face a long time. Then he straightened back up and stuck his hand out.

"Well, what the hell, he can shake hands can't he? Deef or whatever. By God, Chief, you may be big, but you shake my hand or I'll consider it an insult. And it's not a good idea to insult the new bull goose loony of the hospital."

When he said that he looked back over to Harding and Billy and made a face, but he left that hand in front of me, big as a dinner plate.

I remember real clear the way that hand looked: there was carbon under the fingernails where he'd worked once in a garage; there was an anchor tattooed back from the knuckles; there was a dirty Band-Aid on the middle knuckle, peeling up at the edge. All the rest of the knuckles were covered with scars and cuts, old and new. I remember the palm was smooth and hard as bone from hefting the wooden handles of axes and hoes, not the hand you'd think could deal cards. The palm was callused, and the calluses were cracked, and dirt was worked in the cracks. A road map of his travels up and down the West. That palm made a scuffing sound against my hand. I remember the fingers were thick and strong closing over mine, and my hand commenced to feel peculiar and went to swelling up out there on my stick of an arm, like he was transmitting his own blood into it. It rang with blood and power. It blowed up near as big as his, I remember. . . .

"Mr. McMurry."

It's the Big Nurse.

"Mr. McMurry, could you come here please?"

It's the Big Nurse. That black boy with the thermometer has gone and got her. She stands there tapping that thermometer against her wrist watch, eyes whirring while she tries to gauge this new man. Her lips are in that triangle shape, like a doll's lips ready for a fake nipple.

"Aide Williams tells me, Mr. McMurry, that you've been somewhat difficult about your admission shower. Is this true? Please understand, I appreciate the way you've taken it upon yourself to orient with the other patients on the ward, but everything in its own good time, Mr. McMurry. I'm sorry to interrupt you and Mr. Bromden, but you do understand: everyone . . . must follow the rules."

He tips his head back and gives that wink that she isn't fooling him any more than I did, that he's onto her. He looks up at her with one eye for a minute.

"Ya know, ma'am," he says, "ya know—that is the ex-act thing somebody always tells me about the rules. . . ."

He grins. They both smile back and forth at each other, sizing each other up.

" . . . just when they figure I'm about to do the dead opposite."

Then he lets go my hand.

from *One Flew Over the Cuckoo's Nest: The Play*
Dale Wasserman

MCMURPHY: (*Stops short at* CHIEF BROMDEN *strapped in the chair.*) Hooee! What have we got here?

CHESWICK: That's Chief Bromden.

MCMURPHY: What's your story, Big Chief?

BILLY: He can't hear you. He's duh-deaf and dumb.

MCMURPHY: Well, what they got him strapped down for? I don't like that, no, sir. (*As he unstraps the Chief.*) It just ain't dignified. (CHIEF BROMDEN *rises.* MCMURPHY *whistles.*) Say, you get your full growth you're gonna be pretty good-sized. (*Circles* CHIEF BROMDEN *on a tour of inspection.*) What tribe is he?

BILLY: I don't know. He was here when I c-came.

HARDING: According to the doctor, he's a Columbia River Indian . . . one of those who lived up on the water falls? But I believe the tribe is now defunct.

MCMURPHY: That right, Chief? You defunct?

BILLY: He c-can't hear a word you say. (NURSE RATCHED *has entered on this, followed by* WILLIAMS. WARREN *comes out of the Station and joins them.*)

NURSE RATCHED: (*Holding out her hand.*) Mr. McMurphy.

MCMURPHY: (*Shaking hands with her.*) Howdy, Ma'am!

NURSE RATCHED: I'll take that. (*She takes the strap from him, hands it to* WARREN.) Aide Williams tells me you are being difficult.

MCMURPHY: (*Pained.*) Me?

NURSE RATCHED: I understand you refused to take your admission shower?

MCMURPHY: Well, as to that, ma'am, they showered me at the courthouse and last night at the jail, and I swear they'd of washed my ears for me on the way over if they coulda found the facilities. (*Explodes into laughter.*)

NURSE RATCHED: That's quite amusing, Mr. Murphy. But you must realize that our policies are engineered for your cure. Which means cooperation.

MCMURPHY: Ma'am, I'll cooperate from hell to Thursday, but you wouldn't want me to be unpolite? I mean, had to get acquainted with my new buddies?

NURSE RATCHED: (*Ever-smiling.*) Please understand, I do appreciate the way you've taken it upon yourself to . . . orient with other patients? But everything in its own time. You must follow the rules.

MCMURPHY: (*Face close to* NURSE RATCHED's, *smiling brightly.*) Ya know, ma'am—that is the exact thing somebody always tells me about the rules—just when I'm thinkin' a breakin' every one of 'em. (*Lights down fast.*) . . .

Questions

1. What similarities do the works contain?
2. What differences are evident?
3. What purpose did the narrator serve in the novel?
4. How is the narrator's function fulfilled in the drama?

As we see, unlike its close relative narrative prose, a play does not usually employ a narrator to summarize events, to tell how a character looks or moves, or to tell how other characters respond. A playwright, unlike a prose writer, cannot comment overtly on either the behavior of the characters or the actions that occur. Instead, the playwright simply shows us people in action.

When preparing to interpret a play, mental imaging becomes especially important for the interpretive performers as they work to create the scenes. The audience joins with the interpreters in creating scene by accepting the performance conventions used by interpreters and by using their imaginations to co-create the scene.

Components of Drama

Before going on, let's look more closely at the elements a writer uses to create a play.

Plot: What's Happening

A playwright's plot is the "what happens" of the play. It involves the characters in action. In many ways, the play's plot is equivalent to the backbone of one's body, in that it supports his or her work. The plot, normally structured into one or more acts and scenes, usually consists of five main parts: exposition, conflict, crisis, climax, and denouement.

Exposition. Playwrights use **exposition** to provide their audiences with background information about setting, time, characters, or significant past and present happenings. In effect, the exposition sets the scene. Dramatists may use a number of means to transfer expository material to an audience: a prologue, a chorus, a soliloquy, a talkative servant or friend, a telephone conversation, or a character who returns after a lengthy absence. Whatever device is selected, however, the goal is always to ensure audiences have enough information to appreciate and understand fully the unfolding of the play's events.

PERFORMER'S WORKSHOP
Exposition

Read the following expository passages from John Millington Synge's *Riders to the Sea* and Jean Anouilh's *The Lark* carefully. Identify the information that is being revealed and how the playwright has chosen to reveal it.

 ### *Riders to the Sea*
John Millington Synge

NORA: *(in a low voice)* Where is she?
CATHLEEN: She's lying down, God help her, and may be sleeping, if she's able.

(NORA *comes in slowly, and takes a bundle from under shawl.*)

CATHLEEN: *(spinning the wheel rapidly)* What is it you have?
NORA: The young priest is after bringing them. It's a shirt and a plain stocking were got off a drowned man in Donegal.

(CATHLEEN *stops her wheel with a sudden movement, and leans out to listen.*)

NORA: We're to find out if it's Michael's they are, some time herself will be down looking by the sea.
CATHLEEN: How would they be Michael's, Nora? How would he go the length of that way to the far north?
NORA: The young priest says he's known the like of it. "If it's Michael's they are," says he, "you can tell herself he's got a clean

burial by the grace of God, and if they're not his, let no one say a word about them, for she'll be getting her death," says he, "with crying and lamenting."

(*The door which* NORA *half closed is blown open by a gust of wind.*)

CATHLEEN: (*looking out anxiously*) Did you ask him would he stop Bartley going this day with the horses to the Galway fair?

NORA: "I won't stop him," says he, "but let you not be afraid. Herself does be saying prayers half through the night, and the Almighty God won't leave her destitute," says he, "with no son living."

CATHLEEN: Is the sea bad by the white rocks, Nora?

NORA: Middling bad, God help us. There's a great roaring in the west, and it's worse it'll be getting when the tide's turned to the wind. (*She goes over to the table with the bundle.*) Shall I open it now?

CATHLEEN: Maybe she'd wake up on us, and come in before we'd done. (*coming to the table*) It's a long time we'll be, and the two of us crying.

NORA: (*goes to the inner door*) She's moving about on the bed. She'll be coming in a minute.

CATHLEEN: Give me a ladder, and I'll put them up in the turf-loft, the way she won't know of them at all, and maybe when the tide turns she'll be going down to see would he be floating from the east.

(*They put the ladder against the gable of the chimney:* CATHLEEN *goes up a few steps and hides the bundle in the turf-loft.* MAURYA *comes from the inner room.*)

The Lark
Jean Anouilh

(WARWICK *enters and moves through the crowd.*)

WARWICK: Everybody here? Good. Let the trial begin at once. The quicker the judgment and the burning, the better for all of us.

CAUCHON: No, sire. The whole story must be played. Domremy, the Voices, Chinon—

WARWICK: I am not here to watch that children's story of the warrior virgin, strong and tender, dressed in white armor, white standard streaming in the wind. If they have time to waste, they can make the statues that way, in days to come. Different politics may well require different symbols. We might even have to make her a monument in London. Don't be shocked at that, sire. The politics of my government may well require it one day, and what's required,

Englishmen supply. That's our secret, sire, and a very good one, indeed. (*Moves downstage to address the audience.*) Well, let's worry about only this minute of time. I am Beauchamp, Earl of Warwick. I have a dirty virgin witch girl tucked away on a litter of straw in the depths of a prison here in Rouen. The girl has been an expensive nuisance. Your Duke of Burgundy sold her high. You like money in France, Monseigneur, all of you. That's the French secret, sire, and a very good one, indeed. (*He moves toward* JOAN.) And here she is. The Maid. The famous Joan the Maid. Obviously, we paid too much. So put her on trial, and burn her, and be finished.

Questions

1. What expository information is provided in these excerpts?
2. What are the characters in *Riders to the Sea* concerned about? Who are they seeking to protect?
3. Why does Beauchamp directly address the audience in *The Lark?*

Just as a dramatist uses exposition to set the stage for his or her play, so you as an interpreter can use exposition to set the stage for your reading. As in descriptive prose, narrative prose, or poetry, your introduction to a dramatic reading should serve to involve the audience in the world of your selection. It should include important facts about your dramatist, your play, the characters, and the setting; also, it should prepare your audience for the performance by creating a mood that echoes the intent of your literature.

Conflict. Another key element of drama is **conflict.** A conflict is opposition that gives rise to the dramatic action. It creates suspense and keeps the audience involved. For example, a disagreement or argument between persons or forces may serve as a conflict and propel both the story line and the actions of the characters. Conflict in a play precipitates rising action. Conflict may exist within a character, between characters, or between one or more characters and the environment. Conflicts increase tensions and create the play's climaxes.

PERFORMER'S WARM-UP
Clash!

How do you feel when experiencing conflict? Try these exercises.

A. Pantomime a recent internal argument you had with yourself, such as, "I have to study, but I'd rather watch television." Show us which part of you won the struggle.
B. With a partner, improvise a two-person scene in which one person tries to persuade the other to do something against his or her will.

For example, one wants to go to the movie theater, while the other wants to stay home and watch a video.

C. In groups of three, improvise a scene in which two people are competing for the attention of the third individual. What decision does the third individual make?

You should realize that a play often contains a number of conflicts, and each conflict serves to alter the direction of the action. In addition to the play's major conflict, more minor conflicts usually occur in each of the play's scenes and acts. Let's consider in greater depth the possible sources of conflict.

First, conflict may develop from a clash of personalities, wills, ideas, or actions. Second, conflict may develop because of a character's involvement or concern with outside forces. Third, conflict may develop because of a character's involvement or concern with himself or herself. Thus, dramatic conflict may have either a physical or emotional source. The central character in a conflict is referred to as the play's **protagonist;** the forces or people united against the protagonist are the **antagonists.**

Crisis, Climax, and Resolution. A conflict leads to a crucial situation—a **crisis.** The crisis is a turning point in the play. As an interpreter, you will want to use your voice and your body to reflect growing tension as a conflict builds to a crisis; likewise, you will want to use your voice and body to mirror the release in tension that accompanies the resolution of a conflict or crisis. One way to identify the main crisis in a play is to identify the highest point of action in the play, or the **climax.** Once this climax or highpoint is known, you can look back to determine the event(s) that made this climax inevitable.

Thus, the tension level of a play increases and decreases, builds and is released, as it moves through a number of crises. After a series of crises, a decisive situation or a final climax usually emerges. This climax represents the apex of intensity in the work—it is the highest conflict peak of the play. This is the point at which the conflict between the protagonist and the forces that oppose him or her has become so intense that a final solution must be determined. The solution results in either success or defeat for the central character.

The climax also leads to the play's final portion, known as the **resolution** or **denouement.** In the denouement, the dramatist usually untangles and ties off each strand of the plot in order to resolve the questions in the play.

Character: Who's Involved?

Characters make a play come alive; they are the primary means a playwright has to shape a plot. The characters manifest certain physical and verbal behaviors that a playwright uses to shape the action in the work. Thus, plot and character share a symbiotic relationship—that is, each one exists to fulfill the needs of the other.

When creating a character, the interpreter of drama relies on the same methods—the same type of literary fuel—as the actor of drama. However, the interpreter's task is further complicated by the nature of the art. Unlike the typical actor, the interpreter is expected to embody not one character, but an entire cast of characters. Thus, rather than getting to know and feel for a single character, interpreters need to know and feel for all the characters that inhabit their selected scripts.

How can you go about this? You need to begin by discovering the predominant traits, motives, and moods of each character you hope to create. You want to communicate each character's degree of maturity and to re-create each character's style of verbal, vocal, and physical expression. Most of all, you want to use everything the author reveals about a character's attitude toward self, attitude toward surroundings, and attitude toward other individuals who share those surroundings.

Language and Character.   Playwrights divulge information about their characters in a number of different ways. One way is through language—a character reveals a great deal about attitudes and background by what he or she says.

Playwrights use language in much the same way artists use paint, adding color and definition to their characters as they create clear portraits for their audiences. Just as wearing distinctive clothing makes one recognizable, so does speech style. Pay careful attention to each character's speech pattern as you read, study, and prepare to perform a play. Consider the author's word choices and speech rhythms for the character, as well as the ideas the author has the character express. These attributes help communicate a character's basic traits.

Interpreters also need to appreciate and internalize the emotions and the attitudes characters display. These mood-cues serve to distinguish one character from another and to detail each character's mood range. Consequently, you need to be alert to words that indicate mood-tone and to recognize when a character's mood-tone changes. Using these skills, you will empathize with the author's characters, making them live for your audience.

PERFORMER'S WORKSHOP
Meeting a Character Through Language

Read the following passages carefully. What do each character's utterances reveal about who they are?

from *Pygmalion*
George Bernard Shaw

DOOLITTLE: . . . I ask you, what am I? I'm one of the undeserving poor: that's what I am. Think of what that means to a man. It means that he's up against middle class morality all the time. If there's anything going, and I put in for a bit of it, it's always the same story:

"You're undeserving; so you can't have it." But my needs is as great as the most deserving widow's that ever got money out of six different charities in one week for the death of the same husband. I don't need less than a deserving man: I need more. I don't eat less hearty than him; and I drink a lot more. I want a bit of amusement, cause I'm a thinking man. I want cheerfulness and a song and a band when I feel low. Well, they charge me just the same for everything as they charge the deserving. What is middle class morality? Just an excuse for never giving me anything. Therefore, I ask you, as two gentlemen, not to play that game on me. I'm playing straight with you. I ain't pretending to be deserving. I'm undeserving; and I mean to go on being undeserving. I like it; and that's the truth. Will you take advantage of a man's nature to do him out of the price of his own daughter what he's brought up and fed and clothed by the sweat of his brow until she's growed big enough to be interesting to you two gentlemen? Is five pounds unreasonable? I put it to you; and I leave it to you.

Questions

1. To what social class does the speaker belong?
2. Is the speaker happy with his class?
3. At what rate do you believe these lines should be delivered? How does the rate you choose help reflect your impression of the character's internal self? What vocal qualities can you use to help you re-create Doolittle?
4. What physical gestures could you use to help characterize the man?

 from *The Visit*

Friedrich Duerrenmatt

CLAIRE: Mike—Max! (*She claps her hands. Two huge bodyguards come in, left, carrying a sedan chair. She sits in it.*) I travel this way—a bit antiquated, of course. But perfectly safe. Ha! Ha! Aren't they magnificent? Mike and Max. I bought them in America. They were in jail, condemned to the chair. I had them pardoned. Now, they're condemned to my chair. I paid fifty thousand dollars apiece for them. You couldn't get them now for twice the sum. The sedan chair comes from the Louvre. I fancied it so much that the President of France gave it to me. The French are so impulsive, don't you think so, Anton? Go!

(MIKE and MAX *start to carry her off.*)

Questions

1. How do you imagine Claire as she speaks these lines?
2. What type of vocal quality would you attempt to suggest?
3. What gestures could enhance your verbalization?

 ### *A Raisin in the Sun*
Lorraine Hansberry

MAMA: (*still quietly*) Walter, what is the matter with you?

WALTER: Matter with me? Ain't nothing the matter with me!

MAMA: Yes there is. Something eating you up like a crazy man. Something more than me not giving you this money. The past few years I been watching it happen to you. You get all nervous acting and kind of wild in the eyes—(WALTER *jumps up impatiently at her words.*) I said sit there now, I'm talking to you!

WALTER: Mama—I don't need no nagging at me today.

MAMA: Seem like you getting to a place where you always tied up in some kind of knot about something. But if anybody ask you 'bout it you just yell at 'em and bust out of the house and go out and drink somewheres. Walter Lee, people can't live with that. Ruth's a good, patient girl in her way—but you getting to be too much. Boy, don't make the mistake of driving that girl away from you.

WALTER: Why—what she do for me?

MAMA: She loves you.

WALTER: Mama—I'm going out. I want to go off somewhere and be by myself for a while.

MAMA: I'm sorry 'bout your liquor store, son. It wasn't the thing for us to do. That's what I want to tell you about—

WALTER: I got to go out, Mama—

(*He rises.*)

MAMA: It's dangerous, son.

WALTER: What's dangerous?

MAMA: When a man goes outside his home to look for peace.

WALTER: (*beseechingly*) Then why can't there never be no peace in this house then?

MAMA: You done found it in some other house?

WALTER: NO—there ain't no woman! Why do women always think there's a woman somewhere when a man gets restless. (*Coming to her.*) Mama—Mama—I want so many things . . .

MAMA: Yes, son—

WALTER: I want so many things that they are driving me kind of crazy . . . Mama—look at me.

MAMA: I'm looking at you. You are a good-looking boy. You got a job, a nice wife, a fine boy—

WALTER: A job. (*looks at her*) Mama, a job? I open and close car doors all day long. I drive a man around in his limousine and I say, "Yes, sir; no, sir! very good, sir; shall I take the Drive, sir?" Mama, that ain't no kind of a job . . . that ain't nothing at all. (*very quietly*) Mama, I don't know if I can make you understand.

MAMA: Understand what, baby?

WALTER: (*quietly*) Sometimes it's like I can see the future stretched out in front of me—just as plain as day. The future, Mama. Hanging over there at the edge of my days. Just waiting for me—a big, looming blank space—full of nothing. Just waiting for me. (*Pause. Kneeling beside her chair.*) Mama—sometimes when I'm downtown and I pass them cool, quiet looking restaurants where them white boys are sitting and talking 'bout things . . . sitting there turning deals worth millions of dollars . . . sometimes I see guys don't look much older than me—

MAMA: Son—how come you talk so much 'bout money?

WALTER: (*with immense passion*) Because it is life, Mama!

MAMA: (*quietly*) Oh—(*very quietly*) So now it's life. Money is life. Once upon a time freedom used to be life—now it's money. I guess the world really do change. . . .

WALTER: No—it always was money, Mama. We just didn't know about it.

MAMA: No . . . something has changed. (*She looks at him.*) You something new, boy. In my time we was worried about not being lynched and getting to the North if we could and how to stay alive and still have a pinch of dignity too . . . Now here come you and Beneatha—talking 'bout things we ain't even thought about hardly, me and your daddy. You ain't satisfied or proud of nothing we done. I mean that you had a home; that we kept you out of trouble till you was grown; that you don't have to ride to work on the back of nobody's streetcar—You my children—but how different we done become.

WALTER: You just don't understand, Mama, you just don't understand.

MAMA: Son—do you know your wife is expecting another baby? (WALTER *stands, stunned, and absorbs what his mother has said.*) That's what she wanted to talk to you about. (WALTER *sinks down into a chair.*) This ain't for me to be telling—but you ought to know. (*She waits.*) I think Ruth is thinking 'bout getting rid of that child.

WALTER: (*slowly understanding*) No—no—Ruth wouldn't do that.

MAMA: When the world gets ugly enough—a woman will do anything for her family. The part that's already living.

WALTER: You don't know Ruth, Mama, if you think she would do that.

(RUTH *opens the bedroom door and stands there, a little limp.*)

RUTH: (*beaten*) Yes I would too, Walter. (*Pause.*) I gave her a five-dollar down payment.

(*There is total silence as the man stares at his wife and the mother stares at her son.*)

MAMA: (*presently*) Well—(*tightly*) Well—son, I'm waiting to hear you say something . . . I'm waiting to hear you say something . . . I'm waiting to hear how you be your father's son. Be the man he was . . . (*Pause.*) Your wife say she going to destroy your child. And I'm waiting to hear you talk like him and say we a people who give children life, not who destroys them—(*She rises.*) I'm waiting to see you stand up and look like your daddy and say we done give up one baby to poverty and that we ain't going to give up nary another one . . . I'm waiting.

WALTER: Ruth—

MAMA: If you are a son of mine, tell her! (WALTER *turns, looks at her and can say nothing. She continues, bitterly.*) You . . . you are a disgrace to your father's memory. Somebody get me my hat.

Questions

1. What mood-tones characterize the speeches of each character?
2. What attitudes do the characters' words and actions reveal about them? How would you characterize their relationships with others and their relationships to their surroundings?
3. What speaking rhythms would you associate with each of the characters?

Performance Clues

Sometimes a playwright provides stage directions regarding the delivery of certain lines—that is, the kind of feelings the actor or interpreter of literature should experience and relay during the performance. These directions (phrases like "shouts angrily" or "whispers gently") are inserted in parentheses before the character's lines. The oral interpreter, as well as the actor in a production, should internalize the playwright's instructions and demonstrate in performance that these prompts were understood and applied.

Using the directions provided in parentheses, read the following sentences aloud. Demonstrate your understanding of these directions verbally and physically.

(with a hysterical giggle) Look what the monkey's doing!

(harshly) I don't want to go with you. I would not go with you if my life depended upon it.

(as if to a baby) Don't you want to go and get some ice cream?

(with a tinge of sarcasm) You're just so clever; you ought to be on a quiz show.

(very quietly) You can almost hear the sun rise; the day is starting so peacefully.

Questions

1. What vocal actions did you use to support your reading of each sentence?
2. What physical actions did you use to support your interpretations?

The Art of Suggestion and Remembered Action.   A character's personality is also revealed to us through his or her actions, physical behavior, and tension state. Naturally, as an interpreter you cannot mimic a character's every move during a performance, but you can certainly work to suggest to your audience the important movements a character makes.

Just how much does a suggestion involve, and how does the interpreter learn to suggest? Test your own instincts by answering the following questions. As an interpreter, what would you do if, during the scene you chose to perform, one character is supposed to throw a punch at another character? What would you do if, during a scene, one character is supposed to embrace another character?

During your performance, would you stand there and whack at the air or attempt to embrace empty space? Obviously, you would not. But in your rehearsals you might profit by carrying out these precise actions.

A preliminary use of literal action will aid you later in making the transfer to **suggested** or **remembered action.** It is this remembered action that an interpreter relies on during a performance. In other words, once you have "acted out" the action, it is expected that your muscles will be able to recall the dynamic movements they made originally during your literal enactment and that you will experience the emotional tension you first felt at that time. Thus, you and your muscles work together in a performance, even if you choose to muffle their primary reactions. Through physical suggestion, you will allow audience members to complete the action in their minds.

PERFORMER'S WORKSHOP
The Road to Suggestion

Read aloud the following passages from dramas. In the first play, August Strindberg's *The Stronger*, we are introduced to two women who are rivals: Mrs. X and Miss Y.

The Stronger
August Strindberg

The corner of a ladies' cafe. Two little iron tables, a red velvet sofa, several chairs. Enter MRS. X, *dressed in winter clothes, carrying a Japanese basket on her arm.*

MISS Y: (*Sits with a half-empty beer bottle before her, reading an illustrated paper, which she changes later for another.*)

MRS. X: Good afternoon, Amelia. You're sitting here alone on Christmas eve like a poor bachelor!

MISS Y: (*Looks up, nods, and resumes her reading.*)

MRS. X: Do you know it really hurts me to see you like this, alone, in a cafe, and on Christmas eve, too. It makes me feel as I did one time when I saw a bridal party in a Paris restaurant, and the bride sat reading a comic paper, while the groom played billiards with the witnesses. Huh, thought I, with such a beginning, what will follow, and what will be the end? He played billiards on his wedding eve! (MISS Y *starts to speak.*) And she read a comic paper, you mean? Well, they are not altogether the same thing.

(*A* WAITRESS *enters, places a cup of chocolate before* MRS. X *and goes out.*)

MRS. X: You know what, Amelia! I believe you would have done better to have kept him! Do you remember, I was the first to say "Forgive him?" Do you remember that? You would be married now and have a home. Remember that Christmas when you went out to visit your fiancé's parents in the country? How you gloried in the happiness of home life and really longed to quit the theatre forever? Yes, Amelia dear, home is the best place of all—next to the theatre—and as for children—well, you don't understand that.

MISS Y: (*Looks up scornfully.*)

MRS. X: (*Sips a few spoonfuls out of the cup, then opens her basket and shows Christmas presents.*) Now you shall see what I bought for my piggy-wigs. (*Takes up a doll.*) Look at this! This is for Lisa, ha! Do you see how she can roll her eyes and turn her head, eh? And here is Maja's popgun.

(*Loads it and shoots at* MISS Y.)

MISS Y: (*Makes a startled gesture.*)

MRS. X: Did I frighten you? Do you think I would like to shoot you, eh? On my soul, if I don't think you did! If you wanted to shoot me it wouldn't be so surprising, because I stood in your way—and I know you can never forget that—although I was absolutely innocent. You still believe I intrigued and got you out of the Stora theatre, but I didn't. I didn't do that, although you think so. Well, it doesn't make any difference what I say to you. You still believe I did it. (*Takes up a pair of embroidered slippers.*) And these are for my better half. I embroidered them myself—I can't bear tulips, but he wants tulips on everything.

MISS Y: (*Looks up ironically and curiously.*)

MRS. X: (*Putting a hand in each slipper.*) See what little feet Bob has! What? And you should see what a splendid stride he has! You've never seen him in slippers! (MISS Y *laughs aloud.*) Look! (*She makes the slippers walk on the table.*) (MISS Y *laughs loudly.*) And when he is grumpy he stamps like this with his foot. "What! damn those servants who can never learn to make coffee. Oh, now those creatures haven't trimmed the lamp wick properly!" And then there are draughts on the floor and his feet are cold. "Ugh, how cold it is; the stupid idiots can never keep the fire going." (*She rubs the slippers together, one sole over the other.*)

MISS Y: (*Shrieks with laughter.*)

MRS. X: And then he comes home and has to hunt for his slippers which Marie has stuck under the chiffonier—oh, but it's sinful to sit here and make fun of one's husband this way when he is kind and a good little man. You ought to have had such a husband, Amelia. What are you laughing at? What? What? And you see he's true to me. Yes, I'm sure of that, because he told me himself—what are you laughing at?—that when I was touring in Norway that brazen Frederika came and wanted to seduce him! Can you fancy anything so infamous? (*Pause.*) It was lucky that Bob told me about it himself and that it didn't reach me through gossip. (*Pause.*) But would you believe it, Frederika wasn't the only one! I don't know why, but the women are crazy about my husband. They must think he has influence about getting them theatrical engagements, because he is connected with the government. Perhaps you were after him yourself. I didn't used to trust you any too much. But now I know he never bothered his head about you, and you always seemed to have a grudge against him some way.

(*Pause. They look at each other in a puzzled way.*)

MRS. X: Come and see us this evening, Amelia, and show us that you're not put out with us—not put out with me at any rate. I don't know, but I think it would be uncomfortable to have you for an enemy. Perhaps it's because I stood in your way (*more slowly*) or—I really don't know why—in particular.

(*Pause.* MISS Y *stares at* MRS. X *curiously.*)

MRS. X: (*thoughtfully*) Our acquaintance has been so queer. When I saw you for the first time I was afraid of you, so afraid that I didn't dare let you out of my sight; no matter when or where, I always found myself near you—I didn't dare have you for an enemy, so I became your friend. But there was always discord when you came to our house, because I saw that my husband couldn't endure you, and the whole thing seemed as awry to me as an ill-fitting gown— and I did all I could to make him friendly toward you, but with no success until you became engaged. Then came a violent friendship between you, so that it looked all at once as though you both dared show your real feelings only when you were secure—and then— how was it later? I didn't get jealous—strange to say! And I remember at the christening, when you acted as godmother, I made him kiss you—he did so, and you became so confused—as it were; I didn't notice it then—didn't think about it later, either—have never thought about it until—now! (*Rises suddenly.*) Why are you silent? You haven't said a word this whole time, but you have let me go on talking! You have sat there, and your eyes have reeled out of me all these thoughts which lay like raw silk in its cocoon—thoughts— suspicious thoughts, perhaps. Let me see—why did you break your engagement? Why do you never come to our house any more? Why won't you come to see us tonight?

(MISS Y *appears as if about to speak.*)

MRS. X: Hush, you needn't speak—I understand it all! It was because—and because—and because! Yes, yes! Now all the accounts balance. That's it. Fie, I won't sit at the same table with you. (*Moves her things to another table.*) That's the reason I had to embroider tulips—which I hate—on his slippers, because you are fond of tulips; that's why (*throws slippers on the floor*) we go to Lake Malarn in the summer, because you don't like salt water; that's why my boy is named Eskil—because it's your father's name; that's why I wear your colors, read your authors, eat your favorite dishes, drink your drinks—chocolate, for instance; that's why— oh—my God—it's terrible, when I think about it; it's terrible. Everything, everything came from you to me, even your passions. Your soul crept into mine, like a worm into an apple, ate and ate, bored and bored, until nothing was left but the rind and a little black dust within. I wanted to get away from you, but I couldn't;

you lay like a snake and charmed me with your black eyes; I felt that when I lifted my wings they only dragged me down; I lay in the water with bound feet, and the stronger I strove to keep up the deeper I worked myself down, down, until I sank to the bottom, where you lay like a giant crab to clutch me in your claws—and there I am lying now. I hate you, hate you, hate you! And you only sit there silent—silent and indifferent; indifferent whether it's new moon or waning moon, Christmas or New Year's, whether others are happy or unhappy; without power to hate or to love; as quiet as a stork by a rat hole—you couldn't scent your prey and capture it, but you could lie in wait for it! You sit here in your corner of the cafe—did you know it's called "The Rat Trap" for you? And read the papers to see if misfortune hasn't befallen someone, to see if someone hasn't been given notice at the theatre, perhaps; you sit here and calculate about your next victim and reckon on your chances of recompense like a pilot in a shipwreck. Poor Amelia. I pity you, nevertheless, because I know you are unhappy, unhappy like one who has been wounded, and angry because you are wounded. I can't be angry with you, no matter how much I want to be—because you come out the weaker one. Yes, all that with Bob doesn't trouble me. What is that to me, after all? And what difference does it make whether I learned to drink chocolate from you or some one else? (*Sips a spoonful from her cup.*) Besides, chocolate is very healthful. And if you taught me how to dress—tant mieux!— that has only made me more attractive to my husband; so you lost and I won there. Well, judging by certain signs, I believe you have already lost him; and you certainly intended that I should leave him—so as you did with your fiancé and regret as you now regret; but, you see, I don't do that—we mustn't be too exacting. And why should I take only what no one else wants? Perhaps, take it all in all, I am at this moment the stronger one. You received nothing from me, but you gave me much. And now I seem like a thief since you have awakened and find I possess what is your loss. How could it be otherwise when everything is worthless and sterile in your hands? You can never keep a man's love with your tulips and your passions—but I can keep it. You can't learn how to live from your authors, as I have learned. You have no little Eskil to cherish, even if your father's name was Eskil. And why are you always silent, silent, silent? I thought that was strength, but perhaps it is because you have nothing to say! Because you never think about anything! (*Rises and picks up slippers.*) Now I'm going home—and take the tulips with me—your tulips! You are unable to learn from another; you can't bend—therefore, you broke like a dry stalk. But I won't break! Thank you, Amelia, for all your good lessons. Thanks for teaching my husband how to love. Now I'm going home to love him. (*Goes.*)

Questions

1. Which character does the title of the play allude to?
2. How will you reflect this fact in your interpretation?

Continue with the next passage by Neil Simon, which takes a humorous look at an odd couple.

 ### *The Odd Couple*
Neil Simon

(FELIX *comes out of the kitchen carrying a tray with steaming dish of spaghetti. As he crosses behind* OSCAR *to the table, he smells it "deliciously" and passes it close to* OSCAR *to make sure* OSCAR *smells the fantastic dish he's missing. As* FELIX *sits and begins to eat,* OSCAR *takes can of aerosol spray from the bar, and circling the table sprays all about* FELIX, *puts can down next to him and goes back to his newspaper.*)

FELIX: (*Pushing spaghetti away.*) All right, how much longer is this gonna go on?

OSCAR: (*Reading his paper.*) Are you talking to me?

FELIX: That's right, I'm talking to you.

OSCAR: What do you want to know?

FELIX: I want to know if you're going to spend the rest of your life not talking to me. Because if you are, I'm going to buy a radio. (*No reply.*) Well? (*No reply.*) I see. You're not going to talk to me. (*No reply.*) All right. Two can play at this game. (*Pause.*) If you're not going to talk to me, I'm not going to talk to you. (*No reply.*) I can act childish too, you know. (*No reply.*) I can go on without talking just as long as you can.

OSCAR: Then why the hell don't you shut up?

FELIX: Are you talking to me?

OSCAR: You had your chance to talk last night. I begged you to come upstairs with me. From now on I never want to hear a word from that shampooed head as long as you live. That's a warning, Felix.

FELIX: (*Stares at him.*) I stand warned. . . . Over and out!

OSCAR: (*Gets up, taking key out of his pocket and slams it on the table.*) There's a key to the back door. If you stick to the hallway and your room, you won't get hurt. (*Sits back down on couch.*)

FELIX: I don't think I gather the entire meaning of that remark.

OSCAR: Then I'll explain it to you. Stay out of my way.

FELIX: (*Picks up key and moves to couch.*) I think you're serious. I think you're really serious. . . . Are you serious?

OSCAR: This is my apartment. Everything in my apartment is mine. The only thing here that's yours is you. Just stay in your room and speak softly.

FELIX: Yeah, you're serious. . . . Well, let me remind you that I pay half the rent and I'll go into any room I want. (*He gets up angrily and starts towards hallway.*)

OSCAR: Where are you going?

FELIX: I'm going to walk around your bedroom.

OSCAR: (*Slams down newspaper.*) You stay out of there.

FELIX: (*Steaming.*) Don't tell me where to go. I pay a hundred and twenty dollars a month.

OSCAR: That was off-season. Starting tomorrow the rates are twelve dollars a day.

FELIX: All right. (*He takes some bills out of his pocket and slams them down on table.*) There you are. I'm paid up for today. Now I'm going to walk in your bedroom. (*He starts to storm off.*)

OSCAR: Stay out of there! Stay out of my room! (*He chases after him.* FELIX *dodges around the table as* OSCAR *blocks the hallway.*)

FELIX: (*Backing away, keeping table between them.*) Watch yourself! Just watch yourself, Oscar!

OSCAR: (*With a pointing finger.*) I'm warning you. You want to live here, I don't want to see you, I don't want to hear you and I don't want to smell your cooking. Now get this spaghetti off my poker table.

FELIX: Ha! Haha!

OSCAR: What the hell's so funny!

FELIX: It's not spaghetti. It's linguini! (OSCAR *picks up the plate of linguini, crosses to the doorway, and hurls it into the kitchen.*)

OSCAR: Now it's garbage! (*Paces around the couch.*)

FELIX: (*Looks at* OSCAR *unbelievingly.*) What an insane thing to do. You are crazy! . . . I'm a neurotic nut but you are crazy!

OSCAR: I'm crazy, heh? That's really funny coming from a fruitcake like you.

FELIX: (*Goes to kitchen door and looks in at the mess. Turns back to* OSCAR.) I'm not cleaning that up.

OSCAR: Is that a promise?

FELIX: Did you hear what I said? I'm not cleaning it up. It's your mess. (*Looking into kitchen again.*) Look at it. Hanging all over the walls.

OSCAR: (*Crosses up on landing and looks at kitchen door.*) I like it. (*Closes door and paces right.*)

FELIX: (*Fumes.*) You'd just let it lie there, wouldn't you? Until it turns hard and brown and . . . yich. . . . It's disgusting. . . . I'm cleaning it up. (*He goes into the kitchen.* OSCAR *chases after him. There is the sound of a struggle and falling pots.*)

OSCAR: (*Off.*) Leave it alone. . . . You touch one strand of that linguini—and I'm gonna punch you right in your sinuses.

FELIX: (*Dashes out of kitchen with* OSCAR *in pursuit. Stops and tries to calm* OSCAR *down.*) Oscar . . . I'd like you to take a couple of phenobarbital.

OSCAR: (*Points.*) Go to your room! . . . Did you hear what I said? Go to your room!

Questions

1. What adjectives would you use to describe Felix and Oscar?
2. How could you embody these adjectives during a performance?

Now, do the following exercises for the main characters in both of the preceding examples.

A. Walk across the room as you imagine the characters would walk. How do their walks differ?
B. Count from one to twenty as you imagine each of the characters in the passages would count. Give special attention to pitch, rate, volume, and quality.
C. Now, read the passages again, this time taking all the stage directions and dialogue literally. For example, when Felix "gets up angrily and starts towards hallway," get up angrily and start toward the hallway.
D. Read the passages for a third time. This time let your muscles recall where they have just been and what they have just experienced; use the medium of suggestion, rather than the medium of overt or literal action.

As an interpreter, you are expected to project your empathy for a character through your stance, your muscle tone, and your voice. With these tools you can suggest the degree of physical and vocal tension implied in your script. As an interpreter, you are more than simply yourself; you can perform a play—with no need for a supporting cast!

Character Differentiation. The preceding techniques should help you to understand, to visualize, and to present the characters in your play. Once you develop a feel for each character's age, voice tone, state of health, mood intensities, and movement rhythms, then you are ready to help your audience distinguish one character from another in a performance. In addition, you may reinforce the preceding techniques of character differentiation with the recognized technique of character placement.

As we discussed in the previous chapter on narrative prose, an interpreter using the device of character placement identifies a constant angle of address with a specific character. In other words, each character in a scene speaks in a predetermined direction, no matter whom he or she is addressing. This directional technique, when used in conjunction with the other methods we have discussed, enables the audience members to identify the character who is speaking; it also helps them to visualize and to hear the character from their own perceptions. Thus, a working understanding of character placement, together with the posture, facial expression, muscle tone, and vocal cues techniques we have already discussed, is an asset to the interpretative performer.

Setting and Time

Playwrights, like writers of narrative prose, also use setting and time to further enrich and define their works. Unlike the narrative prose writer, however, a dramatist usually places this kind of information in the stage directions that precede each act or scene of the play. This practice further complicates the task of the interpreter because, unlike actors who often work within an artificially created set, the oral interpreter usually works only with the set that exists in his or her mind.

To help re-create this set for an audience and to be sure the audience experiences the desired atmosphere, an interpreter should relate a portion of the stage directions provided by the author. To accomplish this, the oral reader may simply incorporate parts of these descriptions into his or her introduction and transitions. In this way, you can help your audience to internalize the scenic embellishments of the play. You can help them etch the important aspects of time and place into their imaginations and to appreciate how time and location affect the mood-tones that color each of the play's characters. Thus, like playwrights, oral interpreters of plays may also use setting to let their audiences know how environment and atmosphere pervade and permeate a drama.

PERFORMER'S WORKSHOP
Stage Directions

What purposes are fulfilled by the following stage directions excerpted from *Long Day's Journey into Night* by Eugene O'Neill?

It is around half past six in the evening. Dusk is gathering in the living room, an early dusk due to the fog which has rolled in from the Sound and is like a white curtain drawn down outside the windows. From a lighthouse beyond the harbor's mouth, a foghorn is heard at regular intervals, moaning like a mournful whale in labor, and from the harbor itself, intermittently, comes the warning ringing of bells on yachts at anchor.

Questions

1. What kind of atmosphere has the author created in this passage?
2. What does the foghorn sound achieve?

Styles of Drama

Styles of drama, like styles of architecture, painting, or dress, have changed and evolved through the centuries. In fact, it is this constant change in style that makes drama seem new from age to age. During various periods, different dramatic elements are emphasized. For example, the dramatic pendulum swings from simple and sparse plots to extensively developed plots, then back again. Similarly, we find the dramatic pendulum swinging from stereotyped characters to well-rounded individuals and back again. In terms of dialogue, the pendulum has swung from verse dialogue to prose dialogue to no dialogue, then back again. Each age develops its own method of dramatically exhibiting the human condition. Our concern is with how the frequent change in dramatic style affects the oral interpreter. How does the oral interpreter approach the problem of style?

In order for you fully to suggest a specific character to an audience, you first have to immerse yourself into the dramatic period in which the character lives. To do so, you will want to familiarize yourself with the manner and customs of the period. Also, you should attempt to find out how and why the author's characters act, speak, and think as they do. At this point, let us briefly explore a number of different dramatic styles and periods.

The Greek Period

The tragic plays of the Greek period are elevated by verse and formalized by the use of a chorus. Unlike those in other dramatic periods, the characters in a Greek play are not surrounded by furniture, nor do they involve themselves in idle or unimportant conversations. Characters in Greek plays simply do not have time to involve themselves in inconsequential activities—these characters have been placed in the midst of mind-boggling crises.

Thus, when reading Greek tragedy aloud, you will want to communicate these dramatic qualities to your audiences. In order to do this, you will need to exhibit movements characterized by dramatic economy; that is, your movements should be slow, formal, and broad, rather than small, casual, and realistic. You will also want your voice to suit the roles you are portraying; for this you will need to work to capture vocally the rhythmic chants, the lamentations, and the exalted nature of the poetry.

PERFORMER'S WARM-UP
Brown Paper Movement

A. Your instructor will provide you with large sheets of brown wrapping paper. Your goal is to hold the wrapping paper so it is completely extended as you move about your classroom to slow music. The real challenge is to move with the paper without making a sound. Try not to allow the paper to crinkle. This is best accomplished by extending your arms completely.

B. Next, without breaking the silence, fold the sheet of brown paper into a very small package.

Questions

1. What type of movements did you have to make with the paper to avoid making a sound?
2. How might the skills tapped in this exercise help you prepare to interpret plays from the Greek period?

PERFORMER'S WARM-UP
Masks, Voice, and Movement

Wearing a mask you bring to class or create from cardboard, posterboard, or paper, express the following emotions using physical and vocal cues: love, hate, fury, horror, hope, arrogance.

Questions

1. What happened to the size of your physical actions when you wore the mask? To what extent did you find them becoming more sweeping and majestic?
2. How did your voice differ from its normal conversational tone?
3. How might this exercise help you prepare to interpret plays from the Greek period?

Now that you have a feel for the kind of body movements and vocal cues you need to internalize in order to convey the magnitude of the tragedies developed by the ancient Greeks, try this.

PERFORMER'S WORKSHOP
Meet the Greeks

A. Read aloud the following passage from *Antigone* by the Greek playwright Sophocles. In this excerpt, Creon, the uncle of Antigone, has denied her brother Polynices the rite of burial. Antigone risks her life to see that Polynices is properly buried.

CREON: You, you whose face is bent to earth, do you avow, or dis-
avow, this deed?

ANTIGONE: I avow it; I make no denial.

CREON: (*To* GUARD) You can go wherever you will, free and clear of a
grave charge. (*Exit* GUARD) (*To* ANTIGONE) Now, tell me, not in
many words but briefly, did you know that an edict had forbidden
this?

ANTIGONE: I knew it; could I help it? It was public.

CREON: Did you then dare transgress that law?

ANTIGONE: Yes, for it was not Zeus who had published that edict;
not such are the laws set among men by the Justice who dwells
with the gods below. Nor did I deem that your decrees were of such
force that a mortal could override the unwritten and unfailing
statutes of heaven. For their life is not of today or yesterday, but
from all time; no man knows when they were first put forth.

Not through dread of any human pride could I answer to the gods
for breaking these. Die I must; that I knew well (how should I not?)
even without your edicts. But if I am to die before my time I count
that a great gain. If anyone lives as I do, compassed about with
evils, could he find anything but gain in death?

So for me to meet this doom is trifling grief. But if I had suffered
my mother's son to lie in death an unburied corpse, that would have
grieved me; for this I am not grieved. And if my present deeds are
foolish in your sight, it may be that a foolish judge arraigns my folly.

CREON: Yet I would have you know that overstubborn spirits are
most often humbled. It is the stiffest iron, baked to hardness in the
fire, that you will most often see snapped and shivered; and I have
known horses that show temper brought to order by a little curb.
There is no room for pride when you are your neighbor's slave. This
girl was already versed in insolence when she transgressed the laws
that had been set forth; that now done, look, a second insult, to
boast of it and exult in her deed.

Now truly I am no man, she is the man, if this victory shall rest
with her and bring no penalty. No! though she is my sister's child or
nearer to me in blood than any that worships Zeus at the altar of
our house, she and her kinsfolk shall not avoid a doom most dire;
for I charge that other with a like share in the plotting of this burial.

Summon her; I saw her within just now, raving and not mistress
of her wits. So often before the deed, when people plot mischief in
the dark, the mind stands self-convicted in its treason. But this too
is hateful, when one who has been caught in wickedness then seeks
to make the crime a glory.

ANTIGONE: Would you do more than take and slay me?

CREON: No, no more; having that I have all.

ANTIGONE: Why then do you delay? In your discourse there is nothing that pleases me—may there never be—and so my words must needs be unpleasing to you. And yet for glory—how could I have won a nobler than by giving burial to my own brother? All here would own that they thought it well, if their lips were not sealed by fear. Royalty, blessed in so much besides, has the power to do and say what it will.

CREON: In that view you differ from all these Thebans.

ANTIGONE: They also share it, but they curb their tongues for you.

CREON: And are you not ashamed to act apart from them?

ANTIGONE: No; there is nothing shameful in piety to a brother.

CREON: Was it not a brother too that died in the opposite cause?

ANTIGONE: Brother by the same mother and the same sire.

CREON: Why then do you render a grace that is impious in his sight?

ANTIGONE: The dead man will not say that he so deems it.

CREON: Yes, if you make him but equal in honor with the wicked.

ANTIGONE: It was his brother, not his slave, that perished.

CREON: Wasting this land; while he fell as its champion.

ANTIGONE: Nevertheless Hades desires these rites.

CREON: But the good does not desire a like portion with the evil.

ANTIGONE: Who knows but this seems blameless in the world below.

CREON: A foe is never a friend—not even in death.

ANTIGONE: It is not my nature to join in hating, but in loving.

CREON: Pass then to the world of the dead, and if you must needs love, love them. While I live no woman shall rule me.

Questions

1. What kind of characters are you asked to portray?
2. What type of language does each character use?
3. What are each character's chief concerns?
4. With what type of force is each character in conflict?
5. How do you visualize each character's movements?
6. How do you imagine each character's speaking voice?

B. Read the passage aloud again; this time wear a mask.

Questions

1. How did wearing the mask change your reading? Was your pace faster? Slower? Louder? Softer?
2. Did wearing a mask cause you to alter the gestures you used? How?

C. Remove the mask and read the passage aloud for a third time, attempting to maintain the style you achieved when masked.

The Roman Period

While Greek tragedies are usually presented in a slow and stately style, Roman comedies have a rapid and conversational style. The plays in this period were comprised of loosely plotted domestic situations; in fact, the situation comedies we watch on television or see in movies are patterned after them.

The language of the characters in Roman comedies sparkles with wit and humor; the scripts abound in opportunities for expressive gestures or pantomime such as stock comic poses. When reading plays from this period, therefore, you will do well to think of yourself as a clown without makeup, a vaudeville comic, an animated stand-up comic, or a situation comedy star. You will want to utilize a wide variety of facial expressions to help you communicate to your audience the farcical nature of the material. Loosen up and give the following exercise a try.

PERFORMER'S WORKSHOP
Let's Go Roman

Prepare to perform the following passage.

The Ghost
Plautus

(Outside the house of THEOPROPIDES *an elderly and bucolic slave named* GRUMIO *is hammering at the door.)*

GRUMIO: Hey there, Tranio! Come out of that kitchen, will you! . . . Come out, young whipper-snapper! . . . Up to some saucy tricks among the saucepans, I'll be bound . . . Come out here, you master's ruin! By gum, I'll give you what you deserve if I get you out on the farm, may I die if I don't. What are you hiding in there for, you smelly scullion? Come out here, I tell you!

(At last TRANIO *appears—a young and rather elegant slave.)*

TRANIO: Now then, pig, what's all this clatter about? Out in the street too? Where do you think you are? This isn't the country, you know. Get away from this house, please. Go back to your farm. Go and hang yourself, if you like, only stay away from this door. . . . What are you waiting for? *(Starting to pummel him.)* This?
GRUMIO: Hey, hey, steady on. What's that for?
TRANIO: For being alive.

GRUMIO: I can bear it. I only wish the old master would come home—if he ever does come home again, with you eating the life out of him while he's away.

TRANIO: That's a lie—and it doesn't make sense either, woodenhead. How can a person eat the life out of a person when that person's somewhere else?

GRUMIO: You think me a country bumpkin, I dare say—witty city chap that you are—pretty witty city chit. I expect you know you're going to be sent out to the mill yourself before long. Yes, any day now you'll be joining the outdoor staff—the ironclads. Better make the most of your time now, my lad. Drink and be merry, waste your master's goods and make a ruin of your master's fine young son. Drink with your friends all day and night, Greek fashion. Buy your women and set them free. Live like lords, with hangers-on feeding their bellies at your expense. Was this what your master told you to do when he went away? Is this the way he expects to find his house looked after when he comes back? Is this what you call being a good servant, playing fast and loose with your master's property and corrupting your master's son? Corrupted he surely is, for what I know the way he's going on. Not so long ago he was known for the steadiest and best-behaved young man in all Athens; now he's top of a very different class. And that's thanks to your example and teaching.

TRANIO: Is it any business of yours what I am or what I do, damn you? Haven't you got any cattle to look after in the country? If I like drinking and wenching, that's my affair; it's my skin I'm risking, not yours.

GRUMIO: Bold as brass, ain't he?

TRANIO: Jupiter and all the gods strike you dead! Phew, you stink— mud-begotten clod of goat and pig dung; you stink of dog and goat garlic.

GRUMIO: What do you expect? We can't all stink of perfumes like you. We can't all lie on the best couches or feed on the finicky fodder you get. All right—keep your pigeons and poultry and game fish, and let me enjoy the fare that comes my way. You're the lucky one; I'm not. We must take as we find—as long as I can have what good I've got, and you the trouble you're going to get.

TRANIO: You're jealous, Grumio, if you ask me; jealous because I'm doing well and you're not. It's only natural. It's natural for me to keep women and you to keep cows; me to have a good life, you to have a mucky one.

GRUMIO: Gallows-meat, that's what you are, and what you soon will be, if I know anything about it—hustled through the streets under a yoke, with goads through your guts, when the master comes home.

TRANIO: Who knows? It might be you sooner than me.

GRUMIO: It won't because I've not deserved it, as you have and still do.

TRANIO: Cut it out, will you, if you don't want to be exterminated on this spot.

GRUMIO: (*Changing the subject.*) Have you got any greenstuff for me to take out to the cattle? If so, let's have it . . . if you're not eating it . . . (TRANIO *disdains to answer this.*) Oh go to hell then; go on the way you're going; drink, eat your fancy Greek food, fill your bellies with slaughtered flesh—

TRANIO: Shut your mouth and get back to the farm. I have to go to Piraeus for some fish for supper. I'll get some fodder sent over to the farm tomorrow. . . . What are you standing staring at me now for, crossbones?

GRUMIO: That's what they'll be calling you before long, damn me if they won't.

TRANIO: "Before long" they can do what they like, provided things can stay as they are for the present.

GRUMIO: Have it your own way. I know one thing—what's coming to you always comes quicker than what you're looking for.

TRANIO: Leave me alone, will you, and get back to the farm. Remove yourself. I can't waste any more time on you. (TRANIO *goes off along the street.*)

GRUMIO: Off he goes; and don't give tuppence for my warnings. Oh, gods, help me. Let the master come back soon!

Questions

1. What characteristics serve to distinguish Tranio and Grumio from each other?
2. How can you suggest these characteristics vocally and physically during your performance?
3. If you were to cast popular comic actors in these parts, whom would you cast and why?

The Middle Ages

The life of the peasant in medieval times was one of struggle and hardship, while the life of the nobility was one of festivity and amusement. Both types of individuals, however, found joy in drama. Drama in the Middle Ages came out of the church; consequently, the subject matter of plays from this period is usually biblical or ethical in nature.

One type of play prominent in medieval times is the morality drama. In it, concepts such as Vice, Death, Good Deeds, and Riches are personified. The purpose of the morality play is to teach or demonstrate a lesson. The characters in these plays are representative of types rather than individuals; thus, the interpreter should approach these roles with broad or exaggerated body and voice movements.

PERFORMER'S WORKSHOP
Medieval Times

Read the following passage from the morality play *Everyman*. In this play God sends Death to deliver a summons for Everyman. Everyman pleads for more time or for the right to have friends accompany him on his last journey. However, with the exception of Good Deeds, all of his friends (Good Fellowship, Kindred and Goods, Strength, Discretion, and Five Wits) desert him.

 from **Everyman**
Anonymous

MESSENGER: I pray you all give your audience,
And hear this matter with reverence,
By figure a moral play—
The Summoning of Everyman called it is,
That of our lives and ending shows
How transitory we be all day. . . .

DEATH: I am Death, that no man dreadeth,
For every man I 'rest, and no man spareth;
For it is God's commandment
That all to me should be obedient.

EVERYMAN: O Death! thou comest when I had thee least in mind.
In thy power it lieth me to save.
Yet of my good will I give thee, if thou will be kind,
Yea, a thousand pound shalt thou have—
And defer this matter till another day.

DEATH: Everyman, it may not be, by no way.
I set nought by gold, silver, nor riches,
Nor by pope, emperor, king, duke, nor princes.
For, and I would receive gifts great,
All the world I might get.
But my custom is clean contrary:
I give thee no respite. Come hence and not tarry!

EVERYMAN: Alas, shall I have no longer respite?
I may say Death giveth no warning.
To think on thee it maketh my heart sick,

For all unready is my book of reckoning.
But twelve year and I might have a biding,
My counting-book I would make so clear
That my reckoning I should not need to fear.
Wherefore, Death, I pray thee, for God's mercy,
Spare me till I be provided of remedy.

DEATH: Thee availeth not to cry, weep, and pray;
But haste thee lightly that thou were gone that journey,
And prove thy friends, if thou can.
For weet thou well the tide abideth no man,
And in the world each living creature
For Adam's sin must die of nature.

EVERYMAN: Death, if I should this pilgrimage take,
And my reckoning surely make,
Show me, for saint charity,
Should I not come again shortly?

DEATH: No, Everyman. And thou be once there,
Thou mayest never more come here,
Trust me verily.

EVERYMAN: O gracious God in the high seat celestial,
Have mercy on me in this most need!
Shall I have no company from this vale terrestrial
Of mine acquaintance that way me to lead?

DEATH: Yea, if any be so hardy,
That would go with thee and bear thee company.
Hie thee that thou were gone to God's magnificence,
Thy reckoning to give before his presence.
What, weenest thou thy life is given thee,
And thy worldly goods also?

EVERYMAN: I had weened so, verily.

DEATH: Nay, nay, it was but lent thee.
For as soon as thou art go,
Another a while shall have it, and then go therefro,
Even as thou hast done.
Everyman, thou art mad! Thou hast thy wits five,
And here on earth will not amend thy live!
For suddenly I do come.

EVERYMAN: O wretched caitiff! Whither shall I flee,
That I might 'scape endless sorrow?
Now, gentle Death, spare me till tomorrow,
That I may amend me
With good advisement.

DEATH: Nay, thereto I will not consent,
Nor no man will I respite,

But to the heart suddenly I shall smite
Without any advisement.
And now out of thy sight I will me hie;
See thou make thee ready shortly,
For thou mayst say this is the day
That no man living may 'scape away. (*Exit* DEATH.)

Questions

1. How can you characterize Death and distinguish him from Everyman?
2. What type of voice will you use for each of the characters?
3. How will Death and Everyman stand and move?

The Elizabethan Age

Whereas in ancient times people believed that fate controlled them, during the Renaissance people believed they were free to choose their own paths. Therefore, the plays of this period reflect the vitality that characterized the Elizabethan age. Rather than types, individuality of character and humanistic meaning now moved to the forefront.

Characters in Renaissance dramas are seen struggling to actualize their sense of value, and sometimes their struggle gets out of hand. When rehearsing scenes from these plays, you will want to emphasize speech because you will probably wish to communicate both the meaning and the music of the lines. **Soliloquies,** monologues prompted by a character's psychological tensions, were also a common convention of this age. They act much as a flashback would in a film today. When performing a soliloquy, you will want to work to make both visible and audible the inner tensions experienced by the character in order to convince your audience that the words you speak actually live in your mind.

PERFORMER'S WORKSHOP
The Bard

A. Prepare to read the following soliloquy from *Hamlet,* by William Shakespeare. In this play, Hamlet, the Prince of Denmark, mourns the death of his father and the over-hasty remarriage of his mother Gertrude to Claudius, Hamlet's uncle.

HAMLET: O that this too too sullied flesh would melt,
Thaw, and resolve itself into a dew!
Or that the Everlasting had not fixed
His canon 'gainst self-slaughter! Oh, God! God!
How weary, stale, flat and unprofitable
Seem to me all the uses of this world!
Fie on 't, ah, fie! 'Tis an unweeded garden
That grows to seed, things rank and gross in nature
Possess it merely. That it should come to this!
But two months dead! Nay, not so much, not two.
So excellent a King, that was, to this,
Hyperion to a satyr. So loving to my mother
That he might not beteem the winds of heaven
Visit her face too roughly. Heaven and earth!
Must I remember? Why, she would hang on him
As if increase of appetite had grown
By what it fed on. And yet within a month—
Let me not think on 't.—Frailty, thy name is woman!—
A little month, or ere those shoes were old
With which she followed my poor father's body,
Like Niobe, all tears.—Why she, even she—
Oh, God! A beast that wants discourse of reason
Would have mourned longer—married with my uncle,
My father's brother, but no more like my father
Than I to Hercules. Within a month,
Ere yet the salt of most unrighteous tears
Had left the flushing in her galled eyes,
She married. Oh, most wicked speed, to post
With such dexterity to incestuous sheets!
It is not, nor it cannot, come to good.
But break, my heart, for I must hold my tongue!

Questions

1. What attitudes does Hamlet display in this soliloquy?
2. How can you use your voice and your body to suggest these feelings to your audience?
3. What words will you emphasize? Where will you pause?
4. Where will you direct your eye focus? When will you change the direction of your gaze? Why?

B. Now read this excerpt from Shakespeare's *Macbeth*. In this scene, a doctor and a gentlewoman watch as Lady Macbeth enters sleepwalking, after having helped her husband murder King Duncan.

Macbeth

from

William Shakespeare

GENTLEWOMAN: Lo you, here she comes! This is her very guise, and upon my life, fast asleep. Observe her. Stand close.

DOCTOR: How came she by that light?

GENTLEWOMAN: Why, it stood by her. She has light by her continually, 'tis her command.

DOCTOR: You see, her eyes are open.

GENTLEWOMAN: Aye, but their sense is shut.

DOCTOR: What is it she does now? Look how she rubs her hands.

GENTLEWOMAN: It is an accustomed action with her to seem thus washing her hands. I have known her continue in this a quarter of an hour.

LADY MACBETH: Yet, here's a spot.

DOCTOR: Hark! She speaks. I will set down what comes from her, to satisfy my remembrance the more strongly.

LADY MACBETH: Out, damned spot! Out I say! One, two—why, then 'tis time to do 't. Hell is murky. Fie, my lord, fie! A soldier, and afeard? What need we fear who knows it, when none can call our power to account? Yet who would have thought the old man to have had so much blood in him?

DOCTOR: Do you mark that?

LADY MACBETH: The Thane of Fife had a wife. Where is she now? What, will these hands ne'er be clean? No more o' that, my lord, no more o' that. You mar all with this starting.

DOCTOR: Go to, go to. You have known what you should not.

GENTLEWOMAN: She has spoke what she should not, I am sure of that. Heaven knows what she has known.

LADY MACBETH: Here's the smell of the blood still. All the perfumes of Arabia will not sweeten this little hand. Oh, oh, oh!

DOCTOR: What a sigh is there! The heart is sorely charged.

GENTLEWOMAN: I would not have such a heart in my bosom for the dignity of the whole body.

DOCTOR: Well, well, well—

GENTLEWOMAN: Pray God it be, sir.

DOCTOR: This disease is beyond my practice. Yet I have known those which have walked in their sleep who have died holily in their beds.

LADY MACBETH: Wash your hands, put on your nightgown, look not so pale. I tell you yet again, Banquo's buried, he cannot come out on 's grave.

DOCTOR: Even so?

LADY MACBETH: To bed, to bed, there's knocking at the gate. Come, come, come, come, give me your hand. What's done cannot be undone. To bed, to bed, to bed. (*Exit.*)

Questions

1. Why does Lady Macbeth rub her hands?
2. What voice quality will you use to characterize her?
3. How will you use your body to express her tensions?
4. How will you change your eye focus for each of the characters?

Realism

The drama of this style requires very little elaboration or description. The actor in a realistic play is not supposed to be aware of the audience.

Unlike the actor, the oral reader can never fully realize this ideal—the nature of the art form of interpretation simply prevents it. On the other hand, as an interpreter of literature, you can use your voice and body to suggest the little physical and vocal gestures that identify each of the characters you portray. Concentrate on determining the mood and the movement intensities that distinguish your characters from one another. Carefully observe reality so you are able to re-create characters as truthfully as possible by painstakingly selecting details of action and speech to incorporate into your performance.

PERFORMER'S WORKSHOP
Reaching for Realism

Prepare to read aloud the following passage from *A Doll's House* by Henrik Ibsen. In this play, Ibsen addresses the question of a woman's rights and social position through the story of Nora, who is treated like a child by her husband, Torvald Helmer.

 ## *A Doll's House*
Henrik Ibsen

NORA: (*Looking at her watch.*) It's not so late yet. Sit down, Torvald, you and I have much to say to each other. (*She sits at one side of the table.*)

HELMER: Nora, what does this mean? Your cold, set face—

NORA: Sit down. It will take some time; I have much to talk over with you. (HELMER *sits at the other side of the table.*)

HELMER: You alarm me, Nora. I don't understand you.

NORA: No, that is just it. You don't understand me; and I have never understood you—till tonight. No, don't interrupt. Only listen to what I say. We must come to a final settlement, Torvald.

HELMER: How do you mean?

NORA: (*After a short silence.*) Does not one thing strike you as we sit here?

HELMER: What should strike me?

NORA: We have been married eight years. Does it not strike you that this is the first time we two, you and I, man and wife, have talked together seriously?

HELMER: Seriously! Well, what do you call seriously?

NORA: During eight whole years, and more—ever since the day we first met—we have never exchanged one serious word about serious things.

HELMER: Was I always to trouble you with the cares you could not help me to bear?

NORA: I am not talking of cares. I say that we have never yet set ourselves seriously to get to the bottom of anything.

HELMER: Why, my dearest Nora, what have you to do with serious things?

NORA: There we have it! You have never understood me. I have had great injustice done me, Torvald, first by father and then by you.

HELMER: What! by your father and me?—by us, who have loved you more than all the world?

NORA: (*Shaking her head.*) You have never loved me. You only thought it was amusing to be in love with me.

HELMER: Why, Nora, what a thing to say!

NORA: Yes, it is so, Torvald. While I was at home with father, he used to tell me all his opinions, and I held the same opinions. If I had others I concealed them, because he would not have liked it. He used to call me his doll-child, and played with me as I played with my dolls. Then I came to live in your house—

HELMER: What an expression to use about our marriage.

NORA: (*Undisturbed.*) I mean I passed from father's hands into yours. You settled everything according to your taste; and I got the same tastes as you; or I pretended to—I don't know which—both ways perhaps. When I look back on it now, I seem to have been living here like a beggar, from hand to mouth. I lived by performing tricks for you, Torvald. But you would have it so. You and father have done me a great wrong. It is your fault that my life has been wasted.

HELMER: Why, Nora, how unreasonable and ungrateful you are! Haven't you been happy here?

NORA: No, never. I thought I was, but I never was.

HELMER: Not—not happy?

NORA: No, only merry. And you have always been so kind to me. But our house has been nothing but a playroom. Here I have been your doll-wife, just as at home I used to be papa's doll-child. And the children in their turn have been my dolls. I thought it fun when you played with me, just as the children did when I played with them. That has been our marriage, Torvald.

HELMER: There is some truth in what you say, exaggerated and over-strained though it be. But henceforth it shall be different. Playtime is over; now comes the time for education.

NORA: Whose education? Mine, or the children's?

HELMER: Both, my dear Nora.

NORA: Oh, Torvald, you can't teach me to be a fit wife for you.

HELMER: And you say that?

NORA: And I—am I fit to educate the children?

HELMER: Nora!

NORA: Did you not say yourself a few minutes ago you dared not trust them to me?

HELMER: In the excitement of the moment! Why should you dwell upon that?

NORA: No—you are perfectly right. That problem is beyond me. There is another to be solved first—I must try to educate myself. You are not the man to help me in that. I must set about it alone. And that is why I am now leaving you!

HELMER: (Jumping up.) What—do you mean to say—

NORA: I must stand quite alone if I am ever to know myself and my surroundings; so I cannot stay with you.

HELMER: Nora! Nora!

NORA: I am going at once. I daresay Christina will take me in for tonight—

HELMER: You are mad. I shall not allow it. I forbid it.

NORA: It is of no use your forbidding me anything now. I shall take with me what belongs to me. From you I will accept nothing, either now or afterward.

HELMER: What madness!

NORA: Tomorrow I shall go home. . . . I mean to what was my home. It will be easier for me to find some opening there.

HELMER: Oh, in your blind inexperience—

NORA: I must try to gain experience, Torvald.

HELMER: To forsake your home, your husband, and your children! You don't consider what the world will say.

NORA: I can pay no heed to that! I only know that I must do it.

HELMER: It's exasperating! Can you forsake your holiest duties in this way?

NORA: What do you consider my holiest duties?

HELMER: Do you ask me that? Your duties to your husband and your children.

NORA: I have other duties equally sacred.

HELMER: Impossible! What duties do you mean?

NORA: My duties toward myself.

Questions

1. What is the main conflict between husband and wife in this scene?
2. How will you re-create the character of Nora? What attitudes will you try to suggest?
3. How will you re-create the character of Helmer? How does he relate to Nora?

Theatre of the Absurd

Absurdist plays, often referred to as the theatre of the absurd, emphasize the absurdity of existence. The works suggest that it is impossible to be certain about anything: truth is forever elusive and there are no absolutes on which to base behavior. Such a view grew out of post–World War II disillusionment. In absurdist plays, language and dialogue are often reduced to empty clichés, and people are replaced by material objects or are dehumanized in other ways.

When interpreting an absurdist play for an audience, you will once again be called upon to represent types rather than individuals. You will be called upon to mirror the disorder of the world with your voice and your body.

PERFORMER'S WORKSHOP
Adventure in the Absurd

Read the following passage from *The Sandbox* by Edward Albee. In it, the playwright relates how a family has chosen to treat the grandmother.

The Sandbox
Edward Albee

THE SCENE: *The* YOUNG MAN *is alone on stage to the rear of the sandbox. He is doing calisthenics. . . .* MOMMY *and* DADDY *enter from stage left.*

MOMMY: (*motioning to* DADDY) Well, here we are; this is the beach.

DADDY: (*whining*) I'm cold.

MOMMY: (*dismissing him with a little laugh*) Don't be silly; it's as warm as toast. Look at that nice young man over there: he doesn't seem to think it's cold. (*Waves to the* YOUNG MAN) Hello.

YOUNG MAN: (*with an endearing smile*) Hi!

MOMMY: (*looking about*) This will do perfectly . . . don't you think so, Daddy? There's sand there . . . and the water beyond. What do you think, Daddy?

DADDY: (*vaguely*) Whatever you say, Mommy.

MOMMY: (*with the same little laugh*) Well, of course . . . whatever I say. Then it's settled, is it?

DADDY: (*shrugs*) She's your mother, not mine.

MOMMY: I know she's my mother. What do you take me for? (*A pause*) All right, now; let's get on with it. . . . Are you ready, Daddy? Let's go get Grandma.

DADDY: Whatever you say, Mommy.

MOMMY: Of course, whatever I say. . . .

(*After a moment* MOMMY *and* DADDY *reenter, carrying* GRANDMA. *She is borne in by their hands under her armpits; she is quite rigid; her legs are drawn up, her feet do not touch the ground; the expression on her ancient face is that of puzzlement and fear.*)

MOMMY: Don't look at her. Just sit here . . . be very still . . . and wait . . .

GRANDMA: Ah-haaaaaa! Graaaaa! (*Looks for reaction; gets none. Now . . . directly to the audience*) Honestly! What a way to treat an old woman! Drag her out of the house . . . stick her into a car . . . bring her out here from the city . . . dump her in a pile of sand . . . and leave her here to set. I'm eighty-six years old! I was married when I was seventeen. To a farmer. He died when I was thirty . . . I'm a feeble old woman . . . There's no respect around here! There's no respect around!

Questions

1. How do the characters treat the grandmother?
2. How do the characters communicate with each other?
3. What vocal qualities and physical cues will you use to help you express Mommy, Daddy, and Grandma in your interpretation?

IDEA ENCORE

Chapter 6 focused on the interpretation and performance of dramatic literature. It explored the relationship between drama and prose and pointed out their similarities and differences. For example, we learned that in dramatic literature, the characters usually speak for themselves.

The components of a drama include plot, which answers the question "What's happening?" The playwright includes exposition, conflict, crisis/climax, and denouement to articulate the plot or story line to the audience. The question of "Who?" is answered by the characters. Since the meaning of a play is in the dialogue, the characters must use language effectively. Setting and time answer the question of where the play takes place and at what point in time is it happening. The chapter presented suggestions for how to use vocal and physical cues to differentiate characters and enhance your performances.

We explored various styles of dramatic literature including Greek, Roman, Medieval, Elizabethan, Realistic, and Absurd. This brief overview will provide you with the information you need to explore the styles more thoroughly.

By presenting you with opportunities to journey through dramatic literature, the chapter also familiarized you with techniques you need to use when interpreting cuttings from each type.

You can see that the challenge for the interpreter exceeds that of the actor. Actors are called upon to play one of the roles in a play. As an interpreter you are expected to suggest many of the characters in ways that will bring the play to life for the audience. The effective interpreter brings the playwright's ideas and feelings to life in a unique and involving performance.

PERFORMER'S SHOWCASE & JOURNAL
The Play's the Thing

Now apply what you have learned about play analysis, characterization, and dramatic style to a reading that you choose. You should be able to analyze a scene, adapt it to an oral interpretation situation, identify and empathize with each of the characters, and find creative ways to present them to your audience.

Choose a five-minute scene from a play involving no more than three characters to perform for your class. You may choose one of the scenes included in this chapter or one of your own choosing. On the day you re-create your scene, hand in an analysis to your instructor. In your discussion, include answers to the following questions.

1. What is happening in your scene?
2. Where is the scene set? How does the atmosphere affect the action?
3. What is the main conflict in the scene?
4. What characters are involved in the scene?
5. How old are they?
6. How does each character see himself or herself?
7. How do each of the characters relate to the other characters in the play?
8. At what tempo does each character move and speak?
9. What adjectives would you use to describe each of the characters?
10. What physical and vocal gestures will you use to re-create the scene for your audience?

SELECTIONS FOR FURTHER WORK

The following scene is from Marsha Norman's play *'Night, Mother*. In this cutting, Mama tries to convince her daughter Jessie not to kill herself.

 'Night, Mother
Marsha Norman

MAMA: Everything you do has to do with me, Jessie. You can't do anything, wash your face or cut your finger, without doing it to me. That's right! You might as well kill me as you, Jessie, it's the same thing. This has to do with me, Jessie.

JESSIE: Then what if it does! What if it has everything to do with you! What if you are all I have and you're not enough? What if I could take all the rest of it if only I didn't have you here? What if the only way I can get away from you for good is to kill myself? What if it is? I can still do it!

MAMA: (*In desperate tears.*) Don't leave me, Jessie! (JESSIE *stands for a moment, then turns for the bedroom.*) No! (MAMA *grabs her arm.*)

JESSIE: (*Carefully takes her arm away.*) I have a box of things I want people to have. I'm just going to get it for you. You . . . just rest a minute. (*And* JESSIE *is gone and* MAMA *heads for the telephone, but she can't even pick up the receiver this time, and instead stoops to clean up the bottles that have spilled out of the tray.* JESSIE *returns carrying a box that groceries were delivered in. It probably says Hershey Kisses or Starkist Tuna.* MAMA *is still down on the floor cleaning up, hoping that maybe if she just makes it look nice enough,* JESSIE *will stay.*)

MAMA: Jessie, how can I live here without you? I need you! You're supposed to tell me to stand up straight and say how nice I look in my pink dress and drink my milk. You're supposed to go around and lock up so I know we're safe for the night, and when I wake up, you're supposed to be out there making the coffee and watching me get older every day and you're supposed to help me die when the time comes. I can't do that by myself, Jessie. I'm not like you, Jessie. I hate the quiet and I don't want to die and I don't want you to go, Jessie. How can I . . . (*Has to stop a moment.*) How can I get up every day knowing you had to kill yourself to make it stop hurting and I was here all the time and I never even saw it. And then you gave me this chance to make it better, convince you to stay alive, and I couldn't do it. How can I live with myself after this, Jessie?

JESSIE: I only told you so I could explain it, so you wouldn't blame yourself, so you wouldn't feel bad. There wasn't anything you could say to change my mind. I didn't want you to save me. I just wanted you to know.

MAMA: Stay with me just a little longer. Just a few more years. I don't have that many more to go, Jessie. And as soon as I'm dead, you can do whatever you want. Maybe with me gone, you'll have all the quiet you want, right here in the house. And maybe one day you'll put in some begonias up the walk and get just the right rain for them all summer. And Ricky will be married by then and he'll bring your grandbabies over and you can sneak them a piece of candy when their Daddy's not looking and then be real glad when they've gone home and left you to your quiet again.

JESSIE: Don't you see, Mama, everything I do winds up like this. How could I think you would understand? How could I think you would want a manicure? We could hold hands for an hour and then I could go shoot myself? I'm sorry about tonight, Mama, but it's exactly why I'm doing it.

MAMA: If you've got the guts to kill yourself, Jessie, you've got the guts to stay alive.

The following scene is from Shakespeare's comedy *A Midsummer Night's Dream*. In this scene, a group of laborers gathers to rehearse a play they hope to perform for the Duke of Athens and his court. The laborers include Quince the carpenter, Snug the joiner, Bottom the weaver, Flute the bellows-mender, Snout the tinker, and Starveling the tailor.

from *A Midsummer Night's Dream*

William Shakespeare

QUINCE: Is all our company here?

BOTTOM: You were best to call them generally, man by man, according to the scrip.

QUINCE: Here is the scroll of every man's name which is thought fit, through all Athens, to play in our interlude before the Duke and the Duchess on his wedding day at night.

BOTTOM: First, good Peter Quince, say what the play treats on, then read the names of the actors, and so grow to a point.

QUINCE: Marry, our play is "The most lamentable comedy and most cruel death of Pyramus and Thisbe."

BOTTOM: A very good piece of work, I assure you and a merry. Now, good Peter Quince, call forth your actors by the scroll. Masters, spread yourselves.

QUINCE: Answer as I call you. Nick Bottom, the weaver.

BOTTOM: Ready. Name what part I am for, and proceed.

QUINCE: You, Nick Bottom, are set down for Pyramus.

BOTTOM: What is Pyramus? A lover or a tyrant?

QUINCE: A lover, that kills himself, most gallant, for love.

BOTTOM: That will ask some tears in the true performing of it. If I do it, let the audience look to their eyes. I will move storms; I will condole in some measure. To the rest. Yet my chief humor is for a tyrant. I could play Ercles rarely, or a part to tear a cat in, to make all split. . . . A lover is more condoling.

QUINCE: Francis Flute, the bellows-mender.

FLUTE: Here, Peter Quince.

QUINCE: Flute, you must take Thisbe on you.

FLUTE: What is Thisbe? A wandering knight?

QUINCE: It is the lady that Pyramus must love.

FLUTE: Nay, faith, let not me play a woman. I have a beard coming.

QUINCE: That's all one. You shall play it in a mask, and you may speak as small as you will.

BOTTOM: An I may hide my face, let me play Thisbe too. I'll speak in a monstrous little voice: "Thisne, Thisne!" "Ah, Pyramus, my lover dear, thy Thisbe dear, and lady dear."

QUINCE: No, no, you must play Pyramus, and Flute, you Thisbe.

BOTTOM: Well, proceed.

QUINCE: Robin Starveling, the tailor.

STARVELING: Here, Peter Quince.

QUINCE: Robin Starveling, you must play Thisbe's mother. Tom Snout, the tinker.

SNOUT: Here, Peter Quince.

QUINCE: You, Pyramus' father; myself, Thisbe's father; Snug, the joiner, you the lion's part. And I hope here is a play fitted.

SNUG: Have you the lion's part written? Pray you, if it be, give it me, for I am slow of study.

QUINCE: You may do it extempore, for it is nothing but roaring.

BOTTOM: Let me play the lion too. I will roar that I will do any man's heart good to hear me. I will roar that I will make the Duke say, "Let him roar again; let him roar again."

QUINCE: And you should do it too terribly, you would fright the Duchess and the ladies that they would shriek; and that were enough to hang us all.

ALL: That would hang us, every mother's son.

BOTTOM: I grant you, friends, if you should fright the ladies out of their wits, they would have no more discretion but to hang us; but I will aggravate my voice so that I will roar you as gently as any sucking dove. I will roar you an 'twere any nightingale.

QUINCE: You can play no part but Pyramus, for Pyramus is a sweet-faced man, a proper man as one shall see in a summer's day, a most lovely gentlemanlike man. Therefore you must needs play Pyramus.

BOTTOM: Well, I will undertake it. What beard were I best to play it in?

QUINCE: Why, what you will.

BOTTOM: I will discharge it in either your straw-color beard, your orange-tawny beard, your purple-in-grain beard, or your French-crown-color beard, your perfect yellow.

QUINCE: Some of your French crowns have no hair at all, and then you will play barefaced. But masters, here are your parts. (*He distributes parts.*) And I am to entreat you, request you, and desire you to con them by tomorrow night; and meet me in the palace wood, a mile without the town, by moonlight. There will we rehearse; for if we meet in the city, we shall be dogged with company, and our devices known. In the meantime I will draw a bill of properties, such as our play wants. I pray you fail me not.

BOTTOM: We will meet, and there we may rehearse most obscenely and courageously. Take pains, be perfect. Adieu.

QUINCE: At the Duke's oak we meet.

This excerpt is from the final scene of Arthur Miller's *Death of a Salesman*.

Death of a Salesman

Arthur Miller

The Requiem

CHARLEY: It's getting dark, Linda.

(LINDA *doesn't react. She stares at the grave.*)

BIFF: How about it, Mom? Better get some rest, heh? They'll be closing the gate soon.

(LINDA *makes no move. Pause.*)

HAPPY: (*deeply angered*) He had no right to do that. There was no necessity for it. We would've have helped him.

CHARLEY: (*grunting*) Hmmm.

BIFF: Come along, Mom.

LINDA: Why didn't anybody come?

CHARLEY: It was a very nice funeral.

LINDA: But where are all the people he knew? Maybe they blame him.

CHARLEY: Naa. It's a rough world, Linda. They wouldn't blame him.

LINDA: I can't understand it. At this time especially. First time in thirty-five years we were just about free and clear. He only needed a little salary. He was even finished with the dentist.

CHARLEY: No man only needs a little salary.

LINDA: I can't understand it.

BIFF: There were a lot of nice days. When he'd come home from a trip; or on Sundays, making the stoop; finishing the cellar; putting on the new porch; when he built the extra bathroom; and put up the garage. You know something, Charley, there's more of him in that front stoop than in all the sales he ever made.

CHARLEY: Yeah. He was a happy man with a batch of cement.

LINDA: He was so wonderful with his hands.

BIFF: He had the wrong dreams. All, all wrong.

HAPPY: (*almost ready to fight* BIFF) Don't say that.

BIFF: He never knew who he was.

CHARLEY: (*Stopping* HAPPY'S *movement and reply. To* BIFF) Nobody dast blame this man. You don't understand. Willy was a salesman. And for a salesman, there is no rock bottom to the life. He don't put a bolt to a nut, he don't tell you the law or give you medicine. He's a man way out there in the blue, riding on a smile and a shoeshine. And when they start not smiling back—that's an earth-quake. And then you get yourself a couple of spots on your hat, and you're finished. Nobody dast blame this man. A salesman is got to dream, boy, it comes with the territory.

BIFF: Charley, the man didn't know who he was.

HAPPY: (*infuriated*) Don't say that!

BIFF: Why don't you come with me, Happy?

HAPPY: I'm not licked that easily. I'm staying right in this city, and I'm gonna beat this racket! (*He looks at* BIFF, *his chin set.*) The Loman Brothers!

BIFF: I know who I am, kid.

HAPPY: All right, boy. I'm gonna show you and everybody else that Willy Loman did not die in vain. He had a good dream. It's the only dream you can have—to come out number-one man. He fought it out here, and this is where I'm gonna win it for him.

BIFF: (*With a hopeless glance at* HAPPY, *bends toward his mother.*) Let's go, Mom.

LINDA: I'll be with you in a minute. Go on, Charley. (*He hesitates.*) I want to, just for a minute. I never had a chance to say good-by.

CHARLEY *moves away, followed by* HAPPY. BIFF *remains a slight distance up and left of* LINDA. *She sits there, summoning herself. The flute begins, not far away, playing behind her speech.*

LINDA: Forgive me dear. I can't cry. I don't know what it is, but I can't cry. I don't understand it. Why did you ever do that? Help me, Willy, I can't cry. It seems to me that you're just on another trip. I keep expecting you. Willy dear, I can't cry. Why did you do it? I search and search and I search, and I can't understand it, Willy. I made the last payment on the house, today. Today, dear. And there'll be nobody home. (*A sob rises in her throat.*) We're free and clear. (*Sobbing mournfully, released.*) We're free. (BIFF *comes slowly toward her.*) We're free . . . We're free. . . .

BIFF *lifts her to her feet and moves out up right with her in his arms.* LINDA *sobs quietly.* BERNARD *and* CHARLEY *come together and follow them, followed by* HAPPY. *Only the music of the flute is left on the darkening stage as over the house the hard towers of the apartment buildings rise into sharp focus and the curtain falls.*

Chapter 7

The Interpretation of Poetry

Learning Objectives

After completing this chapter, you should be able to

- define poetry
- identify figures of speech in poetry
- discuss how sound devices are used in poetry
- discuss the way rhythm affects the performance of poetry
- demonstrate how meter influences the interpretation of a poem
- discuss and distinguish between three types of poems: lyric, narrative, and dramatic

Poetry. What does it involve? How does it involve you? Poetry describes experience and allows you to share and understand it. Poetry as an oral form is increasing in popularity. Coffee shops, for example, host regular spoken-word and open-mike nights. Even MTV features poetry-performance programs. Poetry helps you develop a clearer perception of life. In fact, you can use poetry to concentrate and intensify your experience, as you use the metallic surface of a reflector to concentrate and intensify light. A poem may help you explore your own contacts with existence; it may help you live more fully and with greater awareness.

The English poet William Wordsworth wrote that "Poetry is the spontaneous overflow of powerful feelings; it takes its origin from emotion recollected in tranquillity." Throughout history, virtually every culture from around the world has used poetry in one form or another to express every emotion and experience imaginable. Poetry, combined with music and dance, is often a part of cultural rituals. Early human societies encountered poetry as you will want to encounter poetry—from the inside, with their whole beings. They worked to establish a congruence between their poetic rites or chants and their inner selves; they participated in the life of a poem by dynamically embodying the poem. Ancient tribes first used poetry for what they considered to be important life functions: poetry praised their gods, incited warriors to battle, celebrated war victories, taunted the defeated, and lamented their dead. Poetry was and still is the voice for desires, fears, prayers, joys, and despairs.

Today, poetry is still an art form that is central to our existence. It serves as a funnel through which all types of impressions and sensations may be filtered—beautiful and ugly, strong and weak, common and proud. Poetry does not discriminate as to subject. It grows out of everything that is of interest or concern to humanity.

The Nature of Poetry

What is poetry? According to poet and critic Matthew Arnold, "Poetry is simply the most beautiful, impressive, and wisely effective mode of saying things." Poetry says a lot in a few words. In reality, what poetry is is redefined by every new poet with every new poem. It is also continually redefined by oral interpreters, for as philosopher-poet Ralph Waldo Emerson noted: "He who reads a poem well is also a poet."

How does poetry differ from the other forms of writing which we have explored? When compared to other forms of writing, poetry is typically more compact—more condensed—more dependent on sound for effect, and more emotionally charged. It cries out for its readers to become involved. In addition, a poet hears the sounds of words like a composer hears the sounds of notes, so poets also are apt to depend on patterned and rhythmic speech—the combination of sound and silence, lighter and heavier stresses. Poets also use figurative language—imagery and symbolism—to enhance the total impact of their work.

While poetry frequently occurs in verse form, words do not need to be written in verse in order to constitute a poem. Verse is a kind of tightly structured writing that usually has a rhythmic pattern and may rhyme. Some forms of poetry, however, such as free verse, are hardly distinguishable from prose.

Like other writers, poets write poems to fulfill a variety of communicative purposes. Through their poems, poets philosophize, persuade, instruct, tell stories, create moods; they fantasize, hypothesize, surprise, and mesmerize.

The cauldron of poetry brims with descriptions of firsthand, observed, or imagined experiences. A skilled poet selects, unites, and restructures the contents of the poetic pot by utilizing certain artistic resources. Let us examine these resources now.

PERFORMER'S WARM-UP
Word Museum

A. As a class, clip words and phrases from newspapers and magazines. Search for interesting nouns and verbs, such as *abandon, glow, parachute, bamboo, peach,* and so on.
B. Write the words on separate cards. Attach each card to objects in your classroom. You will want to label the chalkboard, desks, book bags, pencils, potted plants, and other objects. Join the nouns and verbs to create titles.
C. Next, collect a group of adjective that can be used to describe people: *hidden, frozen, hilarious, super, silly,* and such.
D. Ask each person in the class to create his or her own title by pinning an adjective on himself or herself.
E. As a group, enter the room without talking. Assume that you are in a museum and you are to examine the titles on both the objects and the people.
F. Work with a partner to create a brief spoken performance using some of the titles in the performance area (classroom). Be prepared to respond to each team's performance.

Questions

1. How did you feel entering the word museum?
2. How did you feel with your new title?
3. What titles did you and your partner select for your performance?
4. What was the message that you tried to convey to the audience members?

The Poet's Resources: Language Tools

Poets use a number of specific language tools as resources. These tools cause the words of an effective poem to seem to explode with inner meaning.

Connotation

The first language resource we will consider is **connotation**—the overtones of meaning that surround a word. Unlike denotative meaning which is found in a dictionary, connotative meaning is found in that cluster of personal associations we derive from experience. These associations are initially provided by the poet and then redefined by what we personally bring to the text. Thus, because you cannot look up the connotative meaning, it goes well beyond dictionary definition; instead, connotative meaning represents the writer's personal relationship with a subject or concept. The writer provides us with textual clues regarding that meaning and, as we interpret the text, we internalize the suggestions.

PERFORMER'S WARM-UP
Moving into Connotation

Physically portray each word in the following six word groups. In other words, pantomime your intellectual and emotional responses to each word.

A. firm, stubborn, obstinate
B. neat, fastidious, super-clean
C. slender, skinny, svelte
D. candid, honest, blunt
E. stare, gaze, glare
F. whimper, cry, wail

Questions

1. What do your pantomimes tell you about your reactions to each word in a word group?
2. How were your reactions similar to those of your classmates? How were they different?

To repeat, the meaning of a word goes beyond its dictionary definition. The meaning also resides in the writer's and interpreter's minds and in the minds of each person in an audience. It is extremely important that you let the audience understand what the poet had in mind in selecting a particular term. At least convey what you have decided the word means. You can use not only your voice but also your body to make a relationship with a word clear. You can demonstrate your ability to do this in the next exercise.

PERFORMER'S WORKSHOP
Connotative Reflections

A. Move around the classroom, using your body to express the following words and phrases. When your instructor tells you to freeze, momentarily hold the position in which you find yourself. To benefit most from this exercise, work to internalize the feeling of your position and the meaning the associated concept has for you.

1. tired and weary
2. drooping eyelids
3. drooping eyelids open wide
4. eyes wide open
5. shadow
6. jewels
7. ghastly night

Questions

1. What did each word or phrase make you feel? What images were called to mind? What did you think about?
2. How did you choose to react to each of the word prompts? What do your physical reactions tell you? What did your freeze position tell you about your personal reaction to each word or phrase?

B. Now, read Sonnet 27 by William Shakespeare and consider what kinds of movements might help express the meaning of the poem.

 Sonnet 27

William Shakespeare

Weary with toil, I haste me to my bed,
The dear repose for limbs with travel tired;
But then begins a journey in my head
To work my mind when body's work's expired:
For then my thoughts, from far where I abide,
Intend a zealous pilgrimage to thee,
And keep my drooping eyelids open wide,
Looking on darkness which the blind do see;
Save that my soul's imaginary sight
Presents thy shadow to my sightless view,

Which, like a jewel hung in ghastly night,

Makes black night beauteous and her old face new.

   Lo, thus, by day my limbs, by night my mind,

   For thee and for myself no quiet find.

Questions

1. How might the preceding exercises in turning movement into meaning prepare you to experience this literature?
2. How might they help to prepare you to interpret or perform the poem?
3. What movement adaptations did you make once the poetic context of the word or phrase was revealed?

The meaning you give to a word is based on your background, your experience, and the context of the word. In fact, it is context that serves to refine and alter your verbal perception. Accordingly, by their choice and arrangement of words, poets partially control your affective or emotional responses to their words. They actually channel your defining capabilities in specific directions by encouraging you to make certain mental associations.

Poets are thus concerned with more than the dictionary meaning of words. Of interest to them are the nuances of meaning, the associations, and the variations of mood evoked by specific words placed in specific contexts. Further your understanding by trying the following exercise.

PERFORMER'S WORKSHOP
Word Choices

Read the following poem, "Ozymandias" by Percy Bysshe Shelley, giving careful attention to the word and phrase choices provided. In each case, the word or phrase the poet actually employed is placed first; the second word, in italics, was added for this exercise.

"Ozymandias"

Percy Bysshe Shelley

I met a traveler/*voyager* from an antique/*old* land

Who said: Two vast/*large* and trunkless legs of stone/*rock*

Stand/*are* in the desert . . . Near them, on the sand,

Half sunk/*buried*, a shattered/*broken* visage lies, whose frown,

And wrinkled/*torn* lip, and sneer/*look* of cold command,
Tell that its sculptor/*artist* well those passions/*feelings* read
Which yet survive/*live on*, stamped on these lifeless/*dead* things,
The hand that mocked/*laughed* at them, and the heart that fed:
And on the pedestal/*base* these words appear:
"My name is Ozymandias/*Fred*, king of kings:
Look on my works, ye Mighty/*Strong*, and despair/*cry*!"
Nothing beside remains/*is left*. Round the decay/*rot*
Of that colossal wreck/*mess*, boundless and bare/*empty*
The lone and level/*barren* sands stretch far away.

Questions

1. Why do you believe the poet chose the first word or phrase rather than the hypothetical alternative provided?
2. What does the first word or phrase suggest that the second does not?

You can see that the creative poet is as deliberate about selection of words as a songwriter is about selecting notes. The poet's words must work within the context of the entire piece. Try the next exercise to further solidify your understanding of word choices in poetry.

PERFORMER'S WORKSHOP
Effective Words

Read the following poem by Lucy Smith carefully. Note which words and phrases in "Face of Poverty" you find particularly effective.

"Face of Poverty"
Lucy Smith

No one can communicate to you
The substance of poverty—
Can tell you either the shape,
    Nor the depth,
        nor the breadth

Of poverty—
Until you have lived with her intimately.

No one can guide your fingers
Over the rims of her eye sockets,
Over her hollow cheeks—
Until one day perhaps
In your wife's once pretty face
You see the lines of poverty:
Until you feel
In her now skinny body,
The protruding bones,
The barely covered ribs,
The shrunken breasts of poverty.

Poverty can be a stranger
In a far off land:
An alien face
Briefly glimpsed in a newsreel,
An empty rice bowl
In a skinny brown hand,
Until one bleak day
You look out the window—
And poverty is the squatter
In your own backyard.

Poverty wails in the night for milk,
Not knowing the price of a quart.

It is the stark desperation in your teen-ager's face,
Wanting a new evening gown for the junior prom,
After going through school in rummage store clothes.
It is the glass of forgetfulness sold over the bar.
And poverty's voice is a jeer in the night—
    "You may bring another child
    Into the rat race that is your life;
    You may cut down on food
    To buy contraceptives;

You may see your wife walk alone down some back
    alley route
To a reluctant appointment with an unsterile knife—
Or you may sleep alone."

And one morning shaving
You look in the mirror—
And never again will poverty be alien,
For the face of poverty is not over your shoulder,
The face of poverty is your own.

And hearing the break in your wife's voice
At the end of a bedtime story,
You realize that somewhere along the way
The stock ending in your own story went wrong.
And now you no longer ask
That you and your wife
Will live happily ever after—
But simply that you
And your wife
And your children
Will live.

Questions

1. What associations or overtones adhere to the words you noted? What types of images do these words provoke? How do the words help you experience the poem through your senses?
2. What kind of mood do these words help create?
3. How can you as interpreter harness the suggestive power of these words to enrich your performance of the poem?

Sense Imagery

Poets choose language rich in sense imagery because the words' fresh and vivid images help poets control their impact on readers. As you read more poetry, you will discover that effective poems abound in words relating to the senses.

    The poet wants us to hear the words of the poem, to see the experiences they describe, to smell their nature, to taste their poignancy, to touch their core, to feel their warmth or coolness, and to process them physically with our muscles. The poet asks us to respond to the sensory appeals of the poem and, in doing so, to exist in the poem. Ready your senses for the following exercise.

Read "My Father's Garden" by David Wagoner. Be aware of the sensory appeals of the poem.

"My Father's Garden"
David Wagoner

He would pick flowers for us: small gears and cogwheels
On his way to the open hearth where white-hot steel
Boiled against furnace walls in wait for his lance
To pierce the fireclay and set loose demons
And dragons in molten tons, blazing
Down to the huge satanic cauldrons,
Each day he would pass the scrapyard, his kind of garden.
In rusty rockeries of stoves and brake drums,
In grottoes of sewing machines and refrigerators,
He would pick flowers for us: small gears and cogwheels
With teeth like petals, with holes for anthers,
Long stalks of lead to be poured into toy soldiers,
Ball bearings as big as grapes to knock them down.
He was called a melter. He tried to keep his brain
From melting in those tyger-mouthed mills
Where the same steel reappeared over and over
To be reborn in the fire as something better
Or worse: cannons or cars, needles or girders,
Flagpoles, swords, or plowshares.
But it melted. His classical learning ran
Down and away from him, not burning bright.
His fingers culled a few cold scraps of Latin
And Greek, magna sine laude, for crosswords
And brought home lumps of tin and sewer grills
As if they were his ripe prize vegetables.
Magna sine laude: without great praise.

Now, on a separate sheet of paper, list the following senses. Next to each sense, write the words or phrases in the poem that appeal to that sense. Be certain to include both primary (most prominent) and secondary (those that are implied) appeals.

Sight   Touch
Hearing   Thermal
Smell   Kinetic
Taste   Kinesthetic

Questions

1. Which senses does Wagoner's poem appeal to? Which are the most important sensory images?
2. How does awareness of sensory appeals shape your response to the poem?
3. How might this exercise help you to effectively re-create literature in performance?

Already you have discovered that poetry overflows with vivid imagery. It abounds in sense appeals. It is up to the interpreter, however, to make these images live in performance. As the oral reader, you will discover and process the images that exist in the work. When performing poetry, use the sense impressions provided to guide you in communicating the total experience of the poem.

Figures of Speech

Poets also use **figures of speech** to enrich the meaning and impact of their poems. Figurative language functions as a type of poetic shorthand: in a brief, economical manner the word phrases convey a broader meaning than the words do when used singly. A figure of speech says something in a roundabout way. It provides an alternative to literal statement by allowing people to say one thing and mean something else. Some common word figures are simile, metaphor, personification, hyperbole, paradox, and irony. Let's look at each of these devices.

Simile.   A **simile** is easily identified because it makes an explicit comparison, generally using either the word *like* or *as.* It simply compares the qualities of one thing to the qualities of another.

PERFORMER'S WORKSHOP
The Simile

In the following poem about a guitarist, Frances Cornford uses similes to create a powerful image.

"The Guitarist Tunes Up"
Frances Cornford

With what attentive courtesy he bent
Over his instrument;
Not as a lordly conqueror who could
Command both wire and wood,
But as a man with a loved woman might,
Inquiring with delight
What slight essential things she had to say
Before they started, he and she, to play.

Questions

1. What two things are compared in this poem?
2. Is the comparison an effective one? Why?
3. What performance or behavioral clues does the poet provide the interpreter?

Metaphor. A **metaphor** functions like the simile, except it omits the words *like* or *as.* Thus, it is an even more direct comparison than a simile. For example, the metaphorical equivalent of the simile "that dog looks like a toad" is simply "that dog is a toad." By relating two hitherto unrelated objects and stating something is something else, the poet widens the reader's perception of his or her subject.

PERFORMER'S WORKSHOP
The Metaphor

A. Can you identify the metaphor in this poem title: "The Pretzel Is a Mrs. Weiner"?

Questions

1. How do you imagine Mrs. Weiner looks when she sits or stands? Show your classmates.
2. What type of voice do you think Mrs. Weiner would have? Why?

B. What metaphor is contained in the following short verse about war by Teri Gamble?

> War is a razor
> That cuts into the heart
> And makes it d
>   r
>   i
>   p
>   blood.

Questions

1. What does this poem say about war?
2. How can you embody the metaphor?

C. What does Virginia Woolf's statement "Anonymous . . . was often a woman" tell you about women?

Personification.   The attributing of human qualities to an object, an animal, or an idea is called **personification.** This device enables poets to add vividness and clarity to their creations. It is sometimes difficult to relate to an object, an animal, or an idea, but personification can bring the abstract to life by giving it human characteristics. Check your understanding of this figure of speech with the next exercise.

PERFORMER'S WORKSHOP
Personification

Read aloud Sylvia Plath's poem "Mirror."

"Mirror"
Sylvia Plath

I am silver and exact. I have no preconceptions.
Whatever I see I swallow immediately
Just as it is, unmisted by love or dislike.
I am not cruel, only truthful—
The eye of a little god, four-cornered.
Most of the time I meditate on the opposite wall.

It is pink, with speckles. I have looked at it so long
I think it is a part of my heart. But it flickers.
Faces and darkness separate us over and over.

Now I am a lake. A woman bends over me,
Searching my reaches for what she really is.
Then she turns to those liars, the candles or the moon.
I see her back, and reflect it faithfully.
She rewards me with tears and an agitation of hands.
I am important to her. She comes and goes.
Each morning it is her face that replaces the darkness.
In me she has drowned a young girl, and in me an old woman
Rises toward her day after day, like a terrible fish.

Questions

1. What objects are personified in the poem?
2. How can this language device be used by interpreters to help them fulfill the task of poetic visualization?

Hyperbole.   Overstatement, or **hyperbole,** is the figure of speech poets employ when they make gross, purposeful exaggerations. By exaggerating something out of proportion and making overstatements, the poet helps make a point more vivid for the poem's receivers. Try this.

PERFORMER'S WORKSHOP
Hyperbole

Read the following poem, "To My Mother" by George Barker, being certain to identify the examples of hyperbole.

  "To My Mother"

George Barker

Most near, most dear, most loved and most far,
Under the window where I often found her
Sitting as huge as Asia, seismic with laughter,
Gin and chicken helpless in her Irish hand,

Irresistible as Rabelais, but most tender for
The lame dogs and hurt birds that surround her,—
She is a procession no one can follow after
But be like a little dog following a brass band.

She will not glance up at the bomber, or condescend
To drop her gin and scuttle to a cellar,
But lean on the mahogany table like a mountain
Whom only faith can move, and so I send
O all my faith, and all my love to tell her
That she will move from mourning into morning.

Questions

1. What uses of hyperbole does Barker make in his poem?
2. How does hyperbole aid you in formulating a more precise picture of Barker's mother?
3. How might you apply this understanding to a performance?

Paradox.   Poets use **paradox** to point out apparent contradictions that some-how are true. Thus, this figure of speech allows poets to hint at additional meanings that lie beyond the surface level of their words and prod readers into making fresh connections.

A paradox contains words that appear to describe opposite impulses. For example, in one song by the Eagles, the writer employs a paradox in the lines, "You can check out any time you like, / But you can never leave." The poet Wordsworth also used an apparent contradiction when he wrote, "The child is father of the man." Though each speaker's statement contains seemingly con-tradictory thoughts, the statements are still true in some sense.

PERFORMER'S WORKSHOP
Paradox

Identify the paradox in the following verse from the Bible.

 **John 12:24**

Verily, verily, I say unto you, except a corn of wheat fall into the ground and die, it abideth alone: but if it die, it bringeth forth much fruit.

Questions

1. What is paradoxical in this excerpt?
2. Explain in your own words the thoughts that are true while seemingly at odds.

Oxymoron. An **oxymoron** is even more overtly contradictory or incongruous than a paradox. For example, the military phrases "friendly fire" and "fighting for peace" are oxymorons. The paired words in each phrase have a tensive quality about them, as if they shouldn't be together. In effect, they are self-contradictory.

Irony. **Irony** is a language device used by writers to imply just the opposite of what they say in words. For example, if you say "You're a real sweetheart" with a sneer in your voice, you mean just the opposite. If someone hears you make that statement, they'll know what you really mean by how you sounded when you spoke the words. You can find many examples of irony in poetry and in the routines of many stand-up comics as well.

PERFORMER'S WORKSHOP
Irony

Read "The Unknown Citizen" carefully, noting how the poet W. H. Auden uses irony. How does Auden imply the opposite of what he is saying?

 "The Unknown Citizen"

W. H. Auden

(To JS/07/M/378
This Marble Monument
Is Erected by the State)

He was found by the Bureau of Statistics to be
One against whom there was no official complaint,
And all the reports on his conduct agree
That, in the modern sense of an old-fashioned word,
   he was a saint,
For in everything he did he served the Greater Community.
Except for the War till the day he retired
He worked in a factory and never got fired

But satisfied his employers, Fudge Motors Inc.

Yet he wasn't a scab or odd in his views,

For his Union reports that he paid his dues,

(Our report on his Union shows it was sound)

And our Social Psychology workers found

That he was popular with his mates and liked a drink.

The Press are convinced that he bought a paper every day

And that his reactions to advertisements were normal
in every way.

Policies taken out in his name prove that he was fully insured,

And his Health-card shows he was once in hospital but left
it cured.

Both Producers Research and High-Grade Living declare

He was fully sensible to the advantages of the Installment Plan

And had everything necessary to the Modern Man,

A phonograph, a radio, a car and a frigidaire.

Our researchers into Public Opinion are content

That he held the proper opinions for the time of year;

When there was peace, he was for peace; when there was war,
he went.

He was married and added five children to the population,

Which our Eugenist says was the right number for a parent of his
generation,

And our teachers report that he never interfered with their
education.

Was he free? Was he happy? The question is absurd:

Had anything been wrong, we should certainly have heard.

Questions

1. How is irony used in this poem? What is literally expressed in it?
2. What attitudes lie beneath the surface of the lines?
3. How can you as an interpreter use your body and your voice to
   reflect the irony in the selection?

By using the preceding language devices in various combinations, poets are able to chart verbal maps of experience. It is up to you as an interpretive artist to explore these verbal maps fully. In understanding how poets have used their words to sketch pictures, you will also understand how poets have used their words to touch men and women.

The Poet's Resources: Sound Tools

In order to communicate their works effectively, poets also utilize sound resources with which you will want to familiarize yourself. These sound resources serve to reinforce the tone and meaning of a poem.

Onomatopoeia

How may a poet use sound as a medium of meaning? First of all, the poet may use words that sound like their meaning: *flush, hiss, bark, crash, boom,* and *bubble.* This technique is called **onomatopoeia.** With onomatopoeia, a poet can achieve an immediate connection with a reader or listener, because the very sound of the words suggests their sense.

PERFORMER'S WORKSHOP
Onomatopoeia

Which words in the following excerpt from a poem reinforce their meaning by their sound?

 "Goblin Market"
Christina Rossetti

Laughed every goblin
When they spied her peeping:
Came towards her hobbling,
Flying, running, leaping,
Puffing and blowing,
Chuckling, clapping, crowing,
Clucking and gobbling,
Mopping and mowing,
Full of airs and graces,
Pulling wry faces,
Demure grimaces,
Cat-like and rat-like,
Ratel- and wombat-like,
Snail-paced in a hurry,
Parrot-voiced and whistler,

Helter skelter, hurry skurry,
Chattering like magpies,
Fluttering like pigeons,
Gliding like fishes,—
Hugged her and kissed her,
Squeezed and caressed her:
Stretched up their dishes,
Panniers, and plates:
"Look at our apples
Russet and dun,
Bob at our cherries,
Bite at our peaches,
Citrons and dates,
Grapes for the asking,
Pears red with basking
Out in the sun,
Plums on their twigs;
Pluck them and suck them,
Pomegranates, figs."—

Questions

1. How can you use the sounds in the poem to clarify the meaning of
   the poem?
2. How can you use the sounds to strengthen the impact of your
   performance?

Rhyme

Another important sound resource—**rhyme**—is useful to poets. Besides creating
a rich auditory effect through repetition, rhyme adds emphasis to chosen words.
Besides pleasing our ears, rhyme also helps to organize thoughts and feeling in
a poem by associating words and ideas through their sounds. Rhyme may be
internal, occurring in the middle of a line as it does in this excerpt from
"Tarantella" by Hilaire Belloc: "And the fleas that tease in the high Pyrenees."
Or it may occur, as is customary, at the ends of lines. Edgar Allan Poe uses
rhyme in this way in "Annabel Lee":

It was many and many a year ago,
    In a kingdom by the sea,
That a maiden there lived whom you may know
    By the name of Annabel Lee;—

And this maiden she lived with no other thought
Than to love and be loved by me.

Alliteration, Assonance, and Consonance

Poets use the sound tools of alliteration, assonance, and consonance as unifying devices. **Alliteration** is the repetition of initial consonant sounds, as in "flakes fly faster." **Assonance** is the repetition of identical or closely similar vowel sounds, as in "waste no grave." **Consonance** involves the repetition of final consonant sounds, as in "odds and ends," "friend and fiend." Like rhyme, these sound tools both please our ears and help organize the ideas and images in a poem.

PERFORMER'S WORKSHOP
Sound Surgery

Divide the class into Sound Surgery Teams. Each team has fifteen minutes to "cut into" a portion of Alfred, Lord Tennyson's "The Splendor Falls," from his book-length poem *The Princess*. Locate examples of end rhyme, internal rhyme, alliteration, assonance, and consonance.

 ### "The Splendor Falls"
Alfred, Lord Tennyson

The splendor falls on castle walls
  And snowy summits old in story;
The long light shakes across the lakes
  And the wild cataract leaps in glory.
Blow, bugle, blow, set the wild echoes flying,
Blow, bugle; answer, echoes, dying, dying, dying.

O, hark, O, hear! how thin and clear,
  And thinner, clearer, farther going!
O, sweet and far from cliff and scar
  The horns of Elfland faintly blowing!
Blow, let us hear the purple glens replying,
Blow, bugle; answer, echoes, dying, dying, dying.

O love, they die in yon rich sky,

    They faint on hill or field or river;

Our echoes roll from soul to soul,

    And grow for ever and for ever.

Blow, bugle, blow, set the wild echoes flying,

And answer, echoes, answer, dying, dying, dying.

Questions

1. Which sound devices did you find? Which were used most frequently?
2. How do these sound devices help to carry the meaning of the poem?

The Poet's Resources: Rhythm Tools

Besides using language and sound as artistic resources, the poet also uses **rhythm,** a felt pulse or beat. Like the universe, the human body is constantly engaged in different rhythmic activities. Just as the ocean tides roll in and away from the shore, just as birds seasonally migrate, just as day follows night, so your lungs inflate and deflate, your heart beats steadily, and your blood pulses. In poetry, rhythm emerges as a result of patterns of sounds that speed up or slow down the rate of the utterances. As such, rhythm has a power of its own.

The following exercise should help to improve your understanding of rhythm and its function in poetry.

PERFORMER'S WARM-UP
Feeling Rhythm

A. Feel your own heart beat. What do you notice about it?
B. Take your own pulse. What is its rate per minute?
C. Relax a minute and become aware of your rate of breathing.

Questions

1. In what ways is your heartbeat like the pulse of a poem?
2. What do the acceleration and deceleration of your breathing and heartbeat share in common with poetic rhythms?

PERFORMER'S WORKSHOP
Rap Performance

Rap music has brought chanted poetry very much to the forefront of today's popular culture. Rap artists combine rhythmic poetry with music—a heavy beat and sound—to create an original art form.

A. Have class members who enjoy rap music bring samples to class. If possible, videotape some samples from MTV or similar sources. (Be sure to select segments that contain language you believe is appropriate to your educational setting.)

B. Working in groups, listen closely to one rap performance. Write out the lyrics and distribute them to group members.

C. Working with your group, reproduce the rap sound and the actions that go with it. Perform as if yours was the featured MTV video.

Questions

1. Were you able to reproduce the feeling of the recording?
2. How did the rhythm work for you as you performed?

As an individual, you walk and breathe rhythmically, with certain recurrent or characteristic patterns. So does a poem. Just as the rhythm of one individual is somewhat different from the rhythm of another, so the rhythm of one poem varies from the rhythm of another. In some poems, the rhythm is so unpatterned or slight that a reader may scarcely be aware of it, while in other poems the rhythm is so pronounced or overt that feet are practically forced to tap and hands to clap to it.

Meter

Meter refers to the type of rhythm that can be scanned for stressed and unstressed syllables. Meter is subdivided into patterned **feet,** the units of poetic rhythm. A line in a poem that contains meter is measured by the number of metrical feet it contains. Thus, in metrical poetry a line may be *monometer* (one foot), *dimeter* (two feet), *trimeter* (three feet), *tetrameter* (four feet), *pentameter* (five feet), and so on.

Poems with dominant rhythms are probably written in one of four standard meters or patterns: iambic, trochaic, anapestic, or dactylic. The following exercises will introduce you to the characteristics of these four basic metrical patterns.

PERFORMER'S WORKSHOP
Meeting Meters

A. The meter most commonly used is *iambic*. In poetry that is predominantly iambic, a stressed syllable usually follows an unstressed syllable, as in the words *debate* or *belief*. The most common iambic line length in English is pentameter, or five feet (five sets of unstressed and stressed syllables). Thus, a line of five iambic feet is called *iambic pentameter*.

Iambic is the meter that most nearly approximates the rhythm of ordinary speech. It is the rhythm commonly used by poets from Shakespeare and Milton to contemporary rap artists. Copy the following poem, Shakespeare's Sonnet 73, and scan it, placing unstress (˘) and stress (´) marks appropriately above the syllables. (A sonnet is a fourteen-line poem in iambic pentameter.)

 Sonnet 73

William Shakespeare

> That time of year thou mayst in me behold
> When yellow leaves, or none, or few, do hang
> Upon those boughs which shake against the cold,
> Bare ruin'd choirs, where late the sweet birds sang.
> In me thou seest the twilight of such day
> As after sunset fadeth in the west,
> Which by and by black night doth take away,
> Death's second self, that seals up all in rest.
> In me thou seest the glowing of such fire
> That on the ashes of his youth doth lie,
> As the death-bed whereon it must expire,
> Consum'd with that which it was nourish'd by.
> > This thou perceiv'st, which makes thy love more strong,
> > To love that well, which thou must leave ere long.

Questions

1. Does the poet depart from the predominant iambic pattern at any point(s)? Where?
2. How might changes in the metrical pattern affect the mood of the poem?

B. *Trochaic* rhythm is the reverse of iambic rhythm. It features a stressed syllable followed by an unstressed one, as in the words *mother* or *cancel.* It tends to slow a poem's action or thought. For example, this line from an Edna St. Vincent Millay poem features trochees—one stressed syllable followed by one unstressed: "We were very tired, we were very merry." Similarly, Poe's "The Raven" is predominantly trochaic in rhythm.

Copy and scan this excerpt from "The Raven," placing unstress (˘) and stress (´) marks appropriately above the syllables.

"The Raven"
Edgar Allan Poe

Once upon a midnight dreary, while I pondered, weak and weary,
Over many a quaint and curious volume of forgotten lore—
While I nodded, nearly napping, suddenly there came a tapping,
As of some one gently rapping, rapping at my chamber door.
"'Tis some visitor," I muttered, "tapping at my chamber door—
    Only this and nothing more." . . .

Presently my soul grew stronger; hesitating then no longer,
"Sir," said I, "or Madam, truly your forgiveness I implore;
But the fact is I was napping, and so gently you came rapping,
And so faintly you came tapping, tapping at my chamber door,
That I scarce was sure I heard you"—here I opened wide the door;—
    Darkness there and nothing more.

C. The third standard rhythm is *anapestic.* Each line of an anapestic poem is composed of feet that usually contain two unstressed syllables followed by a stressed syllable (*to the hills, to the woods*). Anapests create a fast-moving effect—almost a gallop. The most usual home of the anapest is in light verse. Note how the following limerick relies on anapestic meter.

A Limerick
Anonymous

A staid schizophrenic named Struther,
When told of the death of his brother,

Said: "Yes, I am sad;

It makes me feel bad,

But then, I still have each other."

The anapest, however, may also be found in serious verse. For example, this excerpt from "The Destruction of Sennacherib" by Gordon, Lord Byron is written in anapestic meter.

 ## "The Destruction of Sennacherib"
Lord Byron

For the Angel of Death spread his wings on the blast,

And breathed in the face of the foe as he passed;

And the eyes of the sleepers waxed deadly and chill,

And their hearts but once heaved, and forever grew still!

D. The least used of the four standard rhythms is the *dactylic,* which contains feet of one stressed and two unstressed syllables (*tenderly, capable*). Unlike the anapestic pattern, it works to produce a monotonous, continuous, steady effect, as in the following excerpt from Henry Wadsworth Longfellow's poem *Evangeline.*

 ## *Evangeline*
Henry Wadsworth Longfellow

It was the month of May. Far down the Beautiful River,

Past the Ohio shore and past the mouth of the Wabash,

Into the golden stream of the broad and swift Mississippi,

Floated a cumbrous boat, that was rowed by Acadian boatmen.

Take a few minutes to scan some of the lyrics in the rap music you examined previously. What poetic patterns are used there?

Besides using meter to provide a background, the poet also employs meter to control the speed and feeling of the lines of the poem. In fact, the poet usually works to match the speed of the poem to the sense of the poem. Consequently, when reading poetry aloud, you need to work to make the basic meter enhance the poem. However, you do not want to exaggerate it—the cost of metrical exaggeration might well be a loss of poetic meaning. When reading or performing poetry, you should permit the meter to provide you with a supportive rhythmic accompaniment, but you should not permit it to dominate or overpower your reading.

Regardless of whether you scan a poem methodically or not, as an interpreter you should always aim to feel the "beat" of your poem, to internalize its rhythm. Eventually, your rhythm and the rhythm of your selection should match.

In order to assure this, you will want to know where the pulse of your poem quickens and where it ebbs. You will want to know at what points you should experience tension and at what points you should experience release. If you cannot mirror these changes in movement, then the poem will not come alive for your audience.

PERFORMER'S WORKSHOP
Rhythm Operations

Read aloud the following poem, "Tarantella" by Hilaire Belloc, paying close attention to the variations in rhythm. (A tarantella is a lively Italian folk dance.)

"Tarantella"
Hilaire Belloc

Do you remember an Inn,
Miranda?
Do you remember an Inn?
And the tedding and the spreading
Of the straw for a bedding,
And the fleas that tease in the High Pyrenees,
And the wine that tasted of the tar?
And the cheers and the jeers of the young muleteers
(Under the dark of the vine verandah)?
Do you remember an Inn, Miranda,
Do you remember an Inn?
And the cheers and the jeers of the young muleteers
Who hadn't got a penny,
And who weren't paying any,
And the hammer at the doors and the Din?
And the Hip! Hop! Hap!
Of the clap
Of the hands to the twirl and the swirl
Of the girl gone chancing,
Glancing,

Dancing,
Backing and advancing,
Snapping of the clapper to the spin
Out and in—
And the Ting, Tong, Tang of the guitar!
Do you remember an Inn,
Miranda?
Do you remember an Inn?

Never more;
Miranda,
Never more.
Only the high peaks hoar;
And Aragon a torrent at the door.
No sound
In the walls of the halls where falls
The tread
Of the feet of the dead to the ground,
No sound:
But the boom
Of the far waterfall like doom.

Questions

1. Where does the pulse of this poem quicken?
2. Where does it ebb? How do you know?
3. Why do you think the poet abruptly changes the rhythm of the work?
4. How can you reflect this change in your performance of the selection before an audience?

Tempo

Some lines in poetry speed and excite, while other lines seem to idle and calm. Like music, poetry possesses both crescendos and diminuendos; thus, you can learn to "play" the poem as you would learn to play a piece of music. A musician reads the time value—full beat, quarter beat, and so on—that a composer has accorded to each note of a composition; an interpreter should read to reflect the time value accorded to an author's words.

Ask yourself whether your poem abounds in long or in short sounds, which words or syllables deserve emphasis or stress, and which words or syllables should be left unstressed. Where has the poet placed rests, or sense pauses? Remember that the absence of sound may also contribute to the creation of a rhythm. By asking and answering such questions, you will discover and reveal the predominant tempo of the poem to your audience.

PERFORMER'S WORKSHOP
Discovering Tempo

A. Read Langston Hughes's "Dream Boogie" aloud, paying close attention to the poem's tempo.

"Dream Boogie"
Langston Hughes

Good morning, daddy!
Ain't you heard
The boogie-woogie rumble
Of a dream deferred?

Listen closely:
You'll hear their feet
Beating out and beating out a—

    You think
    It's a happy beat?

Listen to it closely:
Ain't you heard
something underneath
like a—

    What did I say?

Sure,
I'm happy!
Take it away!

    Hey, pop!
    Re-bop!
    Mop!

    Y-e-a-h!

Questions

1. What type of beat does this poem have? How do you know?
2. Where does the poet accelerate his pace? How can you as an interpreter indicate this acceleration?
3. How can you use the poem's rhythm to reinforce its meaning during performance?

B. Now read the poem "Lines for an Album" by Weldon Kees.

"Lines for an Album"
Weldon Kees

Over the river and through the woods
To grandmother's house we go . . .

She waits behind the bolted door,
Her withered face in thirty pieces,
While blood runs thin, and memory,
An idiot without a name,
Recalls the snows of eighty years,
The daughter whose death was unexplained,
Darkness, blue veins, and broken leases.
Grandmother waits behind the door
(Sight dims beyond the curtain folds)
With her toothless smile and enuresis.
Over the river and through the woods
To grandmother's house we go . . .

Questions

1. How does the rhythm of this poem work to reinforce its meaning and feeling?
2. How can you as an interpreter vary your tempo or pace to help you effectively perform the poem?

C. Test your learning by examining the sound and rhythm used in "O What Is that Sound" by W. H. Auden.

O what is that sound which so thrills the ear
    Down in the valley drumming, drumming?
Only the scarlet soldiers, dear,
    The soldiers coming.

O what is that light I see flashing so clear
    Over the distance brightly, brightly?
Only the sun on their weapons, dear,
    As they step lightly.

O what are they doing with all that gear,
    What are they doing this morning, this morning?
Only their usual maneuvers, dear,
    Or perhaps a warning.

O why have they left the road down there,
    Why are they suddenly wheeling, wheeling?
Perhaps a change in the orders, dear.
    Why are you kneeling?

O haven't they stopped for the doctor's care,
    Haven't they reined their horses, their horses?
Why, they are none of them wounded, dear,
    None of these forces.

O is it the parson they want, with white hair,
    Is it the parson, is it, is it?
No they are passing his gateway, dear,
    Without a visit.

O it must be the farmer who lives so near.
    It must be the farmer so cunning, so cunning?
They have passed the farmyard already, dear,
    And now they are running.

O where are you going? Stay with me here!

    Were the vows you swore deceiving, deceiving?

No, I promised to love you, dear,

    But I must be leaving.

O it's broken the lock and splintered the door,

    O it's the gate where they're turning, turning;

Their boots are heavy on the floor

    And their eyes are burning.

Questions

1. What kinds of sound devices does Auden use? How do they add to the poem's meaning?
2. What tempo would be most appropriate for a performance of this poem? Where would you speed up or slow down?

Thus far in this chapter, you have performed language, sound, and rhythm operations. Notice the use of the word *operations*. Your interpreter's job is, in fact, rather like the job of a surgeon, in that you perform an exploratory operation to discover what is inside the poem. You conduct a search for meaning. During this process you examine the parts that make up the body of the poem and feel the natural rhythm that flows through the poem. And, like a doctor, you should never simply abandon a poem, untreated, to its audience. You are there to breathe life into it as you help it to live for your audience.

Types of Poems

You will need to know, as an interpreter, the types of poems on which you may be asked to operate. Basically, there are three types: lyric, narrative, and dramatic.

In a **lyric poem** a writer describes and shares an intense, subjective emotional experience, picture, or search with a general audience. The poet discloses personal feelings, thoughts, and fears. In effect, the inner self of the poet reaches out to touch the inner self of each reader or auditor of a lyric poem. When performing a lyric poem, make the poet's emotion, picture, or experience visible. Respond to the content of the poem to move your audience. Some common lyric forms include elegies (poems reflecting on death or having a melancholy tone), odes (poems with varied structures that express exultation or high emotions), or sonnets (fourteen-line iambic pentameter verses).

The **narrative poem,** like narrative prose, tells a story or details action that leads to a climax. The structure of this kind of poetry allows the poet to speak through specific characters as well as through a narrator. As a performer of narrative poetry you have a threefold task: first, you want to instill in your audience an understanding of and feeling for the poem's setting. Second, you want to transfer the plot to your audience. And third, you want to reveal the psychological and physical traits of the poem's characters and narrator. Ballads, metrical tales, and epics are three common types of narrative poetry.

Dramatic poetry is related to drama. The ideas, emotions, and action living in this kind of poetry are expressed through the words and behaviors of the characters within the poem. Thus, the dramatic poem is revealed without the aid of a third-person narrator.

PERFORMER'S WORKSHOP
Body Type

Label each of the following poems—Robert Browning's "My Last Duchess," Emily Dickinson's "After Great Pain, a Formal Feeling Comes," and Don Geiger's "Consoling Meditation on the Great Majority: Fathers"—as either lyric, narrative, or dramatic in nature. Be able to state how the "body type" of each poem helps you determine the way you will perform it. How does knowing the "body type" help you to refine your interpretations of the literature?

"My Last Duchess"
Robert Browning

That's my last Duchess painted on the wall,
Looking as if she were alive. I call
That piece a wonder, now: Frà Pandolf's hands
Worked busily a day, and there she stands.
Will 't please you sit and look at her? I said
"Frà Pandolf" by design, for never read
Strangers like you that pictured countenance,
The depth and passion of its earnest glance,
But to myself they turned (since none puts by
The curtain I have drawn for you, but I)
And seemed as they would ask me, if they durst,
How such a glance came there; so, not the first
Are you to turn and ask thus. Sir, 'twas not
Her husband's presence only, called that spot
Of joy into the Duchess' cheek: perhaps

Frà Pandolf chanced to say "Her mantle laps
Over my lady's wrist too much," or "Paint
Must never hope to reproduce the faint
Half-flush that dies along her throat": such stuff
Was courtesy, she thought, and cause enough
For calling up that spot of joy. She had
A heart—how shall I say?—too soon made glad,
Too easily impressed; she liked whate'er
She looked on, and her looks went everywhere.
Sir, 'twas all one! My favor at her breast,
The dropping of the daylight in the West,
The bough of cherries some officious fool
Broke in the orchard for her, the white mule
She rode with round the terrace—all and each
Would draw from her alike the approving speech,
Or blush, at least. She thanked me—good! but thanked
Somehow—I know not how—as if she ranked
My gift of a nine-hundred-years-old name
With anybody's gift. Who'd stoop to blame
This sort of trifling? Even had you skill
In speech—which I have not—to make your will
Quite clear to such an one, and say, "Just this
Or that in you disgusts me; here you miss,
Or there exceed the mark"—and if she let
Herself be lessoned so, nor plainly set
Her wits to yours, forsooth, and made excuse,
—E'en then would be some stooping; and I choose
Never to stoop. Oh sir, she smiled, no doubt,
Whene'er I passed her; but who passed without
Much the same smile? This grew; I gave commands;
Then all smiles stopped together. There she stands
As if alive. Will 't please you rise? We'll meet
The company below, then. I repeat,
The Count your master's known munificence
Is ample warrant that no just pretense
Of mine for dowry will be disallowed;
Though his fair daughter's self, as I avowed

At starting, is my object. Nay, we'll go
Together down, sir. Notice Neptune, though,
Taming a sea-horse, thought a rarity,
Which Claus of Innsbruck cast in bronze for me!

"After Great Pain, a Formal Feeling Comes"
Emily Dickinson

After great pain, a formal feeling comes—
The Nerves sit ceremonious, like Tombs—
The stiff Heart questions was it He, that bore,
And Yesterday, or Centuries before?

The Feet, mechanical, go round—
Of Ground, or Air, or Ought—
A Wooden way
Regardless grown,
A Quartz contentment, like a stone—

This is the Hour of Lead—
Remembered, if outlived,
As Freezing persons, recollect the Snow—
First—Chill—then Stupor—then the letting go—

"Consoling Meditation on the Great Majority: Fathers"
Don Geiger

I saw my father rolled away
in a casket too expensive for my means
(I lived in another town, and somebody else
placed the rush order, but of course I agreed,
so much is our love victim of our fears
that somehow we will have made the dead uncomfortable).
His hair had been darkened nicely and,
stuffed to perfection with embalming fluid,
he made, as the funeral parlor hostess said,
the best prepared one that month.
The men from the office walked up quietly to shake my hand.

I do not think they meant, precisely, to congratulate me,
but it was the only way remaining for them
to show their genuine appreciation of my father.
Two or three of them said they would have known me anywhere,
that I looked just like him,
though I do not know if they meant before or after.
A pastor, seemingly somewhat bewildered
by his own presence in the mortuary chapel,
was nevertheless kindly and general,
as one ought to be in speaking of strangers.
He summarized matters swiftly,
giving a nice account of death's importance to us all,
and stumbling only once in need of some fact
tieing my father's case into basic principles.
Challenged by the occasion, he could not resist
reaching for one rapidly disappearing high note,
but at the graveside he glanced at me uneasily,
as if to wonder if I knew that, as my father taught me,
since only the solitary heart can know its reasons
for the random wailing, the gnashing, the spitting of fingernails,
these miseries, like visions, are most profitable when private.
But insistences in these affairs are many:
making a mawkish scene, it began to rain,
and the thing was done.
The dead gone quick, you might say.
I heard the wet tires roll back like paper horns.
Refusing someone's invitation,
I dined alone and late at my hotel,
to enjoy my rage and fear without interruption.
Feeding relentlessly, I tried to dispel the vision
of water squiggling in the banked earth,
of my father lying alone in the dark
a mountain of menus, welcoming strangers.
I told myself that for him it would be but an episode
in a lifetime of fresh starts from the horizontal position.
I told myself how much he would have enjoyed
our spirited attempts to give him a good send-off.

I told myself that never had he shown such composure in
   a tight place.
I told myself to go ahead and tell myself
what a ruinous old mess he had been for twenty years.
I told myself just as much of a conversation
as I could have without my father there to join in.
The next day, the rain had stopped, the sun rose,
and I with it—to wash, shave, eat, get going.
Outside, a steady wind swept yesterday's litter.
Where they waited for me, I once more shook hands
all the way around, paid everybody off,
and then, as we had done so many times together,
too many times together, too infrequently together,
my father and I moved off together,
shaking the dust of one more friendly town.

Questions

1. How did you label these poems?
2. How might your determination of a poem's "body type" help you
   plan your interpretation?

Remember, when preparing to interpret any poem, the first step is to determine the type of poem that it is. Then, to ensure the success of your interpreting operation, examine the resources the poet used to reveal the meaning of his or her work. When you have accomplished these tasks, you are ready to perform.

IDEA ENCORE

Chapter 7 focused on poetry and the role the performer plays in facilitating the expression of emotion contained in a poem so that audience members may also share fully in the poem's experience. The chapter's central message was that a person who reads a poem well is also a poet.

A poem is compact, condensed, and dependent on sound. It is emotionally charged. As a performer of poetry, you need to participate actively in the exploration of a number of poetic resources, including the language of a poem (connotation, sense imagery, figures of speech such as similes, metaphors, personification, hyperbole, and paradoxes), its sound (onomatopoeia, rhyme, alliteration, assonance, and consonance), and its rhythm (meter and tempo). In addition, you need to be aware of the differing qualities of three key types of poems: lyric, narrative, and dramatic.

PERFORMER'S SHOWCASE & JOURNAL
Poetry in Performance

A. Choose a poem to interpret before the class. You may choose your poem from among those included in the body of this chapter, from the end-of-chapter selections, or from some you find on your own. Be certain to examine your poem thoroughly before attempting to perform it. On the day you are scheduled to read, hand in your analysis, answering the following questions:

1. Why did you choose this poem? What about it appeals to you?
2. What type of experience is described in the poem?
3. What is the poet's attitude toward the subject matter or ideas?
4. What types of language resources does the poet employ? Give specific examples.
5. How does the sound pattern help to support the meaning?
6. How does the rhythm help to support the meaning?

7. What physical responses are called for in the poem?
8. What vocal responses does the poem provoke?
9. In your presentation, what do you want to stimulate your audience to think and feel?
10. What portions of the poem do you feel will be a particular challenge to perform effectively?

B. Choose one poet whose work particularly appeals to and interests you. Once again, it may be a poet included in this chapter, one from the end-of-chapter selections, or an author you discovered on your own. Do some research on your poet. Where did (or does) he or she live, and in what lifestyle? What was the poet's ambition or personal cause? Hold a "Meet the Poets Convention" in class and share your understanding of the poet and at least three of his or her works that you select.

C. Try to increase your insight into poetry by comparing how a variety of poets treat similar themes. Use at least three selections on one theme in your presentation to the class. You may choose from the following poems or from poems you have encountered in other sources.

SELECTIONS FOR FURTHER WORK

"To a Daughter Leaving Home"
Linda Pastan

When I taught you
at eight to ride
a bicycle, loping along
beside you
as you wobbled away
on two round wheels,
my own mouth rounding
in surprise when you pulled
ahead down the curved
path of the park,

I kept waiting
for the thud
of your crash as I
sprinted to catch up,
while you grew
smaller, more breakable
with distance,
pumping, pumping
for your life, screaming
with laughter,
the hair flapping
behind you like a
handkerchief waving
goodbye.

"Gentle Communion"
Pat Mora

Even the long-dead are willing to move.
Without a word, she came with me from the desert.
Mornings she wanders through my rooms
making beds, folding socks.

Since she can't hear me anymore,
Mamande ignores the questions I never knew
to ask, about her younger days, her red
hair, the time she fell and broke her nose
in the snow. I will never know.

When I try to make her laugh,
to disprove her sad album face, she leaves
the room, resists me as she resisted
grinning for cameras, make-up, English.

While I write, she sits and prays,
feet apart, legs never crossed,
the blue housecoat buttoned high
as her hair dries white, girlish
around her head and shoulders.

She closes her eyes, bows her head,
and like a child presses her hands together,
her patient flesh steeple, the skin
worn, like the pages of her prayer book.

Sometimes I sit in her wide-armed
chair as I once sat in her lap.
Alone, we played a quiet I Spy.
She peeled grapes I still taste.

She removes the thin skin, places
the luminous coolness on my tongue.
I know not to bite or chew. I wait
for the thick melt,
our private green honey.

"Spring and Fall: To a Young Child"
Gerard Manley Hopkins

Márgarét, áre you gríeving
Over Goldengrove unleaving?
Leáves, líke the things of man, you
With your fresh thoughts care for, can you?
Áh! ás the heart grows older
It will come to such sights colder
By and by, nor spare a sigh
Though worlds of wanwood leafmeal lie;
And yet you *will* weep and know why.
Now no matter, child, the name:
Sórrow's spríngs áre the same.

Nor mouth had, no nor mind, expressed
What heart heard of, ghost guessed:
It ís the blight man was born for,
It is Margaret you mourn for.

"Status Symbol"

Mari Evans

    i
Have Arrived
    i am the
New Negro
    i
am the result of
President Lincoln
World War I
and Paris
the
Red Ball Express
white drinking fountains
sitdowns and
sit-ins
Federal Troops
Marches on Washington
and
prayer meetings . . .
today
They hired me
it
is a status
job . . .
along
with my papers

They
gave me my
Status Symbol . . .
the
key
to the
White
Locked
JOHN

"next to of course god america i"
E. E. Cummings

"next to of course god america i
love you land of the pilgrims' and so forth oh
say can you see by the dawn's early my
country 'tis of centuries come and go
and are no more what of it we should worry
in every language even deafanddumb
thy sons acclaim your glorious name by gorry
by jingo by gee by gosh by gum
why talk of beauty what could be more
beautiful than these heroic happy dead
who rushed like lions to the roaring slaughter
they did not stop to think they died instead
then shall the voice of liberty be mute?"

He spoke. And drank rapidly a glass of water

"Preface to a Twenty Volume Suicide Note"
Le Roi Jones (Amiri Baraka)

Lately, I've become accustomed to the way
The ground opens up and envelops me
Each time I go out to walk the dog.
Or the broad edged silly music the wind
Makes when I run for a bus . . .

Things have come to that.

And now, each night I count the stars,
And each night I get the same number.
And when they will not come to be counted,
I count the holes they leave.

Nobody sings anymore.

And then last night, I tiptoed up
To my daughter's room and heard her
Talking to someone, and when I opened
The door, there was no one there . . .
Only she on her knees, peeking into

Her own clasped hands.

"Richard Cory"
Edwin Arlington Robinson

Whenever Richard Cory went down town,
We people on the pavement looked at him:
He was a gentleman from sole to crown,
Clean favored, and imperially slim.

And he was always quietly arrayed,
And he was always human when he talked;
But still he fluttered pulses when he said,
"Good-morning," and he glittered when he walked.

And he was rich—yes, richer than a king—
And admirably schooled in every grace:
In fine, we thought that he was everything
To make us wish that we were in his place.

So on we worked, and waited for the light,
And went without the meat, and cursed the bread;
And Richard Cory, one calm summer night,
Went home and put a bullet through his head.

 ### "Welcome to Hiroshima"
Mary Jo Salter

is what you first see, stepping off the train:
a billboard brought to you in living English
by Toshiba Electric. While a channel
silent in the TV of the brain

projects those flickering re-runs of a cloud
that brims its risen columnful like beer
and, spilling over, hangs its foamy head,
you feel a thirst for history: what year

it started to be safe to breathe the air,
and when to drink the blood and scum afloat
on the Ohta River. But no, the water's clear,
they pour it for your morning cup of tea

in one of the countless sunny coffee shops
whose plastic dioramas advertise
mutations of cuisine behind the glass:
a pancake sandwich; a pizza someone tops

with a maraschino cherry. Passing by
the Peace Park's floral hypocenter (where
how bravely, or with what mistaken cheer,
humanity erased its own erasure),

you enter the memorial museum
and through more glass are served, as on a dish
of blistered grass, three mannequins. Like gloves
a mother clips to coatsleeves, strings of flesh

hang from their fingertips; or as if tied
to recall a duty for us, *Reverence*
the dead whose mourners too shall soon be dead,
but all commemoration's swallowed up

in questions of bad taste, how re-created
horror mocks the grim original,
and thinking at last *They should have left it all*
you stop. This is the wristwatch of a child.

Jammed on the moment's impact, resolute
to communicate some message, although mute,
it gestures with its hands at eight-fifteen
and eight-fifteen and eight-fifteen again

while tables of statistics on the wall
update the news by calling on a roll
of tape, death gummed on death, and in the case
adjacent, an exhibit under glass

is glass itself: a shard the bomb slammed in
a woman's arm at eight-fifteen, but some
three decades on—as if to make it plain
hope's only as renewable as pain,

and as if all the unsung
debasements of the past may one day come
rising to the surface once again—
worked its filthy way out like a tongue.

"To Women, As Far as I'm Concerned"
D. H. Lawrence

The feelings I don't have, I don't have.

The feelings I don't have, I won't say I have.

The feelings you say you have, you don't have.

The feelings you would like us both to have, we neither of us have.

The feelings people ought to have, they never have.

If people say they've got feelings, you may be pretty sure they
    haven't got them.

So if you want either of us to feel anything at all

You'd better abandon all idea of feelings altogether.

"The Death of the Ball Turret Gunner"
Randall Jarrell

From my mother's sleep I fell into the State,

And I hunched in its belly till my wet fur froze.

Six miles from earth, loosed from its dream of life,

I woke to black flak and the nightmare fighters.

When I died they washed me out of the turret with a hose.

"miss rosie"
Lucille Clifton

When I watch you

wrapped up like garbage

sitting, surrounded by the smell

of too old potato peels

or

when I watch you

in your old man's shoes

with the little toe cut out

sitting, waiting for your mind

like next week's grocery

I say

when I watch you

you wet brown bag of a woman

who used to be the best looking gal in Georgia

used to be called the Georgia Rose

I stand up

through your destruction

I stand up

"New Mexican Mountain"
Robinson Jeffers

I watch the Indians dancing to help the young corn at Taos
    pueblo. The old men squat in a ring

And make the song, the young women with fat bare arms,
    and a few shame-faced young men, shuffle the dance.

The lean-muscled young men are naked to the narrow loins,
    their breasts and backs daubed with white clay,

Two eagle-feathers plume the black heads. They dance with
    reluctance, they are growing civilized; the old men persuade them.

Only the drum is confident, it thinks the world has not changed;
    the beating heart, the simplest of rhythms,

It thinks the world has not changed at all; it is only a dreamer,
    a brainless heart, the drum has no eyes.

These tourists have eyes, the hundred watching the dance, white
    Americans, hungrily too, with reverence, not laughter;

Pilgrims from civilization, anxiously seeking beauty, religion,
    poetry; pilgrims from the vacuum.

People from cities, anxious to be human again. Poor show how
    they suck you empty! The Indians are emptied,

And certainly there was never religion enough, nor beauty nor
    poetry here . . . to fill Americans.

Only the drum is confident, it thinks the world has not changed.
    Apparently only myself and the strong

Tribal drum, and the rockhead of Taos mountain, remember that
    civilization is a transient sickness.

PART 3

Widening the Art of Interpretation

Chapter 8

Performing Literature for Children

Learning Objectives

After completing this chapter, you should be able to

- demonstrate your understanding of the genre of children's literature
- explain how children's literature compares and contrasts with other forms of literature
- identify the steps the interpreter should follow in preparing to perform children's literature
- discuss the importance of using physical suggestion and vocal variety when performing for children

Qualities you never want to lose or stifle are childhood's spirit of playfulness and the sense of wonder required to tap the imaginative workings of the mind. Yet many of us do suppress these aspects of ourselves. Can your thoughts and reactions reflect those of a child? What, for example, is the figure below?

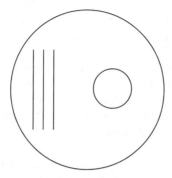

Do you see only a circle surrounding a smaller circle and three lines? If so, consider yourself "grown up." The essence of childhood, the spontaneity and creativity of youth, have escaped you for the moment. However, you can recapture those precious qualities.

Look at the figure again. Can you see an egg and three thin slices of bacon on a plate? Can you see a very neat person's small serving of spaghetti and a single meatball? Most children could see that there is more to this configuration than meets the eye. If you work to keep the child alive in yourself, you will recapture a freshness and inventiveness that will serve you well as an interpreter of literature.

But how can someone become an adult without sacrificing those qualities? Doesn't gaining one necessitate losing the other? Although it is somewhat paradoxical, you can become a grown-up and remain a child. You can do so by carefully tending the spark of childhood that burns within you. You will have to take time to remember growing pains, dragons and monsters, wonder and suspense, wild imaginings, and being afraid.

Chapter 8 will explore some techniques for using literature to regain your childlike spirit. You will discover ways you can use children's literature both to reach children and to widen your scope as an interpretative performer. Reading children's literature to a young audience serves not only to enrich the children's lives, it is an enriching experience for the interpreter as well.

Defining Children's Literature

Children's literature is designed to encourage children to read and appreciate literature. It includes all types of literature: prose, poetry, and drama. Children's literature exists in virtually every culture. It functions to help children see literature as a reflection of human experience. Like literature in general, children's literature may entertain, inspire, and instruct, and it helps children explore the human condition and make sense of their world. As children develop a better understanding of the human experience, they also develop a richer understanding of life.

Children's literature provides children with the opportunity to explore different worlds, real and fantastic, possible and impossible. It also gives them an opportunity to try on different roles—to see how the roles feel and if they fit. It enables children to visualize by helping them formulate pictures in their minds. It also helps them increase their vocabularies by becoming familiar with written language.

What is even more significant, however, is that children's literature affects children's views of themselves. Children's literature has been cited as having an important influence on the development of the self-concepts of children, and studies have shown that children's books have an impact on children's views of gender roles. In fact, surveys of children's books have confirmed that many provide only limited roles for females, an abundance of male characters, and many examples of occupational and gender stereotyping. For example, girls are frequently depicted as attentive and serving others while boys are more apt to be characterized as adventuresome and strong.

Selecting Material for Children

How do you choose literature to interpret for a child audience? In general, children are apt to respond most favorably to literature that contains one or more of the following characteristics: a unified plot; a strong appeal to the imagination; lots of action; suspense; repetition; sensory images they can respond to; vivid and believable characters with whom they can identify or about whom they can fantasize; clever dialogue; use of rhythm, rhyme, and alliteration; a young hero; a villain or monster; and opportunities for them to participate creatively. In order to answer this question for yourself, however, journey back to the days of your own childhood to examine a piece of literature that probably lived in your world with you.

PERFORMER'S WORKSHOP
A Childhood Visit

Read the following excerpt from Mark Twain's *The Adventures of Tom Sawyer.*

The Adventures of Tom Sawyer

from **Mark Twain**

Saturday morning was come, and all the summer world was bright and fresh, and brimming with life. There was a song in every heart; and if the heart was young the music issued at the lips. There was cheer in every face and a spring in every step. The locust trees were in bloom and the fragrance of the blossoms filled the air.

Cardiff Hill, beyond the village and above it, was green with vegetation, and it lay just far enough away to seem a Delectable Land, dreamy, reposeful, and inviting.

Tom appeared on the sidewalk with a bucket of whitewash and a long-handled brush. He surveyed the fence, and all gladness left him and a deep melancholy settled down upon his spirit. Thirty yards of board fence nine feet high! It seemed to him that life was hollow, and existence but a burden. Sighing he dipped his brush and passed it along the topmost plank; repeated the operation, did it again; compared the insignificant whitewashed streak with the far-reaching continent of unwhitewashed fence, and sat down on a tree-box discouraged. Jim came skipping out at the gate with a tin pail, and singing "Buffalo Gals." Bringing water from the town pump had always been hateful work in Tom's eyes before, but now it did not strike him so. He remembered that there was company at the pump. White, mulatto, and negro boys and girls were always there waiting their turns, resting, trading playthings, quarreling, fighting, skylarking. And he remembered that although the pump was only a hundred and fifty yards off, Jim never got back with a bucket of water under an hour; and even then somebody generally had to go after him. Tom said:

"Say, Jim, I'll fetch the water if you'll whitewash some."

Jim shook his head and said:

"Can't, Ma'rs Tom. Ole missis she tole me I got to go an' git dis water an' not stop foolin' roun' wid anybody. She say she spec' Ma'rs Tom gwyne to ax me to whitewash, an' so she tole me go 'long an' 'tend to my own business—she 'lowed *she'd* 'tend to de whitewashin'."

"Oh, never you mind what she said, Jim. That's the way she always talks. Gimme the bucket—I won't be gone only a minute. *She* won't ever know."

"Oh, I dasn't, Ma'rs Tom. Ole missis she'd take an' tar de head off'n me. 'Deed she would."

"*She!* She never licks anybody—whacks 'em over the head with her thimble—and who cares for that, I'd like to know? She talks awful, but talk don't hurt—anyways, it don't if she don't cry. Jim, I'll give you a marble. I'll give you a white alley!"

Jim began to waver.

"White alley, Jim! And it's a bully taw."

"My; dat's a mighty gay marvel, *I* tell you! But Ma'rs Tom, I's powerful 'fraid ole missis—"

"And besides, if you will I'll show you my sore toe."

Jim was only human—this attraction was too much for him. He put down his pail, took the white alley, and bent over the toe with absorbing interest while the bandage was being unwound. In another minute he was flying down the street with his pail and a tingling rear, Tom was whitewashing with vigour, and Aunt Polly was retiring from the field with a slipper in her hand and triumph in her eye.

But Tom's energy did not last. He began to think of the fun he had planned for this day, and his sorrows multiplied. Soon the free boys would come tripping along on all sorts of delicious expeditions, and they would make a world of fun of him for having to work—the very thought of it burnt him like fire. He got out his worldly wealth and examined it—bits of toys, marbles, and trash; enough to buy an exchange of work, maybe, but not half enough to buy so much as half an hour of pure freedom. So he returned his straitened means to his pocket, and gave up the idea of trying to buy the boys. At this dark and hopeless moment an inspiration burst upon him. Nothing less than a great, magnificent inspiration.

He took up his brush and went tranquilly to work. Ben Rogers hove in sight presently; the very boy of all boys whose ridicule he had been dreading. Ben's gait was the hop, skip, and jump—proof enough that his heart was light and his anticipations high. He was eating an apple, and giving a long, melodious whoop at intervals, followed by a deep-toned ding dong dong, ding dong dong, for he was personating a steamboat. As he drew near, he slackened speed, took the middle of the street, leaned far over to starboard, and rounded to ponderously, and with laborious pomp and circumstance; for he was personating the *Big Missouri*, and considered himself to be drawing nine feet of water. He was boat, and captain, and engine-bells combined, so he had to imagine himself standing on his own hurricane-deck giving the orders and executing them:

"Stop her, sir! Ling-a-ling-ling!" The headway ran almost out and he drew up slowly toward the sidewalk. "Ship up to back! Ling-a-ling-ling!" His arms straightened and stiffened down his sides. "Set her back on the stabboard! Ling-aling-ling! Chow! ch-chow-wow-chow!" his right hand meantime describing stately circles, for it was representing a forty-foot wheel. "Let her go back on the labboard! Ling-a-ling-ling! Chow-ch-chow-chow!" The left hand began to describe circles.

"Stop the stabboard! Ling-a-ling-ling! Stop the labboard! Come ahead on the stabboard! Stop her! Let your outside turn over slow! Ling-a-ling-ling! Chow-ow-ow! Get out that headline! Lively now! Come—out with your spring-line—what're you about there! Take a turn round that stump with the bight of it! Stand by that stage, now—let her go! Done with the engines, sir! Ling-a-ling-ling!"

"'Sht! s'sht! sht!" (Trying the gaugecocks.)

Tom went on whitewashing—paid no attention to the steamboat. Ben stared a moment and then said:

"Hi-yi! You're up a stump, ain't you!"

No answer. Tom surveyed his last touch with the eye of an artist, then he gave his brush another gentle sweep, and surveyed the result as before. Ben ranged up alongside of him. Tom's mouth watered for the apple, but he stuck to his work. Ben said:

"Hello, old chap, you got to work, hey?"

Tom wheeled suddenly and said:

"Why, it's you, Ben! I warn't noticing."

"Say—I'm going in a swimming, I am. Don't you wish you could? But of course you'd druther work—wouldn't you? Course you would!"

Tom contemplated the boy a bit, and said:

"What do you call work?"

"Why, ain't that work?"

Tom resumed his whitewashing, and answered carelessly:

"Well, maybe it is, and maybe it ain't. All I know is, it suits Tom Sawyer."

"Oh, come now, you don't mean to let on that you like it?"

The brush continued to move.

"Like it? Well, I don't see why I oughtn't to like it. Does a boy get a chance to whitewash a fence every day?"

That put the thing in a new light. Ben stopped nibbling his apple. Tom swept his brush daintily back and forth—stepped back to note the effect—added a touch here and there—criticized the effect again, Ben watching every move and getting more and more interested, more and more absorbed. Presently he said:

"Say, Tom, let me whitewash a little."

Tom considered; was about to consent; but he altered his mind:

"No, no, I reckon it wouldn't hardly do, Ben. You see, Aunt Polly's awful particular about this fence—right here on the street, you know—but if it was the back fence I wouldn't mind and she wouldn't. Yes, she's awful particular about this fence; it's got to be done very careful; I reckon there ain't one boy in a thousand, maybe two thousand, that can do it the way it's got to be done."

"No—is that so? Oh come, now, lemme just try. Only just a little. I'd let you, if you was me, Tom."

"Ben, I'd like to, honest injun; but Aunt Polly—well, Jim wanted to do it, but she wouldn't let him; Sid wanted to do it, and she wouldn't let Sid. Now, don't you see how I'm fixed? If you was to tackle this fence and any-thing was to happen to it—"

"Oh, shucks; I'll be just as careful. Now lemme try. Say—I'll give you the core of my apple."

"Well, here—No, Ben, now don't. I'm afeard—"

"I'll give you all of it!"

Tom gave up the brush with reluctance in his face, but alacrity in his heart. And while the late steamer *Big Missouri* worked and sweated in the sun, the retired artist sat on a barrel in the shade close by, dangled his legs, munched his apple, and planned the slaughter of more innocents. There was no lack of material; boys happened along every little while; they came to jeer, but remained to whitewash. By the time Ben was fagged out, Tom had traded the next chance to Billy Fisher for a kite, in good repair; and when he played out, Johnny Miller bought in for a dead rat and a string to swing it with; and so on, and so on, hour after hour. And when the middle of the afternoon came, from being a poor poverty-stricken boy in the morning, Tom was literally rolling in wealth. He had, besides the things I have mentioned, twelve marbles, part of a jews' harp, a piece of blue bottle-glass to look through, a spool-cannon, a key that wouldn't unlock anything, a fragment of chalk, a glass stopper of a decanter, a tin soldier, a couple of tadpoles, six fire-crackers, a kitten with only one eye, a brass door-knob, a dog-collar—but no dog—the handle of a knife, four pieces of orange-peel, and a dilapidated old window-sash. He had had a nice, good, idle time all the while—plenty of company—and the fence had three coats of whitewash on it! If he hadn't run out of whitewash, he would have bankrupted every boy in the village.

Tom said to himself that it was not such a hollow world after all. He had discovered a great law of human action, without knowing it, namely, that in order to make a man or a boy covet a thing, it is only necessary to make the thing difficult to attain. If he had been a great and wise philosopher, like the writer of this book, he would now have comprehended that work consists of whatever a body is obliged to do, and that play consists of whatever a body is not obliged to do. And this would help him understand why constructing artificial flowers or performing on a treadmill is work, while rolling nine-pins or climbing Mont Blanc is only amusement. There are wealthy gentlemen in England who drive four-horse passenger-coaches twenty or thirty miles on a daily line, in the summer, because the privilege costs them considerable money; but if they were offered wages for the service that would turn it into work, then they would resign.

The boy mused awhile over the substantial change which had taken place in his worldly circumstances, and then wended toward headquarters to report.

Questions

1. What is the plot of this story? Why is it effective for a child audience?
2. What is its theme?
3. What types of characters people the story?
4. What kind of language does the author use?
5. What uses are made of description?
6. In what ways might an adult audience respond differently from a group of children?

If you want to help children realize that males and females, regardless of their gender, are capable of exhibiting both masculine and feminine characteristics and performing a wide range of roles, then also work to select literature for children that broadens sex-role standards and depicts males and females in less stereotypical ways.

Characteristics of Children's Literature

Effective literature for children is usually rich in imagery. It reaches out to children, as the previous piece by Mark Twain probably reached out to you. A good children's story exercises their senses of sight, smell, taste, touch, and hearing. In imaginative ways, it encourages them to participate in the selection as it appeals to their love of action and adventure.

In addition, a good children's story includes unique or memorable characters with whom the youngsters can identify. It doesn't matter whether the story's characters are people, animals, or objects. If the characters feed children's understanding of themselves and their curiosity about the world, then they fulfill an important function. Children become involved with the characters in a story; they watch and listen to the characters react to their world and attempt to solve problems. Struggles, successes, and needs of the characters are closely attended to by children. In fact, in an effective story the needs of the characters and the needs of the children often overlap.

As an interpreter of children's literature, remember that a child's needs are human needs: acceptance and belonging, control and achievement, love and affection. Stories that illustrate how these needs may be met help children adjust to their world. Accordingly, the world shown in children's literature need not continuously represent an ideal world. From time to time, even imaginary worlds are troubled by problems. Children need not be fed a steady diet of fantasies or fairy tales; realistic stories are also meaningful. The poet Yevgeni Yevtushenko reflects this in lines from his poem "Lies":

> Telling lies to the young is wrong.
>
> Proving to them that lies are true is wrong.
>
> Proving to them that God's in his heaven
>
> and all's well with the world is wrong.
>
> The young know what you mean.
>
> The young are people.

This is not to suggest that children's literature should be disturbing. But literature can do more than simply enrich a child's imagination. Helping in the development of a child's social conscience can be another benefit of children's literature. Nightmares, as well as dreams, are part of life.

As an oral interpreter, respect the literary needs of children. Like adults, children relish the fanciful and delightful, the provoking and sometimes frightening. Thus, literary selection for children is wide open.

PERFORMER'S WORKSHOP
Selecting Children's Literature

Read the following excerpt from Antoine de Saint-Exupéry's *The Little Prince* and consider whether it would work for a child audience.

 from *The Little Prince*

Antoine de Saint-Exupéry

It was then that the fox appeared.

"Good morning," said the fox.

"Good morning," the little prince responded politely, although when he turned around he saw nothing.

"I am right here," the voice said, "under the apple tree."

"Who are you?" asked the little prince, and added, "You are very pretty to look at."

"I am a fox," the fox said.

"Come and play with me," proposed the little prince. "I am so unhappy."

"I cannot play with you," the fox said. "I am not tamed."

"Ah! Please excuse me," said the little prince.

But after some thought, he added:

"What does that mean—'tame'?"

"You do not live here," said the fox. "What is it that you are looking for?"

"I am looking for men," said the little prince. "What does that mean—'tame'?"

"Men," said the fox. "They have guns, and they hunt. It is very disturbing. They also raise chickens. These are their only interests. Are you looking for chickens?"

"No," said the little prince. "I am looking for friends. What does that mean—'tame'?"

"It is an act too often neglected," said the fox. "It means to establish ties."

"'To establish ties'?"

"Just that," said the fox. "To me, you are still nothing more than a little boy who is just like a hundred thousand other little boys. And I have no need of you. And you, on your part, have no need of me. To you, I am nothing more than a fox like a hundred thousand other foxes. But if you tame me, then we shall need each other. To me, you will be unique in all the world. To you, I shall be unique in all the world. . . ."

"I am beginning to understand," said the little prince. "There is a flower . . . I think that she has tamed me. . . ."

"It is possible," said the fox. "On the Earth one sees all sorts of things."

"Oh, but this is not on the Earth!" said the little prince.

The fox seemed perplexed, and very curious.

"On another planet?"

"Yes."

"Are there hunters on that planet?"

"No."

"Ah, that is interesting. . . ." But he came back to his idea.

"My life is very monotonous," he said. "I hunt chickens; men hunt me. All the chickens are just alike, and all the men are just alike. And, in consequence, I am a little bored. But if you tame me, it will be as if the sun came to shine on my life. I shall know the sound of a step that will be different from all the others. Other steps send me hurrying back underneath the ground. Yours will call me, like music, out of my burrow. And then look: you see the grain-fields down yonder? I do not eat bread. Wheat is of no use to me. The wheat fields have nothing to say to me. And that is sad.

"But you have hair that is the color of gold. Think how wonderful that will be when you have tamed me! The grain, which is also golden, will bring me back the thought of you. And I shall love to listen to the wind in the wheat. . . ."

The fox gazed at the little prince, for a long time.

"Please—tame me!" he said.

"I want to, very much," the little prince replied. "But I have not much time. I have friends to discover, and a great many things to understand."

"One only understands the things that one tames," said the fox. "Men have no more time to understand anything. They buy things all ready made at the shops. But there is no shop anywhere where one can buy friendship, and so men have no friends any more. If you want a friend, tame me. . . ."

"What must I do, to tame you?" asked the little prince.

"You must be very patient," replied the fox. "First you will sit down at a little distance from me—like that—in the grass. I shall look at you out of the corner of my eye, and you will say nothing. Words are the source of misunderstandings. But you will sit a little closer to me, every day. . . ."

The next day the little prince came back.

"It would have been better to come back at the same hour," said the fox. " . . . One must observe the proper rites. . . ."

"What is a rite?" asked the little prince.

"Those also are actions too often neglected," said the fox. "They are what make one day different from other days, one hour from other hours. . . ."

So the little prince tamed the fox. And when the hour of his departure drew near—

"Ah," said the fox, "I shall cry."

"It is your own fault," said the little prince. "I never wished you any sort of harm; but you wanted me to tame you. . . ."

"Yes, that is so," said the fox.

"But now you are going to cry!" said the little prince.

"Yes, that is so," said the fox.

"Then it has done you no good at all!"

"It has done me good," said the fox, "because of the color of the wheat fields."

Questions

1. Do you think this selection is suitable for a child audience? Why?
2. What performance challenges mighty you anticipate in preparing this for a child audience?

Preparing to Read for Children

Think back to the literature you were exposed to as a child. What do you remember? Did most of your early exposure come from television? For example, did Miss Piggy, Kermit, and the gang from *Sesame Street* bring stories and ideas alive for you? Did you watch programs like *Reading Rainbow*, *Wishbone*, or Hallmark after-school specials? You are certain to recall children's stories that were alive with animation. Which Disney classics were your favorites?

As you interpret literature for children, you will attempt to create the same involvement and excitement with the literature that Jim Henson and Walt Disney achieved through television and films. Of course, Henson had puppets and Disney had cartoon characters with which to attract and enchant children. How will you use your interpreter's skills to accomplish the same feat?

The methods of preparation you will use to interpret a selection for an audience of children are similar to those you use in preparing to read to your peers. For both types of audience, your aim is to have the individuals meet and merge their lives with the literature you present. While the road you will travel to realize your goal when interpreting for young people differs from the road for your peers, you will find that many of the signposts along the road are familiar.

Work to Understand Your Selection

As a performer of any type of literature, it is essential that you have a complete involvement with and understanding of the selections you hope to perform. Your job as an interpreter of children's literature is more than simply to pass on stories, of course; rather, your goal is to share experience. Allow yourself vicariously and imaginatively to enter children's literature. Experience it, process it, and then make it vivid and alive.

Show Emotion and Feeling

You will want to both physically and vocally illustrate the ways in which the words, events, and characters in the selection interact and affect each other. Present the literature in a manner that precipitates the desired emotional responses in your audiences. To determine what these desired responses are, you must identify with the feelings and attitudes expressed in the selection and then transfer them from your heart and mind to the hearts and minds of your receivers. This requires that you focus on specific images and feelings, vividly imagine the characters, and re-create the experience for the audience.

Make the Characters Believable

How can you make a crafty wolf, a scheming fox, or an impulsive little boy seem real? Begin by imagining yourself as each of the characters in the children's story. You need to be able to express the differences between characters. You need to be able to identify the distinguishing quality of each character, whether it is a mannerism or a voice tone. One at a time, re-create the image of each character during your performance before the audience of children. To succeed at this, you will need to empathize with each character and intuit that character's essence.

Embody the Selection Vocally and Physically

As a performer of children's literature, the demands you must make of your voice and body in performance are significant. When it comes to your voice, you need to vary your rate, timing, pitch, volume, quality, and emphasis as the literature requires. When it comes to your body, you need to suggest the physical expression and demeanor of each character. Children's literature will provide both your voice and your body with a real challenge. You may find that the vocal and physical requirements called for in performing much adult literature seem negligible when compared to the vocal and physical gymnastics the children's storyteller or poet demands. Children's characters do not move only from the neck up. Like the vocal challenges, literature for children offers unique physical challenges as well. Facial expressions are important, but remember, too, the impact of posture and gesture.

As you work, let your particular script serve as your guide. Emphasize the dynamic action in the story, the character's unique qualities, and the rhythm and description in the writing. Make the action of the story physical, using gestures that are overt rather than subtle. Broaden and exaggerate your facial expressions in response to the literature. And finally, make certain that each of the characters has a distinctive voice: shrill, gruff, singsong, rumbling—whatever suits the character.

In order to accept the world of the literature as both important and real, open yourself to a child's boundless world of imagination. In "The World of Imagination," an exhibit in Walt Disney's Epcot Center in Florida, an animated guide named "Figment" takes participants on an intriguing journey through the workings of the imagination. Open yourself to your own imaginative tour, and you will doubtless develop an appreciation for the magic that happens in children's literature.

PERFORMER'S WORKSHOP
Motion and Voice Imaginings

Read the following excerpt from *Alice's Adventures in Wonderland* by Lewis Carroll. Alice encounters some strange characters when she arrives at the "Mad Tea Party."

 ### *Alice's Adventures in Wonderland*
Lewis Carroll

There was a table set out under a tree in front of the house, and the March Hare and the Hatter were having tea at it; a Dormouse was sitting between them, fast asleep, and the other two were using it as a cushion, resting their elbows on it, and talking over its head. "Very uncomfortable for the Dormouse," thought Alice: "only, as it's asleep, I suppose it doesn't mind."

The table was a large one, but the three were all crowded together at one corner of it: "No room! No room!" they cried out when they saw Alice coming. "There's *plenty* of room!" said Alice indignantly, and she sat down in a large arm-chair at one end of the table.

"Have some wine," the March Hare said in an encouraging tone.

Alice looked all round the table, but there was nothing on it but tea. "I don't see any wine," she remarked.

"There isn't any," said the March Hare.

"Then it wasn't very civil of you to offer it," said Alice angrily.

"It wasn't very civil of you to sit down without being invited," said the March Hare.

"I didn't know it was *your* table," said Alice; "it's laid for a great many more than three."

"Your hair wants cutting," said the Hatter. He had been looking at Alice for some time with great curiosity, and this was his first speech.

"You should learn not to make personal remarks," Alice said with some severity: "It's very rude."

The Hatter opened his eyes very wide on hearing this; but all he *said* was, "Why is a raven like a writing-desk?"

"Come, we shall have some fun now!" thought Alice. "I'm glad they've begun asking riddles—I believe I can guess that," she added aloud.

"Do you mean that you think you can find out the answer to it?" said the March Hare.

"Exactly so," said Alice.

"Then you should say what you mean," the March Hare went on.

"I do," Alice hastily replied; "at least—at least I mean what I say— that's the same thing, you know."

"Not the same thing a bit!" said the Hatter. "Why, you might just as well say that 'I see what I eat' is the same thing as 'I eat what I see!'"

"You might just as well say," added the March Hare, "that 'I like what I get' is the same thing as 'I get what I like!'"

"You might just as well say," added the Dormouse, who seemed to be talking in his sleep, "that 'I breathe when I sleep' is the same thing as 'I sleep when I breathe!'"

"It is the same thing with you," said the Hatter, and here the conversation dropped, and the party sat silent for a minute, while Alice thought over all she could remember about ravens and writing-desks, which wasn't much.

The Hatter was the first to break the silence. "What day of the month is it?" he said, turning to Alice: he had taken his watch out of his pocket, and was looking at it uneasily, shaking it every now and then, and holding it to his ear.

Alice considered a little, and said, "The fourth."

"Two days wrong!" sighed the Hatter. "I told you butter wouldn't suit the works!" he added, looking angrily at the March Hare.

"It was the *best* butter," the March Hare meekly replied.

"Yes, but some crumbs must have got in as well," the Hatter grumbled: "you shouldn't have put it in with the bread-knife."

The March Hare took the watch and looked at it gloomily. Then he dipped it into his cup of tea, and looked at it again: but he could think of nothing better to say than his first remark, "It was the *best* butter, you know."

Alice had been looking over his shoulder with some curiosity. "What a funny watch!" she remarked. "It tells the day of the month, and doesn't tell what o'clock it is!"

"Why should it?" muttered the Hatter. "Does *your* watch tell you what year it is?"

"Of course not," Alice replied very readily; "but that's because it stays the same year for such a long time together."

"Which is just the case with *mine*," said the Hatter.

Alice felt dreadfully puzzled. The Hatter's remark seemed to her to have no sort of meaning in it, and yet it was certainly English. "I don't quite understand you," she said, as politely as she could.

"The Dormouse is asleep again," said the Hatter, and he poured a little hot tea on to its nose.

The Dormouse shook its head impatiently, and said, without opening its eyes, "Of course, of course: just what I was going to remark myself."

"Have you guessed the riddle yet?" the Hatter said, turning to Alice again.

"No, I give it up," Alice replied; "what's the answer?"

"I haven't the slightest idea," said the Hatter.

"Nor I," said the March Hare.

Alice sighed wearily. "I think you might do something better with the time," she said, "than wasting it in asking riddles that have no answers."

"If you knew Time as well as I do," said the Hatter, "you wouldn't talk about wasting *it*. It's *him*."

"I don't know what you mean," said Alice.

"Of course you don't!" the Hatter said, tossing his head contemptuously. "I dare say you never even spoke to Time!"

"Perhaps not," Alice cautiously replied: "but I know I have to beat time when I learn music."

"Ah! that accounts for it," said the Hatter. "He won't stand beating. Now, if you only kept on good terms with him, he'd do almost anything you liked with the clock. For instance, suppose it were nine o'clock in the morning, just time to begin lessons: you'd only have to whisper a hint to Time, and round goes the clock in a twinkling! Half-past one, time for dinner!"

("I only wish it was," the March Hare said to itself in a whisper.)

"That would be grand, certainly," said Alice thoughtfully: "but then— I shouldn't be hungry for it, you know."

"Not at first, perhaps," said the Hatter: "but you could keep it to half-past one as long as you liked."

"Is that the way *you* manage?" Alice asked.

The Hatter shook his head mournfully. "Not I!" he replied. "We quarreled last March—just before *he* went mad, you know—" (pointing with his teaspoon at the March Hare) "—it was at the great concert given by the Queen of Hearts, and I had to sing

'Twinkle, twinkle, little bat!
How I wonder what you're at!'

You know the song, perhaps?"

"I've heard something like it," said Alice. . . .

Here the Dormouse shook itself, and began singing in its sleep *"Twinkle, twinkle, twinkle, twinkle—"* and went on so long that they had to pinch it to make it stop.

"Well, I'd hardly finished the first verse," said the Hatter, "when the Queen bawled out 'He's murdering the time! Off with his head!'"

"How dreadfully savage!" exclaimed Alice.

"And ever since that," the Hatter went on in a mournful tone, "he won't do a thing I ask! It's always six o'clock now."

A bright idea came into Alice's head. "Is that the reason so many tea-things are put out here?" she asked.

"Yes, that's it," said the Hatter with a sigh: "It's always tea-time, and we've no time to wash the things between whiles."

"Then you keep moving round, I suppose?" said Alice.

"Exactly so," said the Hatter: "as the things get used up."

"But when you come to the beginning again?" Alice ventured to ask.

"Suppose we change the subject," the March Hare interrupted, yawning. "I'm getting tired of this. I vote the young lady tell us a story."

"I'm afraid I don't know one," said Alice, rather alarmed at the proposal.

"Then the Dormouse shall!" they both cried. "Wake up, Dormouse!" And they pinched it on both sides at once.

The Dormouse slowly opened his eyes. "I wasn't asleep," he said in a hoarse, feeble voice: "I heard every word you fellows were saying."

"Tell us a story!" said the March Hare.

"Yes, please do!" pleaded Alice.

"And be quick about it," added the Hatter, "or you'll be asleep again before it's done. . . ."

A. Imagine you are the March Hare. Move around the room as you believe the March Hare would move. Now, talk as you believe the March Hare would talk. Repeat this sequence for each of the characters in the selection.

B. Try sketching your conception of the world in which the characters operate. Your drawing may be realistic or abstract.

C. Now, prepare to read the selection aloud. Allow yourself to give full expression to the fictional world and to the characters that live in that world. Have fun with the material.

Questions

1. Were your vocal tones and gestures appropriate to each of the characters? Did they serve to distinguish one character from another? How?

2. How was your drawing of the literary world expressed through your performance? In what ways might you actually share your drawing with a child audience? Might the children draw the environment for you after they experience your reading? Could they help by improvising the characters for a second reading?

You can see that the performance of children's literature opens up imaginative vistas for you to share with your audiences. Children love stories. They love to participate. They love to have fun. Have fun yourself, as your imagination takes you into the creative possibilities of children's literature.

IDEA ENCORE

The subject of Chapter 8 was performing literature for children. If you are going to succeed at performing for young audience members, you first need to get in touch with the child inside yourself. To this end, the chapter provided you with numerous opportunities to familiarize yourself with techniques designed to help you release the childlike spirit within you so that you might free it easily during your performances.

The chapter also described characteristics that make literature particularly appropriate for children and suggested steps that you, the interpreter, can take to best prepare to perform for children. What is especially important is that you demonstrate the willingness to use your imagination to remember, explore, and share.

PERFORMER'S SHOWCASE & JOURNAL
A Collage of Readings

Choose a selection to perform for a neighboring elementary school class or for the children's reading hour at your local library. In order to ensure that no two students perform the same selection, clear your choice with your instructor. Consider these questions both before and after your performance of your children's literature. Note your responses in your journal.

1. Why did you select this piece of literature for interpretation?
2. What did you do to adapt the material to the requirements of oral performance?
3. Describe your work techniques as you rehearsed the material. How do they differ from the way you have rehearsed material for adult audiences?
4. Describe the response you received from your peers as you shared the material with them.
5. How did you feel when approaching your child audience? Were you nervous? Confident?

6. How did the children respond to the material? In what ways were their reactions similar to that of adults? In what ways were their reaction different?
7. What changes would you make if you were to present the material for another group of children?

SELECTIONS FOR FURTHER WORK

"Sick"
Shel Silverstein

"I cannot go to school today,"
Said little Peggy Ann McKay.
"I have the measles and the mumps,
A gash, a rash and purple bumps.
My mouth is wet, my throat is dry,
I'm going blind in my right eye.
My tonsils are as big as rocks,
I've counted sixteen chicken pox
And there's one more—that's seventeen,
And don't you think my face looks green?
My leg is cut, my eyes are blue—
It might be instamatic flu.
I cough and sneeze and gasp and choke,
I'm sure that my left leg is broke—
My hip hurts when I move my chin,
My belly button's caving in,
My back is wrenched, my ankle's sprained,
My 'pendix pains each time it rains.
My nose is cold, my toes are numb,
I have a sliver in my thumb.

My neck is stiff, my spine is weak,

I hardly whisper when I speak.

My tongue is filling up my mouth,

I think my hair is falling out.

My elbow's bent, my spine ain't straight,

My temperature is one-o-eight.

My brain is shrunk, I cannot hear,

There is a hole inside my ear.

I have a hangnail, and my heart is—what?

What's that? What's that you say?

You say today is . . . Saturday?

G'bye, I'm going out to play!"

 from *The Secret Garden*

Frances Hodgson Burnett

In each century since the beginning of the world, wonderful things have been discovered. In the last century more amazing things were found out than in any century before. In this new century, hundreds of things still more astounding will be brought to light. At first people refuse to believe that a strange new thing can be done, then they begin to hope it can be done, then they see it can be done—then it is done and all the world wonders why it was not done centuries ago. One of the new things people began to find out in the last century was that thoughts—just mere thoughts—are as powerful as electric batteries—as good for one as sunlight is, or as bad for one as poison. To let a sad thought or a bad one get into your mind is as dangerous as letting a scarlet fever germ get into your body. If you let it stay there after it has got in you, you never get over it as long as you live.

So long as Mistress Mary's mind was full of disagreeable thoughts about her dislikes and sour opinions of people and her determination not to be pleased by or interested in anything, she was a yellow-faced, sickly, bored and wretched child. Circumstances, however, were very kind to her, though she was not at all aware of it. They began to push her about for her own good. When her mind gradually filled itself with robins, and moorland cottages crowded with children, with queer crabbed old gardeners and common little Yorkshire housemaids, with springtime and with secret gardens coming alive day by day, and also with a boy and his "creatures," there was no room left for the disagreeable thought which affected her liver and her digestion and made her yellow and tired.

So long as Colin shut himself up in his room and thought only of his fears and weakness and his detestation of people who looked at him and reflected hourly on humps and early death, he was a hysterical half-crazy little hypochondriac who knew nothing of the sunshine and the spring and also did not know that he could get well and could stand up on his feet if he tried to do it. When new beautiful thoughts began to push out the old hideous ones, life began to come back to him, his blood ran healthily through his veins and strength poured into him like a flood. His scientific experiment was quite practical and simple, and there was nothing weird about it at all. Much more surprising things can happen to anyone who, when a disagreeable or discouraged thought comes into his mind, just has the sense to remember in time and push it out by putting in an agreeable determinedly courageous one. Two things cannot be in one place.

"The Bremen Town Musicians"
The Brothers Grimm

A certain man owned a donkey who for many years helped him haul sacks to the mill without becoming fatigued. Finally, however, the donkey's strength was sapped and it was no longer able to work. Accordingly, its master began to think about how he could best reduce the amount of money he paid for the beast's keep. But the donkey, sensing there was mischief in the air, ran away and started on the road to Bremen. There he planned on becoming a town musician.

After he had been journeying a short while, he came upon a hound, who was lying panting on the road as though he was on his last legs.

"Well, what are you panting so for, Growler?" said the donkey.

"Ah," said the hound, "just because I am so old, and every day I get weaker. Also, since I can no longer keep up with the pack, my master decided to kill me, so I made my exit. But now how am I to earn my bread and stay alive?"

"Do you know what?" said the donkey. "I am going to Bremen and shall there become a town musician. Come and join me in making music. I shall play the lute, and you can beat the kettledrum."

The hound agreed and they traveled on.

After a while, they came upon a cat sitting in the road, with a face as long as a twenty foot scarf.

"Well, why are you so ornery, Whiskers?" asked the donkey.

"Who can be cheerful when he is in as much need as I?" said the cat. "I am getting on in years and my teeth are dull, and I prefer to sit by the stove and purr instead of hunting and chasing mice. Just because of this my mistress wanted to drown me. I made myself scarce, but now I don't know where to go."

"Come with us to Bremen," said the donkey. "You are a great hand at serenading, so you can also become a town musician."

The cat agreed and joined them.

Next the runaways passed by a yard where a barnyard rooster was sitting on the door, crowing with all its might.

"You crow so loud you make my ears ring and my skin get goosebumps," said the donkey. "What is wrong?"

"Since Sunday visitors are coming tomorrow, my owner has no pity, and she has ordered the cook to make me into soup. So I shall have my neck wrung tonight. Therefore, I am crowing with all my might while I still can."

"Come with us, Red-comb," said the donkey. "We are going to Bremen and you will find a much happier fate awaiting you there. You have a clear voice, and when we all make music together, you will add quality to our song."

The rooster allowed himself to be persuaded and all four friends went off together. They could not, however, reach the town in one day, and when evening came they were in a wood where they decided to spend the night. The donkey and the hound lay under a big tree. The cat and the rooster settled themselves in the branches, the rooster flying right up to the top, which he believed was the safest place for him. Before going to sleep he looked in every direction. Suddenly it seemed that he saw a light burning in the distance. He called out to his colleagues that there must be a house not far off, since he clearly saw a light.

"Okay," said the donkey. "Let us set out and head for it; the entertainment here is very poor anyway."

The hound thought the house might contain some bones or meat, and that would please him, so they all set out in the direction of the light. They soon saw it shining more clearly and getting bigger and bigger, till they arrived at a brightly lit robbers' den. The donkey, being the tallest, approached the window and peered in.

"What do you see, old Jackass?" asked the rooster.

"What do I see?" answered the donkey. "Why, a table covered with luscious food and drink, and robbers seated at it enjoying themselves."

"That would just suit us," said the rooster.

"Yes, if we were only in there," responded the donkey.

Then the animals put their heads together in order to decide how to drive the robbers out. At last they hit upon a plan.

The donkey was to take up his position with his forefeet on the window sill, the hound was to jump on his back, the cat to climb up onto the hound, and finally, the rooster was to fly up and stand on the cat's head. When they were thus arranged, at a given signal they all began to perform their music. The donkey hee-hawed, the hound woofed, the cat meowed, and the rooster cock-a-doodle-dooed. They crashed through the window, splintering the panes. The robbers were startled by the horrendous noise. They thought that the devil was coming to join them; so they ran into the forest for fear of their lives. Then the four animals sat down at the table and had themselves a feast; they ate as though they had not eaten in weeks. When they had finished, they put out the light and looked for sleeping quarters.

The donkey lay down on a pile of straw, the hound in back of the door, the cat on the hearth near the warm ashes, and the rooster flew up to the rafters. Their long journey had tired them, so they all soon fell asleep.

When midnight had come and gone, the robbers noticed from afar that the light was no longer burning and that all seemed quiet. The chief robber said, "We should not have been scared by a false alarm." And he ordered one of his fellow robbers to go and examine the house.

Finding all quiet, the messenger went into the kitchen to light a candle. And mistaking the cat's glowing, fiery eyes for live coals, he held a match close to them in order to light it. But the cat would not put up with this— it flew at his face, clawed and scratched. The robber was startled and scared out of his wits; he quickly attempted to run away.

He tried first to get out of the back door, but the hound, who was lying there, jumped up and bit his leg. As he ran across the pile of straw in front of the house, the donkey gave him a good sound kick with his rear legs; while the rooster who had awakened at the uproar cried out from his rafter "Cock-a-doodle-doo."

At this, the robber ran back to his chief as quick as his legs would carry him. He said, "There is an awful witch in the house who breathed on me and then scratched me with her long fingers. Behind the door there stands a man with a knife, who stabbed me, while in the yard lies a black monster who hit me with a club. To top it off, upon the roof the judge is seated, and he called out, 'Bring the devil here!' So I ran away as fast as I could."

From that day on, the robbers did not dare approach the house; this pleased the four Bremen musicians so much that they decided never to leave their house again.

 ## "The Rich Man and the Poor Man"
Anonymous

A poor man went to his rich friend,
And said, with gracious smile:
"I've come to ask if you would lend
Your ass to me awhile."

"My ass, alas, is out today,"
The rich man made reply.
"At nine o'clock it went away,
I don't know where or why."

"Too bad, too bad," the poor man said,
"I'll bid you, then, good day,"
But at that moment, in the shed,
An ass began to bray.

"You lied to me!" the poor man cried.
"'My ass is out' forsooth!
But even if its master lied,
The ass has told the truth."

"I lied?!"—the rich man's face grew red—
"I cannot let that pass!
It's me you should believe, instead
Of trusting a mere ass!"

The poor man turned without a word
And climbed the pathway steep.
On coming to a grove he heard
The bleating of a sheep.

The thirsty sheep had left the flock
In search of water cool
It now was standing by a rock,
And drinking at a pool.

The poor man caught it, tied its feet,
And put it on his back.
He then continued in the heat
To climb the rugged track.

The rich man came that afternoon:
"You stole my sheep, they say.
I want it back and want it soon,
I want it straightaway."

"No sheep of yours is in my shed,
Go search another place,"
The poor man to the rich one said,
And turned away his face.

The rich man was about to go,
When from behind a wall,
He heard a bleat he seemed to know—
A most familiar call.

"My sheep is here!" he roared in rage.
"I hear it calling me.
It's a disgrace for one your age
To lie so shamelessly!"

"You trust that foolish sheep in there?"
The poor man calmly said.
"Far better would it be, I swear,
To trust your friend instead."

"The Emperor's New Clothes"

Hans Christian Andersen

Many years ago there was an Emperor who was so excessively fond of new clothes that he spent all his money on them. He cared nothing about his soldiers, nor for the theatre, nor for driving in the woods except for the sake of showing off his new clothes. He had a costume for every hour in the day, and instead of saying as one does about any other King or Emperor, "He is in his council chamber," here one always said, "The Emperor is in his dressing-room."

Life was very gay in the great town where he lived; hosts of strangers came to visit it every day, and among them one day two swindlers. They gave themselves out as weavers, and said that they knew how to weave the most beautiful stuffs imaginable. Not only were the colors and patterns unusually fine, but the clothes that were made of these stuffs had the peculiar quality of becoming invisible to every person who was not fit for the office he held, or if he was impossibly dull.

"Those must be splendid clothes," thought the Emperor. "By wearing them I should be able to discover which men in my kingdom are unfitted for their posts. I shall distinguish the wise men from the fools. Yes, I certainly must order some of that stuff to be woven for me."

He paid the two swindlers a lot of money in advance so that they might begin their work at once.

They did put up two looms and pretended to weave, but they had nothing whatever upon their shuttles. At the outset they asked for a quantity of the finest silk and the purest gold thread, all of which they put into their own bags while they worked away at the empty looms far into the night.

"I should like to know how these weavers are getting on with the stuff," thought the Emperor; but he felt a little queer when he reflected that anyone who was stupid or unfit for his post would not be able to see it. He certainly thought that he need have no fears for himself, but still he thought he would send somebody else first to see how it was getting on. Everybody in the town knew what wonderful power the stuff possessed, and everyone was anxious to see how stupid his neighbor was.

"I will send my faithful old minister to the weavers," thought the Emperor. "He will be best able to see how the stuff looks, for he is a clever man and no one fulfills his duties better than he does!"

So the good old minister went into the room where the two swindlers sat working at the empty loom.

"Heaven preserve us!" thought the old minister, opening his eyes very wide. "Why, I can't see a thing!" But he took care not to say so.

Both the swindlers begged him to be good enough to step a little nearer, and asked if he did not think it a good pattern and beautiful coloring. They pointed to the empty loom, and the poor old minister stared as hard as he could but he could not see anything, for of course there was nothing to see.

"Good heavens!" thought he, "it is possible that I am a fool? I have never thought so and nobody must know it. Am I not fit for my post? It will never do to say that I cannot see the stuffs."

"Well, sir, you don't say anything about the stuff," said the one who was pretending to weave.

"Oh, it is beautiful! quite charming!" said the old minister looking through his spectacles; "this pattern and these colors! I will certainly tell the Emperor that the stuff pleases me very much."

"We are delighted to hear you say so," said the swindlers, and then they named all the colors and described the peculiar pattern. The old minister paid great attention to what they said, so as to be able to repeat it when he got home to the Emperor.

Then the swindlers went on to demand more money, more silk, and more gold, to be able to proceed with the weaving; but they put it all into their own pockets—not a single strand was ever put into the loom, but they went on as before weaving at the empty loom.

The Emperor soon sent another faithful official to see how the stuff was getting on, and if it would soon be ready. The same thing happened to him as to the minister; he looked and looked, but as there was only the empty loom, he could see nothing at all.

"Is not this a beautiful piece of stuff?" said both the swindlers, showing and explaining the beautiful pattern and colors which were not there to be seen.

"I know I am not a fool!" thought the man, "so it must be that I am unfit for my good post! It is very strange though! However, one must not let it appear!" So he praised the stuff he did not see, and assured them of his delight in the beautiful colors and the originality of the design. "It is absolutely charming!" he said to the Emperor. Everybody in the town was talking about this splendid stuff.

Now the Emperor thought he would like to see it while it was still on the loom. So accompanied by a number of selected courtiers, among whom were the two faithful officials who had already seen the imaginary stuff, he went to visit the crafty imposters, who were working away as hard as ever they could at the empty loom.

"It is magnificent!" said both the honest officials. "Only see, Your Majesty, what a design! What colors!" And they pointed to the empty loom, for they thought no doubt the others could see the stuff.

"What!" thought the Emperor; "I see nothing at all! This is terrible! Am I a fool? Am I not fit to be Emperor? Why, nothing worse could happen to me!"

"Oh, it is beautiful!" said the Emperor. "It has my highest approval!" and he nodded his satisfaction as he gazed at the empty loom. Nothing would induce him to say that he could not see anything.

The whole suite gazed and gazed, but saw nothing more than all the others. However, they all exclaimed with His Majesty, "It is very beautiful!" and they advised him to wear a suit made of this wonderful cloth on the occasion of a great procession which was just about to take place. "It is magnificent! gorgeous! excellent!" went from mouth to mouth; they were all equally delighted with it. The Emperor gave each of the rogues an order of knighthood to be worn in their buttonholes and the title of "Gentlemen Weavers."

The swindlers sat up the whole night, before the day on which the procession was to take place, burning sixteen candles, so that people might see how anxious they were to get the Emperor's new clothes ready. They pretended to take the stuff off the loom. They cut it out in the air with a huge pair of scissors, and they stitched away with needles without any thread in them. At last they said, "Now the Emperor's new clothes are ready!"

The Emperor, with his grandest courtiers, went to them himself, and both the swindlers raised one arm in the air, as if they were holding something, and said, "See, these are the trousers, this is the coat, here is the mantle!" and so on. "It is as light as a spider's web. One might think one had nothing on, but that is the very beauty of it!"

"Yes!" said all the courtiers, but they could not see anything, for there was nothing to see.

"Will Your Imperial Majesty be graciously pleased to take off your clothes," said the imposters, "so that we may put on the new ones, along here before the great mirror?"

The Emperor took off all his clothes, and the imposters pretended to give him one article of dress after the other, of the new ones which they had pretended to make. They pretended to fasten something around his waist and to tie on something; this was the train, and the Emperor turned round and round in front of the mirror.

"How well His Majesty looks in the new clothes! How becoming they are!" cried all the people round. "What a design, and what colors! They are most gorgeous robes!"

"The canopy is waiting outside which is to be carried over Your Majesty in the procession," said the master of the ceremonies.

"Well, I am quite ready," said the Emperor. "Don't the clothes fit well?" and then he turned round again in front of the mirror, so that he would seem to be looking at his grand things.

The chamberlains who were to carry the train stooped and pretended to lift it from the ground with both hands, and they walked along with their hands in the air. They dared not let it appear that they could not see anything.

Then the Emperor walked along in the procession under the gorgeous canopy, and everybody in the streets and at the windows exclaimed, "How beautiful the Emperor's new clothes are! What a splendid train! And they fit to perfection!" Nobody would let it appear that he could see nothing, for then he would not be fit for his post, or else he was a fool.

None of the Emperor's clothes had been so successful before.

"But he has got nothing on," said a little child.

"Oh, listen to the innocent," said its father; and one person whispered to the other what the child had said. "He has nothing on; a child says he has nothing on!"

"But he has nothing on!" at last cried all the people.

The Emperor writhed, for he knew it was true, but he thought "the procession must go on now," so he held himself stiffer than ever, and the chamberlains held up the invisible train.

"Macavity, the Mystery Cat"

T. S. Eliot

Macavity's a Mystery Cat: he's called the Hidden Paw—
For he's the master criminal who can defy the Law.
He's the bafflement of Scotland Yard, the Flying Squad's despair:
For when they reach the scene of crime—Macavity's not there!

Macavity, Macavity, there's no one like Macavity,
He's broken every human law, he breaks the law of gravity.
His powers of levitation would make a fakir stare,
And when you reach the scene of crime—*Macavity's not there!*
You may seek him in the basement, you may look up in the air—
But I tell you once and once again, *Macavity's not there!*

Macavity's a ginger cat, he's very tall and thin;
You would know him if you saw him, for his eyes are sunken in.
His brow is deeply lined with thought, his head is highly domed;
His coat is dusty from neglect, his whiskers are uncombed.
He sways his head from side to side, with movements like a
    snake;
And when you think he's half asleep, he's always wide awake.

Macavity, Macavity, there's no one like Macavity,
For he's a fiend in feline shape, a monster of depravity.
You may meet him in a by-street, you may see him in the
    square—
But when a crime's discovered, then *Macavity's not there!*

He's outwardly respectable. (They say he cheats at cards.)
And his footprints are not found in any file of Scotland Yard's.
And when the larder's looted, or the jewel-case is rifled,
Or when the milk is missing, or another Peke's been stifled,
Or the greenhouse glass is broken, and the trellis past repair—
Ay, there's the wonder of the thing! *Macavity's not there!*

And when the Foreign Office find a Treaty's gone astray,
Or the Admiralty lose some plans and drawings by the way,

There may be a scrap of paper in the hall or on the stair—
But it's useless to investigate—*Macavity's not there!*
And when the loss has been disclosed, the Secret Service say:
"It must have been Macavity!"—but he's a mile away.
You'll be sure to find him resting, or a-licking of his thumbs,
Or engaged in doing complicated long division sums.

Macavity, Macavity, there's no one like Macavity,
There never was a Cat of such deceitfulness and suavity.
He always has an alibi, and one or two to spare:
At whatever time the deed took place—MACAVITY WASN'T
    THERE!
And they say that all the Cats whose wicked deeds are widely
    known,
(I might mention Mungojerrie, I might mention Griddlebone)
Are nothing more than agents for the Cat who all the time
Just controls their operations: the Napoleon of Crime!

"The Rat's Daughter"

Japanese Fable

There lived once in Japan a rat and his wife who came from an old and noble family. They had one beautiful and clever daughter of whom they were very proud. She could gnaw through the hardest wood and run like the wind. Her coat was a lovely soft silky brown and her pointed teeth shone like pearls. Many of the other young female rats envied her good looks.

Her proud parents expected her to marry well. Her father was a rat through and through and happily dreamed of his daughter marrying a handsome young rat from their own group. There was a particularly fine specimen that he thought would be suitable: a young rat with long moustaches that touched the ground and whose family was even nobler and older than his own.

The rat's mother had very different ideas, however. She despised all rats outside her own family and could not consider that any of them would be good enough for her own darling daughter.

"My daughter shall never marry a mere rat," she declared, holding her head high. "With her beauty and talents she has a right to marry someone better than that."

So the husband and wife quarreled day and night about who would make a suitable husband for their child. But they never even thought to ask their daughter what she herself thought.

At last the wife said:

"I think only the mighty and powerful Sun is good enough for my child—let us pay him a visit."

The husband reluctantly agreed and they set off with their daughter to visit the Sun in his golden palace. Once there the wife looked up at the Sun and said bravely:

"Noble king, here is our precious daughter and we are offering her to you in marriage as we know that you are the most powerful being on earth, and only you will be worthy of her."

Now the Sun was amused at this proposal but he hadn't the slightest intention of marrying anybody, least of all a rat, so he said carefully:

"It is very kind of you to offer your beautiful daughter to me, but I really cannot accept—after all I am not really the most powerful being on earth: the Cloud is. He can pass over me and stop my light whenever he wishes." At that moment the Cloud did indeed cover the Sun and he was blocked from view.

The husband and wife agreed to ask the Cloud immediately. Certainly, they thought, the Cloud was more powerful than the Sun, as at any time he could cover the Sun whether the Sun wanted this or not.

The Cloud was rather taken aback when the rats offered their daughter to him in marriage. He did not want to offend the couple, but he did not want to marry a rat—even a very beautiful one—and so he said:

"It is kind of the Sun to describe me as the most powerful being in the world, but he really isn't right. The Wind is far more powerful than I am, watch this—" and at that moment a great gust of Wind blew the Cloud across the sky.

The husband and wife saw that the Wind was more powerful than the Cloud and asked him if he would like to marry their darling daughter. The Wind was secretly appalled at the idea—he was far too busy traveling around the world to be stuck in one place and married to a rat. So he said in a great booming voice:

"The Cloud is quite right—I am more powerful than he is but I am not more powerful than that Wall over there. He has the power to stop me in my flight. Ask him to marry your daughter."

The three rats all stared at the huge brick wall looming over them.

The wife said:

"Well, Wall, as you are the most powerful being, we can offer you the hand of our beautiful daughter in marriage."

The Wall was considering this proposal when all at once there was a terrible wailing noise. It was the young female rat.

"I don't want to marry a Wall!" she cried. "How can you all be so cruel and not consider my feelings? I would have married the Sun, or the Cloud or the Wind, because that was what you wished, but not an ugly old Wall!"

The Wall was somewhat hurt at this outburst and declared that he had no wish to marry a rat anyway.

"It is quite true," he said, "that I can stop the Wind, but there is some-one who is more powerful than I—that is the rat who lives under me. He can reduce me to powder, simply by gnawing with his teeth. A fine young male rat would surely make the best companion for your daughter."

The young female rat was delighted at this suggestion and said she would love to marry the handsome young rat with the moustaches that touched the ground, whom her father had suggested in the first place. Her mother was happy to agree now that she knew how powerful rats really were.

So they all returned home. The lady rat married the handsome rat with the moustaches and a wonderful wedding celebration was enjoyed by all.

Chapter 9

Performing Literature from Around the World

Learning Objectives

After completing this chapter, you should be able to

- use literature as a means of traveling to another culture
- discuss how the cultures of other countries is reflected in their literature
- share your understanding of the cultures and literature of other countries with an audience
- perform literature from a different culture

Technology—telecommunications, communication satellite systems, the fax, the Internet, and e-mail—has made our lives easier. Have you also considered how this technology has shrunk our world? We can get in touch virtually instantly with people in all but the remotest corners of the world. The concept of our being part of a global community is now a reality. As a result, every day we discover that we have things in common with people of different countries and cultures.

And yet, we are different from one another as well. Recall the Vulcan greeting in the television series *Star Trek:* "Greetings! I am pleased to see that we are different. May we together become greater than the sum of both of us." In order to live harmoniously in today's global village, we must make a huge leap from suspicion to mutual respect and understanding for others. As an interpreter of literature, you are in an enviable position both to increase your understanding of the various cultures that make up our world and to share that understanding with audiences.

Nearly three hundred years ago, the poet Bashō wrote:

> Nearing Autumn's close.
>
> My neighbor—
>
> How does he live, I wonder?

Many of the literary selections included in the other chapters are by American authors. In this chapter, you will focus on the literature of other countries and learn about their diverse cultures, discovering what is different and what we have in common. Through analyzing and interpreting literature from around the world, you will learn that we share basic emotions—joy, fear, sorrow, love, anger. Performing the literature of other countries will help you understand your place in the global community as well as the cultures and peoples in other parts of the world.

Using Literature in Performance as a Cultural Bridge

People have always been curious about how other people live and think. Experiencing the literature of the United States as an interpreter makes it possible for you to connect with and share the feelings of the people of this land. Your interpretation is a key to making connections with and gaining entry into the minds and emotions of people of different nations too.

John F. Kennedy said: "Our most basic common link is that we all inhabit this planet." Certainly, we are all alike, and yet, we are all different. The effective interpreter of literature appreciates similarities and accepts differences. Your intercultural encounters with literature will enable you to establish contact with people from around the globe. Through interpreting the literature of cultures from around the world, you gain a greater understanding of the fact that reality is not the same for all people. You also increase your chances for developing new and different ways of looking at the world. After all, literature is the lens through which we see a culture.

Use your interpretative art to examine literature from around the world. In studying a variety of works, you can come to appreciate the ideas, beliefs, customs, and attitudes that characterize each group of people. In this way you can come to know something about the people and to understand that people in other societies view themselves and the world differently.

For example, different cultures exhibit different attitudes toward the concepts of time and nature. Such attitudes, as well as the behaviors through which these attitudes are manifested, reveal themselves in the literature of that culture. For example, past-oriented cultures stress the importance of prior events. They value history, tradition, and established religions. In addition, they strongly believe that the past should guide them in making decisions and identifying truth. In contrast, present-oriented cultures contend that it is the present moment that contains the most significance. For them it is the here and now that counts, not some vague, amorphous future. Future-oriented cultures keep their eye on the future, plan for it, and are optimistic about it. For them, the future will be more fulfilling and better than the present. They believe it is where they will find the most happiness.

Exploring Cultural Variability

By familiarizing ourselves with the literature of other cultures, we develop a better understanding of how cultures are similar and how they differ. Two key variables essential to understanding cultural similarities and differences are individualism versus collectivism and low- and high-context communication.

Individualism Versus Collectivism. If a culture promotes **individualism,** it gives precedence to the goals of individuals. Individuals are supposed to look after themselves and immediate family members. "I" assumes a greater importance than "we." Included among the cultures which tend to be predominantly individualistic are Ireland, Italy, Sweden, Canada, and the United States.

In contrast, if a culture promotes **collectivism,** it stresses the importance of the group, emphasizing harmony and cooperation and requiring that individuals conform to and fit into the group. For example, in Kenyan culture, the tribe is paramount; no one is an isolated individual. Other cultures in which collectivism tends to predominate are Argentina, China, India, Japan, Korea, Mexico, and Saudi Arabia. In general, Arab, African, Asian, and Latin cultures tend to be collectivistic.

Low- and High-Context Communication. A **low-context message** is one in which a message is very explicitly coded, affording little room for ambiguity. Communication between members of a culture that values low-context messages tends to be clear and direct. People "get to the point."

In contrast, a **high-context message** tends to be rather indirect instead of explicit. Persons in a culture that relies on high-context messages expect other members of the culture to understand them without their having to be specific. They talk around points.

In general, low-context communication is prevalent in individualistic cultures, while high-context communication predominates in collectivistic cultures.

Establishing Cultural Connections

A Confucian saying tells us, "Human beings draw close to one another by their common nature, but habits and customs keep them apart." The interpretation of literature gives you the opportunity to explore those different habits and customs and to find ways to help your audience understand and identify with them. As theorist Edward T. Hall points out, "There is not one aspect of human life that is not touched and altered by culture. This means personality, how people express themselves, the way they think, how they move, how problems are solved . . . as well as how economic and government systems are put together and function." Culture teaches you how to act, feel, and believe, as it helps you to distinguish proper from improper behavior.

Remember, oral interpretation is a social art. Widening your literary maps will allow your audiences to experience the commonality of all humanity through a variety of cultures.

Chapter **9** Performance Applications

IDEA ENCORE

Every day technology brings us closer together, and we are finally recognizing that what connects us to our fellow inhabitants of this planet are the feelings that lie beneath the surface. We discover those emotions in literature, and, more and more, the literature of other cultures reach out and speak to us.

This chapter focused on the great diversity of literary texts and the development of empathy for the cultures and writers of literature from backgrounds different from that of the works considered in other chapters. The chapter suggested that literature can become a cultural bridge and facilitate our appreciation of cultural variability. It is by establishing cultural connections through the interpretation of literature that we enable audiences to experience both the diversity and the commonality of all humanity.

PERFORMER'S SHOWCASE & JOURNAL
A World's Fair of Literature

Divide the class into small groups. Each group should select a foreign country to explore in terms of literature and culture. Each member of your group should select a piece of literature from that part of the world. To begin your search for your individual selection for performance, you may first consider the sampling of cuttings from world literature in this chapter. However, you should also explore other possibilities in a world literature anthology, do research at the library, or check with your foreign language department for recommendations on literature available in translation. In addition to sharing your interpretation of literature with your class, your group may also consider bringing in samples of your chosen country's culture—foods, clothing, or recordings of music representative of that country.

As you analyze the following literature and rehearse your performance, consider how the different cultures represented compare and contrast with that of the United States. For each selection, write in your notebook your responses to the following questions.

1. What type of experience is being described in the literature?
2. What theme or themes are treated?
3. What types of characters, if any, are revealed in the literature? What attitudes, beliefs, and ideas do these characters express?
4. What moods are highlighted in your interpretation?
5. What does the literature tell you about the foreign country, its culture, and its inhabitants?
6. What feelings do you want your audience to experience as you share your interpretation of the literature with them?

SELECTIONS FOR FURTHER WORK

"Out of Darkness"

Alex La Guma (South Africa)

The smell of unwashed bodies and sweaty blankets was sharp, and the heat in the cell hung as thick as cotton wool. The man on the rope mat beside me turned, grunted, and flung a long arm across my face.

"How do you do?" he said, waking up and giggling.

"Very well," I replied soothingly, for he was a little mad.

In the dark the other bodies turned, cursed, and tried to settle back into perspiring sleep.

"Did Joey bring the eggs?"

I could make out the dim shapeless bulge of his body curled up on the mat. He had entered the seventh year of his ten-year sentence for culpable homicide, and being shut up so long had unhinged him somewhat. He was neither staring mad nor violent. His insanity was of a gentle quality that came in spells. It was then that he would talk. Otherwise he was clamped up tight and retired, like a snail withdrawn into its shell. He was friendly enough but it was the friendliness of a man on the other side of a peephole.

To the rest of the inmates he was known as Ou Kakkelak, Old Cockroach, and was either the butt of their depraved humour or was completely ignored. He took everything with a gentle smile. From parts of his conversations during his spells I gained the impression that he was an educated man and might have been a schoolmaster before he had committed his crime. . . .

"Is the heat troubling you?" I asked, as kindly as I could make it. "It's damn hot, isn't it?" He did not reply. I decided to do a little probing. "You speak of Cora now and then. Who is she?" But he turned on his side and was asleep again.

In the morning there was the usual shouting and clanging of doors. Blankets were folded; the long line of convicts streamed down to the yards. The guards stood by, lashing out with their leather belts. . . .

We squatted, packed into the cement yard, and breakfasted on the mealie meal and black, bitter coffee. Old Cockroach sat near me, smiling his gentle, vacant smile and wolfing his food.

I saw him again when we were locked up after supper. He sank down in his place beside me. Around us secret cigarettes were emerging. . . . Figures in washed-out red shirts and canvas shirts packed the floor of the cell.

"Here we are," Old Cockroach said and giggled at me. "The wreckage which mankind, on its onward march, left behind."

"Well," I answered, smiling at him. "Perhaps it's better to say that we are the results of mankind's imperfections."

"Perhaps. Perhaps. I wonder where Joey is tonight?" He sat with his knees drawn up and his long arms clasped about his shins, gazing vacantly about at the faces around him. "Ah, there he is now."

I looked and said, "That's Smiley Abrams. Remember? That's not Joey. That's Smiley Abrams."

"Oh, ja. He's here for murder. I believe he's killed three people in his lifetime. They got him for the last one. An ape-man roaming a jungle. Here he is king. In a cave the cave man is king."

He fell silent again. . . . I sat with my back against the concrete wall and looked at Old Cockroach. He was tall and thin and bony, folded up now like a carpenter's ruler. His skin was as dark as burnt leather, and he had slightly negroid features and kinky hair going gray, close to his skull, like a tight-fitting cap. . . .

"Cora," he rambled. "I think. . . . "

"She'll turn up on visiting day," I told him, although I knew she would not . . . because nobody had ever visited him for as long as I had been in. I began to wish I could learn more about him. . . .

The sun faded beyond the barred windows like lights being dimmed in a theatre. It had become hot again in the casern, and from the bucket latrine came the sharp, acrid smell of ammonia. Old Cockroach lay back on his mat and pulled the thin blanket up to his waist. He did not seem to feel the heat, but just lay there. . . . It was as if he had drawn an invisible armor around himself. . . .

The next night started much the same. The heat was overpowering, and the stench of bodies increased quickly. Men fought and clawed around the water buckets, snarling like jackals around their carrion. The cave man, Smiley Abrams, hurled men from the center of the turmoil, growling and snapping at his cringing subjects. . . .

"A slave has revolted," Old Cockroach observed in a voice as gentle as the fall of dust. "Do you know that the whole of mankind's history consists of a series of revolutions?"

"You're an educated man, Old Cockroach," I said. "You don't belong here. How did you come to kill anybody? If you don't mind me asking."

"I used to be a schoolmaster," he replied, confirming my old suspicion. Then his mind wandered again, and he murmured, "I hope Joey brings that book he borrowed last week. *Treasure Island.* Have you ever read *Treasure Island?*"

. . .The brawl around the water buckets had subsided, since they both had been emptied. . . . Men sat around, hunched stark naked under the light, exploring their clothes and blankets for lice. . . .

Old Cockroach had settled down on his blankets and I could hear him scratching himself. . . . From all around us grunts, curses, and tiny cries came like suppressed voices out of hell.

". . . Cora," Old Cockroach's voice came out of the dark, quiet as the trickle of sweat. "Cora."

"Take it easy, old man," I murmured. . . .

I decided to probe a little more. "By the way, who is Cora?"

Silence. Then he said, "Hullo, Joey. I'm glad you've come. I'll tell you a story. Would you like to listen to a story?"

"Okay. That would be fine."

"All right, then, it was a long time ago. A very long time ago, I think. I was in love with her. You don't think this is going to be a silly story, do you?"

"Certainly not."

"I was a teacher at a junior school and was doing a varsity course in my spare time. And I was in love with Cora. She was beautiful. . . . Her skin was soft and smooth and the color of rich cream. She was almost white you see. I was in love with her. . . . "

He was silent again while the sounds of sleep went on around us. When he went on his voice had taken on a dullness. "Then she began to find that she could pass as white, and I was black. She begun to go to the white places . . . Places where I couldn't take her. . . . She drifted away from me, but I kept on loving her.

"I talked to her, pleaded with her. But she wouldn't take any notice of what I said. I became angry. I wept. I raved . . . I groveled. . . . But it wasn't of any use. She said I was selfish and trying to deny her the good things of life. . . .

"In the end she turned on me. She told me to go to hell. She slapped my face and called me a black nigger. . . . "

"Then you lost your head and killed her," I said quietly. "That's why you're here now.'"

"Oh no," Old Cockroach answered. "I could never have done that to Cora. I did lose my head, but it was Joey whom I killed. He said I was a damn fool for going off over a damn play-white. . . . So I hit him, and he cracked his skull on something. Ah, here's Joey now. Hullo, Joey. I hope you've brought my book. . . ."

"Telephone Conversation"
Wole Soyinka (Nigeria)

The price seemed reasonable, location
Indifferent. The landlady swore she lived
Off premises. Nothing remained
But self-confession. "Madam," I warned,
"I hate a wasted journey—I am—African."
Silence. Silenced transmission of
Pressurized good-breeding. Voice, when it came,
Lipstick-coated, long gold-rolled
Cigarette-holder pipped. Caught I was, foully.
"HOW DARK?". . . I had not misheard . . . "ARE YOU LIGHT
OR VERY DARK?" Button B. Button A. Stench
Of rancid breath of public hide-and-speak.
Red booth. Red pillar box. Red double-tiered
Omnibus squelching tar. It *was* real! Shamed
By ill-mannered silence, surrender
Pushed dumbfoundment to beg simplification.
Considerate she was, varying the emphasis—
"ARE YOU DARK? OR VERY LIGHT?" Revelation came.
"You mean—like plain or milk chocolate?"
Her assent was clinical, crushing in its light
Impersonality. Rapidly, wave-length adjusted,
I chose. "West African sepia"—and as afterthought,
"Down in my passport." Silence for spectroscopic
Flight of fancy, till truthfulness clanged her accent
Hard on the mouthpiece. "WHAT'S THAT?" conceding
"DON'T KNOW WHAT THAT IS." "Like brunette."
"THAT'S DARK, ISN'T IT?" "Not altogether.
Facially, I am brunette, but madam, you should see
the rest of me. Palm of my hand, soles of my feet

Are a peroxide blonde. Friction, caused—

Foolishly madam—by sitting down, has turned

My bottom raven black—One moment, madam!"—sensing

Her receiver rearing on the thunderclap

About my ears——"Madam," I pleaded, "wouldn't you rather

See for yourself?"

"The Blind Dog"

R. K. Narayan (India)

It was not a very impressive or high-class dog; it was one of those commonplace dogs one sees everywhere—color of white and dust, tail mutilated at a young age by God knows whom, born in the street, and bred on the leavings and garbage of the marketplace. He had spotty eyes and undistinguished carriage and needless pugnacity. Before he was two years old he had earned the scars of a hundred fights on his body. When he needed rest on hot afternoons he lay curled up under the culvert at the Eastern gate of the market. In the evenings he set out on his daily rounds, loafed in the surrounding streets and lanes, engaged himself in skirmishes, picked up edibles on the roadside, and was back at the market gate by nightfall.

This life went on for three years. And then occurred a change in his life. A beggar, blind of both eyes, appeared at the market gate. An old woman led him up there early in the morning, seated him at the gate, and came up again at midday with some food, gathered his coins, and took him home at night.

The dog was sleeping near by. He was stirred by the smell of food. He got up, came out of his shelter, and stood before the blind man, wagging his tail and gazing expectantly at the bowl, as he was eating his sparse meal. The blind man swept his arms about and asked: "Who is there?" At which the dog went up and licked his hand. The blind man stroked its coat gently tail to ear and said: "What a beauty you are. Come with me—" He threw a handful of food which the dog ate gratefully. It was perhaps an auspicious moment for starting a friendship. They met every day there, and the dog cut off much of its rambling to sit up beside the blind man and watch him receive alms morning to evening. In course of time observing him, the dog understood that the passersby must give a coin, and whoever went away without dropping a coin was chased by the dog; he tugged the edge of their clothes by his teeth and pulled them back to the old man at the gate and let go only after something was dropped in his bowl. . . .

"Babiy Yar"

Yevgeni Yevtushenko (Russia)

Over Babiy Yar
there are no memorials.
The steep hillside like a rough inscription.
I am frightened.
Today I am as old as the Jewish race.
I seem to myself a Jew at this moment.
I, wandering in Egypt.
I, crucified. I perishing.
Even today the mark of the nails.
I think also of Dreyfus. I am he.
The Philistine my judge and my accuser.
Cut off by bars and cornered,
ringed round, spat at, lied about;
the screaming ladies with the Brussels lace
poke me in the face with parasols.
I am also a boy in Belostok,
the dropping blood spreads across the floor,
the public-bar heroes are rioting
in an equal stench of garlic and of drink.
I have no strength, go spinning from a boot,
shriek useless prayers that they don't listen to;
with a cackle of "Thrash the kikes and save Russia!"
the corn-chandler is beating up my mother.
I seem to myself like Anna Frank
to be transparent as an April twig
and am in love, I have no need for words,
I need for us to look at one another.
How little we have to see or to smell
separated from foliage and the sky,
how much, how much in the dark room
gently embracing each other.

They're coming. Don't be afraid.
The booming and banging of the spring.
It's coming this way. Come to me.
Quickly, give me your lips.
They're battering in the door. Roar of the ice.
Over Babiy Yar
rustle of the wild grass.
The trees look threatening, look like judges.
And everything is one silent cry.
Taking my hat off
I feel myself slowly going grey.
And I am one silent cry
over the many thousands of the buried;
am every old man killed here,
every child killed here.
O my Russian people, I know you.
Your nature is international.
Foul hands rattle your clean name.
I know the goodness of my country.
How horrible it is that pompous title
the anti-semites calmly call themselves,
Society of the Russian People.
No part of me can ever forget it.
When the last anti-semite on the earth
is buried for ever
let the International ring out.
No Jewish blood runs among my blood,
but I am as bitterly and hardly hated
by every anti-semite
as if I were a Jew. By this
I am a Russian.

"Invasion"
Roman Podolny (Russia)

One fine spring day in the year 2074, She and He sat on a bench in the midst of a tropical forest, preserved as a sanctuary. Their little go-everywhere plane dozed quietly under a nearby palm.

Even the wind was still, not to disturb them. And there was not another living soul for a hundred kilometers around. But at the moment when His lips came close to Hers, there was a strange hiss, some unknown force thrust them apart, and on the bench between them appeared, from heaven knows where, a bearded little old man.

Instantly grasping the situation, the stranger said in a frightened voice:

"Forgive me, I had no intention. . . . " But he quickly recovered his self-possession and changed from apologetic to solemn tones. "You will, of course, forgive my intrusion when you learn that I am a visitor from the distant past. . . . "

He had not finished his sentence when the young man crossed his arms and clasped his own shoulders, whispering in despair:

"I must be cursed! Another one!" He turned to the girl. "I swear I had nothing to do with it."

"I understand," she said coldly.

"But I don't!" protested the visitor. "Why don't you welcome me?"

The young man mastered himself sufficiently to answer:

"For the six millionth time? It's enough that we welcomed the first one."

"But I have invented a machine for traveling into the future! I was the first to test it!"

"Congratulations," he said drily. "We studied you at school. . . . But your machine . . . well . . . I mean, those who left later came earlier. It happens. Don't upset yourself. Better tell me something," and the young man's gloomy face brightened. "Why is it that visitors from the past always appear in the most inconvenient times? After all, this sends the whole theory of probability into the antiworld. Even the Council of the Wise cannot make head or tail of it. Couldn't something be done about it?"

"It's the fourth time he was interrupted just as he was going to say he loves me," She sighed resentfully.

"Again, forgive me. . . . As for your question . . . If you studied me at school, you know that the time machine does not travel with the passenger. It merely shoots him forward, across so many years—approximately, of course. And the properties of space-time are such that a man who travels in time also moves in space, and it's impossible to foresee. . . . " The great inventor was now speaking in the manner of a lecturer.

"We know it without you," said the young man, evidently losing all interest in his neighbor.

"Um . . . excuse me, but what about me now? I'm sure you have already invented a machine for traveling back into the past? I would like to go home."

"Ah, if we had! All the six million of you only wanted to take a peek at the future and then go home. If they didn't would so many have come? Every one of them was desperately eager to go back to his relatives and friends as soon as possible. Eight years ago, after the first visits, the Council of the Wise transferred forty million physicists and mathematicians to work on this problem. True, some of them felt that such a machine was impossible because it would violate the law of cause and effect, but we're used to manipulating natural laws. And meantime, until the problem is solved, the great Nurden suggested sending our guests further into the future—into a time when people have learned to travel back and forth in time. We've sent on nearly four million. But then a poet suddenly asked a question: 'If travel into the past is possible, how is it that no one has come to us from the future?' And so we had to liquidate the whole project. And we stopped sending our visitors into the future: that would have meant merely shoving our own problems onto someone else's shoulders."

"What problems?"

"What problems? Don't we have to console you, and give you medical care, and spend decades retraining you?" . . .

The great Nurden stepped onto the podium and looked at the audience with his kindly eyes.

"I think," he began, "that I can bring you good news. According to our calculations, the last of the six million, twenty-four thousand, five hundred and thirty-three persons sent into our era from the year 1974 has just arrived. The second invasion will take place about two centuries hence. We must accept those who have been sent three hundred years into the future. But in the next two centuries we shall have time to prepare. . . . "

The podium on which Nurden stood rocked violently. And the physicist received a most painful jab in the side as a badly embarrassed young man appeared next to him.

"You, Nikolay?" the great man gasped. "But you were the first to arrive from the past, eight years ago, and we immediately dispatched you into the future. . . . "

"Forgive me, they must have miscalculated," the uninvited guest whispered miserably. "I never meant. . . . "

Oemaru (Japan)

I sit like Buddha
　　but the mosquitoes
　　　keep biting.

Bashō (Japan)

Clouds come from time to time—
　　and bring to men a chance to rest
　　　from looking at the moon.

Buson (Japan)

The piercing chill I feel:
　　my dead wife's comb, in our bedroom,
　　　under my heel . . .

Issa (Japan)

At the butterflies
　　the caged bird gazes, envying—
　　　just watch its eyes!

Chibo (Japan)

Even the sparrows
　　can hardly lift their feet
　　　in the hot sand.

"Serves You Right, Beggar"

Hsu Chih-Mo (China)

"Kindhearted ladies, charitable sirs,"

    The northwest wind slashes his face like a sharp
    knife.

"Give me a little bit of your leftovers, just a little bit!"

    A patch of dark shadow curls up near the gate.

"Have pity, my wealthy lord, I'm dying of hunger,"

    Inside the gate there are jade cups, warm fire and
    laughter.

"Have pity, my lord of good fortunes, I'm dying of cold."

    Outside the gate the northwest wind chuckles,

      "Serves you right, beggar!"

I am but a pile of black shadows, trembling,

Lying like a worm on the frontage road of humanity;

I wish only a bit of the warmth of sympathy

To shelter what's left of me, after repeated carving. . . .

 "A Withered Tree"

Han Yü (China)

Not a twig or a leaf on the old tree,

Wind and frost harm it no more.

A man could pass through the hole in its belly,

Ants crawl searching under its peeling bark.

Its only lodger, the toadstool which dies in a morning,

The birds no longer visit in the twilight.

But its wood can still spark tinder.

It does not care yet to be only the void at its heart.

"The Pawnshop"
Chu Hsiang (China)

Beauty runs a pawnshop,
Accepting only the hearts of men.
When the time comes for them to redeem their belongings,
She has already closed the door.

from "To Hiroshima"
Ai Ch'ing (China)

You should be a beautiful harbor
With mountains on three sides, and one side open to a plain.
Embraced by the hills, your city
Spreads like a fan southward.
Seven streams feed the bay,
Warm and moist sea breezes come from the south
To cheer the blossoms blanketing the seashore,
Where seaweeds drape their tassels and ribbons.
Hiroshima, you are an ancient city
Scented with sandalwood.
Over the years your thousands of residents
Have worked diligently, like bees.
The noise of berthing boats filled the days,
And songs and music accompanied the long nights.

None of them ever wanted war—
These common Japanese workers and farmers,
Of Nagasaki or Hiroshima,
None of them ever wanted war.
They nursed no hatred
Against the Chinese or the Malayans.

The Japanese never sought a rubber plant in Ceylon,
Or a coconut plantation in Java,
Or a colony on the Mekong River,
To support any claim to a conqueror's fame.
These people gained nothing from the war;
The war fattened other people,
Not them.
Yet, one morning
When sirens had just stirred people awake,
A sudden flash, without any noise,
Slashed the sky from the east westward.
Everyone knew disaster had arrived.

The survivors
Have become deformed, mostly—
As if meant to tell the world
Of their experience of horror . . . .

Hiroshima, you are the eyewitness,
You must rise from the disaster.
Your existence itself is a declaration,
For you have recorded the cruelty of war.
You must speak in defense of peace,
And tell the world,
How the dead died,
And how the survivors live.

Today—Silence, please, everybody,
Let Hiroshima speak.

"On My Short-Sightedness"
Prem Chaya (Thailand)

To my short-sighted eyes,
The world seems better far
Than artificial aid

To sight would warrant it:
The earth is just as green,
The sky a paler blue;
Many a blurred outline
Of overlapping hue;
Shapes, forms are indistinct;
Distance a mystery;
Often a common scene
Conceals a new beauty;
Ugliness is hidden
In a curtain of mist;
And hard, cruel faces
Lose their malignity.
So do not pity me
For my short-sighted eyes;
They see an unknown world
Of wonder and surprise.

 "They Closed Her Eyes"

Gustavo Adolfo Becquer (Spain)

They closed her eyes
That were still open;
They hid her face
With a white linen,
And, some sobbing,
Others in silence,
From the sad bedroom
All came away.

The night light in a dish
Burned on the floor;
It threw on the wall
The bed's shadow,
And in the shadow

One saw sometime
Drawn in sharp line
The body's shape.

The dawn appeared.
At its first whiteness
With its thousand noises
The town awoke.
Before that contrast
Of light and darkness,
Of life and strangeness
I thought a moment.
My God, how lonely
The dead are!

"The Other Wife"

Colette (France)

"Table for two? This way, Monsieur, Madame, there is still a table next to the window, if Madame and Monsieur would like a view of the bay."

Alice followed the maître d'.

"Oh, yes. Come on, Marc, it'll be like having lunch on a boat on the water . . ."

Her husband caught her by passing his arm under hers. "We'll be more comfortable over there."

"There? In the middle of all those people? I'd much rather . . ."

"Alice, please."

He tightened his grip in such a meaningful way that she turned around. "What's the matter?"

"Shh . . ." he said softly, looking at her intently, and led her toward the table in the middle.

"What is it, Marc?"

"I'll tell you, darling. Let me order lunch first. Would you like the shrimp? Or the eggs in aspic?"

"Whatever you like, you know that."

They smiled at one another, wasting the precious time of an overworked maître d', stricken with a kind of nervous dance, who was standing next to them, perspiring.

"The shrimp," said Marc. "Then the eggs and bacon. And the cold chicken with a romaine salad. *Fromage blanc?* The house specialty? We'll go with the specialty. Two strong coffees. My chauffeur will be having lunch also, we'll be leaving again at two o'clock. Some cider? No, I don't trust it . . . Dry champagne."

He sighed as if he had just moved an armoire, gazed at the colorless midday sea, at the pearly white sky, then at his wife, whom he found lovely in her little Mercury hat with its large, hanging veil.

"You're looking well, darling. And all this blue water makes your eyes look green, imagine that! And you've put on weight since you've been traveling . . . It's nice up to a point, but only up to a point!"

Her firm, round breasts rose proudly as she leaned over the table.

"Why did you keep me from taking that place next to the window?"

Marc Seguy never considered lying. "Because you were about to sit next to someone I know."

"Someone I don't know?"

"My ex-wife."

She couldn't think of anything to say and opened her blue eyes wider.

"So what, darling? It'll happen again. It's not important."

The words came back to Alice and she asked, in order, the inevitable questions. "Did she see you? Could she see that you saw her? Will you point her out to me?"

"Don't look now, please, she must be watching us. . . . The lady with brown hair, no hat, she must be staying in this hotel. By herself, behind those children in red . . ."

"Yes, I see."

Hidden behind some broad-brimmed beach hats, Alice was able to look at the woman who, fifteen months ago, had still been her husband's wife.

"Incompatibility," Marc said. "Oh, I mean . . . total incompatibility! We divorced like well-bred people, almost like friends, quietly, quickly. And then I fell in love with you, and you really wanted to be happy with me. How lucky we are that our happiness doesn't involve any guilty parties or victims!"

The woman in white, whose smooth, lustrous hair reflected the light from the sea in azure patches, was smoking a cigarette with her eyes half closed. Alice turned back toward her husband, took some shrimp and butter, and ate calmly. After a moment's silence she asked: "Why didn't you ever tell me that she had blue eyes, too?"

"Well, I never thought about it!"

He kissed the hand she was extending toward the bread basket and she blushed with pleasure. Dusky and ample, she might have seemed somewhat coarse, but the changeable blue of her eyes and her wavy, golden hair made her look like a frail and sentimental blonde. She vowed overwhelming gratitude to her husband. Immodest without knowing it, everything about her bore the overly conspicuous marks of extreme happiness.

They ate and drank heartily, and each thought the other had forgotten the woman in white. Now and then, however, Alice laughed too loudly, and Marc was careful about his posture, holding his shoulders back, his head up. They waited quite a long time for their coffee, in silence. An incandescent river, the straggled reflection of the invisible sun overhead, shifted slowly across the sea and shone with a blinding brilliance.

"She's still there, you know," Alice whispered.

"Is she making you uncomfortable? Would you like to have coffee somewhere else?"

"No, not at all! She's the one who must be uncomfortable! Besides, she doesn't exactly seem to be having a wild time, if you could see her . . ."

"I don't have to. I know that look of hers."

"Oh, was she like that?"

He exhaled his cigarette smoke through his nostrils and knitted his eyebrows. "Like that? No. To tell you honestly, she wasn't happy with me."

"Oh, really now!"

"The way you indulge me is so charming, darling . . . It's crazy . . . You're an angel . . . You love me . . . I'm so proud when I see those eyes of yours. Yes, those eyes . . . She . . . I just didn't know how to make her happy, that's all. I didn't know how."

"She's just difficult!"

Alice fanned herself irritably, and cast brief glances at the woman in white, who was smoking, her head resting against the back of the cane chair, her eyes closed with an air of satisfied lassitude.

Marc shrugged his shoulders modestly.

"That's the right word," he admitted. "What can you do? You have to feel sorry for people who are never satisfied. But we're satisfied . . . Aren't we, darling?"

She did not answer. She was looking furtively, and closely, at her husband's face, ruddy and regular; at his thick hair, threaded here and there with white silk; at his short, well-cared-for hands; and doubtful for the first time, she asked herself, "What more did she want from him?"

And as they were leaving, while Marc was paying the bill and asking for the chauffeur and about the route, she kept looking, with envy and curiosity, at the woman in white, this dissatisfied, this difficult, this superior. . . .

"Locked In"

Ingemar Gustafson (Norway)

All my life I lived in a coconut.
It was cramped and dark.
Especially in the morning when I had to shave.
But what pained me most was that I had no way
to get into touch with the outside world.
If no one out there happened to find the coconut,
if no one cracked it, then I was doomed
to live all my life in the nut, and maybe even die there.
I died in the coconut.
A couple of years later they found the coconut,
cracked it and found me shrunk and crumbled inside.
"What an accident!"
"If only we had found it earlier . . ."
"Then maybe we could have saved him."
"Maybe there are more of them locked in like that . . ."
"Whom we might be able to save,"
they said, and started knocking to pieces every coconut
within reach.
No use! Meaningless! A waste of time!
A person who chooses to live in a coconut!
Such a nut is one in a million!
But I have a brother-in-law who
lives in an
acorn.

Chapter **10**

Using Documentary Material for Oral Interpretation

Learning Objectives

After completing this chapter you should be able to

- discuss how the differences between a speech, essay, biography, autobiography, diary, letter, personal narrative, news reports, and video- and audiotape affect the interpreter's performance of such works
- identify how the time period of documentary material influences the interpretation and performance of a selection
- analyze documentary material for oral interpretation
- use the necessary techniques to perform nonfiction oral interpretation

Would you like to stand beside Abraham Lincoln as he delivers the Gettysburg Address? To walk beside Helen Keller as she conquers the darkness? To rise with William Faulkner to accept the Nobel Prize for literature? Do you have the courage to use everyday life and virtually any human activity as a catalyst for dramatic and poetic performance? Do you feel prepared to shape the material of history and current events into an interpretation performance?

Nonfiction text allows you to share compelling moments in your own life and the lives of the people behind history—the thoughts, cares, and hopes of men and women in real-life drama. In effect, nonfiction prose holds a mirror up to life, reflecting personal visions of the past, the present, and even the future.

By including selections of nonfiction texts in your literary storehouse, you will widen your experience as an interpreter. Experience is reflected not only in fictional prose, poetry, and drama but also in speeches, letters, diaries, essays, personal narratives, cultural rituals, Internet chat rooms and cyberspace bulletin boards, newspapers, magazines, radio and television news broadcasts, trial transcripts, interviews, biographies, and autobiographies, as well as in recordings of everyday conversations. Clearly, our notion of "text" is a broad one. Our lives themselves may supply "texts" for study.

The experiences detailed in such works are as intriguing and interesting as the experiences detailed in short stories, novels, poems, and plays. Indeed, it has been said many times that fact is often stranger than fiction. Thus, documentary materials may contain as much intensity as fictional prose, as much immediacy as drama, and as much personal revelation as lyric poetry.

Let us briefly sample some of the documentary materials available to you as an interpreter. Remember, the writers of these documentary materials served as historians, reflecting in their many writings the fears, concerns, hopes, values, and mores of their ages. Regardless of when these authors lived, their comments on and responses to life may help us in understanding ourselves and our times.

The Public Speech

A great speech lives on after its delivery and often deals with significant movements that change the course of history. A public speech is neither created nor delivered in a vacuum; thus, it cannot be fully understood unless one understands the individual who wrote it and the circumstances that provoked it as well. Every speaker reflects the age in which he or she lives. Memorable speakers, however, also affect the beliefs and patterns of life to come by making universal appeals or reflecting universal concerns.

PERFORMER'S WORKSHOP
Analyzing a Speech

Read the following speeches carefully. Then, working with classmates in small groups, select one speech for further study. After discussing the selected speech as a group, answer the questions on page 289.

Author Mark Twain delivered this speech in 1882.

 "Advice to Youth"

Mark Twain

Being told I would be expected to talk here, I inquired what sort of a talk I ought to make. They said it should be something suitable to youth—something didactic, instructive; or something in the nature of good advice. Very well; I have a few things in my mind which I have often longed to say for the instruction of the young; for it is in one's tender early years that such things will best take root and be most enduring and most valuable. First, then, I will say to you, my young friends—and say it beseechingly, urgingly—

Always obey your parents, when they are present. This is the best policy in the long run; because if you don't, they will make you. Most parents think they know better than you do; and you can generally make more by humoring that superstition than you can by acting on your own better judgment.

Be respectful of your superiors, if you have any; also to strangers, and sometimes to others. If a person offends you, and you are in doubt as to whether it was intentional or not, do not resort to extreme measures; simply watch your chance and hit him with a brick. That will be sufficient. If you shall find that he had not intended any offense, come out frankly and confess yourself in the wrong when you struck him; acknowledge it like a man, and say you didn't mean to. Yes, always avoid violence; in this age of charity and kindness, the time has gone by for such things. Leave dynamite to the low and unrefined.

Go to bed early, get up early—this is wise. Some authorities say get up with one thing, some with another. But a lark is really the best thing to get up with. It gives you a splendid reputation with everybody to know that you get up with the lark; and if you get the right kind of a lark, and work at him right, you can easily train him to get up at half-past nine, every time—it is no trick at all.

Now as to the matter of lying. You want to be very careful about lying; otherwise you are nearly sure to get caught. Once caught, you can never again be, in the eyes of the good and the pure, what you were before. Many a young person has injured himself permanently through a singly clumsy and ill-finished lie, the result of carelessness born of incomplete training. Some authorities hold that the young ought not to lie at all. That, of course, is putting it rather stronger than necessary; still, while I cannot go quite so far as that, I do maintain, and I believe I am right, that the young ought to be temperate in the use of this great art until practice and experience shall give them that confidence, elegance, and precision which alone can make the accomplishment graceful and profitable. Patience, diligence, painstaking attention to detail—these are the requirements; these, in time, will make the student perfect; upon these, and upon these only, may he rely as the sure foundation for future eminence. Think what tedious years of study, thought, practice, experience went to the equipment of that peerless old master who was able to impose upon the whole world the lofty and sounding maxim that, "Truth is mighty and will prevail"—the most majestic compound fracture of fact which any of woman born has yet achieved. For the history of our race, and each individual's experience, are sown thick with evidences that a truth is not hard to kill, and that a lie well told is immortal. There in Boston is a monument to the man who discovered anesthesia; many people are aware, in these latter days, that that man didn't discover it at all, but stole the discovery from another man. Is this truth mighty, and will it prevail? Ah, no, my hearers, the monument is made of hardy material, but the lie it tells will outlast it a million years. An awkward, feeble, leaky lie is a thing which you ought to make it your unceasing study to avoid; such a lie as that has no more real permanence than an average truth. Why, you might as well tell the truth at once and be done with it. A feeble, stupid, preposterous lie will not live two years—except it be a slander upon somebody. It is indestructible, then, of course, but that is no merit of yours. A final word: begin your practice of this gracious and beautiful art early—begin now. If I had begun earlier, I could have learned how.

Never handle firearms carelessly. The sorrow and suffering that have been caused through the innocent but heedless handling of firearms by the young! Only four days ago, right in the next farmhouse to the one where I am spending the summer, a mother, old and gray and sweet, one of the loveliest spirits in the land, was sitting at her work, when her young son crept in and got down an old, battered, rusty gun which had not been touched for many years, and was supposed not to be loaded, and pointed it at her, laughing and threatening to shoot. In her fright she ran screaming and pleading toward the door on the other side of the room; but as she passed him he placed the gun almost against her very breast and pulled the trigger! He had supposed it was not loaded. And he was right: it wasn't. So there wasn't any harm done. It is the only case of the kind I ever heard of. Therefore, just the same, don't you meddle with old unloaded firearms; they are the most deadly and unerring things that have ever been created by man. You don't have to take any pains at all, with them; you don't have to have a rest, you don't have to have any sights on the gun, you don't have to take aim, even. No, you just pick out a relative and bang away, and you are sure to get him. A youth who can't hit a cathedral at thirty yards with a Gatling gun in three-quarters of an hour, can take up an old empty musket and bang his mother every time, at a hundred. Think what Waterloo would have been if one of the armies had been boys armed with old rusty muskets supposed not to be loaded, and the other army had been composed of their female relations. The very thought of it makes me shudder.

There are many sorts of books; but good ones are the sort for the young to read. Remember that. They are a great, an inestimable, an unspeakable means of improvement. Therefore be careful in your selection, my young friends; be very careful; confine yourself exclusively to Roberson's *Sermons*, Baxter's *Saint's Rest*, *The Innocents Abroad*, and works of that kind.

But I have said enough. I hope you will treasure the instructions which I have given you, and make them a guide to your feet and a light to your understanding. Build your character thoughtfully and painstakingly upon these precepts; and by and by, when you have got it built, you will be surprised and gratified to see how nicely and sharply it resembles everybody else's.

Writer Cecile Larson delivered this speech in 1980 to commemorate a massacre.

 ## "The 'Monument' at Wounded Knee"
Cecile Larson

We Americans are big on monuments. We build monuments in memory of our heroes. Washington, Jefferson, and Lincoln live on in our nation's capital. We erect monuments to honor our martyrs. The Minute Man still stands guard at Concord. The flag is ever raised over Iwo Jima. Sometimes we even construct monuments to commemorate victims. In Ashburn Park downtown there is a monument to those who died in the yellow fever epidemics. However, there are some things in our history that we don't memorialize. Perhaps we would just as soon forget what happened. Last summer I visited such a place—the massacre site at Wounded Knee.

In case you have forgotten what happened at Wounded Knee, let me refresh your memory. On December 29, 1890, shortly after Sitting Bull had been murdered by the authorities, about 400 half-frozen, starving, and frightened Indians who had fled the nearby reservation were attacked by the Seventh Cavalry. When the fighting ended, between 200 and 300 Sioux had died—two-thirds of them women and children. Their remains are buried in a common grave at the site of the massacre.

Wounded Knee is located in the Pine Ridge Reservation in southwestern South Dakota—about a three-hour drive from where Presidents

Washington, Jefferson, Theodore Roosevelt, and Lincoln are enshrined in the granite face of Mount Rushmore. The reservation is directly south of the Badlands National Park, a magnificently desolate area of wind-eroded buttes and multicolored spires.

We entered the reservation driving south from the Badlands Visitor's Center. The landscape of the Pine Ridge Reservation retains much of the desolation of the Badlands but lacks its magnificence. Flat, sun-baked fields and an occasional eroded gully stretch as far as the eye can see. There are no signs or highway markers to lead the curious tourist to Wounded Knee. Even the Rand-McNally Atlas doesn't help you find your way. We got lost three times and had to stop and ask directions.

When we finally arrived at Wounded Knee, there was no official historic marker to tell us what had happened there. Instead there was a large, handmade wooden sign—crudely lettered in white on black. The sign first directed our attention to our left—to the gully where the massacre took place. The mass grave site was to our right—across the road and up a small hill.

Two red-brick columns topped with a wrought-iron arch and a small metal cross form the entrance to the grave site. The column to the right is in bad shape: cinder blocks from the base are missing; the brickwork near the top has deteriorated and tumbled to the ground; graffiti on the columns proclaim an attitude we found repeatedly expressed about the Bureau of Indian Affairs—"The BIA sucks!"

Crumbling concrete steps lead you up to the mass grave. The top of the grave is covered with gravel, punctuated by unruly patches of chickweed and crabgrass. These same weeds also grow along the base of the broken chain-link fence that surrounds the grave, the "monument," and a small cemetery.

The "monument" itself rests on a concrete slab to the right of the grave. It's a typical, large, old-fashioned granite cemetery marker, a pillar about six feet high topped with an urn—the kind of gravestone you might see in any cemetery with graves from the turn of the century. The inscription tells us that it was erected by the families of those who were killed at Wounded Knee. Weeds grow through the cracks in the concrete at its base.

There are no granite headstones in the adjacent cemetery, only simple white wooden crosses that tell a story of people who died young. There is no neatly manicured grass. There are no flowers. Only the unrelenting and unforgiving weeds.

Yes, Americans are big on monuments. We build them to memorialize our heroes, to honor our martyrs, and sometimes, even to commemorate victims. But only when it makes us feel good.

Civil rights leader and Nobel Peace Prize winner Dr. Martin Luther King Jr. delivered his famous "I Have a Dream" speech at a rally at the Lincoln Memorial in Washington, D.C., on August 28, 1963. The following excerpt is from the end of the speech.

I am not unmindful that some of you have come here out of great trials and tribulations. Some of you have come fresh from narrow jail cells. Some of you have come from areas where your quest for freedom left you battered by the storms of persecution and staggered by the winds of police brutality. You have been the veterans of creative suffering.

Continue to work with the faith that unearned suffering is redemptive. Go back to Mississippi, go back to Alabama, go back to South Carolina, go back to Georgia, go back to Louisiana, go back to the slums and ghettos of our Northern cities, knowing that somehow this situation can and will be changed. Let us not wallow in the valley of despair.

I say to you today, my friends, though, even though we face the difficulties of today and tomorrow, I still have a dream. It is a dream deeply rooted in the American dream. I have a dream that one day this nation will rise up, live out the true meaning of its creed: "We hold these truths to be self-evident, that all men are created equal." . . .

I have a dream that my four little children will one day live in a nation where they will not be judged by the color of their skin but by the content of their character.

I have a dream today. . . . I have a dream that one day every valley shall be exalted, and every hill and mountain shall be made low. The rough places will be made plain, and the crooked places will be made straight. And the glory of the Lord will be revealed, and all flesh shall see it together. This is our hope. This is the faith that I go back to the South with. With this faith we will be able to hew out of the mountain of despair a stone of hope. With this faith we will be able to transform the jangling discords of our nation into a beautiful symphony of brotherhood. With this faith we will be able to work together, to pray together, to struggle together, to go to jail together, to stand up for freedom together, knowing that we will be free one day.

This will be the day when all of God's children will be able to sing with new meaning, "My country, 'tis of thee, sweet land of liberty, of thee I sing. Land where my fathers died, land of the pilgrim's pride, from every mountainside, let freedom ring." And if America is to be a great nation, this must become true. So let freedom ring from the prodigious hilltops of New Hampshire. Let freedom ring from the mighty mountains of New York. Let freedom ring from the heightening Alleghenies of Pennsylvania. Let freedom ring from the snow-capped Rockies of Colorado. Let freedom ring from the curvaceous slopes of California.

But not only that. Let freedom ring from Stone Mountain of Georgia. Let freedom ring from Lookout Mountain of Tennessee. Let freedom ring from every hill and molehill of Mississippi, from every mountainside, let freedom ring. . . .

When we allow freedom to ring—when we let it ring from every village and every hamlet, from every state and every city, we will be able to speed up that day when all of God's children, black men and white men, Jews and Gentiles, Protestants and Catholics, will be able to join hands and sing in the words of the old Negro spiritual, "Free at last, Free at last, Great God Almighty, We are free at last."

Questions

1. How does this speech contribute to your understanding of the period in which it was written?
2. How does this speech contribute to your understanding of the speaker?
3. What message does the speech have for today?

Performing the Speech

How do you perform a public speech? As an interpreter of public speeches, aim to make your audience one with the original audience of your chosen speaker. To do this you must directly address and include your listeners in the world of your literature as you share with them the logical and emotional content of the manuscript. Your voice and body will help you re-create the speech and will suggest the bearing of the original speaker as well. Work hard to reflect visibly and vocally the emotions, attitudes, and images inherent in the work you chose, because in history, as in performance, much depends upon not only what is said but on how it is said.

Approach the performance of the public speech as you have approached the performance of literature in general. Decide which words to emphasize, at what points to change your rate, at what points to increase or decrease your volume, and when to pause for effect. When will you incorporate gesture, how should you move, and how might your face reflect the material you are interpreting? If it is appropriate, use suggestive bits of costuming, visual aids, or music from the era of your speech maker to set the stage for sharing your documentary script with the audience.

PERFORMER'S WORKSHOP
Re-creating a Speech

Divide the class into small groups, each of which will work on one of the following speeches. Select one person from your small group to perform your group's assigned speech for the class. Help prepare him or her to successfully re-create the speech by rehearsing with group members as a team. Also answer the questions on page 294.

This speech was delivered by the Seneca chief Sagoyewatha, also known as Red Jacket, in 1805, after a white missionary had addressed a council of the Iroquois Confederation chiefs.

from "To the Council"
Sagoyewatha (Red Jacket)

Friend and Brother:—It was the will of the Great Spirit that we should meet together this day. He orders all things and has given us a fine day for our council. He has taken His garment from before the sun and caused it to shine with brightness upon us. Our eyes are opened that we see clearly; our ears are unstopped that we have been able to hear distinctly the words you have spoken. . . .

Brother, this council fire was kindled by you. It was at your request that we came together at this time. We have listened with attention to what you have said. You requested us to speak our minds freely. This gives us great joy; for we now consider that we stand upright before you and can speak what we think. All have heard your voice and all speak to you now as one man. Our minds are agreed. . . .

Brother, listen to what we say. There was a time when our forefathers owned this great island. Their seats extended from the rising to the setting sun. The Great Spirit had made it for the use of Indians. He had created the buffalo, the deer, and other animals for food. He had made the bear and the beaver. Their skins served us for clothing. He had scattered them over the country and taught us how to take them. He had caused the earth to produce corn for bread. All this He had done for His red children because He loved them. If we had some disputes about our hunting-ground they were generally settled without the shedding of much blood.

But an evil day came upon us. Your forefathers crossed the great water and landed on this island. Their numbers were small. They found friends and not enemies. They told us they had fled from their own country for fear of wicked men and had come here to enjoy their religion. They asked for a small seat. We took pity on them, granted their request, and they sat down among us. We gave them corn and meat; they gave us poison in return.

The white people, brother, had now found our country. Tidings were carried back and more came among us. Yet we did not fear them. We took them to be friends. They called us brother. We believed them and gave them a larger seat. At length their numbers had greatly increased. They wanted more land; they wanted our country. Our eyes were opened and our minds became uneasy. Wars took place. Indians were hired to fight against Indians, and many of our people were destroyed. They also brought liquor among us. It was strong and powerful, and has slain thousands.

Brother, our seats were once large and yours were small. You have now become a great people, and we have scarcely a place left to spread our blankets. You have got our country, but are not satisfied; you want to force your religion upon us. . . .

Brother, you say there is but one way to worship and serve the Great Spirit. If there is but one religion, why do you white people differ so much about it? . . .

Brother, we do not understand these things. We are told that your religion was given to your forefathers and has been handed down from father to son. We also have a religion which was given to our forefathers and has been handed down to us, their children. We worship in that way. It teaches us to be thankful for all the favors we receive, to love each other, and to be united. We never quarrel about religion.

Brother, the Great Spirit has made us all, but He has made a great difference between His white and His red children. He has given us different complexions and different customs. To you He has given the arts. To these He has not opened our eyes. We know these things to be true. Since He has made so great a difference between us in other things, why may we not conclude that He has given us a different religion according to our understanding? The Great Spirit does right. He knows what is best for His children; we are satisfied.

Brother, we do not wish to destroy your religion or take it from you. We only want to enjoy our own. . . .

Brother, you have now heard our answer to your talk, and this is all we have to say at present. As we are going to part, we will come and take you by the hand, and hope the Great Spirit will protect you on your journey and return you safe to your friends.

President Ronald Reagan delivered this eulogy after the explosion of the space shuttle *Challenger* in January 1986.

 ## "Tribute to the Crew of the Space Shuttle *Challenger*"
Ronald Reagan

We come together today to mourn the loss of seven brave Americans, to share the grief that we all feel, and perhaps in that sharing, to find the strength to bear our sorrow and the courage to look for the seeds of hope.

Our nation's loss is first a profound personal loss to the family and the friends and the loved ones of our shuttle astronauts. To those they left behind—the mothers, the fathers, the husbands and wives, brothers and sisters, yes, and especially the children—all of America stands beside you in your time of sorrow.

What we say today is only an inadequate expression of what we carry in our hearts. Words pale in the shadow of grief; they seem insufficient even to measure the brave sacrifice of those you loved and we so admired. Their truest testimony will not be in the words we speak, but in the way they led their lives and in the way they lost their lives—with dedication, honor, and an unquenchable desire to explore this mysterious and beautiful universe.

The best we can do is remember our seven astronauts, our Challenger Seven, remember them as they lived, bringing life and love and joy to those who knew them and pride to a nation.

They came from all parts of this great country—from South Carolina to Washington State; Ohio to Mohawk, New York; Hawaii to North Carolina to Concord, New Hampshire. They were so different; yet in their mission, their quest, they held so much in common.

We remember Dick Scobee, the commander who spoke the last words we heard from the space shuttle *Challenger*. He served as a fighter pilot in Vietnam earning many medals for bravery and later as a test pilot of advanced aircraft before joining the space program. Danger was a familiar companion to Commander Scobee.

We remember Michael Smith, who earned enough medals as a combat pilot to cover his chest, including the Navy Distinguished Flying Cross, three Air Medals, and the Vietnamese Cross of Gallantry with Silver Star in gratitude from a nation he fought to keep free.

We remember Judith Resnik, known as J.R. to her friends, always smiling, always eager to make a contribution, finding beauty in the music she played on her piano in her off-hours.

We remember Ellison Onizuka, who as a child running barefoot through the coffee fields and macadamia groves of Hawaii dreamed of someday traveling to the Moon. Being an Eagle Scout, he said, had helped him soar to the impressive achievements of his career.

We remember Ronald McNair, who said that he learned perseverance in the cottonfields of South Carolina. His dream was to live aboard the space station, performing experiments and playing his saxophone in the weightlessness of space. Well, Ron, we will miss your saxophone; and we will build your space station.

We remember Gregory Jarvis. On that ill-fated flight he was carrying with him a flag of his university in Buffalo, New York—a small token, he said, to the people who unlocked his future.

We remember Christa McAuliffe, who captured the imagination of the entire nation; inspiring us with her pluck, her restless spirit of discovery; a teacher, not just to her students, but to an entire people, instilling us all with the excitement of this journey we ride into the future.

We will always remember them, these skilled professionals, scientists, and adventurers, these artists and teachers and family men and women; and we will cherish each of their stories, stories of triumph and bravery, stories of true American heroes.

On the day of the disaster, our nation held a vigil by our television sets. In one cruel moment our exhilaration turned to horror; we waited and watched and tried to make sense of what we had seen. That night I listened to a call-in program on the radio; people of every age spoke of their sadness and the pride they felt in our astronauts. Across America we are reaching out, holding hands, and finding comfort in one another.

The sacrifice of your loved ones has stirred the soul of our nation and through the pain our hearts have been opened to a profound truth: The future is not free; the story of all human progress is one of a struggle against all odds. We learned again that this America, which Abraham Lincoln called the last, best hope of man on Earth, was built on heroism and noble sacrifice. It was built by men and women like our seven star voyagers, who answered a call beyond duty, who gave more than was expected or required, and who gave little thought to worldly reward.

We think back to the pioneers of an earlier century, the sturdy souls who took their families and their belongings and set out into the frontier of the American West. Often they met with terrible hardship. Along the Oregon Trail, you could still see the gravemarkers of those who fell on the way. But grief only steeled them to the journey ahead.

Today the frontier is space and the boundaries of human knowledge. Sometimes when we reach for the stars, we fall short. But we must pick ourselves up again and press on despite the pain. Our nation is indeed fortunate that we can still draw on immense reservoirs of courage, character, and fortitude; that we're still blessed with heroes like those of the space shuttle *Challenger.*

Dick Scobee knew that every launching of a space shuttle is a technological miracle. And he said, "If something ever does go wrong, I hope that doesn't mean the end to the space shuttle program." Every family member I talked to asked specifically that we continue the program, that that is what their departed loved one would want above all else. We will not disappoint them.

Today we promise Dick Scobee and his crew that their dream lives on, that the future they worked so hard to build will become reality. The dedicated men and women of NASA have lost seven members of their family. Still, they, too, must forge ahead with a space program that is effective, safe, and efficient, but bold and committed.

Man will continue his conquest of space. To reach out for new goals and ever greater achievements—that is the way we shall commemorate our seven *Challenger* heroes.

Dick, Mike, Judy, El, Ron, Greg, and Christa—your families and your country mourn your passing. We bid you goodbye; we will never forget you. For those who knew you well and loved you, the pain will be deep and enduring. A nation, too, will long feel the loss of her seven sons and daughters, her seven good friends. We can find consolation only in faith, for we know in our hearts that you who flew so high and so proud now make your home beyond the stars, safe in God's promise of eternal life.

May God bless you all and give you comfort in this difficult time.

American political activist and writer Susan B. Anthony delivered her speech "On Woman's Right to Suffrage" in 1873 to mobilize support for women's right to vote.

 ## "On Woman's Right to Suffrage"

Susan B. Anthony

Friends and Fellow Citizens—I stand before you to-night under indictment for the alleged crime of having voted at the last presidential election, without having a lawful right to vote. It shall be my work this evening to prove to you that in thus voting, I not only committed no crime, but, instead, simply exercised my citizen's rights, guaranteed to me and all United States citizens by the National Constitution, beyond the power of any State to deny.

The preamble of the Federal Constitution says:

"We, the people of the United States, in order to form a more perfect union, establish justice, insure domestic tranquility, provide for the common defense, promote the general welfare, and secure the blessings of liberty to ourselves and our posterity, do ordain and establish this Constitution for the United States of America."

It was we, the people; not we, the white male citizens; nor yet we, the male citizens; but we, the whole people, who formed the Union. And we formed it, not to give the blessings of liberty, but to secure them; not to the half of ourselves and the half of our posterity, but to the whole people—women as well as men. And it is a downright mockery to talk to women of their enjoyment of the blessings of liberty while they are denied the use of the only means of securing them provided by this democratic-republican government—the ballot. . . .

Webster, Worcester and Bouvier all define a citizen to be a person in the United States, entitled to vote and hold office.

The only question left to be settled now is: Are women persons? And I hardly believe any of our opponents will have the hardihood to say they are not. Being persons, then, women are citizens; and no State has a right to make any law that shall abridge their privileges or immunities. Hence, every discrimination against women in the constitutions and laws of the several States is to-day null and void, precisely as is every one against negroes.

Questions

1. How did each of the speakers reflect the period and setting in which the speech was originally presented?
2. What audience moods did each interpreter try to evoke?
3. What did the interpreters do to transfer the intellectual and emotional meanings of their speeches to the audience?
4. What did they do that hindered or impeded the communication of meaning?

The Essay

Like a public speech, an essay also reflects the mood and spirit of the time in which it was written. Through essays, writers share their ideas, their experiences, and their impressions of events, places, or people. In this way, you can experience the lifestyle and attitudes of individuals you do not know personally. Just as a speech reveals the speaker, so an essay reveals its author.

The focus of an essay is not on make-believe happenings, though fictional devices sometimes help authors develop and communicate a philosophy or statement. Although the writers of essays may not have intended for their works to be read aloud, oral performance certainly provides a viable avenue to appreciation.

While essays are usually built around the exploration of a single subject, they run the gamut from humorous to expository to personal. The **humorous essay,** for example, relies on satire, irony, wit, or other comic techniques to deliver its message. In contrast, the central purpose of the **expository essay** is to instruct or inform. And the **personal essay** relays the firsthand experience of the writer. Each type of essay was probably written with an external rather than purely internal audience in mind, and one goal of the essayist is to involve audience members in a consideration of a subject of common interest.

When interpreting an essay, consider your responsibility to be threefold. First, determine how the essay mirrors the time and setting of its writing. Second, determine the central idea and mood of the work. Third, determine what the essay says about people and their values. In addition, before you perform the work, ask yourself how much of the writer's personality you should reflect in your re-creation of his or her work.

Participate in the next exercise to develop your essay-reading skills.

PERFORMER'S WORKSHOP
Analyzing the Essay

Read each of the following essays carefully, noting how each writer uses language and tone to appeal to his or her audience. Then divide the class into small groups and select one of the essays to consider and perform. Choose a member of your group to present the chosen essay and work as a team to help that individual prepare adequately. Pay close attention to the distinctive qualities of each essay. Also answer the questions on page 302.

Irish poet, wit, and clergyman Jonathan Swift published his pamphlet *A Modest Proposal* in 1729. It is an elaborate satire on the conditions in eighteenth-century Ireland, then under English rule.

A Modest Proposal

Jonathan Swift

For Preventing the Children of Poor People in Ireland From Being a Burden to Their Parents or Country, and For Making Them Beneficial to the Public

It is a melancholy object to those who walk through this great town or travel in the country, when they see the streets, the roads, and cabin doors, crowded with beggars of the female sex, followed by three, four, or six children, all in rags and importuning every passenger for an alms. These mothers, instead of being able to work for their honest livelihood, are forced to employ all their time in strolling to beg sustenance for their helpless infants, who, as they grow up, either turn thieves for want of work, or leave their dear native country to fight for the Pretender in Spain, or sell themselves to the Barbados.

I think it is agreed by all parties that this prodigious number of children in the arms, or on the backs, or at the heels of their mothers, and frequently of their fathers, is in the present deplorable state of the kingdom a very great additional grievance; and therefore whoever could find out a fair, cheap, and easy method of making these children sound, useful members of the commonwealth would deserve so well of the public as to have his statue set up for a preserver of the nation.

But my intention is very far from being confined to provide only for the children of professed beggars; it is of a much greater extent, and shall take in the whole number of infants at a certain age who are born of parents in effect as little able to support them as those who demand our charity in the streets.

As to my own part, having turned my thoughts for many years upon this important subject, and maturely weighed the several schemes of other projectors, I have always found them grossly mistaken in their computation. It is true, a child just dropped from its dam may be supported by her milk for a solar year, with little other nourishment; at most not above the value of two shillings, which the mother may certainly get, or the value in scraps, by her lawful occupation of begging; and it is exactly at one year old that I propose to provide for them in such a manner as instead of being a charge upon their parents or parish, or wanting food and raiment for the rest of their lives, they shall on the contrary contribute to the feeding, and partly to the clothing of many thousands.

There is likewise another great advantage in my scheme, that it will prevent those voluntary abortions, and that horrid practice of women murdering their bastard children, alas, too frequent among us, sacrificing the poor innocent babes, I doubt, more to avoid the expense than the shame, which would move tears and pity in the most savage and inhuman breast.

The number of souls in this kingdom being usually reckoned one million and a half, of these I calculate there may be about two hundred thousand couples whose wives are breeders; from which number I subtract thirty thousand couples who are able to maintain their own children, although I apprehend there cannot be so many under the present distresses of the kingdom; but this being granted, there will remain a hundred and seventy thousand breeders. I again subtract fifty thousand for those women who miscarry, or whose children die by accident or disease within the year. There only remain a hundred and twenty thousand children of poor parents annually born. The question therefore is, how this number shall be reared and provided for, which, as I have already said, under the present situation of affairs, is utterly impossible by all the methods hitherto proposed. For we can neither employ them in handicraft or agriculture; we neither build houses (I mean in the country) nor cultivate land. They can very seldom pick up a livelihood by stealing till they arrive at six years old, except where they are of towardly parts; although I confess they learn the rudiments much earlier, during which time they can however be looked upon only as probationers, as I have been informed by a principal gentleman in the county of Cavan, who protested to me that he never knew above one or two instances under the age of six, even in a part of the kingdom so renowned for the quickest proficiency in that art.

I am assured by our merchants that a boy or girl before twelve years old is no salable commodity; and even when they come to this age they will not yield above three pounds, or three pounds and half a crown at most on the Exchange; which cannot turn to account either to the parents or the kingdom, the charge of nutriment and rags having been at least four times that value.

I shall now therefore humbly propose my own thoughts, which I hope will not be liable to the least objection.

I have been assured by a very knowing American of my acquaintance in London, that a young healthy child well nursed is at a year old a most delicious, nourishing, and wholesome food, whether stewed, roasted, baked, or boiled; and I make no doubt that it will equally serve in a fricassee or a ragout.

I do therefore humbly offer it to public consideration that of the hundred and twenty thousand children, already computed, twenty thousand may be reserved for breed, whereof only one fourth part to be males, which is more than we allow to sheep, black cattle, or swine; and my reason is that these children are seldom the fruits of marriage, a circumstance not much regarded by our savages, therefore one male will be sufficient to serve four females. That the remaining hundred thousand may at a year old be offered in sale to persons of quality and fortune through the kingdom, always advising the mother to let them suck plentifully in the last month, so as to render them plump and fat for a good table. A child will make two dishes at an entertainment for friends; and when the family dines alone, the fore or hind quarter will make a reasonable dish, and seasoned with a little pepper or salt will be very good boiled on the fourth day, especially in winter.

I have reckoned upon a medium that a child just born will weigh twelve pounds, and in a solar year if tolerably nursed increaseth to twenty-eight pounds.

I grant this food will be somewhat dear, and therefore very proper for landlords, who, as they have already devoured most of the parents, seem to have the best title to the children. . . .

Born in 1880, Helen Keller lost her senses of sight and hearing during a childhood illness. She regained her ability to communicate thanks to a devoted teacher, Anne Sullivan Macy (whose work is commemorated in the play *The Miracle Worker* by William Gibson), and went on to become a famous lecturer and writer. In "Three Days to See," she urges readers to consider their own facilities.

from "Three Days to See"
Helen Keller

I have often thought it would be a blessing if each human being were stricken blind and deaf for a few days at sometime during his early adult life. Darkness would make him more appreciative of sight; silence would teach him the joys of sound.

Now and then I have tested my seeing friends to discover what they see. Recently I was visited by a good friend who had just returned from a long walk in the woods, and I asked her what she had observed. "Nothing in particular," she replied. I might have been incredulous had I not been accustomed to such responses, for long ago I became convinced that the seeing see little.

How was it possible, I asked myself, to walk for an hour through woods and see nothing worthy of note? I who cannot see find hundreds of things to interest me through mere touch. I feel the delicate symmetry of a leaf. I pass my hands lovingly about the smooth skin of a silver birch, or the rough shaggy bark of a pine. In spring I touch the branches of trees hopefully in search of a bud, the first sign of awakening Nature after her winter's sleep. I feel the delightful velvety texture of a flower, and discover its remarkable convolutions; and something of the miracle of Nature is revealed to me. . . .

Perhaps I can best illustrate by imagining what I should most like to see if I were given the use of my eyes, say, for just three days. . . . If, by some miracle, I were granted three seeing days, to be followed by a relapse into darkness, I should divide the period into three parts.

On the first day, I should want to see the people whose kindness and gentleness and companionship have made my life worth living. First I should like to gaze long upon the face of my dear teacher, Mrs. Anne

Sullivan Macy, who came to me when I was a child and opened the outer world to me. I should want not merely to see the outline of her face, so that I could cherish it in my memory, but to study that face and find in it the living evidence of the sympathetic tenderness and patience with which she accomplished the difficult task of my education. . . .

The first day would be a busy one. I would call to me all my dear friends and look long into their faces, imprinting upon my mind the outward evidences of beauty that is within them. I should let my eyes rest, too, on the face of a baby, so that I could catch a vision of the eager, innocent beauty which precedes the individual's consciousness of the conflicts which life develops. . . .

When dusk had fallen, I should experience the double delight of being able to see by artificial light, which the genius of man has created to extend the power of his sight when Nature decrees darkness.

The next day—the second day of sight—I should arise with the dawn and see the thrilling miracle by which night is transformed into day. I should behold with awe the magnificent panorama of light with which the sun awakens the sleeping earth.

This day I should devote to a hasty glimpse of the world, past and present. I should want to see the pageant of man's progress, the kaleidoscope of the ages. How can so much be compressed into one day? Through museums. . . .

The evening of my second day of sight I should spend at a theatre or at the movies. Even now I often attend theatrical performances of all sorts, but the action of the play must be spelled into my hand by a companion. But how I should like to see with my own eyes the fascinating figure of Hamlet, or the gusty Falstaff amid colorful Elizabethan trappings!

The following morning, I should again greet the dawn . . . this according to the terms of my imagined miracle, is to be my third and last day of light. I shall have no time to waste in regrets or longings; there is too much to see. The first day I devoted to my friends, animate and inanimate. The second revealed to me the history of man and Nature. Today I shall spend in the workaday world of the present, amid the haunts of men going about the business of life . . . on the evening of that last day, I should again run away to the theatre, to a hilariously funny play, so that I might appreciate the overtones of comedy in the human spirit.

At midnight my temporary respite from blindness would cease, and permanent night would close in on me again.

I who am blind can give one hint to those who see: use your eyes as if tomorrow you would be stricken blind. And the same method can be applied to the other senses. . . . But of all the senses, I am sure that sight must be the most delightful.

William L. Laurence was a crew member on the plane that dropped the atomic bomb on Nagasaki in 1945, which gives his essay an interesting perspective.

"Atomic Bombing of Nagasaki"

William L. Laurence

With the atomic-bomb mission to Japan, August 9 (Delayed)—We are on our way to bomb the mainland of Japan. Our flying contingent consists of three specially designed B-29 Superforts, and two of these carry no bombs. But our lead plane is on its way with another atomic bomb, the second in three days, concentrating in its active substance an explosive energy equivalent to twenty thousand and, under favorable conditions, forty thousand tons of TNT.

We have several chosen targets. One of these is the great industrial and shipping center of Nagasaki . . . [on] one of the main islands of the Japanese homeland. . . .

I watched the assembly of this man-made meteor during the past two days and was among the small group of scientists and Army and Navy representatives privileged to be present at the ritual of its loading in the Superfort last night, against a background of threatening black skies torn open at intervals by great lightning flashes.

It is a thing of beauty to behold, this "gadget." Into its design went millions of man-hours of what is without doubt the most concentrated intellectual effort in history. Never before had so much brain power been focused on a single problem.

This atomic bomb is different from the bomb used three days ago with such devastating results on Hiroshima.

I saw the atomic substance before it was placed inside the bomb. By itself it is not at all dangerous to handle. . . .

The briefing at midnight revealed the extreme care and the tremendous amount of preparation that had been made to take care of every detail of the mission, to make certain that the atomic bomb fully served the purpose for which it was intended. . . .

The briefing period ended with a moving prayer by the chaplain. We then proceeded to the mess hall for the traditional early-morning breakfast before departure on a bombing mission. . . .

We took off at 3:50 this morning and headed northwest on a straight line for the Empire. . . . On we went through the night. . . . The first signs of dawn came shortly after five o'clock. Sergeant Curry, of Hoopeston, Illinois, who had been listening steadily on his earphones for radio reports, while maintaining a strict radio silence himself, greeted it by rising to his feet and gazing out the window. . . .

"Think this atomic bomb will end the war?" he asks hopefully.

"There is a very good chance that this one may do the trick," I assured him, "but if not, then the next one or two surely will. . . ."

By 5:50 it was really light outside. . . .

Our genial bombardier, Lieutenant Levy, comes over to invite me to take his front-row seat in the transparent nose of the ship, and I accept eagerly. . . . At that height the vast ocean below and the sky above seem to merge into one great sphere. . . .

My mind soon returns to the mission I am on. Somewhere beyond these vast mountains of white clouds ahead of me there lies Japan, the land of our enemy. In about four hours from now one of its cities, making weapons of war for use against us, will be wiped off the map by the greatest weapon ever made by men. In one tenth of a millionth of a second, a fraction of time immeasurable by any clock, a whirlwind from the skies will pulverize thousands of its buildings and tens of thousands of its inhabitants. . . .

Captain Bock informs me that we are about to start our climb to bombing altitude. . . . We reached our altitude at nine o'clock. . . .

We reached Yakushima at 9:12 and there, about four thousand feet ahead of us, was *The Great Artiste* with its precious load. . . .

We started circling. We saw little towns on the coastline, heedless of our presence. We kept on circling, waiting for the third ship in our formation. . . .

We flew southward down the channel and at 11:33 crossed the coastline and headed straight for Nagasaki, about one hundred miles to the west. Here again we circled until we found an opening in the clouds. It was 12:01 and the goal of our mission had arrived.

We heard the prearranged signal on our radio, put on our arc welder's glasses and watched tensely the maneuverings of the strike ship about half a mile in front of us.

"There she goes!" someone said.

Out of the belly of *The Great Artiste* what looked like a black object went downward. Captain Bock swung around to get out of range; but even though we were turning away in the opposite direction, and despite the fact that it was broad daylight in our cabin, all of us became aware of a giant flash that broke through the dark barrier of our arc welder's lenses and flooded our cabin with intense light.

We removed our glasses after the first flash, but the light still lingered on. . . . A tremendous blast wave struck our ship and made it tremble from nose to tail. . . .

Observers in the tail of our ship saw a giant ball of fire rise as though from the bowels of the earth, belching forth enormous white smoke rings. Next they saw a giant pillar of purple fire, ten thousand feet high, shooting skyward with enormous speed.

By the time our ship had made another turn in the direction of the atomic explosion the pillar of purple fire had reached the level of our altitude. Only about forty-five seconds had passed. Awestruck, we watched it shoot upward like a meteor coming from the earth instead of from outer space, becoming ever more alive as it climbed skyward through the white clouds. It was no longer smoke, or dust, or even a cloud of fire. It was a living thing, a new species being born right before our incredulous eyes.

At one stage of its evolution, covering millions of years in terms of seconds, the entity assumed the form of a giant square totem pole, with its base about three miles long, tapering off to about a mile at the top. Its bottom was brown, its center was amber, its top white. But it was a living totem pole, carved with many grotesque masks grimacing at the earth.

Then, just when it appeared as though the thing had settled down into a state of permanence, there came shooting out of the top a giant mushroom that increased the height of the pillar to a total of forty-five thousand feet. The mushroom top was even more alive than the pillar, seething and boiling in a white fury of creamy foam, sizzling upward and then descending earthward, a thousand Old Faithful geysers rolled into one.

It kept struggling in an elementary fury, like a creature in the act of breaking the bonds that held it down. In a few seconds it had freed itself from its gigantic stem and floated upward with tremendous speed, its momentum carrying it into the stratosphere to a height of about sixty thousand feet.

But no sooner did this happen when another mushroom, smaller in size than the first one, began emerging out of the pillar. It was as though the decapitated monster was growing a new head.

As the first mushroom floated off into the blue it changed its shape into a flower-like form, its giant petals curving downward, creamy white outside, rose-colored inside. . . . Much living substance had gone into those rainbows. The quivering top of the pillar was protruding to a great height through the white clouds, giving the appearance of a monstrous prehistoric creature with a ruff around its neck, a fleecy ruff extending in all directions, as far as the eye could see.

Questions

1. What is the central idea of the chosen essay?
2. What is its mood or tone?
3. How does the language of the essay reflect its tone?
4. How does the work reflect the concerns of both the author and the times in which it was written?
5. How might the oral reader use the techniques of interpretation to make the essay live for the audience?

Biography and Autobiography

Although both biography and autobiography document the life and history of one man or woman, they do so in very different ways. **Autobiography** is authored by and told from the point of view of the subject himself or herself. **Biography** is authored by and told from the point of view of someone other than the subject. Before examining them in detail, take a few moments to read the samples that follow.

PERFORMER'S WORKSHOP
Character Portraits

Read the following passages carefully, giving special attention to point of view.

 Down These Mean Streets
Piri Thomas

I had been walking around since 9 P.M. My thoughts were boiling. Poppa ain't ever gonna hit me again. I'm his kid, too, just like James, Jose, Paulie, and Sis. But I'm the one that always gets the blame for everything. I'm sorry Momma's gotta worry, but she gotta understand that it wasn't my fault.

"Caramba," I muttered aloud, "I'm getting hungry."

The streets of Harlem make an unreal scene of frightened silence at 2 A.M. Like everything got a layoff from noise and hassling. Only the rumbling of a stray car passing by or the shy foraging of a cat or dog make the quietness bearable—especially to a twelve-year-old kid whose ability to make noise had got him a whipping from his poppa.

I could see Poppa's face, tired and sleepy. . . .

I could feel my mouth making the motions of wanting to say something in my defense. Of how it wasn't my fault that Jose had almost knocked the toaster off the table, and how I had tried to save it from falling, and in trying had finished knocking it to the floor along with a large jar of black coffee. But I just couldn't get the words out. Poppa just stood there, eyes swollen and hurting from too much work, looking at a river of black coffee. He didn't give me a chance. Even before the first burning slap of his belt awakened tears of pain, I was still trying to get words out that would make everything all right again. The second whap of the belt brought words of pain to my lips, and my blind running retreat was a mixture of tears and "I hate you."

 The Old Gentleman
Gilbert Highet

The old gentleman was riding round his land. He had retired several years ago, after a busy career; but farming was what he liked, and he knew that the best way to keep farms prosperous was to supervise them in person. So, although he was approaching seventy, he rode round his property for four or five hours, several days each week. It was not easy for

Biography and Autobiography   303

him, but it was not difficult either. He never thought whether a thing was easy or difficult. If it ought to be done, it would be done. Besides, he had always been strong. Although his hair was white and his eyes were dimming, he stood a good six feet and weighed 210 pounds. He rose at four every morning. It was December now, Christmas was approaching, snow was in the air, frost and snow on the ground. This month he had been away from home on a toilsome but necessary trip, and in the hard weather he had been able to ride over his farms very seldom. Still, he liked to see them whenever he could. The land was quiet; yet a great deal of work remained to be done.

There was much on the old gentleman's mind. His son had come home from college in some kind of disturbance and uneasiness, unwilling to go back again. Perhaps he should be sent elsewhere—to Harvard, or William and Mary? Perhaps he should have a private tutor? . . . Meanwhile, in order to teach him habits of quiet and undistracted industry, "I can (the old gentleman wrote to a friend), and I believe I do, keep him in his room a certain portion of the twenty-four hours." But even so, nothing would substitute for the boy's own will power, which was apparently defective. The grandchildren, too, were sometimes sick, because they were spoiled. Not by their grandmother, but by their mother. The old gentleman's wife never spoiled anyone: indeed, she wrote to Fanny to warn her, saying emphatically, "I am sure there is nothing so pernicious as over charging the stomach of a child."

He thought hard and long about the state of the nation. Although he had retired from politics, he was often consulted, and he kept closely in touch. One advantage of retirement was that it gave him time to think over general principles. Never an optimist, he could usually see important dangers some time before they appeared to others. This December, as he rode over the stiff clods under the pale sky, he was thinking over two constant threats to his country. One was the danger of disputes between the separate States and the central government. (Congress had just passed a law designed to combat sedition, and two of the States had immediately denounced it as unconstitutional. This could lead only to disaster.) The other problem was that respectable men were not entering public life. They seemed to prefer to pursue riches, to seek their private happiness, as though such a thing were possible if the nation declined. The old gentleman decided to write to Mr. Henry, whom he considered a sound man, and urge him to reenter politics: he would surely be elected if he would consent to stand; and then, with his experience, he could do much to bridge the gap between the federal government and the States.

The old gentleman stopped his horse. With that large, cool, comprehensive gaze which every visitor always remembered, he looked round the land. It was doing better. Five years ago his farms had been almost ruined by neglect and greed. During his long absence the foremen had cropped them too hard and omitted to cultivate and fertilize, looking for quick and easy profits. Still, even before retiring, he had set about restoring the ground to health and vigor: first, by feeding the soil as much as possible, all year round; second by "a judicious succession of crops"; and third, most important of all, by careful regularity and constant application. As he put it in a letter, "To establish good rules, and a regular system, is the life and the soul of every kind of business." Now the land was improving every year. It was always a mistake to expect rapid returns. To build up a nation and to make a farm out of the wilderness, both needed long, steady, thoughtful, determined application; both were the work of the will.

Long ago, when he was only a boy, he had copied out a set of rules to help in forming his manners and his character—in the same careful way as he would lay out a new estate or survey a recently purchased tract of land. The last of the rules he still remembered. Keep alive in your breast that little spark of celestial fire called Conscience. Some of the philosophers said that the spark from heaven was reason, the power of the intellect, which we share with God. The old gentleman did not quarrel with them, but he did not believe them. He knew that the divine fire in the spirit was the sense of duty, the lawfulness which orders the whole universe, the power of which a young poet then alive was soon to write:

> Thou dost preserve the stars from wrong;
> And the most ancient heavens, through Thee,
>   are fresh and strong.

His mind turned back over his long and busy life. He never dreamed or brooded, but he liked to note things down, to plan them and record them. Now, on this cold December day, he could recall nearly every Christmas he had ever spent: sixty at least. Some were peaceful, some were passed in deadly danger, many in war, some in strange lonely places, some in great assemblies, some in happiness and some in anguish of soul, none in despair.

One of the worst was Christmas Day of twenty-one years before. That was early in the war, a bad time. It snowed four inches on Christmas. His men were out in the open, with no proper quarters. Although he started them on building shelters, an aggressive move by the enemy made them stand to arms and interrupt all other work for nearly a week. And they had no decent uniforms, no warm coats, no strong shoes, no regular supplies, two days without meat, three days without bread, almost a quarter of his entire force unfit for duty. He was receiving no supplies from the government, and he was actually meeting opposition from the locals. They had sent up a protest against keeping the troops in service during the winter. Apparently they thought you could raise an army whenever you needed one—not understanding that this little force was the only permanent barrier between them and foreign domination. He had replied with crushing energy to that protest. In a letter to the President of Congress, he wrote:

> I can assure those gentlemen that it is a much easier and less distressing thing to draw remonstrances in a comfortable room by a good fireside than to occupy a cold, bleak hill, and sleep under frost and snow without clothes or blankets. However, although they seem

to have little feeling for the naked and distressed soldiers, I feel superabundantly for them, and from my soul I pity those miseries which it is neither in my power to relieve or prevent.

He ended with his well-known, strongly and gracefully written signature, G. WASHINGTON.

Questions

1. What is being described in each of the selections?
2. Who is the speaker of each passage?
3. What is the dominant point of view in each passage?
4. How can you as an interpreter re-create these passages for an audience? In what ways do you alter your performance when you change from autobiographical to biographical material?

Exploring the Differences between Biography and Autobiography

An autobiography presents a literary self-portrait in which the writer describes his or her own life and times. Thus, in the excerpt from *Down These Mean Streets,* the autobiographical point of view is almost always first person, rather than third person, as is usual in biographical works. In addition, the author of an autobiography writes from a dual perspective: his or her words are reflective of both past and present attitudes. This duality complicates the task of the interpreter who seeks to re-create such works. Consequently, when interpreting autobiographical literature, your goal is to suggest your author-subject's outlooks and behaviors at various points in his or her lifetime. How does the author-subject experience himself or herself and others? How does your author-subject react to various events and people helpful to him or her? Share details such as these with your audience.

Like autobiography, biography also presents a literary portrait of an individual; in biography, though, that portrait has been carefully sketched in the words of another individual who came to know the subject well through interviews or research. How does an interpreter approach the task of re-creating biographical material for an audience? First, realize that just as two artists will paint portraits of the same subject in contrasting ways, so will "word sketches" of a subject differ. How much can they differ? Take a new look at a familiar personality by reading the following opinion.

PERFORMER'S WORKSHOP
Biographical Perspectives

As you read the following passage from an editorial by Russell Baker, consider what it tells you about the famous Little Miss Muffett.

"An Opinion: An Analysis of Miss Muffet"
from **Russell Baker**

Little Miss Muffet, as everyone knows, sat on a tuffet eating her curds and whey when along came a spider who sat down beside her and frightened Miss Muffet away. While everyone knows it, the significance of the event had never been analyzed until a conference of thinkers recently brought their special insights to bear upon it. Following are excerpts from the transcript of their discussion:

SOCIOLOGIST: Miss Muffet is nutritionally underprivileged, as evidenced by the subminimal diet of curds and whey upon which she is forced to subsist, while the spider's cultural disadvantage is evidenced by such phenomena as legs exceeding standard norms, odd mating habits and so forth.

In this instance, spider expectations lead the culturally disadvantaged to assert demands to share the tuffet with the nutritionally underprivileged. Due to a communications failure, Miss Muffet assumes without evidence that the spider will not be satisfied to share her tuffet, but will also insist on eating her curds and whey. . . .

MILITARIST: Second-strike capability, sir! That's what was lacking. If Miss Muffet had developed a second-strike capability instead of squandering her resources on curds and whey, no spider on earth would have dared launch a first strike capable of carrying him right to the heart of her tuffet. I am confident that Miss Muffet had adequate notice from experts that she could not afford both curds and whey and at the same time support an early-spider-warning system. . . .

BOOK REVIEWER: Written on several levels, this searing, sensitive exploration of the arachnid heart illuminates the agony and splendor of Jewish family life with a candor that is at once breathtaking in its simplicity and soul-shattering in its implied ambiguity. Some will doubtless be shocked to see such subjects as tuffets and whey discussed without flinching, but hereafter writers too timid to call a tuffet a tuffet will no longer. . . .

EDITORIALIST: Why has the Government not seen fit to tell the public all it knows about the so-called curds-and-whey affair? It is not enough to suggest that this was merely a random incident involving a lonely spider and a young diner. . . .

PSYCHIATRIST: Little Miss Muffet is, of course, neither little, nor a miss. These are obviously the self she has created in her own fantasies to escape the reality that she is a . . . divorcee whose superego makes it impossible for her to sustain a normal relationship with any man, symbolized by the spider. . . .

STUDENT: Little Miss Muffet, tuffets, curds, whey and spiders are what's wrong with education today. They're all irrelevant. Tuffets are irrelevant. Curds are irrelevant. Whey is irrelevant. . . .

CHILD: This is about a little girl who gets scared by a spider.

(The child was sent home when the conference broke for lunch. It was agreed that the child was too immature to add anything to the sum of human understanding and should not return until he had grown up.)

Questions

1. What do the respondents' comments concerning Miss Muffet tell you about each respondent?
2. How do the respondents reveal their own biases?

Although the conference on Miss Muffet never actually occurred (so far as we know), the imagined results are probably only slightly exaggerated. The Miss Muffet piece emphasizes that there simply is no such thing as a completely objective human being. Thus, when re-creating a portion of a biography, be certain that your own preconceptions of the person or subject do not hinder you in internalizing the impressions of your author. In other words, when re-creating a selection from a biography, work to share your author's concept—not your own—of his or her subject. Be accurate in determining the writer's perspective or frame of reference; you want to reflect faithfully the author's attitude toward the subject in order to embody the tensions, feelings, qualities, and events the author chose to emphasize. Consider the author's orientation and biases regarding the subject of the following biographies.

PERFORMER'S WORKSHOP
Biographies

Read the following selections written about the assassination of President John F. Kennedy.

Through Russian Eyes: President Kennedy's from *1036 Days*
Anatolii Andreievich Gromyko

It was late autumn in Texas. The sky was filled with threatening greyish clouds, and it drizzled. The sun, it seemed, would not hearten Texans on the morning of November 22, 1963. But later that morning the weather began to clear, and by eleven a bright southern sun was sparkling over Dallas.

Air Force Two landed at the Dallas airport at 11:35 A.M. Lyndon Johnson, Vice-President of the United States of America, was aboard. Five minutes later the shadow of a second plane, Air Force One, appeared on the runway. That aircraft carried the 45-year-old President of the United States, John Fitzgerald Kennedy. . . .

The President's airplane slowly taxied to the airport terminal. It is hard to say what Kennedy was thinking as he prepared to leave the aircraft, in front of which a large welcoming crowd had already gathered. There is every reason to believe, however, that at the bottom of his heart he felt an ominous foreboding about his journey. . . .

Kennedy's wife, Jacqueline, and Kenneth O'Donnell, his close friend, shared his apprehension. It was no accident that the three, while having breakfast at their hotel before flying to Dallas on the morning of November 22, discussed a highly unusual topic: the personal risks Kennedy was taking during his public appearances. Kennedy remarked that "if somebody really wanted to shoot the President of the United States of America, it would not be a very difficult task. All he would have to do is to climb a tall building, have a telescopic rifle, and nobody could do anything to prevent such an attempt. . . ."

The President did not realize how close he came to the truth.

The main reason for Kennedy's journey to Texas was his desire to bolster his prestige in this southern state, the birthplace of Vice-President Johnson, on the eve of the 1964 presidential elections. In the 1960 election, Kennedy almost lost Texas to Richard Nixon, the Republican party candidate. . . .

Now Kennedy was in Dallas. At 11:50 A.M., local time, the motorcade set out from the airport for the city. Kennedy and his wife were seated in the back of the first car; in the jump-seats were Governor Connally and his wife. In the front seat were two Secret Service agents to protect the President. Immediately behind Kennedy's car was another which held eight additional security agents. . . .

The suburbs were behind them. The President's motorcade entered Main Street, the principal artery of Dallas' business district, which crosses it from east to west. The welcoming crowds had swollen in number. Squinting in the sunlight, Kennedy gazed with curiosity at the spectators lining the sidewalks who had come—if not to welcome him—at least to look at the President of the United States. Nothing appeared to foreshadow danger.

At the end of Main, the presidential procession turned right on Houston Street. Ahead, at the intersection of Houston and Elm Streets, stood a seven-floor red brick building, a book depository. The clock on one building now showed the time as 12:30 P.M. The President's car slowly turned left onto Elm Street.

Seconds later, sharp shots rang out in quick succession. Eyewitnesses to Kennedy's assassination later maintained that the shots had been fired from the book depository as well as from the railroad viaduct. . . . John Kennedy was fatally wounded in the neck and head. . . .

Naturally, since Kennedy's assassination, the question of who actually murdered the President has preoccupied everyone. And to this day the question remains essentially unanswered. It appears as though all traces of the crime have vanished.

It is generally known that Lee Harvey Oswald, the person charged with Kennedy's assassination, was shot within the Dallas police station by the owner of a night club, one Jack Ruby, who later died in a prison hospital. . . . How could it happen that the only American apprehended as the apparent perpetrator of the crime was liquidated literally before the eyes of everyone, and, naturally, can no longer furnish any evidence. . . ?

from *The Death of a President*
William Manchester

12:22. Main and Ervay.

A dozen young people surged into the street; from his curbside command post Dallas' husky Inspector Herbert Sawyer gave a signal and a clutch of patrolmen closed in, pressing them back. The Secret Service showed signs of activity. . . .

On the left loomed the Mercantile Building and the Neiman Marcus department store. The seventh floor of the Mercantile Building was the headquarters of H. L. Hunt, Dallas' billionaire. Flanked by two secretaries, Hunt stared down as the President gaily saluted the mob in front of Walgreen's.

12:23. Main and Akward.

Forrest Sorrels, in the lead car, heard shouts of "The President's coming!" He craned his neck and muttered to Lawson, "My God, look at the people hanging out the windows!"

Clint Hill was watching the windows. So was Yarborough, and he didn't like them. The Senator was delighted by the throngs on the sidewalks. Next to the President, he was the most exuberant campaigner in the motorcade. . . .

12:24. Main and Field.

Jim Hosty, the local FBI agent in charge of Lee Oswald's file, had his wish. He saw Kennedy from the curb and then stepped into the Alamo Grill for lunch. His day, he felt, was made.

12:26. Main and Poydras.

. . . Liz Carpenter, listening to the echoing roars, crowed, "Well, this pulls the rug out from under . . . Barry Goldwater!"

12:28. Main and Market.

The neighborhood began to deteriorate. They were entering a seamy section of bail-bond shops, bars, a public gym. It occurred to Yarborough that anyone could drop a pot of flowers on Kennedy from an upper story. It will be good to have the President out of this, he thought, and then he saw that they were nearly at the end. . . .

12:29. Main and Houston.

. . . Nellie, surprised and delighted at Dallas' showing, twisted in her jump seat. "You sure can't say Dallas doesn't love you, Mr. President," she said jubilantly. Kennedy smiled and answered, "No, you can't."

12:30. Houston and Elm.

. . . Sorrels was saying to Curry, "Five more minutes and we'll have him there." Noting that there was only a handful of spectators ahead, Lawson alerted the four-to-twelve shift. He radioed the Trade Mart that they would reach there in five minutes. Then he automatically scanned the overpass. . . .

The pool car was approaching it. Kilduff, misreading the sign on the front of the warehouse, said to Merriman Smith, "What the hell is a Book Repository?"

Back on Main Street Evelyn Lincoln was saying, "Just think—we've come through all of Dallas and there hasn't been a single demonstration." One of Liz Carpenter's local friends laughed. "That's Dallas," she said. . . .

The Lincoln moved ahead at 11.2 miles an hour. It passed the tree. . . . Momentarily the entire car was obscured. But it was no longer hidden from the sixth-floor corner window. It had passed the last branch.

Brend's five-year-old boy timidly raised his hand. The President smiled warmly. He raised his hand to wave back.

There was a sudden, sharp, shattering sound. . . .

The President was wounded, but not fatally. A 6.5 millimeter bullet had entered the back of his neck, bruised his right lung, ripped his windpipe, and exited at his throat, nicking the knot of his tie. . . .

And now it was too late. Howard Brennan, open-mouthed, saw Oswald take deliberate aim for his final shot. . . . Crooking his arm, Oswald drew a fresh bead with his Italian rifle. Ready on the left, ready on the right, all ready on the firing line, his Marine Corps instructors had shouted on the San Diego range, signaling the appearance of rapid-fire targets. He was ready now. They had also told him to hold his front sight at six o'clock on an imaginary clock dial. It was there, and steady. His target, startlingly clear in the cross hairs of his telescopic sight, was eighty-eight yards away.

He squeezed the trigger.

The First Lady, in her last act as First Lady, leaned solicitously toward the President. His face was quizzical. She had seen that expression so often, when he was puzzling over a difficult press conference question. Now, in a gesture of infinite grace, he raised his right hand, as though to brush back his tousled chestnut hair. But the motion faltered. The hand fell back limply. He had been reaching for the top of his head. But it wasn't there any more.

The radio reports continued to assert that the president had been injured and was alive.

I suddenly realized that for the first time in my life I was late for an appearance in court. The trial was to have been continued five minutes earlier. I rushed to the courtroom not sure of what I would encounter there, but certain that the trial would not go forth that day. I explained to the judge that the president had been shot and that he had died. He was unmoved. He had heard about it; the case would go forward. "Let's move along with this trial," he said.

I hesitated. "Call your next witness, Mr. Lane. We have work to do." My client testified. The jury apparently was satisfied with his explanation, for at the close of the day he was acquitted.

I hurried from the courthouse aware that I was, several hours after the assassination, one of the least knowledgeable persons in the country about the details of the historic event that had transpired earlier that day. I was eager to rush to my office to a television set and telephone.

With a briefcase in one hand and a topcoat in the other, I ran down the massive stone steps, stepping around an elderly gentleman who was walking slowly in the same direction. He turned and said, "Well, Lane, do you think he did it alone?" I recognized a judge of my acquaintance, a distinguished though somewhat irascible jurist for whom I had great respect and at least a modicum of fondness. Identifying with Rip van Winkle as he rose, I responded, "Who, sir? Did what?"

"Do you think Oswald killed the president?" he asked.

I explained that I had just tried a case and had heard nothing about the details of the assassination. The judge waved away my response, clearly ruling it to be irrelevant. He stopped walking, looked at me, and said:

"He couldn't very well shoot him from the back and cause an entrance wound in his throat, could he?"

The rhetorical question required no response. He continued:

"The doctors said the throat wound was an entrance wound. It'll be an interesting trial. I want to see how they answer that question."

More than a quarter of a century later, the question—how could Oswald shoot Kennedy from the back from the front?—remains without adequate response.

Questions

1. What do the preceding excerpts tell you about each author's orientation toward John F. Kennedy?

2. What occurrences has each writer chosen to emphasize? Why do you believe these choices were made?
3. How do the comments in the excerpts reveal each writer's biases?
4. What challenges would you face in recreating the material during a performance?

Diaries and Letters

Diaries and letters allow intimate glimpses into the lives and times of individuals, providing an interpreter of literature with stimulating performance material. In a diary, a writer speaks to himself or herself; in a letter, he or she speaks to another person. Consequently, the two forms of literature reflect differences in communication processes—differences an interpreter must mirror in performance.

When recreating a diary entry, you seek to suggest an intrapersonal transaction is taking place; in effect, the person talking to himself or herself. You allow your audience to overhear your speaker's meditations; however, be certain you don't sound as if you are engaging in subvocal musings. Adequate voice projection is a necessity for the audience to hear and understand the speaker. Although it is thoughts you are communicating, remember that you are thinking aloud.

On the other hand, when re-creating a letter or a series of letters, you want to suggest an interpersonal communication transaction is occurring. Place your scene out front and speak to your recipient as if he or she were seated in your audience. When interpreting letters, be certain you determine the kind of relationship the writer shared with the letter's recipient. Often, the style and content of the letter will offer clues, but you will probably find it both interesting and beneficial to research the relationship.

When interpreting either a diary entry or a letter, be certain you comprehend how these documents reflect their author's daily life and concerns. Interpreting material of such a personal nature necessitates an empathic understanding of the author and his or her environmental influences.

PERFORMER'S WORKSHOP
Intimate Glimpses

Read the following passages carefully. Think about what the content of each selection reveals about its author.

from *Letters to a Black Boy*
Bob Teague

Dear Adam,
    Question the mysteries that you
        do not understand
    Question the answers that
        quickly come to hand
    Question your teachers, yourself
        and what you see
    Question him, question her
    Question me.

Despite your daddy's desire simply to guide you through the maze, there will be times when I am guilty of pushing and preaching. My excuse is that I cannot forget that the black skin you got from me will force you to waste a kingsize slice of your lifetime climbing invisible barriers, imagining other barriers where none exist, fending off affronts—real and imagined—to your dignity, proving that you are human, disproving that you are inferior, living down stereotypes, protesting injustice, choking down helpless rage, waiting for freedom, and adjusting to the knowledge that you will still be waiting when you die.

All those distractions, of course, will rob you of more time and energy than any man can afford to lose from his search for personal fulfillment, from learning to help, to share, to build, to laugh, to dream, to love.

And that is why with a sense of desperation I pound away, trying to instill in you the notion that the real concerns of living have no relation to the color of your skin; that besides learning to cope with the distractions that come with being black in this society, you must also face the more fundamental distractions that plague all men. . . .

Dear Adam,

We have just lived through the longest night of our lives. The black patron saint, the Rev. Dr. Martin Luther King, Jr., was assassinated, mourned and buried. We also survived the violent aftermath of black brothers by the thousands blindly searching for revenge.

Dr. King's passage from living symbol to entombed martyr required only six unaccountably sunny days. The passage of black vigilantes from stunned mourners to bitter marauders and finally back to men required a week of accountably ugly nights. . . .

My main impression is that we watched the complete horror from beginning to end, sitting slumped in front of our television screen. . . . The four of us in the living room sob openly. There is no attempt to comfort one another. There is no attempt to hide our tears. . . .

Eventually, we are swept by the screen into the mournful trek to the cemetery. His coffin lies on the bed of a creaking mule-drawn cart. A symbol of his commitment to the poor. . . .

At last they lower his body—and a part of us—into the grave. We will weep yet again upon reading the epitaph engraved on his white marble tomb:

> "Free at last, free at last
> Thank God Almighty
> I'm free at last."

Anne Frank and her family, German-born Jews, went into hiding in Holland in 1942 to try to escape deportation to the Nazi concentration camps. Anne kept a diary of their time in hiding. This excerpt is from her diary entry for July 15, 1944, just a few weeks before the family was betrayed and transported to the camps. Anne died in Bergen-Belsen in 1945, only a few months before the camp was liberated.

Anne Frank: The Diary of a Young Girl

Anne Frank

"Deep down, the young are lonelier than the old." I read this in a book somewhere and it's stuck in my mind. As far as I can tell, it's true.

So if you're wondering whether it's harder for the adults here than for the children, the answer is no, it's certainly not. Older people have an opinion about everything and are sure of themselves and their actions. It's twice as hard for us young people to hold on to our opinions at a time when ideals are being shattered and destroyed, when the worst side of human nature predominates, when everyone has come to doubt truth, justice and God.

Anyone who claims that the older folks have a more difficult time in the Annex doesn't realize that the problems have a far greater impact on us. We're much too young to deal with these problems, but they keep thrusting themselves on us until, finally, we're forced to think up a solution, though most of the time our solutions crumble when faced with the facts. It's difficult in times like these: ideals, dreams and cherished hopes rise within us, only to be crushed by grim reality. It's a wonder I haven't abandoned all my ideals, they seem so absurd and impractical. Yet I cling to them because I still believe, in spite of everything, that people are truly good at heart.

It's utterly impossible for me to build my life on a foundation of chaos, suffering and death. I see the world begin slowly transformed into a wilderness, I hear the approaching thunder that, one day, will destroy us too, I feel the suffering of millions. And yet, when I look up at the sky, I somehow feel that everything will change for the better, that this cruelty too shall end, that peace and tranquility will return once more. In the meantime, I must hold on to my ideals. Perhaps the day will come when I'll be able to realize them!

Yours, Anne M. Frank

Questions

1. What do the preceding passages tell you about the individuals who wrote them? What personal traits or qualities were revealed?
2. What performance techniques would help to re-create these materials for an audience?

Remember, your aim as interpreter is to match the style of your performance to the style and content of the literature. Use your rehearsal period to decide the vocal and physical gestures you will adopt to indicate the author's attitudes and feelings. Select facial expressions, gestures, movements, and voice qualities carefully to exhibit the essence and personality of the work.

Oral History and Tales of Everyday Life

Today, oral histories, personal narratives, taped interviews, news broadcasts, and radio and television documentaries function as storehouses for the important events of our age. Interpreters should pay special attention to these materials because the public or private monologues and dialogues recorded on them are, in fact, drama in our time. For example, over fifty years ago, interviewers from the Federal Writers' Project traveled throughout the South talking to and recording on audiotape the memories of former slaves. Through their efforts, they preserved the words of men like Fountain Hughes, who matter of factly said, "My grandfather belonged to Thomas Jefferson," and women like Delia Garlic who recalled, "Us just prayed for strength to endure it to the end. We didn't expect nothing but to stay in bondage till we died." Similar videotapes exist containing the testimonies of survivors of the Holocaust. While these audio- and videotapes themselves elicit a visceral reaction from those who listen to them, the interpretive performer can also make these kinds of texts come alive during performances.

Storytelling is part of our everyday lives. Personal narratives involve and intrigue us. They help us make sense of our experience by enable us to engage in retrospective sense-making. They provide us with a natural means of figuring out what has happened to us. One user of personal narrative observes, "I write to record what others erase when I speak, to rewrite the stories others have miswritten about me, about you." By re-creating and performing personal narratives, interpreters help others see with clarity the times in which they live; they also help equip their listeners with the sensitivity they need to know the individuals who have affected their society.

The oral reader's task is to bring alive "stored" speech and experience. According to some, the telling and consuming of personal narratives is becoming

a defining condition of our culture. There are things we learn through performances of personal narratives that we might never come to appreciate were they
revealed to us in other ways. The telling, in effect, links the experience and the
story. To paraphrase the words of Walter Benjamin, the storyteller takes what he
or she tells from experience—his or her own or that reported by others. And he
or she in turn makes it the experience of those who are listening to the tale.

PERFORMER'S WORKSHOP
The Drama of Our Times

Read the following excerpts and think about how they reflect the drama
and conflicts of the late twentieth century and today.

"Life at 'Jeff': Tough Students Wonder Where Childhood Went"

"New York Times," March 7, 1992

New Yorkers and indeed the nation were shocked when two students were gunned down in the hallway of Thomas Jefferson High
School in East New York, Brooklyn, on February 26. Khalil
Sumpter, a 15-year-old student, was arrested and charged with the slayings
of Tyrone Sinkler, 16, and Ian Moore, 17.

For the 1,800 students who attend "Jeff," in one of the poorest and most
violent sections of the city, murder and mayhem are as much a feature of
teen-age life as pep rallies and proms.

To learn more about the lives, hopes and fears of these "children of
war," as their principal calls them, the *New York Times* invited Thomas
Jefferson students to a discussion this week.

Even as city officials called for such measures as more metal detectors
in the schools, many of the students said the problems went far beyond
guns, ultimately to a kind of erosion of the spirit.

MARIANA BRYANT: Last night we was looking through my junior high
school yearbook and my friend pointed out a number of people in that
book that was dead.

Q: About how many would you estimate?

MARIANA: Ten, all guys from eighth and ninth grade.

CAROLINE GRIFFITH: There was a shooting around my building over this
girl. I was on my way to school. Two guys were going with one girl, so after
one found out then he just pulled out his gun and shot him. . . . The one
that got shot was 17.

SEAN WILLIAMS: One of the guys that died from this school was Wesley. . . . He got shot in a barbershop right across the street on Pennsylvania. . . . I think he was 16.

He was caught on the wrong side of Pennsylvania Avenue, the demarcation line in long-running guerrilla warfare between those who live in the Linden housing project and those who live "on the other side."

NEREIDA TORRES: I had a boyfriend that recently died. He got killed right there across the street at a party over an argument and they decided, well, if they couldn't get him to fight . . . He wasn't a punk. Why you gone fight over an argument, something stupid? So they just decided just to come up and kill him. . . . They shot him in the neck.

NORVEN CHARLES: A couple of months ago there was a drive-by shooting and one of my friends died.

KAREEM SMITH: I already got shot. . . . I ran into this kid that I had a little problem with.

Q: Larry, how many do you know who have been shot?

LARRY BUGETT: A lot. That's all I can say is a lot of people I know.

Q: More than five?

LARRY: More than 20. People that's 18 and under. Cause we used to be in a posse called V.I.P.: Vanderveer International Posse.

Q: Over what period of time were these people shot?

LARRY: Like two years, three years. Some is dead. Some crippled. Some of them is still selling. Some of them is in jail now.

The students, boys and girls, say they have to walk the streets ever mindful that there are certain blocks that are unsafe for them because of ongoing gang rivalries and "beef" that someone may have with them personally.

Q: How do you know what the rules are, that you can walk on one side of a street and not the other side?

EUGENE ROBICHAUX: Examples. They make examples of people. They catch somebody and kill 'em and then you know: don't be over on this side.

Q: Are you afraid that you could be the next victim?

MARIANA: I'm afraid. Right now it's a dispute between these two guys, a rivalry over two gangs. My brother said he was sitting in a barbershop and they came in there and shot through the window. . . . It gets to the point where I don't walk up that block no more because I heard the guys that cut hair there, they've got to wear bulletproof vests.

SHAWN: I got one.

Q: Where did you get a bulletproof vest?

SHAWN: My uncle.

Kareem said that he also has a bulletproof vest that he bought for "a buck fifty"—that is, $150—after telling his mother he needed the money for new sneakers.

KAREEM: I wear it on Fridays and Saturdays. . . . Sometimes I wear it when I'm going off my block, out my projects. Like if I'm going to Bed-Stuy to see this other chick, I wear my vest.

Q: Isn't that an awful way to have to live, to have to wear a bulletproof vest when you leave home for parties or dates?

KAREEM: No, if you want to be safe.

Q: Why don't you carry a gun?

KAREEM: Cause you'll get arrested for carrying a gun, not for wearing a bulletproof vest.

Q: What about a knife?

KAREEM: I don't carry no knife. What am I going to do: stab the bullet?

But there is a more deeply-rooted anger that seems to lead to an ever escalating level of violence.

Q: Why are people so angry, angry enough to kill?

SHAWN: The main reason is somebody in their family probably got shot or got murdered, and they just go out and have revenge on everybody they don't like.

RETISHA: I think it's peer pressure. It's a lot of guys that hang around other people just to be in the crowd. . . . Some people just got guns to have them and then a lot of them use them. Then the ones that do use them don't know how to use them. That's how a lot of innocent bystanders get killed, too.

Everyone wants some kind of "rep" or reputation—and one way to earn one for being tough is to carry a gun, the teen-agers said. No one wants to be seen as a "herb" or wimp.

SEAN: If a guy steps on your foot, it's one of your peers says, "Oh, you gone let that happen to you? He stepped on your foot." You know, you have the right mind that's like, "I'm gone ignore that." But your friend says, "You ain't gone do nothing about that?" That puts you to the limit. You be like "Ahh, what I'm gone do?" It gets you thinking and you say something: "Yo, what the hell are you doing?" or something like that. You start, you know, to break.

NATHANIEL EDWARDS: Say I was walking in the hallway and somebody bumped me and they meant to bump me. And now, me, I'm the herb. I will turn and I will walk away from them. Next day, he gone bump me again. Now it's a Friday, right? And he comes and bump me and he says, "Yo, what's up, man? If you keep walking away, we'll keep bothering you." . . . You can fight right there, but a gun gone come in sooner or later.

Disputes can start over what the teenagers acknowledge to be "the stupidest things." Kareem Smith said he almost fought a friend who tried to grab his cheeseburger.

Some Thomas Jefferson students cope with the violence around them by staying indoors as much as possible, whether home or school. Others say they try to suppress their feelings altogether. Nathaniel Edwards has a different way.

NATHANIEL: It hurts me, but I hardly cry because I take everything as a joke. That's how I protect myself. I can't be taking nothing too seriously because that's when you sit down and sob and you mope. That's what makes you commit suicide, too, you know? So I just make jokes.

"Death of Innocence"

Frank Bruni

Listening to the wild stories her classmates brought back from the beaches of spring break last year, Jennifer Swartout feared some of them were true.

She wasn't jealous.

She was panicky.

The boys who counted their sexual conquests, the girls who gulped birth control pills, didn't they know?

Swartout did.

She had watched AIDS lay waste to her favorite uncle, her godfather, left emaciated and addlebrained by the disease at age 35.

He died last September.

In November, Swartout made an appointment with her school principal, Rodney Hosman, at Livonia Churchill High.

"This is going to sound strange," she told him. "But please, just listen."

She told Hosman that this year, the week before spring break, there should be a senior class assembly about AIDS.

It should be blunt and forceful, because she didn't want any of her friends ever to get the gruesome disease. They should learn a little fear, a lot of caution.

Swartout offered to coordinate the project. That night, she phoned the president of the school's Parent, Teacher, and Student Association, a woman she had never met.

In subsequent days, she talked to health teachers. She told them that whatever AIDS education she had gotten in the 10th grade wasn't gripping enough—she couldn't even remember it. How could the assembly go further?

She got answers and help. Next month, just before school lets out for a week's recess, most of the 388 seniors will gather in the auditorium, listen to guest speakers infected with the virus that causes AIDS, and be told how to save themselves.

They also will hear Swartout's story. The 17-year-old girl will stand up before her classmates and talk about losing her uncle to AIDS, an experience she felt compelled to keep secret while it was happening because some people view the disease as a shameful curse.

"I don't know—maybe 98 percent of the seniors won't listen," Swartout said. "But that's OK. When you've seen the kind of pain I've seen, you just feel that if you can save one person or make a few people think, 'I better be careful,' that's great."

Before the assembly, a note will go to the parents of every senior, letting them know their children can be excused, said Hosman. He said some parents don't want their kids hearing candid talk about AIDS and sexual behavior.

But Hosman believes the assembly is important. He said that while most teenagers have a good scientific grasp of what AIDS is, they don't feel its threat or impact in any direct way.

For Swartout, it was particularly important for teenagers to know. They seemed oblivious to AIDS.

"They hear about it so much it becomes part of the background noise," she said. "It blends in with all the other crises in the world."

"But if you've watched a person die this way, it just becomes so urgent that people understand how serious it is."

"Instant Intimacy"
Roxana Robinson

Generally, the rule in the subway is silence. This is not, of course, to say that you are in a silent world. You are in a metal car weighing several tons, riding on rimless metal wheels, driven by crackling electrical charges and surrounded by hard, reverberant surfaces. The noise, especially on corners, when all the moving metal parts of the train seem to rub horridly together, is high, piercing and cacophonous enough to drive you mad. So that simply standing alone in the subway car, without anyone else in it, you are under a kind of attack.

But your own silence is the rule. When the car is full, there may be 60 or 70 complete strangers crammed into it, any one of whom may be poised on the brink of madness. Your neutral request that he move over may be all that's needed to send him down into a black pit of manic rage. And not only will he hurtle downward, he'll try to pull you with him. So silence and no eye contact. Eyes are often raised upward in studious attention, as though Michelangelo's last and little known commission had been discovered on the curved white ceiling of the No. 6 train. Or focused discreetly on the floor. This is safer than the ceiling, because looking downward partly conceals your face and throat: no one can cast his mad eyes across your features, measuring your cheeks for slashes, your neck for fingers. Silence and anonymity are the rule that most people obey.

Which is why it is so startling when someone breaks it, plunging a carful of strangers into unsettling intimacy.

Last week I was standing in the middle of a fullish car that stopped at Grand Central. As the crowd outside pushed its way in, a man among it fell. I saw him go down, just as he was stepping into the car: I saw his head slide downward. He was falling down onto the tracks, through that narrow opening between car and platform. As he went down, he gave a wordless shout—a loud, low, dull cry. Everyone turned, electrified. Everyone saw him going, sliding away from the world. He was grabbed by the people closet to him: suddenly we were together in this. Suddenly we were all survivors, connected, and one of us was in peril. There was the man's head, slipping downward in the crowd, and in all of our minds was the unspeakable notion of being on the tracks, in that lethal black underworld between platform and train. Urgency flashed through us: the man was grabbed by his arms and his elbows and his shoulders and pulled magically back up. He was saved; he stood. He was terrified, but upright. He moved inside the car to stand directly in front of me.

He was a white man in his 40's, gray-haired, grizzled and stout, wearing black plastic-rimmed glasses, a white T-shirt and a brown leather jacket. He looked like a deliveryman, perhaps, someone used to taking orders, not giving them. He took hold of the pole and stared at me. His face was 10 inches from mine. He began talking. His voice was still loud and urgent, but oddly low, dull, without variation.

"I fell down, I fell down," he roared. "I fell down between the train." He was looking into my eyes.

"I know," I said, "but you're all right now."

At once he frowned. His eyes were black with fear, his pupils huge. "I didn't hurt myself, did I? I'm all right, aren't I? My leg isn't broken or nothing, is it?"

"No," I said steadily. "You're all right."

"I'm all right, aren't I?" he repeated, loud and plangent. He was desperate.

"You're all right," I said. I looked deeply and directly into his eyes, as you never do in the subway with strangers. "You're all right now."

"They pushed me," he roared mournfully. "I fell down."

"They pulled you up again," I answered. "You're all right now. Your leg isn't hurt. You're all right."

His fear was contagious. I felt as though I were soothing a frightened horse, as though my own certainty was all that would save us both from rocketing helplessly down into terror. But the man had chosen to stand in front of me. This was my task, just as it had been the task of those at the door to grab his arms, his elbows, his shoulders and pull him powerfully to safety as he slid screaming down.

Now it was my task to look into his eyes and tell him that, though all his fears were real, though we were surrounded by demonic tumult and silent stranger, though we were hurtling, dangerously through the darkness, though we were continually at risk of losing our places and falling out of the world, still, just at this moment, because of luck and of that sudden reflex of humanity that strikes a crowd like a flash of lightening, galvanizing and electrifying us and revealing us as our true selves, we were all right. We were fine.

Questions

1. What challenges must you meet in order to effectively re-create each of the preceding selections?
2. How does the tone of each passage reflect the times it describes?
3. What is the relationship between the speaker and the audience?
4. What can an interpreter bring to these passages that simply reading or replaying an audio- or videotape of them cannot bring? How might you combine multimedia with your performance to heighten the impact of the pieces?

IDEA ENCORE

This chapter explored nonfiction literature, including public speech, essay, biography and autobiography, diaries and letters, video- and audiotape, oral history, and tales of everyday life. We discussed how to analyze each literary type, and we focused on the various techniques you, the interpreter, must use to prepare a selection for performance. As you read today's paper, flip through a magazine, or watch a speech on C-Span, keep your eyes and ears open for nonfiction material that you can use as a performer to bring important themes and ideas alive for your audiences.

PERFORMER'S SHOWCASE & JOURNAL
Performance Documentary

Choose an individual, living or dead, whose attitudes, thoughts, and personality you would enjoy sharing with the rest of the class. In your journal, write how you would present that person through the performance of documentary materials reflecting that character's life experiences and ideals.

Make certain that the person you choose is prominent enough so that there is a fairly wide range of documentary material—published material by or about that person—from which to draw for purposes of interpretation. Just a few of the individuals whom you might consider for performance are: Frederick Douglass, Winston Churchill, Anne Frank, Malcolm X, Stephen Spielberg, Janet Reno, Stephen Hawking, or other well-known persons.

SELECTIONS FOR FURTHER WORK

 from ***Women in Politics***

Lady Nancy Astor

My entrance into the House of Commons was not, as some thought, in the nature of a revolution. It was an evolution. My husband was the one who started me off on this downward path—from the fireside to public life. If I have helped the cause of women, he is the one to thank, not me.

A woman in the House of Commons! It was almost enough to have broken up the House. I don't blame them—it was equally hard on the woman as it was on them. A pioneer may be a picturesque figure, but they are often rather lonely ones. I must say for the House of Commons, they bore their shock with dauntless decency. No body of men could have been kinder and fairer to a "pirate" than they were. When you hear people over here trying to run down England, please remember that England was the first large country to give the vote to women and that the men of England welcomed an American born woman in the House with a fairness and a justice which, at least, this woman never will forget. . . .

Now, why are we in politics? What is it all about? Something much bigger than ourselves. Schopenhauer was wrong in nearly everything he wrote about women—and he wrote a lot, but he was right in one thing. He said, in speaking of women, "the race is to her more than the individual," and I believe that it is true. I feel somehow we do care about the race as a whole, our very nature makes us take a forward vision; there is no reason why women should look back; mercifully we have no political past; we have all the mistakes of sex legislation with its appalling failures to guide us.

We should know what to avoid, it is no use blaming the men—we made them what they are—and now it is up to us to try and make ourselves—the makers of men—a little more responsible in the future. We realize that no one sex can govern alone. I believe that one of the reasons why civilization has failed so lamentably is that it has had a one-sided government. Don't let us make the mistake of ever allowing that to happen again.

I can conceive of nothing worse than a man-governed world except a woman-governed world—but I can see the combination of the two going forward and making civilization more worthy of the name of civilization based on Christianity, not force. A civilization based on justice and mercy.

I feel men have a greater sense of justice and we of mercy. They must borrow our mercy and we must use their justice. We are new brooms; let us see that we sweep the right rooms.

"The Gettysburg Address"
Abraham Lincoln

Four score and seven years ago our fathers brought forth on this continent a new nation, conceived in liberty, and dedicated to the proposition that all men are created equal.

Now we are engaged in a great civil war, testing whether that nation or any nation so conceived and so dedicated can long endure. We are met on a great battlefield of that war. We have come to dedicate a portion of that field, as a final resting place for those who here gave their lives that that nation might live. It is altogether fitting and proper that we should do this.

But, in a larger sense, we cannot dedicate—we cannot consecrate—we cannot hallow—this ground. The brave men, living and dead, who struggled here, have consecrated it, far above our poor power to add or detract. The world will little note nor long remember what we say here, but it can never forget what they did here. It is for us, the living, rather, to be dedicated here to the unfinished work which they who fought here have thus far so nobly advanced.

It is rather for us to be here dedicated to the great task remaining before us—that from these honored dead we take increased devotion to that cause for which they gave the last full measure of devotion; that we here highly resolve that these dead shall not have died in vain; that this nation, under God, shall have a new birth of freedom; and that government of the people, by the people, for the people shall not perish from the earth.

"Acceptance of the Nobel Prize"
William Faulkner

I feel that this award was not made to me as a man, but to my work—a life's work in the agony and sweat of the human spirit, not for glory and least of all for profit, but to create out of the materials of the human spirit something which did not exist before. So this award is only mine in trust. It will not be difficult to find a dedication for the money part of it commensurate with the purpose and significance of its origin. But I would like to do the same with the acclaim too, by using this moment as a pinnacle from which I might be listened to by the young men and women already dedicated to the same anguish and travail, among whom is already that one who will some day stand where I am standing.

Our tragedy today is a general and universal physical fear so long sustained by now that we can even bear it. There are no longer problems of the spirit. There is only one question: When will I be blown up? Because of this, the young man or woman writing today has forgotten the problems of the human heart in conflict with itself which alone can make good writing because only that is worth writing about, worth the agony and the sweat.

He must learn them again. He must teach himself that the basest of all things is to be afraid; and, teaching himself that, forget it forever, leaving no room in his workshop for anything but the old verities and truths of the heart, the universal truths lacking which any story is ephemeral and doomed—love and honor and pity and pride and compassion and sacrifice. Until he does so, he labors under a curse. He writes not of love but of lust, of defeats in which nobody loses anything of value, and victories without hope and worst of all, without pity or compassion. His griefs grieve on no universal bones, leaving no scars. He writes not of the heart but of the glands.

Until he relearns these things, he will write as though he stood among and watched the end of man. I decline to accept the end of man. It is easy enough to say that man is immortal simply because he will endure: that when the last ding-dong of doom has clanged and faded from the last worthless rock hanging tideless in the last red and dying evening, that even then there will still be one more sound: that of his puny inexhaustible voice, still talking. I refuse to accept this. I believe that man will not merely endure: he will prevail. He is immortal, not because he alone among creatures has an inexhaustible voice, but because he has a soul, a spirit capable of compassion and sacrifice and endurance. The poet's, the writer's, duty is to write about these things. It is his privilege to help man endure by lifting his heart, by reminding him of the courage and honor and hope and pride and compassion and pity and sacrifice which have been the glory of his past. The poet's voice need not merely be the record of man, it can be one of the props, the pillars to help him endure and prevail.

from *Revolution from Within*

Gloria Steinem

When I was living in India on a fellowship after college, a kind Indian friend took me aside and suggested I might consider saying "South Asia," "Southeast Asia," and the like, instead of the "Near" and "Far East." It was the first time I'd ever realized that "Near" and "Far" assumed Europe as the center of the world.

Ever since then, I've noticed that the process of discovering and esteeming a true self is remarkably similar for a person or a race, a group or a nation. When women began to call themselves "Mary Jones" instead of

"Mrs. John Smith," for example, they were doing the same thing as formerly colonized countries that stopped identifying themselves in relation to Europe. When India and England continued their Commonwealth and other relationships after India's independence, one might say that, as George Sand once suggested men and women do, they had broken the marriage bond and reformed it as an equal partnership. When "Negroes" became "blacks" and then "African Americans" in the United States, it was part of a long journey from the humiliation of slavery to a pride of heritage. When I myself started to say "we" instead of "they" when speaking of women, it was a step toward self-esteem that was at least as important as identifying with one's true ethnic heritage. It was also my Declaration of Interdependence.

No matter who we are, the journey toward recovering the self-esteem that should have been our birthright follows similar steps: a first experience of seeing through our own eyes instead of through the eyes of others (for instance, the moment when an Algerian first looked in defiance at a French soldier, or when a woman stops being defined by the male gaze); telling what seemed to be shameful secrets, and discovering they are neither shameful nor secret (from the woman who has survived childhood sexual abuse to the man whose bottomless need for power hides weakness); giving names to problems that have been treated as normal and thus have no names (think of new terms like homophobia, battered women, or Eurocentrism); bonding with others who share similar experiences (from groups of variously abled people to conferences of indigenous nations); achieving empowerment and self-government (from the woman who has a room and income of her own to the nation that declares its independence); bonding with others in shared power (think of democratic families, rainbow coalitions, or the principles of the United Nations); and finally, achieving a balance of independence and interdependence, and taking one's place in a circle of true selves.

Plain Speaking: An Oral Biography of Harry S Truman

Merle Miller

. . . Mr. President, can you tell me about the day Franklin Roosevelt died?

"It is a day . . . it's a time I can even now not think about without feeling very deep emotion.

"It was an ordinary day in the Senate, and I presided. I usually presided most of the time when I was Vice President. Senator Wiley . . . was making a speech about something. I forget what it was about; it didn't make any difference with Wiley. He could go on forever about nothing. And so I wrote a letter to Mamma. . . .

Dear Mamma and Mary:

I am trying to write you a letter from the desk of the President of the Senate while a windy Senator is making a speech on a subject with which he is in no way familiar. . . .

. . . Turn on your radio tomorrow night at 9:30 your time, and you'll hear Harry make a Jefferson Day address to the nation. . . . It will be followed by the President, whom I'll introduce.

"Along about, oh I guess it was probably half past four or a quarter of five, Sam Rayburn called. He'd been in Texas, and he called and said there was a meeting of the Board of Education."

The Board of Education was the name of a group of legislators who dropped into Rayburn's private office from time to time after a legislative session to share stories and drink a little bourbon and tap water. Rayburn, a bachelor from Texas, was Speaker of the House.

". . . and so I went over, and before I could sit down . . . Sam told me that Steve Early (Roosevelt's press secretary) had called and wanted me to call right back. I did, and Early said to come right over to the White House and to come to the front entrance, and he said to come up to Mrs. Roosevelt's suite on the second floor. I didn't think much about it. I just supposed that the President had come back from Georgia (Roosevelt died at Warm Springs, Georgia) and was going to be at Bishop Atwood's funeral. . . . Roosevelt was an honorary pallbearer, and I just supposed that was what had happened.

"And so I went over to the White House, and Mrs. Roosevelt . . . Mrs. Roosevelt . . . she told me that . . . the President . . . was dead."

For a moment Mr. Truman was unable to continue.

When he could, he said, "I was able . . . I told Steve Early to call the Cabinet, and they started phoning for the Chief Justice (Harlan F. Stone) and members of Congress.

"I went over to the office of the President in the West End of the White House and tried to call my wife and daughter. I had a hard time getting them, but I finally did, and they came, and the Chief Justice was there, and all the others, including the Cabinet, and everybody was crying.

"They had just an awful time finding a Bible. I'm sure there were plenty of them in the family living quarters of the White House, but down in the executive wing they had a terrible time finding one, and the Chief Justice was waiting to swear me in.

"Finally, they found one in the office I believe it was of Bill Hassett, who was Roosevelt's secretary. . . .

". . . Anyway, that's the one I was sworn in on . . . I was sworn in—there was a clock on the mantel—and I was sworn in at 7:09. Exactly at 7:09 on April 12, 1945, and that's all the time it took for me to become President of the United States. . . ."

In Search of Light: The Broadcasts of Edward R. Murrow

Edited by Edward Bliss Jr.

April 15, 1945

. . . Permit me to tell you what you would have seen, and heard, had you been with me on Thursday. It will not be pleasant listening. If you are at lunch, or if you have no appetite to hear what Germans have done, now is a good time to switch off the radio, for I propose to tell you of Buchenwald. It is on a small hill about four miles outside Weimar, and it was one of the largest concentration camps in Germany, and it was built to last. As we approached it, we saw about a hundred men in civilian clothes with rifles advancing in open order across the fields. There were a few shops; we stopped to inquire. We were told that some of the prisoners had a couple of SS men cornered in there. We drove on, reached the main gate. The prisoners crowded up behind the wire. We entered.

And now, let me tell this in the first person, for I was the least important person there, as you shall hear. There surged around me an evil-smelling horde. Men and boys reached out to touch me; they were in rags and the remnants of uniform. Death had already marked many of them, but they were smiling with their eyes. I looked out over that mass of men to the green fields beyond where well-fed Germans were ploughing.

A German, Fritz Kersheimer, came up and said, "May I show you round the camp? I've been here ten years." An Englishman stood to attention, saying, "May I introduce myself, delighted to see you, and can you tell me when some of our blokes will be along?" I told him soon and asked to see one of the barracks. It happened to be occupied by Czechoslovakians. When I entered, men crowded around, tried to lift me to their shoulders. They were too weak. Many of them could not get out of bed. I was told that this building had once stabled eighty horses. There were twelve hundred men in it, five to a bunk. The stink was beyond all description.

When I reached the center of the barracks, a man came up and said, "You remember me. I'm Peter Zenkl, one-time mayor of Prague." I remembered him, but did not recognize him. . . .

As I walked down to the end of the barracks, there was applause from the men too weak to get out of bed. It sounded like the hand clapping of babies; they were so weak. The doctor's name was Paul Heller. He had been there since 1938.

As we walked out into the courtyard, a man fell dead. Two others—they must have been over sixty—were crawling toward the latrine. I saw it but will not describe it.

In another part of the camp they showed me the children, hundreds of them. Some were only six. One rolled up his sleeve, showed me his number. It was tatooed on his arm. D-6030, it was. The others showed me their numbers; they will carry them till they die.

An elderly man standing beside me said, "The children, enemies of the state." I could see their ribs through their thin shirts. The old man said, "I am Professor Charles Richer of the Sorbonne." The children clung to my hands and stared. We crossed to the courtyard. Men kept coming up to speak to me and touch me, professors from Poland, doctors from Vienna, men from all Europe. Men from the countries that made America.

We went to the hospital; it was full. The doctor told me that two hundred had died the day before. . . . Dr. Heller pulled back the blankets from a man's feet to show me how swollen they were. The man was dead. Most of the patients could not move. . . .

I asked to see the kitchen; it was clean. The German in charge had been a Communist, had been at Buchenwald for nine years, had a picture of his daughter in Hamburg. He hadn't seen her for almost twelve years, and if I got to Hamburg, would I look her up? He showed me the daily ration—one piece of brown bread about as thick as your thumb, on top of it a piece of margarine as big as three sticks of chewing gum. That, and a little stew, was what they received every twenty-four hours. . . .

Dr. Heller, the Czech, asked if I would care to see the crematorium. He said it wouldn't be very interesting because the Germans had run out of coke some days ago and had taken to dumping the bodies into a great hole nearby. Professor Richer said perhaps I would care to see the small courtyard. I said yes. . . . The wall was about eight feet high; it adjoined what had been a stable or garage. We entered. It was floored with concrete. There were two rows of bodies stacked up like cordwood. They were thin and very white. Some of the bodies were terribly bruised, though there seemed to be little flesh to bruise. . . . I tried to count them as best I could and arrived at the conclusion that all that was mortal of more than five hundred men and boys lay there in two neat piles.

There was a German trailer which must have contained another fifty, but it wasn't possible to count them. . . . It appeared that most of the men and boys had died of starvation. . . . But the manner of death seemed unimportant. Murder had been done at Buchenwald. God alone knows how many men and boys have died there during the last twelve years. . . .

As I left that camp, a Frenchman who used to work for Havas in Paris came up to me and said, "You will write something about this, perhaps?" And he added, "To write about this you must have been here at least two years, and after that—you don't want to write any more."

I pray you to believe what I have said about Buchenwald; I have reported what I saw and heard, but only part of it. For most of it I have no words. . . .

Chapter **11**

Ensemble Approaches
to Interpretation

Learning Objectives

After completing this chapter, you should be able to

- define ensemble
- define group interpretation
- discuss and demonstrate the following types of focus: out-front, onstage, and mixed
- incorporate the use of multimedia into an ensemble interpretation performance

Ensemble interpretation may be defined as group interpretation. When two or more performers set out to bring a literary selection alive, what advantages would the group have over an individual interpretation? Would you anticipate any limitations in interpreting as a group? To prepare yourselves for working as a group, try the following exercise.

PERFORMER'S WARM-UP
Ensemble Machines

Working in small groups of five or six members, choose one of the following objects to create together. Work as a unit, but each group member must play a unique part in your group's creation. You may use both voice and movement to help you suggest to the audience your group creation of one of the items listed:

washing machine
people-eating machine
computer
air hammer
CD player
telephone
car
wheel

Questions

1. How were you able to coordinate your efforts to create a machine?
2. What were the barriers that had to be overcome?

The Nature of Ensemble Reading

An ensemble is a group of individuals who work together to produce an effect or achieve a mutual goal. An ensemble of interpreters is, in fact, a literary performing team. Their team goal is to re-create literature. In doing so, the group must share or effectively communicate to audiences all the experiences that exist in selected pieces of literature.

Ensemble performers are expected to utilize the skills they acquired as solo readers and to apply them to the needs of the group. In ensemble interpretation, the emphasis must be on the interdependence of the group members rather than on the independence of any individual interpreter. It is the performing effects that the group is able to create—not an individual's expertise—that must be the focus of ensemble interpretation.

Many of the aesthetic principles and techniques that characterize the art of solo interpretation also characterize the art of ensemble reading. For example, both forms of interpretation use presentational staging approaches—that is, neither form attempts to create the illusion of reality. In fact, a presentational style of staging serves to distinguish the ensemble interpreter from the actor. The goal of the interpreter, unlike the goal of the actor, is to present or to suggest literary experience to an audience. It is not to represent that experience for the audience, as the actor is charged to do. Thus, the techniques and the devices of both ensemble and solo interpretation remind the audience that art, rather than life, is being portrayed on the stage; in both forms of interpretation, the emphasis is placed on suggestion—not explicitness.

The interpreter's task, whether he or she works alone or in an ensemble, is to help make the literature live for the audience. Interpreters do not accomplish this by acting out an event or experience in an atmosphere created by lifelike sets and elaborate costumes. Instead, interpreters use their bodies and their voices to make literature real for an audience. As is true for an interpreter working alone, ensemble interpretation requires both reading and performing abilities and careful analysis of a selection for its effect.

Members of your performing ensemble should agree on the dominant ideas, moods, and attitudes of the literature to be presented. You need to agree on specifics, such as the ways that timing, volume, and pitch may be used to support the meaning of the literature. You also need to discuss and agree on ways that visible action will be used to reinforce the content of the literature. Finally, you need to reach a consensus regarding the effect the ensemble wants its presentation to have on the audience. You must satisfy these conditions as a group in order to work well together to suggest the sensory, emotional, and cognitive experiences in the chosen selection or selections.

Performers who belong to an ensemble may be compared to musicians who belong to orchestras. A musician's responsibility broadens when he or she joins an orchestra. The same is true for the performers who join an ensemble. No longer are the performers responsible only for themselves; rather, they work together with and for their group. Orchestra members learn to blend their instruments to create a unified sound. Performers must learn to blend their performing efforts as well. Work together with group members to do the following exercises.

PERFORMER'S WARM-UP
Word Combos

Working in small groups, each unit should select one of the following words to express. Voice and choreographed movement are your group's communication instruments.

jealousy
gossip
war
strength
weakness
sympathy

Combine your efforts with other group members' so the experiences represented in the chosen word are fully realized through your performance. Your group may be able to create your presentation by speaking the word only once, or you may decide to repeat the word many times in different ways to bring it alive for your audience.

Questions

1. How did your group work to physicalize and vocalize your word image?
2. How does this exercise help you realize your role as a member of a performing ensemble?

Focus in Ensemble Readings

Ensemble groups need to decide upon the kind of eye interaction in performance that the script's readers will have with each other and with the audience. Interactional choices include total out-front focus, total onstage focus, and a mixture of out-front and onstage focus.

Out-Front Focus

The **out-front focus,** also known as indirect interaction, is the type of focus usually employed by solo interpreters when they read from works involving numerous characters. This same technique can be used in ensemble performance. An out-front focus simply requires that each of the reader/characters speak to or address the other reader/characters as if they were situated out front, or in the audience, rather than on the stage. Using this type of focus technique, readers establish an indirect interactional contact with each other.

Offstage or out-front focus does not mean the readers establish eye contact with the members of the audience, however. It indicates only that the readers are placing the imagined scene and the imagined characters of that scene in the realm of the audience. On the other hand, if one reader is functioning as narrator, he or she may look directly into the eyes of the audience members at certain points in the performance.

Onstage Focus

Onstage focus requires that the readers relate to each other on the stage. This type of focus makes the interactions or conversations among the readers more natural and direct.

A mixture of out-front and onstage focus can be used in works that seem to call for a combination of approaches. A change of focus can be used to achieve variety in staging techniques and to heighten various effects of the literature. For example, some scenes—especially those containing descriptions of the environment or descriptions of the characters' inner thoughts—work best with an out-front focus. With this technique the scene is actually directed physically closer to the audience members, reaching out to draw them into the literature. Some scenes, however, may be more effective if performed with an onstage focus. This focus allows the audience members to appreciate the script's forward movements, since they can both see and hear the relations and interactions among the readers.

Members of a performing ensemble should freely vary and mix the types of focus they use. But keep in mind that directorial decisions regarding focus should be made only after a careful and thorough textual analysis. Consider the following analogy.

Imagine that your interpretative ensemble is a giant pair of eyes. These eyes must wear eyeglasses to perfect their vision. The prescription for the eyeglass lenses changes according to the observational situation the eyes are placed in. Thus, sometimes the eyes need to wear lenses designed for nearsighted people, so the scene they are to observe receives onstage focus. When the eyes need lenses designed for farsighted people, the scene they are to observe is placed in the midst of the audience. In some situations, however, the eyes need to wear bifocals—lenses that allow a rapid switch from a nearsighted correction to a farsighted correction; that is, the ensemble of readers moves from an onstage focus to an out-front or indirect focus. The type of lens (focus) prescribed by the doctor (director) for the eyes (ensemble of readers) depends on the situation (the literature) the eyes are observing (staging). Check your understanding of the concept of focus with this exercise.

PERFORMER'S WORKSHOP
Bifocus

Read the following excerpt from Bertolt Brecht's play *The Good Woman of Setzuan* carefully. How does this excerpt lend itself to a mixed focus or bifocus approach? Determine where you would focus in each segment of the selection.

The Good Woman of Setzuan

Bertolt Brecht

WONG: I sell water here in the city of Setzuan. It isn't easy. When water is scarce, I have long distances to go in search of it, and when it is plentiful, I have no income. But in our part of the world there is nothing unusual about poverty. Many people think only the gods can save the situation. And I hear from a cattle merchant—who travels a lot—that some of the highest gods are on their way here at this very moment. Informed sources have it that heaven is quite disturbed at all the complaining. I've been coming out here to the city gates for three days now to bid these gods welcome. I want to be the first to greet them. What about those fellows over there? No, no they work. And that one there has ink on his fingers, he's no god, he must be a clerk from the cement factory. Those two are another story. They look as though they'd like to beat you. But gods don't need to beat you, do they? (THREE GODS *appear.*) What about those three? Old-fashioned clothes—dust on their feet—they must be gods! (*He throws himself at their feet.*) Do with me what you will, illustrious ones!

FIRST GOD: *(with an ear trumpet)* Ah! (*He is pleased.*) So we were expected?

WONG: *(giving them water)* Oh, yes. And I knew you'd come.

FIRST GOD: We need somewhere to stay the night. You know of a place?

WONG: The whole town is at your service, illustrious ones! What sort of a place would you like?

(The GODS *eye each other.*)

FIRST GOD: Just try the first house you come to, my son.

WONG: That would be Mr. Fo's place.

FIRST GOD: Mr. Fo.

WONG: One moment! (*He knocks at the first house.*)

VOICE FROM MR. FO'S: No!

(WONG *returns a little nervously.*)

WONG: It's too bad. Mr. Fo isn't in. And his servants don't dare do a thing without his consent. He'll have a fit when he finds out who they turned away, won't he?

FIRST GOD: *(smiling)* He will, won't he?

Questions

1. Why does this work lend itself to a mixed-focus approach?
2. At what points in the preceding selection would you employ an onstage focus? Where would you employ an out-front focus? Why?

Action, Movement, and Physical Arrangement

In general, movement or overt action in ensemble interpretation is kept to a minimum. This is not to say that the readers do not use their bodies to help them communicate—of course they do—but the movement is selective. Avoid movement for the sake of movement. Ensemble interpreters should deliberate before deciding upon appropriate gestures and movements for performance. They should select only those physical actions that will help to illustrate emotions and intellectual meanings inherent in their script.

Besides understanding the ways that muscle tone and facial expressions aid in communication as a member of an ensemble, you need to appreciate the ways in which body position, head levels, and stage areas can be combined to help display the literature.

Body position is an important source of emphasis in performance. Facing audiences signifies one thing, turning your back to them indicates something else. Ensemble readers often use these two basic body positions to represent their entrances and exits. Rather than actually turning their backs to their audience, the readers sometimes indicate their exit simply by lowering their heads. Using another technique, readers may freeze their positions to indicate that they have temporarily withdrawn from the developments on the stage.

Varying the heights or **head levels** of the readers is a means to providing emphasis and contrast in a performance. As an interpreter, you may sit, stand, kneel, or lie on the floor or on artificial levels such as chairs or stools. Arranging characters on levels helps the audience in its perceptions of the literary text by suggesting the relative physical stature or importance of the characters.

PERFORMER'S WARM-UP

The Chair

Explore all the different parts of this exercise. You may want to photograph the various positions you assume in the following exercises for further study.

A. On your own, try to determine all the different body positions you can assume when working with a single, sturdy chair whose four feet remain on the floor at all times.

B. Now, with a partner explore all the different ways the two of you can vary your body positions or levels using the same chair. Again, the four feet of the chair must remain firmly planted on the floor at all times.

C. Finally, explore the different group pictorial arrangements that can be created with two or three chairs and six to eight people. Hint: Do not hesitate to use more than the central portion of the performing area.

Questions

1. Did you sit on the chair? Stand on it? Lean against it? Sit with your back against it? Lie under it? Crouch on it? Hide behind it? Straddle it? What messages were sent by each of the different positions you assumed?

2. How did the addition of one other person affect the possibilities? How did the addition of the group affect the possibilities?

3. How could these different positions or levels be used to clarify the actions, character attitudes, or general meaning of selected scripts?

4. If you chose to take photographs, did the resulting pictures send the message you thought you were sending? Do the photographs give you ideas for additional ways to structure the physical arrangements for ensemble performance? How?

Although ensemble interpreters do not engage in a great deal of overt movement in performance, the number of group arrangements that can be created to illustrate and refine the script is almost infinite. Stools, orange crates, barrels, and other simple platform devices provide instant level variety.

How would the addition of facial expressions and body gestures alter the possibilities available to your group? Find out by exploring the next exercise.

PERFORMER'S WARM-UP
Refining Group Pictures

Repeat each section of the preceding chair exercise. This time, add facial expressions and body gestures to the pictures created by your various arrangements. Again, you may want to photograph your efforts for future examination.

Questions

1. How do the pictures change in meaning when physical gestures and facial expressions are added to them?

2. How would you title the pictures resulting from your group's arrangements? Would any depict an emotion such as anger? Friendship? Jealousy? Jubilance?

Adding appropriate facial expressions and gestures to group members helps to define or suggest the meaning of the created picture. Rather than evolving moods spontaneously or randomly, as in the previous two exercises, the performing group will look to the literature to precipitate the mood intensities and psychological relations they seek to re-create.

Multimedia Devices

Ensemble interpreters sometimes employ multimedia devices to help them share meaning with their audience. Film, slides, recordings, and live music may be incorporated into performances. Such embellishments, however, should never be employed as gimmicks. Use them only when they will enhance the literary experience.

A simple but effective technique is to use an overhead projector, 8-1/2-by-11-inch transparencies, and magic markers. Create some abstract images on the transparencies and project them on the wall. Experiment with people moving around and through the images. Standard black-and-white copiers make transparencies of photographs and drawings that can be used by performers. Color copiers also provide transparencies of paintings and photographs.

When it is possible to darken the room, 35-millimeter slides can be used. An enlarged photograph of an object can also become the backdrop for your presentation. Pictures from books (prepared as overhead transparencies) can prove to be effective additions as well. For example, a picture of the writer could serve as part of the environment for a reading of some of his or her works. Photographs of the performers taken in other locations may also be used to help emphasize the message in the literature.

In addition, audiotapes can set the mood for a reading. Use sound to support your presentation by suggesting the appropriate environment: a noisy crowd, applause, wind in the trees, or even the voice of the writer.

Selective use of videotape enhances performances as well. Select video excerpts that make a point early. Then turn them off or pause them in freeze frame. This allows the audience to focus clearly on the literature and the message the interpreters are presenting. Some performers have also experimented with large-screen projections and PowerPoint presentations as a part of an ensemble performance.

Of course, the risks with technology are that it can break down or become too obtrusive and obscure the actual performance. Employing the technology requires both time and effort; gathering and effectively integrating such materials into a presentation is challenging. If time and technical expertise among group members allow it, experiment with multimedia devices. Otherwise, focus on the presentation itself. Media could be incorporated later in the presentation development process, if desired.

Ensemble Performance of Poetry: Choral Speaking

Choral speaking is group interpretation of poetry. It is one of the two basic styles of ensemble performance. It provides group readers with a unique performing experience, and it uses the techniques discussed earlier in this chapter. In choral speaking, individuals in the ensemble understand and express—sometimes collectively—the ideas, emotions, and moods inherent in their poetic selection.

Choral speakers help to illustrate a poem by dividing the poetic material into various voices or phrases. This division, if applied to appropriate literary material, usually works to illuminate the work. When choosing literature for choral interpretation, interpreters should adhere to the following guidelines.

1. The material should allow for the possibility of organized mass effects.
2. The material should be enhanced by the addition of an ensemble.

Once these two conditions are met, the main tasks of the ensemble are to decide how the lines of the poem can best be divided and assigned for reading. There are a number of traditional choral-speaking structures to guide you as you make these decisions. One approach is to divide the ensemble group into solo speaker(s) and a chorus. This type of structure lends itself to poems that include a refrain or repetitive passage. The goal of the chorus when reading a refrain is to reinforce the moods that exist in the poem. Try this exercise to check your understanding.

PERFORMER'S WORKSHOP
Refrain Work

Read the following ballad.

 ## "There Was a Frog"
Anonymous

There was a frog lived in a well,
Whipsee diddle-dee dandy dee;
There was a frog lived in a well,
And a merry mouse in a mill,
With a harum, scarum, diddle dum darum,
Whipsee diddle-dee dandy dee.

This frog he would a-wooing ride,
Whipsee diddle-dee dandy dee;

This frog he would a-wooing ride,
And on a snail he got astride,
With a harum, scarum, diddle dum darum,
Whipsee diddle-dee dandy dee.

He rode till he came to my Lady Mouse Hall,
Whipsee diddle-dee dandy dee;
He rode till he came to my Lady Mouse Hall,
And there he did both knock and call,
With a harum, scarum, diddle dum darum,
Whipsee diddle-dee dandy dee.

"Miss Mouse, Miss Mouse, I'm come to thee,"
Whipsee diddle-dee dandy dee;
"Miss Mouse, Miss Mouse, I'm come to thee,
To see if thou canst fancy me,"
With a harum, scarum, diddle dum darum,
Whipsee diddle-dee dandy dee.

"Oh answer I will give you none,"
Whipsee diddle-dee dandy dee;
"Oh answer I will give you none
Until my Uncle Rat comes home,"
With a harum, scarum, diddle dum darum,
Whipsee diddle-dee dandy dee.

And when her Uncle Rat came home,
Whipsee diddle-dee dandy dee;
And when her Uncle Rat came home,
"Who's been here since I've been gone?"
With a harum, scarum, diddle dum darum,
Whipsee diddle-dee dandy dee.

"There's been a worthy gentleman,"
Whipsee diddle-dee dandy dee;
"There's been a worthy gentleman,
That's been here since you've been gone."
With a harum, scarum, diddle dum darum,
Whipsee diddle-dee dandy dee.

The frog he came whistling through the brook,
Whipsee diddle-dee dandy dee;
The frog he came whistling through the brook,
And there he met with a dainty duck.
With a harum, scarum, diddle dum darum,
Whipsee diddle-dee dandy dee.

The duck she swallowed him up with a quack,
Whipsee diddle-dee dandy dee;
The duck she swallowed him up with a quack,
So there's an end of my history book.
With a harum, scarum, diddle dum darum,
Whipsee diddle-dee dandy dee.

Questions

1. How would you divide the poem for the group and the individual reader?
2. What mood or moods will you suggest as you interpret each refrain?
3. How can you use time and emphasis to help establish the tone and share the ideas?

When reading a poem with a refrain, the ensemble group may be divided into two parts, with one part reading the verses and the other part reading the refrain. This arrangement is commonly employed in religious services, in poems that contain questions or answers, or when a balance between two groups of voices is desired. This vocal balance may be attained by contrasting male and female voices, by contrasting pitch levels, or by contrasting vocal levels.

You can see that the choral speaking ensemble is very much like a singing ensemble or chorus. In fact, in early rehearsals it may be prudent to have a member of the group actually "conduct" the reading as a choral conductor would direct a musical performance. As your group becomes more proficient with the material, the conductor will no longer be necessary. Practice more choral reading using the following poem.

PERFORMER'S WORKSHOP
Chorus Ensemble

Here is another ballad that works well when the ensemble group is divided into two parts. Rehearse and perform it with your group.

"Lord Randall"

Anonymous

O, where have you been, Lord Randall, my son?
O, where have you been, my handsome young man?
I have been to the wild wood, mother make my bed soon,
For I'm weary with hunting, and fain would lie doon.

Where got ye your dinner, Lord Randall, my son?
Where got ye your dinner, my handsome young man?
I dined with my true love; mother make my bed soon,
For I'm weary with hunting and fain would lie doon.

What got you to your dinner, Lord Randall, my son?
What got you to your dinner, my handsome young man?
I got eels boiled in brew; mother make my bed soon,
For I'm weary with hunting, and fain would lie doon.

What became of your bloodhounds, Lord Randall, my son?
What became of your bloodhounds, my handsome young man?
They swelled and they died; mother make my bed soon,
For I'm weary with hunting, and fain would lie doon.

O, I fear you are poisoned, Lord Randall, my son!
O, I fear you are poisoned, my handsome young man!
O, yes, I am poisoned, mother make my bed soon,
For I'm sick at the heart and fain would lie doon.

Questions

1. How does this structure help to communicate the literature?
2. What effect can you achieve by a two-part division of your ensemble? What would be the most effective division of the voices?

Sometimes the literature is enhanced if the choral group is divided into three or more parts. This type of division allows for finer discriminations in pitch and quality. Work as a group or as an entire class to bring the following poem to life.

PERFORMER'S WORKSHOP
The Trio

Your choral team or teacher will choose a conductor to facilitate this performance. This is a much more advanced experience that will require the concentration of everyone in the choral group, which will be divided into three subgroups. The three subgroups are indicated by the numbers 1, 2, and 3 below. Subgroups read the lines next to their number at the same time. Rehearse each group separately. Then put them together as if a round were being sung.

"Trio"
Tobie Lurie

1   This is a poem for three voices
2   This is a poem
3

1   that asks each voice   to listen
2   for three voices
3

1   to create silence
2   that asks each voice
3   This is a poem

1
2   to listen
3   for three voices   that asks each voice

1   and to feel.
2   to create silence
3   to listen

1   That shows by doing
2   and to feel.
3   to create silence

```
1   that poems      can be read
2      That shows      by doing
3

1   together      to enhance meaning.
2
3   and to feel.      That shows

1            This is a poem
2   that poems      can be read together
3      by doing

1               that becomes three poems
2   to enhance meaning.
3      that poems

1         when given to
2         This is a poem
3   can be read      together

1   three voices
2         that becomes three poems
3      to enhance meaning.

1   each voice bringing      its quality
2
3      This is      a poem

1   into the whole      and adding
2      when given      to three voices
3

1      to poetry
2            each voice
3   that becomes three poems

1         the dimension
2            bringing its
3   when given to three voices

1      of dialogue.
2   quality      into the whole
3         each voice
```

1   This is a poem   that says
2   and adding
3 bringing its quality

1   we
2 to poetry   the dimension   of dialogue.
3   into the whole

1 should come together
2
3   and adding to poetry

1   celebrate together
2 This is a poem
3   the dimension

1   create together
2   that says
3 of dialogue   This is a poem

1   and understand
2 we should come together
3   that says

1 together.
2   celebrate together
3   we should come together

1   This is a poem
2 create together
3   celebrate together

1   a simple poem
2 and understand together.
3   create together

1   which I hope
2 This is a poem
3   and understand together.

1   succeeds in expressing
2 a simple poem
3   This is a poem

1	the idea
2	which I hope succeeds in expressing
3	a simple poem

1	that the human voice is an instrument
2	the idea
3	which I hope

1	
2	that the human voice
3	succeeds in expressing the idea

1	of infinite possibilities.
2	is an instrument
3	that the human voice

1	is an instrument of infinite possibilities
2	of infinite possibilities. is an instrument of infinite possibilities
3	is an instrument of infinite possibilities

Questions

1. How does dividing the poem into three sections help to communicate its meaning?
2. What special skills does the interpreter need to develop in order to function as an effective member of the "Trio" ensemble?
3. How would you stage this reading? Where would you position the three groups?

Sequential Speaking Structure

Choral-speaking teams can be divided into four or even more groups to accommodate other pieces of literature. In such instances, the choral-speaking group members could place themselves in a wide variety of areas for the presentation. For example, the groups can be positioned in the four corners of the room or in an area that includes multilevels, such as balconies or stairs. Keep in mind, however, that the divisions and locations of the readers must spring from the literature. They should not chosen arbitrarily.

Often a poem calls for a **sequential speaking structure.** This type of structure allows an individual from the ensemble to interpret a single line or a stanza, followed by another individual and another line, and so on. As you might imagine, it is a difficult structure to utilize effectively, for the individuals of the performing team must be sure when delivering their lines that they do not break the continuity or destroy the flow of the work. Try sequential speaking with some classmates in the exercise that follows.

PERFORMER'S WORKSHOP
Sequential Work

A. Divide the class into groups of eight members. Each member will select a syllable from the following sentence:

I am part of an ensemble.

Each person will speak aloud the syllable he or she is assigned as it occurs in the sentence. Try to express clearly the meaning of the sentence as your group maintains vocal continuity. As much as possible, make the sentence sound as if it is being spoken by one person. (If your class does not divide evenly into groups of eight, try groups of four, with each member selecting two syllables.)

B. Now, prepare as a group to use the sequential approach to read aloud the following poem, from Ecclesiastes in the Bible. Divide up the words and syllables and assign them to each group member, as was done in the first part of this exercise. Note that each of the lines in the poem carries a specific image that relates to the main idea of the poem.

Ecclesiastes 3:1–3:8

To everything there is a season, and a time to every purpose under the heaven:
A time to be born, and a time to die;
A time to plant, and a time to pluck up that which is planted;
A time to kill, and a time to heal;
A time to break down, and a time to build up;
A time to weep, and a time to laugh;
A time to mourn, and a time to dance;
A time to cast away stones, and a time to gather stones together;
A time to embrace, and a time to refrain from embracing;
A time to get, and a time to lose;
A time to keep, and a time to cast away;
A time to rend, and a time to sew;
A time to keep silence, and a time to speak;

A time to love, and a time to hate;

A time of war, and a time of peace;

To everything there is a season, and a time to every purpose under the heaven.

Questions

1. What techniques did you have to use in order to give the impression that a single individual was speaking?
2. What challenges did these exercises present to you as an interpreter?
3. How does a sequential approach support the tone and meaning of the poem?
4. What gestures could a group use to enhance the poetic statements?

An entire poem may also be spoken in unison. When adopting this structure, the ensemble again aims for the effect of a single voice. Thoughts and feelings need to be perfectly blended as timing, tone, and volume are carefully controlled. Work as a group to realize the dominant mood and ideas within the selection. The Japanese haiku, or short lyric poem, lends itself to this approach.

PERFORMER'S WORKSHOP
Unison Work

Divide the class into two groups. Each group should select one of the following two short poems to perform using a unison approach.

Haiku
Issa

The old, plump bullfrog
held his ground and stared at me—
what a sour face!

"Buffalo Dusk"
Carl Sandburg

The buffaloes are gone.

And those who saw the buffaloes are gone.

Those who saw the buffaloes by thousands and how

they pawed the prairie sod into dust with their
hoofs, their great heads down, pawing on in a
great pageant of dusk,
Those who saw the buffaloes are gone.
And the buffaloes are gone.

Questions

1. What mood did your group work to create?
2. How were timing, phrasing, stress, and movement coordinated?

You should recognize that the five preceding structures—solo/chorus, two-part chorus, trio, sequential, and unison—do not tell the whole story of choral speaking. As an ensemble performer, experiment with these structures, using them in various combinations or patterns. Create a new speaking structure for use by your own ensemble to match and enhance a literary selection. Check your understanding of choral speaking by participating in the following exercise.

PERFORMER'S WORKSHOP
A Choral Ensemble

Divide the class into several groups and choose one of the following poems to perform. Each group should adapt its selection for choral presentation. You should also be familiar with the remaining literature selections so you can analyze the strengths and weaknesses of the other groups' presentations.

"What's That Smell in the Kitchen?"
Marge Piercy

All over America women are burning dinners.
It's lambchops in Peoria; it's haddock
in Providence; it's steak in Chicago;
tofu delight in Big Sur; red
rice and beans in Dallas.
All over America women are burning
food they're supposed to bring with calico
smile on platters glittering like wax.
Anger sputters in her brainpan, confined

but spewing out missiles of hot fat.
Carbonized despair presses like a clinker
from a barbecue against the back of her eyes.
If she wants to grill anything, it's
her husband spitted over a slow fire.
If she wants to serve him anything
it's a dead rat with a bomb in its belly
ticking like the heart of an insomniac.
Her life is cooked and digested,
nothing but leftovers in Tupperware.
Look, she says, once I was roast duck
on your platter with parsley but now I am Spam.
Burning dinner is not incompetence but war.

"Love Your Enemy"
Yusef Iman

Brought here in slave ships and pitched overboard.
Love your enemy.
Language taken away, culture taken away.
Love your enemy.
Work from sun up to sun down.
Love your enemy.
Work for no pay.
Love your enemy.
Last hired, first fired.
Love your enemy.
Rape your mother.
Love your enemy.
Lynch your father.
Love your enemy.
Bomb your churches.
Love your enemy.
Forced to fight his wars.
Love your enemy.
Pay the highest rent.
Love your enemy.

Sell you rotten food.

Love your enemy.

Sell dope to your children.

Love your enemy.

Forced to live in the slums.

Love your enemy.

Dilapidated schools.

Love your enemy.

Puts you in jail.

Love your enemy.

Bitten by dogs.

Love your enemy.

Water hose you down.

Love your enemy.

    Love.

    Love.

    Love.

    Love.

    Love.

    Love, for everybody else.

But when will we love ourselves?

"The Walrus and the Carpenter"
Lewis Carroll

The sun was shining on the sea,
    Shining with all his might;
He did his very best to make
    The billows smooth and bright—
And this was odd, because it was
    The middle of the night.

The moon was shining sulkily,
    Because she thought the sun
Had got no business to be there
    After the day was done—
"It's very rude of him," she said,
    "To come and spoil the fun!"

The sea was wet as wet could be,
  The sands were dry as dry.
You could not see a cloud, because
  No cloud was in the sky:
No birds were flying overhead—
  There were no birds to fly.

The Walrus and the Carpenter
  Were walking close at hand;
They wept like anything to see
  Such quantities of sand.
"If this were only cleared away,"
  They said, "it *would* be grand!"

"If seven maids with seven mops
  Swept it for half a year,
Do you suppose," the Walrus said,
    "That they could get it clear?"
"I doubt it," said the Carpenter,
  And shed a bitter tear.

"O Oysters, come and walk with us!"
  The Walrus did beseech.
"A pleasant walk, a pleasant talk,
  Along the briny beach;
We cannot do with more than four,
  To give a hand to each."

The eldest Oyster looked at him,
  But never a word he said;
The eldest Oyster winked his eye,
  And shook his heavy head—
Meaning to say he did not choose
  To leave the oyster-bed.

Questions

1. What in the selection led your group to develop its specific speaking structure?
2. How did your group choose to use rhythm, volume, and pitch to support the meaning of the poem?

3. What visible action, if any, did your ensemble employ to enhance the performance?
4. How could you change your presentation to increase its effectiveness?

PERFORMER'S WORKSHOP
Concrete Poetry for Choral Speaking

Choral speaking techniques may also be used to aid in the re-creation of a nontraditional kind of literature called "concrete poetry." Concrete poems are visual structures that work to create a sensory experience in the perceiver. They are intended to affect the minds, eyes, ears, and bodies of their readers. Thus, concrete poems are not merely read, they are felt. In fact, they are not merely felt, they are played with.

Divide the class into groups and take some time to explore the following concrete poems by Eugen Gomringer. Then prepare one of the poems for performance.

```
ping   pong
       ping   pong   ping
       pong   ping   pong
              ping   pong
```

```
silencio   silencio   silencio
silencio   silencio   silencio
silencio              silencio
silencio   silencio   silencio
silencio   silencio   silencio
```

```
                    w           w
              d           i
        n           n           n
    i           d           i           d
w                           w
```

Questions

1. In what ways can an ensemble group make the concepts inherent in the poems live for an audience?
2. For which poems would movement be appropriate?
3. How could eye and head movements be used to reflect the poems' content?

Ensemble Performance of Poetry: Choral Speaking

A second style of ensemble performance is known as **chamber theater,** which is group interpretation of narrative prose. The text of the narrative tale is maintained, but the scenes of the story often are located onstage, rather than out front. This adds the impact and immediacy of drama to the performance, while leaving the original narrative form intact. In chamber theater, the narrator of the written story is the narrator of the staged version as well. His or her point of view is manifested in the presentation onstage. The narrator thus assumes a major role in a chamber theater production.

A chamber theater performance style usually works best with stories in which the narrator functions as a liaison between the characters and their world. This performing style does not work as well in stories told mostly in scene—where there is little, if any, narration. In chamber theater the narrator usually delivers his or her lines with an out-front focus. This kind of focus is also shared by the story's characters as they express their own unspoken thoughts or engage in indirect discourse.

The characters will probably shift to an onstage focus when interacting directly with each other. Thus, chamber theater does more than simply dramatize a narrative text; rather, it preserves the mode of narrative writing and combines it with a theater-performance style. Consequently, in chamber theater the narrator continues to serve descriptive and reflective functions, summarizing and clarifying events in the world of the literature.

In addition, chamber theater actually provides the narrator with the opportunity to physicalize his or her relationship to the characters. For example, the narrator can work physically near a specific character—in effect, moving in for a close-up. Or the narrator can freely roam about the stage, stopping at a particular vantage point in order to identify with a number of characters. The narrator can operate objectively and can physically separate himself or herself from the scene of the action. In these ways the audience feels and understands the presence and the point of view of the narrator, so that his or her proper function is served.

PERFORMER'S WORKSHOP
Chamber Theater Concepts

Chamber theater works well for children or adults, as the following selections illustrate. Read each selection carefully.

The following excerpt from a chamber-theater adaptation of *The Cat and the Mouse Together* by the Brothers Grimm colorfully illustrates the key concepts of chamber theater and would be sure to delight a child audience.

The Cat and the Mouse Together

Brothers Grimm

Cast of Characters:

NARRATOR: a skillful storyteller, male or female

CAT: a proud, adventuresome animal

MOUSE: a meek, loyal friend

Setting:

A chair is placed to the right of the performing area at the front of the classroom. The chair represents a chosen hiding place in a church. The narrator sits on a stool to the left of the stage; the MOUSE *and the* CAT *when at home perform up center-stage.*

NARRATOR: A cat met a mouse (*while* NARRATOR *speaks, action described is pantomimed by the characters*); after getting to know the mouse a bit, the cat professed such great love and affection for the mouse that the mouse consented to live and keep house with him. (MOUSE *puts on an apron.*) The cat was a wise animal and always thought ahead.

CAT: "We must prepare our food for the winter," said the cat, "or we shall go hungry. (*Adamant*) And you, little mouse, are not to leave the house or you'll be caught in a trap."

NARRATOR: So they put their heads together (CAT *and* MOUSE *do this*) and they decided to make a pot of food to store for the winter. (*Pantomime filling the pot.*) Then, they debated for a long while about where to place the pot for safety. (*An argument between the cat and the mouse is pantomimed.*)

CAT: Finally, the cat suggested that the church was probably the safest site to store their pot.

NARRATOR: So they agreed to put the pot under the church's altar. (*While the* NARRATOR *speaks, the* CAT *and the* MOUSE *pantomime carrying their pot to the church. They walk around in a large circle three times until they finally arrive at the chair.*) They also agreed not to touch it until they were really in need. When the pot was safely hidden, they traveled back home again (*we see them retracing their steps*), pleased that they had made a wise decision. However, before long the cat was seized with a great desire to eat from that giant pot of food.

CAT: (*brightly*) "Listen to me, dear mouse," said he. "My cousin has asked me to act as godfather to her newborn son. The little feller is white with brown spots, and the christening is set for this afternoon. So, let me go to it, if you will, while you stay at home and keep house."

MOUSE: (*kindly*) "Why, of course," answered the mouse. "By all means you can go. And when you're eating and drinking all the refreshments, think a bit of me. I would really enjoy a drop of sweet, red wine."

NARRATOR: But there was not a bit of truth in all of this. The cat had no cousin, and certainly, he had not, therefore, been asked to serve as godfather. (*As the* NARRATOR *starts to speak, the* MOUSE, *out of the scene, turns her back to the audience; the* CAT, *however, skips around in a large circle and finishes at the chair. He pantomimes the action described by the* NARRATOR.) Instead, he went to the church, dragged out the hidden pot, and licked all the tasty morsels off the top. (*After eating, the cat starts to leisurely retrace his steps, pantomiming as the narrator indicates.*) The cat took a stroll over the rooftops of the town, saw some of his friends, relaxed in the sun and licked his whiskers whenever he thought of the pot of food. And, when evening came, he arrived home.

MOUSE: (*indulgently*) "Here you are at last," said the mouse. "I hope you've had a great time!"

CAT: "Not bad," answered the cat.

MOUSE: "And what did your cousin choose to name the child?"

CAT: "Top-off," said the cat quite dryly.

MOUSE: "Top-off!" cried the mouse. "What an odd name! Is it widely used in your family?"

CAT: "Does it matter? It's not any worse than Crumbpicker, like your godchild."

NARRATOR: They laughed together. However, it was not long before the cat was again seized with a yearning for the pot of food.

CAT: "I'm afraid I'm going to have to ask you to do me a favor," intoned the cat sweetly to the mouse. "Will you keep house alone again for a day? I have once more been asked to serve as godfather, and this new child has a white ring about its neck. In all good conscience, I cannot refuse."

NARRATOR: So the innocent little mouse agreed. (*As the* NARRATOR *speaks the next lines, the* CAT *creeps around the stage in a circle three times, until he once again reaches the chair.*) The cat departed and crept along by the town wall, until he reached the church where . . . he went directly to the pot of food and proceeded to eat half of it. (*The cat pantomimes this.*)

CAT: "Nothing tastes so good as what one keeps to oneself." (*The* CAT *contentedly pats his tummy, and starts to retrace his steps home.*)

NARRATOR: When the cat reached home . . .

MOUSE: . . . the mouse asked him what name had been given to the child.

CAT: "Half-Gone," answered the cat.

MOUSE: "Half-Gone!" screeched the mouse. "What a strange, strange name."

NARRATOR: Events returned to normal. (*The* CAT *and* MOUSE *are cleaning.*) However, within a few days, the cat's mouth again began to water for the hidden pot of food.

CAT: (*He approaches the* MOUSE *happily.*) "Good things always come in threes," he said to her. "Believe it or not, I once again have to act as godfather. This new little one is jet-black with white feet. Such an event doesn't happen every day. You will permit me to go and serve, won't you?"

MOUSE: "Top-Off, Half-Gone!" murmured the mouse. "They're such odd names, I cannot help but ponder them."

CAT: (*firmly*) "That's because you always stay at home in your gray dress and hairy tail, never journeying the world."

NARRATOR: (*As the* NARRATOR *starts to speak, the* CAT *starts to run in a circle as before, only this time his manner is quite exaggerated; he stops when he reaches the chair.*) So once again the mouse stayed home alone and cleaned the house while the greedy cat ran to the church to finish downing the pot of food.

CAT: (*After eating*) "Now all is completed, and my mind is at rest." (*The* CAT *slinks back home; he looks quite full, quite content, and displays a self-satisfied smile.*)

MOUSE: When he arrived the mouse asked what name had been given to the third child.

CAT: "It won't please you any more than any of the other names. It's called All-Gone."

MOUSE: "All-Gone! What an unheard of name! I never met anyone named that. All-Gone! What in heavens can it mean?" And shaking her head, she curled herself up and went to sleep.

CAT: After that the cat was not again asked to act as godfather.

NARRATOR: When the winter arrived (*the* CAT *and the* MOUSE *pantomime putting on coats, scarves and hats*), and there was no more food to be found outdoors . . .

MOUSE: . . . the mouse began to think of their hidden treasure. "Come cat, we'll go get our pot of food. I'm sure it will just hit the spot!"

CAT: "Of course it will," said the cat bravely. "Let's go."

NARRATOR: So they set out. (*The* CAT *and the* MOUSE *shiver through the streets, walking together in a circle as before, until they reach the chair.*) When they reached the church, they went behind the altar, and they found the pot. . . .

MOUSE: . . . But it was standing empty. (*Very deliberately*) "Oh, now I know what it all meant. Some partner and friend you have been. Instead of acting as a godfather, you have acted as a diner. First, Top-Off! Then Half-Gone! Then—"

CAT: "Hold your tongue!" screamed the cat. "One more word and I'll eat you, too!"

MOUSE: The poor little mouse couldn't help it. (*Quickly*) Out came the words "All-Gone—"

CAT: —and the cat leaped upon her and made an end of her.

NARRATOR: (casually) And that is the way of the world.

Zapp! is a business-management novel written by William C. Byham and Jeff Cox. In their tale, which is directed at business managers and supervisors, Byham and Cox tell the story of Ralph Rosco and his supervisor Joe Mode, who get "zapped" into a new way of looking at corporate excellence. The cutting that follows was adapted for chamber theater.

from *Zapp!*
William C. Byham and Jeff Cox

NARRATOR 1:   Once upon a time, in a magic land called America, there lived a normal guy named Ralph Rosco.

NARRATOR 2:   Ralph worked in Department N of the Normal Company in Normalburg, USA. For years, Normal had been a leading manufacturer of normalators, those amazing devices which are so fundamental to society as we know it.

NARRATOR 3:   As you might expect, just about everything was normal at Normal, including the understanding of who was normally supposed to do what:

NARRATOR 1:   Managers did the thinking.

NARRATOR 2:   Supervisors did the talking.

NARRATOR 3:   And employees did the doing.

NARRATOR 1:   That was the way it had always been—ever since Norman Normal had invented the normalator and founded the company—and so everybody just assumed that was the way it should always be.

NARRATOR 2:   Ralph was your normal type of employee. He came to work. He did the jobs his supervisor told him to do. At the end of the day he dragged himself home to get ready to do it all again.

NARRATOR 3:   When friends or family asked him how he liked his work, Ralph would say:

RALPH: Oh, it's all right, I guess. Not very exciting, but I guess that's normal. Anyway, it's a job, and the pay is OK.

NARRATOR 1:   Ralph worked on a subsystem of what was technically termed the guts of the Normal normalator.

NARRATOR 2:   One day on his way back from lunch, Ralph happened to be thinking about the guts of the normalator, and, well, he was simply (*lightning-like cracking sound*)

ZAPPED!

by an idea so original and so full of promise that his head nearly exploded with excitement!

RALPH: Wowee! Zowee!! Yeah!!!

NARRATOR 3:   The Normal employees around him were shocked!

NARRATOR 1:   In his excitement, Ralph totally forgot that probably nobody would listen, and he ran down the hall to explain his idea to his supervisor, Joe Mode.

JOE: It doesn't sound to me like the Normal way to do things. Don't you think if that idea is good, the Normal Research and Development people would have thought of it? But, tell you what, when I get time, I'll kick it upstairs and we'll see what happens. Maybe they'll form a task force to look into it.

NARRATOR 2:   How do you feel about that, Ralph?

NARRATOR 3:   Ralph was tempted to tell Joe that he didn't want his idea to be kicked anywhere by anybody. . . .

NARRATOR 1:   But being normal, Ralph didn't tell Joe anything. He just nodded and went back to work.

NARRATOR 2:   Of course, Joe Mode soon forgot about Ralph's idea. But Ralph did not. And because of that, something very abnormal began to take place. Weeks passed, but little by little, from an old normalator evolved a new device, one that Ralph proudly called:

RALPH: THE RALPHOLATOR!

NARRATOR 3:   Naturally, Ralph just had to try it out. He typed a command on his desktop computer.

NARRATORS 1, 2, 3:   (*A whining sound is heard*) A high-pitched whine began to emanate from the strange machine. Ralph gripped the arms of the chair, grinned, and vanished as he was ZAPPED in a powerful flash!

NARRATOR 1:   A few hours later, Joe Mode was looking for Ralph, but Ralph was not around. He entered Ralph's work area and was astounded at the tangles of wires running everywhere.

JOE: What's all this?

NARRATORS 1, 2, 3:   He sat down in Ralph's chair, and in doing so, his elbow hit the return key on the computer. There was a high-pitched whine, a blinding flash of light, and Joe Mode was ZAPPED into the 12th Dimension!

Questions

1. What kind of role did the narrator(s) assume in each piece?
2. How might your use of onstage and offstage focus enhance performance?

Readers Theater

A third style of ensemble interpretation is **readers theater,** which is group interpretation of drama or dramatic poetry. This mode is similar to the other ensemble modes examined thus far in that it is nonrepresentational. It relies on the physical and vocal abilities of the readers for its effects. The role of the audience members is to picture and complete the dramatic presentation in their imaginations.

As with the other ensemble forms, there is no single way to stage readers theater. The group should work at finding the staging techniques that best illustrate and express the nature of their selection. For example, a readers-theater group may adopt an onstage focus (the type of focus usually used in a fully staged production), an out-front focus (the type of focus usually used in solo-interpretation events), or a combination of offstage and onstage focus (the type of focus usually used in chamber theater). The ensemble should investigate all performance possibilities before settling on the most effective manner of staging and re-creating the literature.

Readers-theater groups must also be concerned with the narrator's role. What stage directions must he or she reveal to the audience? Should the individual performers function as characters and as narrators? Demonstrate your own creativity by adapting the following material for readers theater.

PERFORMER'S WORKSHOP
Experiencing Readers Theater

The following selections from Clark Gesner's *You're a Good Man, Charlie Brown* (based on the comic strip *Peanuts* by Charles Schulz) and from Richard Brinsley Sheridan's *The Rivals* have been successfully staged for readers theater. Read them carefully.

 You're a Good Man, Charlie Brown
Clark Gesner

CHARLIE BROWN: I think lunchtime is about the worst time of the day for me. Always having to sit here alone. Of course, sometimes mornings aren't so pleasant, either—waking up and wondering if anyone would really miss me if I never got out of bed. Then there's the night, too—lying there and thinking about all the stupid things I've done during the day. And all those hours in between—when I do all those stupid things. Well, lunchtime is among the worst times of the day for me.
Well, I guess I'd better see what I've got. (*He opens the bag, unwraps a sandwich, and looks inside.*) Peanut butter. (*He bites and chews.*) Some psychiatrists say that people who eat peanut but-

ter sandwiches are lonely. I guess they're right. And if you're really lonely, the peanut butter sticks to the roof of your mouth. (*He munches quietly, idly fingering the bench.*) Boy, the PTA sure did a good job of painting these benches. (*He looks off to one side.*) There's that cute little red-headed girl eating her lunch over there. I wonder what she'd do if I went over and asked her if I could sit and have lunch with her. She'd probably laugh right in my face. It's hard on a face when it gets laughed in. There's an empty place next to her on the bench. There's no reason why I couldn't just go over and sit there. I could do that right now. All I have to do is stand up. (*He stands.*) I'm standing up. (*He sits.*) I'm sitting down. I'm a coward. I'm so much of a coward she wouldn't even think of looking at me. She hardly ever does look at me. In fact, I can't remember her ever looking at me. Why shouldn't she look at me? Is there any reason in the world why she shouldn't look at me? Is she so great and am I so small that she couldn't spare one little moment just to . . . (*He freezes.*) She's looking at me. (*In terror he looks one way, then another.*) She's looking at me.

(His head looks all around, frantically trying to find something else to notice. His teeth clench. Tension builds. Then, with one motion, he pops the paper bag over his head. LUCY *and* PATTY *enter.)*

LUCY: No, Patty, you're thinking of that other dress, the one I wore to Lucinda's party. The one I'm talking about was this very light blue one and had a design embroidered around the waist.

PATTY: I don't remember that dress.

LUCY: (*Takes a pencil and draws matter-of-factly on the bottom of the paper bag*) Something like this. The skirt went out like this and it had these puffy sleeves and a sash like this.

PATTY: Oh, yes, I remember.

LUCY: Yes, well that was the dress I was wearing last week when I met Frieda and she told me she'd seen one just like it over at . . . (*The girls have exited.* CHARLIE BROWN *sits immobile as their voices fade.*)

CHARLIE BROWN: (*The paper bag still pulled over his head.*) Lunchtime is among the worst times of the day for me. . . .

In *The Rivals*, Captain Absolute, posing as Ensign Beverley, woos Lydia Languish, a sentimental heiress. Lydia is guarded by her aunt, Mrs. Malaprop—a woman renowned for using long words incorrectly. Mrs. Malaprop is unaware that Absolute and Beverley are one and the same.

The Rivals

Richard Brinsley Sheridan

MRS. MALAPROP, *with a letter in her hand, and* CAPTAIN ABSOLUTE

MRS. MALAPROP: Your being Sir Anthony's son, Captain, would itself be a sufficient accommodation; but from the ingenuity of your appearance, I am convinced you deserve the character here given of you.

CAPTAIN ABSOLUTE: Permit me to say, Madam, that as I never yet have had the pleasure of seeing Miss Languish, my principal inducement in this affair at present is the honor of being allied to Mrs. Malaprop; of whose intellectual accomplishments, elegant manners, and unaffected learning, no tongue is silent.

MRS. MALAPROP: Sir, you do me infinite honor! I beg, Captain, you'll be seated. (*sit*) Ah! few gentlemen now-a-days know how to value the ineffectual qualities in a woman! Men have no sense now but for the worthless flower of beauty!

ABSOLUTE: It is but too true, indeed, Ma'am. Yet I fear our ladies should share the blame—they think our admiration of beauty so great, that knowledge in them would be superfluous. Thus, like garden-trees, they seldom show fruit till time has robbed them of the more specious blossom. Few, like Mrs. Malaprop and the orange-tree, are rich in both at once!

MRS. MALAPROP: Sir—you overpower me with good breeding. (*aside*) He is the very pineapple of politeness!—you are not ignorant, Captain, that this giddy girl has somehow contrived to fix her affections on a beggarly, strolling, eavesdropping Ensign, whom none of us have seen, and nobody knows anything of.

ABSOLUTE: Oh, I have heard the silly affair before. I'm not at all prejudiced against her on that account.

MRS. MALAPROP: You are very good, and very considerate, Captain. I am sure I have done everything in my power since I exploded the affair! Long ago I laid my positive conjunctions on her never to think on the fellow again; I have since laid Sir Anthony's proposition before her; but I'm sorry to say, she seems resolved to decline every particle that I enjoin her.

ABSOLUTE: It must be very distressing, indeed, Ma'am.

MRS. MALAPROP: Oh! it gives me the hydrostatics to such a degree! I thought she had persisted from corresponding with him; but behold this very day I have interceded another letter from the fellow! I believe I have it in my pocket.

ABSOLUTE: (*aside*) Oh the devil! my last note.

MRS. MALAPROP: Aye, here it is.

ABSOLUTE: (*aside*) Aye, my note, indeed! Oh the little traitress Lucy!

MRS. MALAPROP: There, perhaps you may know the writing. (*gives him the letter*)

ABSOLUTE: I think I have seen the hand before—yes, I certainly must have seen this hand before—

MRS. MALAPROP: Nay, but read it, Captain.

ABSOLUTE: (*reads*) "My soul's idol, my adored Lydia!"—Very tender, indeed!

MRS. MALAPROP: Tender! aye, and profane, too, o' my conscience!

ABSOLUTE: "I am excessively alarmed at the intelligence you send me, the more so as my new rival"—

MRS. MALAPROP: That's you, Sir.

ABSOLUTE: "has universally the character of being an accomplished gentleman, and a man of honour."—Well, that's handsome enough.

MRS. MALAPROP: Oh, the fellow had some design in writing so.

ABSOLUTE: That he had, I'll answer for him, Ma'am.

MRS. MALAPROP: But go on, Sir—you'll see presently.

ABSOLUTE: "As for the old weather-beaten she-dragon who guards you"—Who can he mean by that?

MRS. MALAPROP: Me! Sir—me!—he means me! There—what do you think now? But go on a little further.

ABSOLUTE: Impudent scoundrel!—"it shall go hard but I will elude her vigilance, as I am told that the same ridiculous vanity which makes her dress up her coarse features, and deck her dull chat with hard words which she don't understand"—

MRS. MALAPROP: There, Sir! an attack on my language! What do you think of that?—an aspersion upon my parts of speech! Was ever such a brute! Sure if I reprehend anything in this world, it is the use of my oracular tongue, and a nice derangement of epitaphs!

ABSOLUTE: He deserves to be hanged and quartered! Let me see— "same ridiculous vanity—"

MRS. MALAPROP: You need not read it again, Sir.

ABSOLUTE: I beg pardon, Ma'am—"does also lay her open to the grossest deceptions from flattery and pretended admiration"—an impudent coxcomb!— "so that I have a scheme to see you shortly with the old harridan's consent, and even to make her a go-between in our interviews."—Was ever such assurance!

MRS. MALAPROP: Did you ever hear anything like it? He'll elude my vigilance, will he? Yes, yes! ha! ha! He's very likely to enter these doors! We'll try who can plot best!

ABSOLUTE: So we will, Ma'am—so we will. Ha! ha! ha! A conceited puppy, ha! ha! ha! Well, but Mrs. Malaprop, as the girl seems so infatuated by this fellow, suppose you were to wink at her corresponding with him for a little time—let her even plot an elopement with him—then do you connive at her escape—while I, just in the nick, will have the fellow laid by the heels, and fairly contrive to carry her off in his stead.

MRS. MALAPROP: I am delighted with the scheme; never was anything better perpetrated!

ABSOLUTE: But, pray, could not I see the lady for a few minutes now? I should like to try her temper a little.

MRS. MALAPROP: Why, I don't know—I doubt she is not prepared for a visit of this kind. There is a decorum in these matters.

ABSOLUTE: O Lord! she won't mind me—only tell her Beverley—

MRS. MALAPROP: Sir!—

ABSOLUTE: (aside) Gently, good tongue.

MRS. MALAPROP: What did you say of Beverley?

ABSOLUTE: Oh, I was going to propose that you should tell her, by way of jest, that it was Beverley who was below—she'd come down fast enough then—ha! ha! ha!

MRS. MALAPROP: 'Twould be a trick she well deserves. Besides, you know the fellow tells her he'll get my consent to see her—ha! ha! ha! Let him if he can, I say again. (calling) Lydia, come down here!—He'll make me a go-between in their interviews!—ha! ha! ha!—Come down, I say, Lydia!—I don't wonder at your laughing, ha! ha! ha!—his impudence is truly ridiculous. . . .

Questions

1. How would you physically set the stage for each production?
2. What kind of focus would you employ if you were to stage each excerpt?
3. What type of costuming would you suggest?
4. What kind of movement and how much of it would you have the characters use in each scene?

Ensembles for Children

The wealth of literature for children and young people provides another source for ensemble performers. Libraries and bookstores house an extensive variety of materials for the interpretative group. Children's poetry is great fun to perform. Short stories can be produced as children's chamber theater, and plays can be staged in a readers-theater style for young audiences. A well-rehearsed, well-performed program for children is rewarding for both performers and audience.

Try this. Work with your group to choose some piece of literature you all enjoyed when you were young. Next, stage it for an audience of children.

IDEA ENCORE

This chapter focused on ensemble approaches to interpretation. Ensemble or group interpretation is another exciting way to explore and perform literature.

Three divisions of the ensemble approach were described: choral reading, chamber theater, and readers theater. Each kind of performance requires an understanding of group dynamics and the ability to build group cohesiveness. In an ensemble performance, while the individual performer is still important, it is how the individual contributes to the group that is paramount.

For ensemble performance to succeed, the members of the group must be adept at using both onstage and out-front focus, skilled at suggesting action and movement, attuned to the importance of physical arrangement, and creative in their use of multimedia devices.

PERFORMER'S SHOWCASE & JOURNAL
The Ensemble and Children

Working with group members, select one of the following options to perform for children.

Option 1: Choose a number of poems to stage and present chorally for a young audience.
Option 2: Choose an appropriate short story to present in chamber-theater style for a young audience.
Option 3: Choose a scene or scenes from a play. Using readers-theater techniques, stage that portion of the play for a young audience.

If possible, arrange for an audience of appropriate age to visit your classroom and watch your performances, or take your performances on tour to nearby schools. In your journal, make notes on the audience's reactions to your performance as well as your assessment of your interpretation.

You can see that ensemble performances of literature have much to offer both the performers and their audiences. Working with others to bring literature alive is both challenging and satisfying. Because it takes time, effort, and commitment to develop effective presentations, ensemble performance is for mature, motivated performers who truly want to explore themselves and their chosen literature. And in the process, they often have fun!

SELECTIONS FOR FURTHER WORK

 "I Hear America Singing"
Walt Whitman

I hear America singing, the varied carols I hear;

Those of mechanics, each one singing his as it should be blithe and strong,

The carpenter singing his as he measures his plank or beam,

The mason singing his as he makes ready for work, or leaves off work,

The boatman singing what belongs to him in his boat, the deck-hand singing on the steamboat deck,

The shoemaker singing as he sits on his bench, the hatter singing as he stands,

The wood-cutter's song, the ploughboy's on his way in the morning, or at noon intermission or at sundown,

The delicious singing of the mother, or of the young wife at work, or of the girl sewing or washing,

Each singing what belongs to him or her and to none else,

The day what belongs to the day—at night the party of young fellows, robust, friendly,

Singing with open mouths their strong melodious songs.

"Cool Tombs"
Carl Sandburg

When Abraham Lincoln was shoveled into the tombs, he forgot
the copperheads and the assassin . . . in the dust, in the cool
tombs.

And Ulysses Grant lost all thought of con men and Wall Street,
cash and collateral turned ashes . . . in the dust, in the cool
tombs.

Pocahontas' body, lovely as a poplar, sweet as a red haw in
November or a pawpaw in May, did she wonder? does she
remember? . . . in the dust, in the cool tombs?

Take any streetful of people buying clothes and groceries, cheer-
ing a hero or throwing confetti and blowing tin horns . . . tell
me if the lovers are losers . . . tell me if any get more than the
lovers . . . in the dust . . . in the cool tombs.

"Death Snips Proud Men"
Carl Sandburg

Death is stronger than all the governments because the
governments are men, and men die, and then death laughs:
"Now you see 'em, now you don't."

Death is stronger than all proud men and so death snips
proud men on the nose, throws a pair of dice and says:
"Read 'em and weep."

Death sends a radiogram every day: "When I want you I'll
drop in"—and then one day he comes with a master-
key and lets himself in and says: "We'll go now."

Death is a nurse mother with big arms: "'Twon't hurt you
at all; it's your time now; you just need a long sleep,
child; what have you had anyhow better than sleep?"

Chapter

Approaches to
Organizing a Program

Learning Objectives

After completing this chapter, you should be able to

- identify the steps involved in creating a program
- distinguish between the following two kinds of programs: solo and counterpoint
- discuss staging techniques to use when presenting a program
- present a program individually and as part of an ensemble

In the performance art of oral interpretation, as in the arts of painting and sculpture, the overall effect of the performance is often greater than the sum of its parts. Just as artists mix shades, textures, shapes, and colors to make a statement, a work of art, performers of literature can mix genres and moods, orchestrating several selections or cuttings to produce a program. Flexible and practiced interpreters may present their audiences with many different types of literary experiences. Following are some creative approaches to organizing a program.

The Solo Program

An interpreter who organizes a solo program should cluster literary genres and selections in a way that permits the audience to discover new meanings in the performed literature and, ideally, to develop new insights into life. The interpreter who works alone is, in effect, more than an individual—he or she offers a range of experience. A solo performer may assume a limitless number of faces during the course of a program, because the range of literature he or she may draw from is also limitless.

In some ways, the job of an oral interpreter in a solo program is comparable to that of a stand-up comic. In performance, comics portray a variety of characters who live in their minds or in their material, while interpreters bring to life characters from literature. The performer of literature is free to present a much wider range of material, of course—not just material that is meant to elicit laughter. However, the solo performer of literature and the stand-up comic have something very much in common. They are alone on stage for an extended period of time, armed only with words and their performance ability to interest their audiences.

The solo performer today is not limited to the classroom or the stage. Performers sometimes work with art, electronic images, dance, and music to add impact to the messages being presented. As a solo performer you have a great responsibility to your audience to create a piece that is worth the time and energy of your audience. You also have a tremendous amount of material from which to choose. The solo performer today is truly in a position where he or she can develop striking and memorable presentations.

Like individual readings, a solo program may be effective or dull. An effective program results from a script attached with a sense of textual unity. To achieve this quality of textual cohesion, an interpreter must choose selections that illuminate a single central idea. The focus could be on themes like America today, dreams, windows, age, youth, war, faces, friendship, animals, memories, the political person, the social person, learning, poverty, homelessness, or growing up—to name just a few possibilities.

An alternative to choosing a theme to unify the program is to select a particular writer's work as your focus. In this case, you would probably approach the works of your chosen author chronologically or topically—that is, you might investigate the growth and changes in your author's artistic techniques over time, or you might illuminate the major issues or concepts that recur throughout the author's works. Some particularly successful author programs have explored Oscar Wilde ("It's a Wilde, Wilde World"); Mark Twain ("A Man of Many Faces"); Edgar Allan Poe ("A Poe Pourri"); Emily Dickinson ("A Woman Alone"); and Lorraine Hansberry ("The Black Experience"). Numerous authors' works and lives await your creative exploration.

As mentioned in the chapter on documentary interpretation, the focus of your program might be on a particular historical period or personality. There are infinite topic possibilities awaiting your personal approach. Consider using slides, sound, or appropriate images to support your program. Clearly, there are myriad opportunities for the program builder.

Organizing the Program

The program's introduction should establish the theme, set the tone, and prepare the audience to receive, process, and respond to the literature selected. For example, the following passage served as the introduction to a program on the theme of inhumanity:

> The inhumane treatment of human beings is a topic that should concern us all today since its occurrence is far too frequent. Indeed, if anything, the brutality that has persisted throughout history has become progressively worse—not better. It is to this brutality or inhumanity that I address myself today.

This introduction admirably fulfills its function because it establishes the unifying thread of the entire program—inhumanity—and readies the audience to expect literature on this topic.

An introduction need not be "heavy" or moral in its implication, however. In setting the mood, it should reinforce the statement you wish to make to your audience with your program. For example, the following lines served as the opening to a program focusing on Mark Twain, the person and the writer:

> Mark Twain included this notice at the beginning of his most famous novel, *The Adventures of Huckleberry Finn:* "Persons attempting to find a motive in this narrative will be prosecuted; persons attempting to find a moral in it will be banished; persons attempting to find a plot in it will be shot." I say the same to you today concerning the program I have developed on "Mark Twain: A Man of Many Faces."

In addition to having an introduction, every successful program builds toward a climax and creates a unified effect overall. A unified effect does not imply sameness, however. In fact, most effective programs are characterized not by sameness but by variety. Talented musicians sing and play a variety of styles and moods in their concerts. Use variety in your program to hold your audience's interest.

Choosing the Selections

When possible, intermingle selections of varying lengths and tones. Proper juxtaposition of materials will help to underscore the theme of your program. For example, the program on inhumanity included the following three works: "More Light! More Light!" by Anthony Hecht, an excerpt from *Man's Search for Meaning* by Viktor Frankl, and "All There Is to Know About Adolph Eichmann" by Leonard Cohen. The works varied in length, tone, and genre, yet they served to illustrate perfectly the interpreter's theme.

In program planning, adhere to three general rules:

1. The first selection of your program should capture your audience's attention.
2. The selection strongest in emotional impact should be the climax of your program.
3. The selection that best summarizes your theme should conclude your program.

PERFORMER'S WORKSHOP
Mark Twain: A Man of Many Faces

To illustrate these concepts of program planning, examine the Twain program referred to in the previous paragraphs. As you consider the program, look for concepts that can guide you in developing your own material.

After introducing the general theme of her Mark Twain, the interpreter stated: "Unlike most men, Samuel Clemens never did renounce his boyhood. He lived youth, and he greatly enjoyed playing. One of Twain's favorite youthful characters was Huck Finn. Thus, I would like to begin with a selection from Twain's most renowned work, *The Adventures of Huckleberry Finn.*"

The Adventures of Huckleberry Finn
Mark Twain

You don't know about me, without you have read a book by the name of "The Adventures of Tom Sawyer," but that ain't no matter. That book was made by Mr. Mark Twain, and he told the truth, mainly. There was things which he stretched, but mainly he told the truth. . . .

Now, the way that the book winds up, is this: Tom and me found the money that the robbers hid in the cave, and it made us rich. We got six thousand dollars apiece—all gold. It was an awful sight of money when it was piled up. Well, Judge Thatcher, he took it and put it out at interest, and it fetched us a dollar a day apiece, all the year round—more than a body could tell what to do with. The Widow Douglas, she took me for her son, and allowed she would civilize me; but it was rough living in the house all the time, considering how dismal regular and decent the widow was in all her ways; and so when I couldn't stand it no longer, I lit out. I got into my old rags . . . and was free and satisfied. But Tom Sawyer, he hunted me up and said he was going to start a band of robbers, and I might join if I would go back to the widow and be respectable. So I went back.

The widow she cried over me, and called me a poor lost lamb, and she called me a lot of other names, too, but she never meant no harm by it. She put me in them new clothes again, and I couldn't do nothing but sweat and sweat, and feel all cramped up. Well, then, the old thing commenced again. The widow rung a bell for supper, and you had to come on time. When you got to the table you couldn't go right to eating, but you had to wait for the widow to tuck down her head and grumble a little over the victuals, though there warn't really anything the matter with them. That is, nothing only everything was cooked by itself. In a barrel of odds and ends it is different; things get mixed up, and the juice kind of swaps around, and the things go better.

After supper she got out her book and learned me about Moses and the Bulrushers; and I was in a sweat to find out all about him; but by-and-by she let it out that Moses had been dead a considerable long time; so then I didn't care no more about him; because I don't take no stock in dead people.

Pretty soon I wanted to smoke, and asked the widow to let me. But she wouldn't. She said it was a mean practice and wasn't clean, and I must try to not do it any more. That is just the way with some people. They get down on a thing when they don't know nothing about it. Here she was a bothering about Moses, which was no kin to her, and no use to anybody, being gone, you see, yet finding a power of fault with me for doing a thing that had some good in it. And she took snuff too; of course that was all right, because she done it herself.

Her sister, Miss Watson, a tolerable slim old maid, with goggles on, had just come to live with her, and took a set at me now, with a spelling-book. She worked me middling hard for about an hour, and then the widow made her ease up. I couldn't stood it much longer. Then for an hour it was deadly dull, and I was fidgety. Miss Watson would say, "Don't put your feet up there, Huckleberry"; and "don't scrunch up like that, Huckleberry—set up straight"; and pretty soon she would say, "Don't gap and stretch like that, Huckleberry—why don't you try to behave?" Then she told me all about the bad place, and I said I wished I was there. She got mad, then, but I didn't mean no harm. All I wanted was to go somewheres; all I wanted was a change, I warn't particular. She said it was wicked to say what I said; said she wouldn't say it for the whole world; she was going to live so as to go to the good place. Well, I couldn't see no advantage in going where she was going, so I made up my mind I wouldn't try for it. . . .

Now she had got a start, and she went on and told me all about the good place. She said all a body would have to do there was to go around all day long with a harp and sing, forever and ever. So I didn't think much of it. But I never said so. I asked her if she reckoned Tom Sawyer would go there, and, she said, not by a considerable sight. I was glad about that because I wanted him and me to be together. . . .

Since the interpreter's first selection ended with Huck expressing a kinship for his friend Tom, it was natural that her next selection would come from *The Adventures of Tom Sawyer*. She introduced the selection in the following manner:

Tom Sawyer was another of Twain's favorites; he also serves to represent another face of Samuel Clemens. In fact, all his life Mark Twain was Tom Sawyer, that is, when he was not pretending to be someone else. At the outset of this novel Twain told his readers: "Although my book is intended mainly for the entertainment of boys and girls, I hope it will not be shunned by men and women on that account, for part of my plan has been to try to pleasantly remind adults of what they once were themselves, and of how they felt and thought and talked, and what queer enterprises they sometimes engaged in." Let us now join Twain as he describes Tom Sawyer preparing to show off at Sunday School in front of his "beloved Becky" and her great and famous father, Judge Thatcher.

 ### *The Adventures of Tom Sawyer*
Mark Twain

The sun rose upon a tranquil world, and beamed down upon the peaceful village like a benediction. Breakfast over, Aunt Polly had family worship: it began with a prayer built from the group of solid courses of Scriptural quotations, welded together with a thin mortar of originality. . . .

Then Tom girded up his loins, so to speak, and went to work to "get his verses." . . . Tom bent all his energies to the memorizing of five verses, and he chose part of the Sermon on the Mount, because he could find no verses that were shorter. . . . Mary took his book to hear him recite, and he tried to find his way through the fog:

"Blessed are the—a—a"

"Poor—"

"Yes—poor; blessed are the poor—a—a"

"In spirit—"

"In spirit; blessed are the poor in spirit, for they—they—"

"Theirs—"

"For theirs. Blessed are the poor in spirit for theirs is the kingdom of heaven. Blessed are they that mourn, for they—they—"

"Sh—"

"For they—a—"

"S—H—A—"

"For they S—H—Oh, I don't know what it is!"

"Shall!"

"Oh, shall! for they shall—for they shall—a—a—shall mourn—a—a—blessed are they that shall—they that—a—they that shall mourn, for they shall—a—shall what? Why don't you tell me, Mary?—What do you want to be so mean for?"

"Oh, Tom, you poor thick-headed thing, I'm not teasing you. I wouldn't do that. You must go and learn it again. . . ."

And he did "tackle it again" . . . he did it with such spirit that he accomplished a shining success.

(Tom was then ready to go to Sunday School.)

Sabbath-school hours were from nine to half past ten. . . . At the door Tom dropped back a step and accosted a Sunday-dressed comrade:

"Say, Billy, got a yaller ticket?"

"Yes."

"What'll you take for her?"

"What'll you give?"

"Piece of lickrish and a fish-hook."

"Less see 'em."

Tom exhibited. They were satisfactory, and the property changed hands. Then Tom traded a couple of white alleys for three red tickets, and some small trifle or other for a couple of blue ones. He waylaid other boys as they came, and went on buying tickets of various colors ten or fifteen minutes longer. He entered the church, now, with a swarm of clean and noisy boys and girls, proceeded to his seat and started a quarrel with the first boy that came handy. The teacher, a grave, elderly man, interfered; then turned his back a moment and Tom pulled a boy's hair in the next bench, and was absorbed in his book when the boy turned around, stuck a pin in another boy, presently, in order to hear him say "Ouch!" and got a new reprimand from his teacher. Tom's whole class were of a pattern—restless, noisy, and troublesome. When they came to recite their lessons, not one of them knew his verses perfectly, but had to be prompted all along. However, they worried through, and each got his reward—in small blue tickets, each with a passage of Scripture on it; each blue ticket was pay for two verses of the recitation. Ten blue tickets equaled a red one, and could be exchanged for it; ten red tickets equaled a yellow one; for ten yellow tickets the superintendent gave a very plainly bound Bible (worth forty cents in those easy times) to the pupil. . . . Only the older pupils managed to keep their tickets and stick to their tedious work long enough to get a Bible, and so the delivery of one of these prizes was a rare and noteworthy circumstance; the successful pupil was so great and conspicuous for that day that on the spot every scholar's heart was fired with a fresh ambition that often lasted a couple of weeks. . . .

In due course the superintendent stood up in front of the pulpit, with a closed hymn-book in his hand and his forefinger inserted between its leaves, and commanded attention. When a Sunday-school superintendent makes his customary little speech, a hymn-book in the hand is as necessary as is the inevitable sheet of music in the hand of a singer who stands forward on the platform and sings a solo at a concert—though why is a mystery: for neither the hymn-book nor the sheet of music is ever referred to by the sufferer. . . . He began after this fashion:

"Now, children, I want you all to sit up just as straight and pretty as you can and give me all your attention for a minute or two. There—that is it. That is the way good little boys and girls should do. I see one little girl who is looking out of the window—I am afraid she thinks I am out there somewhere—perhaps up in one of the trees making a speech to the little birds. (Applausive titter.) I want to tell you how good it makes me feel to see so many bright clean little faces assembled in a place like this, learning to do right and be good." And so forth and so on. It is not necessary to set down the rest of the oration. It was of a pattern which does not vary, and so it is familiar to us all. . . .

A good deal of whispering had been occasioned by an event which was more or less rare—the entrance of visitors; lawyer Thatcher, accompanied by a very feeble and aged man; a fine, portly, middle-aged gentleman with iron-gray hair; and a dignified lady who was doubtless the latter's wife. The lady was leading a child. . . . The next moment [Tom] was "showing off" with all his might—cuffing boys, pulling hair, making faces—in a word, using every art that seemed likely to fascinate a girl and win her applause. . . .

The visitors were given the highest seat of honor, and as soon as Mr. Walter's speech was finished, he introduced them to the school. . . . There was only one thing wanting to make Mr. Walter's ecstasy complete, and that was a chance to deliver a Bible prize and exhibit a prodigy. Several pupils had a few yellow tickets, but none had enough—he had been around the star pupils inquiring. . . .

And now at this moment, when hope was dead, Tom Sawyer came forward with nine yellow tickets, nine red tickets, and ten blue ones, and demanded a Bible. This was a thunderbolt out of a clear sky. Walter was not expecting an application from this source for the next ten years. But there was no getting around it—here were the certified checks, and they were good for their face. Tom was therefore elevated to a place with the Judge and the other elect. . . . It was the most stunning surprise of the decade, and so profound was the sensation that it lifted the new hero up to the judicial one's altitude. . . . The boys were all eaten up with envy—but those that suffered the bitterest pangs were those who perceived too late that they themselves had contributed to this hated splendor by trading tickets to Tom for the wealth he had amassed in selling whitewashing privileges. . . .

The prize was delivered to Tom with as much effusion as the superintendent could pump up under the circumstances; but it lacked somewhat of the true gush, for the poor fellow's instinct taught him that there was a mystery here that could not well bear the light, perhaps; it was simply preposterous that this boy had warehoused two thousand sheaves of Scriptural wisdom on his premises—a dozen would strain his capacity, without a doubt. . . .

Tom was introduced to the Judge, but his tongue was tied; his breath would hardly come, his heart quaked—partly because of the awful greatness of the man, but mainly because he was her parent. . . . The Judge put his hand on Tom's head and called him a fine little man, and asked him what his name was. The boy stammered, gasped, and got it out:

"Tom. . . ."

"Fine boy. Fine, manly little fellow. Two thousand verses is a great many—very, very great many. And you never can be sorry for the trouble you took to learn them; for knowledge is worth more than anything there is in the world; it's what makes great men and good men; you'll be a great man and a good man yourself, some day, Thomas, and then you'll look back and say, It's all owing to the previous Sunday-school privileges of my boyhood—it's all owing to my dear teachers that taught me to learn. . . . That is what you will say, Thomas—and you wouldn't take any money for those two thousand verses—no indeed you wouldn't. And now you wouldn't mind telling me and this lady some of the things you've learned—no, I know you wouldn't. . . . Now, no doubt you know the names of all the twelve disciples. Won't you tell us the names of the first two that were appointed?"

Tom was tugging at a button-hole and looking sheepish. He blushed now, and his eyes fell. Mr. Walter's heart sank within him. . . . Yet he felt obliged to speak up and say:

"Answer the gentlemen, Thomas—don't be afraid."

Tom still hung fire.

"Now I know you'll tell me," said the lady. "The names of the first two disciples were—"

"DAVID AND GOLIATH!"

Let us draw the curtain of charity over the rest of the scene.

Because this last selection poked mild fun at religion, the interpreter chose her next passage from Twain's satirical piece *Letters from the Earth*. Let's take a look at this excerpt now.

Letters from the Earth
Mark Twain

His [man's] heaven is like himself: strange, interesting, astonishing grotesque. I give you my word, it has not a single feature in it that he actually values. It consists—utterly and entirely—of diversions which he cares next to nothing about, here in the earth, yet is quite sure he will like in heaven. Isn't it curious? Isn't it interesting? You must not think I am exaggerating, for it is not so. I will give you details.

Most men do not sing, most men cannot sing, most men will not stay where others are singing if it be continued more than two hours. Note that.

Only about two men in a hundred can play upon a musical instrument, and not four in a hundred have any wish to learn how. Set that down.

Many men pray, not many of them like to do it. A few pray long, the others take a short cut. . . .

Now then, you have the facts. You know what the human race enjoys, and what it doesn't enjoy. It has invented a heaven out of its own head all by itself: guess what it is like! . . . Very well, I will tell you about it.

1. First of all, I recall to your attention the extraordinary fact . . . that the human being, like the immortals, naturally places sexual intercourse far and away above all other joys—yet he has left it out of his heaven! The very thought of it excites him; opportunity sets him wild; in this queer state, he will risk life, reputation, everything. . . . To make good that opportunity and ride it to the overwhelming climax. . . . Yet it is actually as I have said: it is not in their heaven; prayer takes its place. . . .

2. In man's heaven, everybody sings! The man who did not sing on earth sings there; the man who could not sing on earth is able to do it there. . . . And everybody stays; whereas on the earth the place would be empty in two hours. . . .

3. Meantime, every person is playing on a harp—those millions and millions!—whereas not more than twenty in a thousand could play an instrument on the earth, or ever wanted to. . . .

He is a Marvel—man is! I would I knew who invented him. . . .

The next portion of the interpreter's program was devoted to exploring Twain's ideas concerning the government, slavery, and the human race. Selections were drawn from *A Connecticut Yankee in King Arthur's Court*, *Pudd'nhead Wilson*, *The Adventures of Huckleberry Finn*, and an essay entitled "The Art of Inhumation." The interpreter concluded this section of her program with excerpts from some of Twain's works that contained comments on the general behavior of men and their affinity for war.

I have been studying the traits and dispositions of the "lower animals" (so-called), and contrasting them with the traits and dispositions of man. I find the result humiliating to me. . . . It is now plain to me that Darwin's theory ought to be vacated in favor of a new and truer one, this new and truer one to be named the Descent of Man from the Higher Animals. . . .

In the course of my experiments I convinced myself that among the animals man is the only one that harbors insults and broods over them, waits till a chance offers, then takes revenge. The passion of revenge is unknown to the higher animals. . . .

Indecency, vulgarity, obscenity—these are strictly confined to man: he invented them. Among the higher animals there is no trace of them. They hide nothing: they are not ashamed. . . .

The higher animals engage in individual fights, but never in organized masses. Man is the only animal that deals in the atrocity of atrocities, War. He is the only one that gathers his brethren about him and goes forth in cold blood and with calm pulse to exterminate his kind. He is the only animal that for sordid wages will march out . . . and help to slaughter strangers of his own species who have done him no harm and with whom he has no quarrel. . . . Man has done this in all ages. . . . And in the intervals between campaigns he washes the blood off his hands and works for "the universal brotherhood of man"—with his mouth. . . .

It seems plain to me that whatever he is, he is not a reasoning animal. His record is the fantastic record of a maniac. . . . This is a matter for thought; and for serious thought. And it is full of grim suggestion: that we are not as important, perhaps, as we had all along supposed we were.

The next selection, a biting indictment of human savagery, served as the climax of the interpreter's program.

from "The War Prayer"

Mark Twain

It was a time of great and exalting excitement. The country was up in arms, the war was on, in every breast burned the holy fire of patriotism; the drums were beating, the bands playing. . . .

Sunday morning came—next day the battalions would leave for the front; the church was filled; the volunteers were there, their young faces alight with martial dreams—visions of the stern advance, the gathering momentum, the rushing charge, the flashing sabers. . . . the fierce pursuit, the surrender!—then home from the war, bronzed horses, welcomed, adored, submerged in golden seas of glory! With the volunteers sat their dear ones, proud, happy, and envied by the neighbors and friends who had no sons and brothers to send forth to the field of honor. . . . The service proceeded. . . .

Then came the "long" prayer. . . . The burden of its supplication was that an ever merciful and benignant Father of us all would watch over our noble young soldiers, and aid, comfort, and encourage them in their patriotic work . . . bear them in His mighty hand, make them strong and confident, invincible in the blood onset; help them to crush the foe, grant to them and to their flag and country imperishable honor and glory—

An aged stranger entered and moved with slow and noiseless step up the main aisle, his eyes fixed upon the minister, his long body clothed in a robe that reached to his feet, his head bare, his white hair descending in a frothy cataract to his shoulders, his seamy face unnaturally pale, pale even to ghastliness. . . .

The stranger touched (the minister's) arm, motioned him to step aside—which the startled minister did—and took his place. . . . Then in a deep voice he said:

"I come from the Throne—bearing a message from Almighty God. . . . He has heard the prayer of His servant your shepherd, and will grant it if such shall be your desire after I, His messenger, shall have explained to you its import. . . . For it is like unto many of the prayers of men, in that it asks for more than he who utters it is aware of. . . .

"You have heard your servant's prayer—the uttered part of it. I am commissioned of God to put into words the other part of it—that part which the pastor—and also you in your hearts—fervently prayed silently. . . .

"O Lord our Father, our young patriots, idols of our hearts, go forth to battle—be Thou near them! With them—in spirit—we also go forth from the sweet peace of our beloved firesides to smite the foe. O Lord our God, help us to tear their soldiers to bloody shreds with our shells; help us to cover their smiling fields with the pale forms of their patriot dead; help us to drown the thunder of the guns with the shrieks of their wounded, writhing in pain; help us to lay waste their humble homes with a hurricane of fire; help us to wring the hearts of their unoffending widows with unavailing grief; help us to turn them out roofless with their little children to wander unfriended the wastes of their desolate land in rags and hunger and thirst . . . for our sakes who adore thee, Lord, blast their hopes, blight their lives . . . make heavy their steps, water their way with their tears, stain the white snow with blood of their wounded feet! We ask it in the spirit of love, of Him Who is the Source of Love, and Who is the ever faithful refuge and friend of all that are sore beset and seek His aid with humble and contrite hearts. Amen.

(After a pause) "Ye have prayed it; if ye still desire it, speak! The messenger of the Most High waits."

It was believed afterward that the man was a lunatic, because there was no sense in what he said.

The interpreter concluded the Twain presentation with an excerpt from a letter to the editor written by Twain and entitled "Amended Obituaries."

 "Amended Obituaries"
Mark Twain

Sir, I am approaching seventy; it is in sight; it is only three years away. Necessarily, I must go soon. It is but matter-of-course wisdom, then, that I should begin to set my worldly house in order now, so that it may be done calmly and with thoroughness. . . . Of necessity, an obituary is a thing which cannot be so judiciously edited by any hand as by that of the subject of it. . . . In considering this matter . . . it has seemed to me wise to take such measures as may be feasible, to acquire, by courtesy of the press, access to my standing obituaries, with the privilege—if this is not asking too much—of editing, not their Facts, but their Verdicts. . . .

It is my desire that the journals and periodicals as have obituaries of me lying in their pigeonholes, with a view to sudden use someday, will not wait longer, but will publish them now, and kindly send me a marked copy. . . .

P.S.—For the best Obituary—one suitable for me to read in public, and calculated to inspire regret—I desire to offer a Prize, consisting of a portrait of me done entirely by myself, in pen and ink. . . . The ink warranted to be the kind used by the very best artists.

By interspersing humor, satire, and gloom in her program, the interpreter sketched Twain's many faces for her audience. At the conclusion of her presentation, she stated: "Twain himself designed my program for me when he wrote: 'Pessimists are born, not made, optimists are born, not made; but no man is born either pessimistic wholly or optimistic wholly; perhaps he is pessimistic along certain lines and optimistic along certain lines. That is my case.'"

Questions

1. In selecting the program, what did the performer do that you enjoyed?
2. In what ways would you alter the program? Are there materials you would omit? What other materials would you consider incorporating? Why?
3. What challenges would you face in developing a program of this length?

Note that the performer used planned transitions to tie each of the selections to the central idea of her program and to emphasize the thematic unity of the presentation. Her transitions, like her introduction, were succinct—sometimes a few words, sometimes a few sentences, but rarely longer. Thus, her transitions provided the audience with a bridge on which to travel from the mood and content of one selection to the mood and content of the next. Her transitions helped her create a unified effect within the program.

Visuals and Performance

Some performers choose to incorporate visuals and even sound into their programs. For example, in a documentary program titled "Vietnam Voices," the performer uses letters and other materials to bring the ten-year tragedy of the war in Vietnam to life for audiences. Video clips of war scenes that were common on the evening news begin the presentation. Slides of drawings by combat veterans set the scene for several of the pieces. A photo of the Vietnam Memorial helps provide the "tomb" feeling from which the letters flow.

Some performers use computer projections in their programs. If the equipment is available, it may be worth your time to experiment with it as a way of creating mood, showing a photograph of the author or presenting other visual material. An overhead projector provide similar support. Simply have photographs or other art copied on acetate slides at your local copy shop.

If you decide to use slides, including PowerPoint–type projections, be sure that they support the performance and do not dominate it. Your task is always to bring the literature alive.

Now it is your turn to develop a program. Read the details below regarding your assignment.

PERFORMER'S WORKSHOP
The Many Faces of Literature

Your task is to build a twelve- to fifteen-minute sustained, well-integrated presentation on a theme or subject of your choice. Consider variety, development, and climax when selecting and arranging your material.

Put thought and effort into your introduction, transitions, and conclusion. Remember, too, to keep them brief. On the day you are to perform, hand into your instructor your answers to these questions.

Questions

1. What is the theme you seek to present in your presentation?
2. What problems or challenges did your program present to you as an interpreter? Be specific.
3. What would you like your presentation to stimulate your audience to feel, think, or do?

The Ensemble Program

An ensemble, too, can perform the kind of program discussed above. Selections are carefully assigned among the ensemble readers and staging decisions are made. The same sorts of techniques used by the individual performer would be used to develop a program for an ensemble.

The balance of this chapter will explore an innovative type of program that may be developed and performed by an ensemble of readers.

The Counterpoint Program

A **counterpoint program** consists of two or more independent works related by a thematic thread. These works are interwoven with each other and by an ensemble of readers to form a single, harmonic creation. When creating a counterpoint program, the group of readers has a fourfold task to complete:

1. They must decide upon a theme, central idea, or statement to share with the audience.
2. They must search out a number of literary selections that comment on, or relate to, their chosen theme.
3. They must integrate the materials in an arrangement that yields a "new" work.
4. They must stage this new work using a readers theater or chamber theatre approach.

Given those tasks, counterpoint program staging techniques usually include some movement, suggestive use of gesture, and vocal effects.

In a counterpoint program, one selection usually serves as the base, or carpet, for the other selections. Thus, when performing counterpoint you need not use the whole of any selection, unless you wish to. For example, the poem "Patterns" by Amy Lowell and the poem "War Is Kind" by Stephen Crane have been effectively counterpointed. (These poems are included in their entirety elsewhere in this text.) When counterpointed, the poems can be intermeshed as in the following program.

Counterpoint Program

Amy Lowell and Stephen Crane

Chorus of Soldiers

Because your lover threw wild hands toward the sky

Do not weep, maiden, for war is kind

Because your lover threw wild hands toward the sky

And the affrighted steed ran on alone,
Do not weep.
War is kind.

Woman
I walk down the garden paths,
And all the daffodils
Are blowing, and the bright blue squills.
I walk down the patterned garden-paths
In my stiff, brocaded gown.
With my powdered hair and jeweled fan,
I too am a rare
Pattern. As I wander down
The garden paths.

Chorus of Soldiers
(echoes these phrases under words of woman)
Do not weep
Do not weep
War is kind
War is kind
(repeated)

Woman
My dress is richly figured,
And the train
Makes a pink and silver stain
On the gravel, and the thrift
Of the borders.
Just a plate of current fashion,
Tripping by in high-heeled, ribboned shoes.
Not a softness anywhere about me,
Only whalebone and brocade.
And I sink on a seat in the shade
Of a lime tree. For my passion
Wars against the stiff brocade.

Chorus of Soldiers

(*Chorus maintains beat by marching in place*)

War is kind

War is kind

Woman

And I weep;

For the lime-tree is in blossom

And one small flower has dropped upon my bosom.

Chorus of Soldiers

Do not weep

War is kind

Do not weep

War is kind.

Woman

And I weep

And I weep

I too am a rare pattern

And I weep

I too am a rare pattern

And I weep

Chorus of Soldiers

Hoarse, booming drums of the regiment,

Little souls who thirst for fight,

These men were born to drill and die.

The unexplained glory flies above them,

Great is the battle-god, great, and his kingdom—

A field where a thousand corpses lie.

Woman

I would be the pink and silver as I ran along the paths,

And he would stumble after,

Bewildered by my laughter.

I should see the sun flashing from his sword-hilt and the buckles
on his shoes.

Chorus of Soldiers

(*marching in place*)
These men were born
to drill and die
to drill and die

Woman

Underneath the fallen blossom
In my bosom,
Is a letter I have hid.
It was brought to me this morning by a rider from the Duke.
"Madam, we regret to inform you that Lord Hartwell
Died in action Thursday se'nnight."

Chorus of Soldiers

Do not weep
War is kind
War is kind
Do not weep
Do not weep
War is kind
The affrighted steed ran on alone
War is kind

Woman

In a month he would have been my husband.
In a month, here, underneath this lime,
We would have broke the pattern;
He for me, and I for him,
He as Colonel, I as Lady,
On this shady seat.

Chorus of Soldiers

Do not weep maiden
For war is kind
. . . your lover threw
wild hands toward the sky

Raged at his breast,
    gulped and died
    gulped and died
    gulped and died.

Woman
In Summer and in Winter I shall walk
Up and down
Up and down
The patterned garden-paths
In my stiff, brocaded gown.
I shall go

Chorus of Soldiers
Swift blazing flag of the regiment
eagle with crest of red and gold
These men were born to
    drill and die
    drill and die

Woman
Up and down
In my gown.
Gorgeously arrayed,
Boned and stayed.
For the man who should loose me is dead,
Fighting with the Duke in Flanders,
In a pattern called a war.
Christ! What are patterns for?
Christ! What are patterns for?
What are patterns for?

Chorus of Soldiers
    drill and die
War is kind
War is kind
    drill and die
    raged at his breast
    died

And a field where a thousand
　　corpses lie, corpses lie
War is kind!
War is kind!
War is kind!

Clearly, the message about the passion and pain of war is as relevant in an age of high-technology warfare as it was in an earlier era.

PERFORMER'S WORKSHOP
Counterpointing

Using cuttings from three different selections of literature on the same theme, create a counterpoint program. You may use selections from this text or other sources.

Questions

1. How did your group integrate the selections? Which work served as the base? At what points in your base work did you incorporate the other works?
2. How did your ensemble divide among its members the lines of the "new" work? Why?
3. What type of statement emerged from your performance?
4. What staging techniques did you use?

Counterpoint programs present performers with numerous opportunities for creative experimentation and artistic exploration. Each of the groups in your class probably evolved a different counterpoint scheme or pattern.

An original program developed with counterpoint techniques may include a variety of genres and selection lengths. Prose, poetry, essays, and drama may all be freely combined and mixed. Counterpoint programming is thus invaluable experience for every interpretive performer.

IDEA ENCORE

The focus of chapter 12 was on programming. Two types of programs were surveyed: the solo program and the counterpoint program. Examples of each type were provided.

In addition to providing an overview of organizational strategies, the chapter also contained a discussion of staging techniques. The solo performance provides the greatest challenge to the individual interpreter. It is his or her job to select an important theme, develop it, rehearse it, and bring it alive for the audience. The creative use of the performer, the material, and available technology will be the challenge for the performer of today and tomorrow.

PERFORMER'S SHOWCASE & JOURNAL
Counterpoint Study

Working with a group, choose a theme to explore using at least two selections and counterpoint techniques. Be sure to choose your literature (from this book or of your own choosing) carefully and to plan your performance thoughtfully. Structure your performance to illustrate your group's central idea.

Questions

1. What theme did you decide upon?
2. What piece of literature became the base of the counterpoint?
3. How did you work to integrate the second piece or other pieces of literature into the performance? How successful do you think you were in this endeavor?

Thoughts on Making Literature Come Alive

Throughout this book you explored the art of oral performance. In doing so, you probably came to know yourself in new ways. Experiencing literature brought this about. You used your body, voice, and senses to bring literature to life—both for yourself and for others. In prose, poetry, drama, literature for children, literature from diverse cultures, and even documentary materials, you found fuel for oral interpretation programs.

We hope your journeys into literature have been fruitful and worthwhile, both for you and for your audiences. Oral interpretation is entertaining as well as challenging. Continue to use the techniques you learned in this class to reach yourself and others through literature. Take a few minutes, now, to complete this last Performer's Journal.

PERFORMER'S SHOWCASE & JOURNAL
Not the Last Word

Reflect on your experiences as an oral interpreter. Then answer these questions.

1. What have you discovered about literature since beginning this course? What have you discovered about the performance of literature?
2. How have your experiences influenced your perception of oral interpretation? To what extent do you believe effective communicators are really effective performers too? Explain.
3. Think back to the sensory experiences from exercises early in this course. Is their place in performance more clear to you now? Which exercise would you like to try again, and why?
4. Are there some pieces of literature you would like to read now that you would not have considered reading before taking this course? Explain.
5. Of all the literature you have experienced, what is your favorite? Which pieces of literature will continue to live in your life?
6. If you were to take this course again, how would your attitude or behavior toward literature be different?
7. Can you envision yourself performing literature for others again? In what circumstances?
8. How does the oral performance of literature fit in with your career and life goals? Can you see a place for it in business? In education?

When we began this book, we asked you to make a commitment to grow as a person through literature and to share the world of literature with an audience. This is an ongoing challenge: it takes a thoughtful and dedicated interpreter/performer to keep the literature alive!

The following fiction and poetry selections are suitable for use with nearly any warm-up or workshop exercise in this text.

Fiction Selections

 from ***Family Life in America***

Robert Benchley

The living room in the Twillys' house was so damp that thick, soppy moss grew all over the walls. It dripped on the picture of Grandfather Twilly that hung over the melodeon, making streaks down the dirty glass like sweat on the old man's face. It was a mean face. Grandfather Twilly had been a mean man and had little spots of soup on the lapel of his coat. All his children were mean and had soup spots on their clothes.

Grandma Twilly sat in the rocker over by the window, and as she rocked the chair snapped. It sounded like Grandma Twilly's knees snapping as they did whenever she stooped over to pull the wings off a fly. She was a mean old thing. Her knuckles were grimy and she chewed crumbs that she found in the bottom of her reticule. You would have hated her. She hated herself. But most of all she hated Grandfather Twilly.

"I certainly hope you're frying good," she muttered as she looked up at his picture.

"Hasn't the undertaker come yet, Ma?" asked young Mrs. Wilbur Twilly petulantly. She was boiling water on the oilheater and every now and again would spill a little of the steaming liquid on the baby who was playing on the floor. She hated the baby because it looked like her father. The hot water raised little white blisters on the baby's red neck and Mabel Twilly felt short, sharp twinges of pleasure at the sight. It was the only pleasure she had had for four months.

"Why don't you kill yourself, Ma?" she continued. "You're only in the way here and you know it. It's just because you're a mean old woman and want to make trouble for us that you hang on."

Grandma Twilly shot a dirty look at her daughter-in-law. She had always hated her. Stringy hair, Mabel had. Dank, stringy hair. Grandma Twilly thought how it would look hanging at an Indian's belt. But all that she did was to place her tongue against her two front teeth and make a noise like the bathroom faucet.

Wilbur Twilly was reading the paper by the oil lamp. Wilbur had watery blue eyes and cigar ashes all over his knees. The third and fourth buttons of his vest were undone. It was too hideous.

He was conscious of his family seated in chairs about him. His mother, chewing crumbs. His wife Mabel, with her stringy hair, reading. His sister Bernice, with projecting front teeth who sat thinking of the man who came every day to take away the waste paper. Bernice was wondering how long it would be before her family would discover that she had been married to this man for three years.

How Wilbur hated them all. It didn't seem as if he could stand it any longer. He wanted to scream and stick pins into every one of them and then rush out and see the girl who worked in his office snapping rubber bands all day. He hated her too, but she wore side-combs.

 ## "How Light Belief Bringeth Damage"
Bidpai

Two skillful thieves one night entered the house of a wealthy knight, no less wise than worshipped in the community. The gentleman, hearing the noise of their feet in the house, awakened and suspected that they were thieves. They were upon the point of opening the door of the chamber wherein he lay, when he jogged his wife, awakened her, and whispered, "I hear the noise of thieves who have come to rob us. I would have you, therefore, ask me straight, and with great insistence, whence and by what means I came by all I own. Ask me loudly and earnestly, and, as I shall appear reluctant, you must plead and wheedle until, at length, I shall succumb and tell you." The Lady, his wife, being wise and subtle, began in this manner to question her husband—"O, dear sir. Grant me one thing this night that I have for so long desired to know. Tell me how you have come by all these goods you now possess." He, speaking at random and carelessly, scarce answered. Finally, after she kept pleading, he said, "I can but wonder, Madam, at what moves you to know my secrets. Be contented then, to live well, to dress well, and to be waited upon and served. I have heard that all things have ears, and that many things are spoken which are later repented. Therefore, I pray you, hold your peace."

But even this did not deter the Lady. Sweetly and lovingly enticing, she besought him to tell her. Finally, wearying of her speech, the knight said, "All we have—and I charge you to say nothing of this to anyone—is stolen. Indeed, of all I own I got nothing truly." The Lady, unbelieving, so berated her husband that he answered farther, "You think what I have already told you is a wonder. Listen then. Even in my cradle, I delighted in stealing and filching. And I lived among thieves so that my fingers might never be idle. One friend among them loved me so well that he taught me a rare and singular trick. He taught me a conjuration which I made to the moonbeams—enabling me to embrace them suddenly. Thus I sometimes came down upon them from a high window—or served myself with them to go up again to the top of the house. So I used them as I would. The Moon, hearing my conjuration seven times, showed me all the money and treasure of the house and with her beams I flew up and down. And thus, good wife, I made me rich. Now, no more."

One of the thieves, listening at the door, heard all that was said and bore it away. Because the knight was known to be a man of credit and integrity, the thieves believed his story. The chief thief, desirous to prove in deeds what he had heard in words, repeated the conjuration seven times, and then, embracing the moonbeams, he cast himself upon them thinking to go from window to window, and he fell headlong to the ground. The Moon, however, favored him so that he was not killed, but broke his legs and one arm. He cried aloud in his pain and at his stupidity in trusting too much to another's words.

 ## "Tears, Idle Tears"
Elizabeth Bowen

Frederick burst into tears in the middle of Regent's Park. His mother, seeing what was about to happen, had cried: "Frederick, you can't— in the middle of Regent's Park!" Frederick, knees trembling, butted towards his mother a crimson convulsed face, as though he had the idea of burying himself in her. She whipped out a handkerchief and dabbed at him with it under his grey felt hat, exclaiming meanwhile in fearful mortification: "You really haven't got to be such a baby!" Her tone attracted the notice of several people, who might otherwise have thought he was having something taken out of his eye.

He was too big to cry: the whole scene was disgraceful. He wore a grey flannel knickerbocker suit and looked like a schoolboy; though in fact he was seven, still doing lessons at home. . . . His tears were a shame of which she could speak to no one; no offensive weakness of body could have upset her more.

 ## "A Wicked Boy"
Anton Chekhov

Ivan Ivanych Lapkin, a young man of nice appearance, and Anna Semionovna Zamblitskaia, a young girl with a little turned-up nose, went down the steep bank and sat down on a small bench. The bench stood right by the water among some thick young osier bushes. What a wonderful little place! Once you'd sat down, you were hidden from the world—only the fish saw you, and the water-tigers, running like lightning over the water. The young people were armed with rods, nets, cans of worms, and other fishing equipment. Having sat down, they started fishing right away.

"I'm glad we're alone at last," Lapkin began, looking around. "I have to tell you a lot of things, Anna Semionovna . . . an awful lot . . . when I saw you the first time. . . . You've got a bite . . . when I saw you for the first time . . . then I understood what I'm living for, understood where my idol was—to whom I must devote my honest, active life . . . that must be a big one that's biting. . . . Seeing you, I feel in love for the first time, feel passionately in love! Wait before you give it a jerk . . . let it bite harder. . . . Tell me, my darling, I adjure you, may I count on—not on reciprocity, no! I'm not worthy of that, I dare not even think of that—may I count on . . . Pull!"

Anna Semionovna raised her hand with the rod in it, yanked, and cried out. A little silvery-green fish shimmered in the air.

"My Lord, a perch! Ah, ah. . . . Quickly! It's getting free!"

The perch got free of the hook, flopped through the grass toward its native element . . . and plopped into the water!

In pursuit of the fish, Lapkin somehow inadvertently grabbed Anna Semionovna's hand instead of the fish, inadvertently pressed it to his lips. . . . She quickly drew it back, but it was already too late; their mouths inadvertently merged in a kiss. It happened somehow inadvertently. Another kiss followed the first, then vows and protestations. . . . What happy minutes! However, in this earthly life there is no absolute happiness. Happiness usually carries a poison in itself, or else is poisoned by something from outside. So this time, too. As the young people were kissing, a laugh suddenly rang out. They glanced at the river and were stupefied: a naked boy was standing in the water up to his waist. This was Kolia, a schoolboy, Anna Semionovna's brother. He was standing in the water, staring at the young people and laughing maliciously.

"Ah-ah-ah . . . you're kissing?" he said. "That's great! I'll tell Mama."

"I hope that you, as an honest young man. . . ." muttered Lapkin, blushing. "It's low-down to spy, and to tell tales is foul and detestable. . . . I assume that you, as an honest and noble young man. . . ."

"Give me a ruble and then I won't tell!" said the noble young man. "Or else I will."

Lapkin pulled a ruble out of his pocket and gave it to Kolia. Kolia squeezed the ruble in his wet fist, whistled, and swam off. And the young people didn't kiss any more that time.

The next day Lapkin brought Kolia some paints and a ball from town, and his sister gave him all her empty pill-boxes. After that they had to give him some cuff-links with dogs' heads on them. The wicked boy obviously liked all these things very much and, in order to get still more, he started keeping his eye on them. Wherever Lapkin and Anna Semionovna went, he went too. He didn't leave them alone for a minute.

"The bastard!" Lapkin gnashed his teeth. "So little and already such a real bastard! What's he going to be like later?"

All through June, Kolia made life impossible for the poor lovers. He threatened to tell on them, kept his eye on them, and demanded presents; it all wasn't enough for him, and he finally started talking about a pocket watch. And what then? They had to promise the watch.

One time at dinner when the waffle cookies were being passed, he suddenly burst out in a guffaw, winked an eye, and asked Lapkin:

"Shall I tell? Huh?"

Lapkin blushed terribly and started eating his napkin instead of the cookie. Anna Semionovna jumped up from the table and ran into the other room.

And the young people found themselves in this position until the end of August, until the very day when, at last Lapkin proposed to Anna Semionovna. Oh what a happy day that was! Having talked to the parents of his bride, and having received their consent, Lapkin first of all ran out into the garden and started looking for Kolia. Once he had found him, he almost sobbed from delight and seized the wicked boy by the ear. Anna Semionovna, who had also been looking for Kolia, ran up, and seized him by the other ear. And you really ought to have seen what joy was written all over the lovers' faces as Kolia cried and begged them:

"Dearest, darling, angels, I'll never do it again! Ow, ow! Forgive me!"

And afterwards they both admitted that during the whole time they had been in love with each other they had never once felt such happiness, such breath-taking bliss as during those moments when they were pulling the wicked boy's ears.

"Hills Like White Elephants"
Ernest Hemingway

The hills across the valleys of the Ebro were long and white. On this side there was no shade and no trees and the station was between two lines of rails in the sun. Close against the side of the station there was the warm shadow of the building and a curtain, made of strings of bamboo beads, hung across the open door into the bar, to keep out the flies. The American and the girl with him sat at a table in the shade, outside the building. It was very hot and the express from Barcelona would come in forty minutes. It stopped at this junction for two minutes and went on to Madrid.

"What should we drink?" the girl asked. She had taken off her hat and put it on the table.

"It's pretty hot," the man said.

"Let's drink beer."

"Dos cervezas," the man said into the curtain.

"Big ones?" a woman asked from the doorway.

"Yes. Two big ones."

The woman brought two glasses of beer and two felt pads. She put the felt pads and the beer glasses on the table and looked at the man and the girl. The girl was looking off at the line of hills. They were white in the sun and the country was brown and dry.

"They look like white elephants," she said.

"I've never seen one," the man drank his beer.

Metamorphosis

Franz Kafka

As Gregor Samsa awoke one morning from uneasy dreams he found himself transformed in his bed into a gigantic insect. He was lying on his hard, as it were armor-plated, back, and when he lifted his head a little he could see his dome-like belly divided into stiff arched segments on top of which the bed quilt could hardly keep in position and was about to slide off completely. His numerous legs, which were pitifully thin compared to the rest of his bulk, waved helplessly before his eyes.

What happened to me? he thought. It was no dream. His room, a regular human bedroom, only rather too small, lay quiet between the four familiar walls. . . .

Gregor's eyes turned next to the window, and the overcast sky—one could hear raindrops beating on the window gutter—made him melancholy. What about sleeping a little longer and forgetting all this nonsense, he thought, but it could not be done, for he was accustomed to sleeping on his right side, and in his present condition he could not turn himself over.

"The Dead Wife"

Native American Folktale

Once there was a man and his wife who lived on the edge of a large forest. They were Red Indians, but after they were married they chose to live apart from the rest of their tribe who had settled many miles away.

They lived in quiet harmony together. He would catch fish in the river nearby or hunt for food in the forest, while his wife worked at home cooking and sewing.

One day, when the man returned from his hunting, he found his wife had fallen ill with a violent fever. He nursed her as well as he knew how, but after a few days she died in her sleep.

The man wept for many weeks. He could not get used to being without his wife. In the end he felt so lonely he made a wooden doll of about the same height and size as his wife had been and then he dressed the doll with his wife's clothes. He carved a face out of the wood, and pretended it was his wife come back to him. Night after night he would sit by the fire with the doll and talk gently to it as he used to talk to his wife. He looked after the doll carefully and would brush away any ashes that happened to fall on the doll from the fire.

He was always busy during the day now, as he had to cook and mend as well as go out hunting for food. But in the evenings he would sit quietly by the fire with the wooden doll and tell it of the day's happenings, and so a year passed by.

One evening he came back from hunting and found that some wood had been collected and left by his home, and he did not remember having done it himself. He thought he must have forgotten. But the next night when he returned home not only had there been wood gathered, but there was a merry fire burning, and by the fire sat not the doll, but his own dear wife. He was too astonished to speak, but simply gazed at his wife in wonder. After a short while she said to him: "Dear husband, the Great Spirit took pity on you, because you could not be comforted after my death and you did not forget me. So he let me come back to you, but on one condition: you must not stretch out your hand and touch me till we have seen the rest of our people—if you do, I shall die."

The man's heart was filled with tender happiness, and he said: "Dear wife, we must go at once to our tribe."

However, snow fell thick and fast all that night, and they were not able to travel for several days. The man longed to hold his wife, but he remembered her words and did not go near her.

At last they started on their journey, having prepared some deer's flesh to take with them. They traveled for five days, and they had one more day's journey to complete, when once again, a terrible snow blizzard started. They stopped to rest for the night and lay down on their skins to sleep. But the heart of the man was stirred by his wife lying so close to him and he stretched out his arms to her. She waved him away and said, "We haven't seen our people yet. It is too early." But this time he did not listen and he put his arms around her—and found he was clutching the wooden doll.

When he saw what had happened, he pushed it away from him in horror and anger and ran and ran until he finally came upon his tribe, where he lay down and wept and told them his story. Some people doubted, so he took them to the place where they had rested and there lay the doll. They saw footprints left in the snow by two people—but the prints of one were like that of a doll.

"The Cariboo Café"

Helena Maria Viramontes

He's got lice. Probably from living in the detainers. Those are the rooms where they round up the children and make them work for their food. I saw them from the window. Their eyes are cut glass, and no one looks for sympathy. They take turns, sorting out the arms from the legs, heads from the torsos. Is that one your mother? one guard asks, holding a mummified head with eyes shut tighter than coffins. But the children no longer cry. They just continue sorting as if they were salvaging cans from a heap of trash. They do this until time is up and they drift into a tunnel, back to the womb of sleep, while a new group comes in. It is all very organized. I bite my fist to keep from retching. Please God, please don't let Geraldo be there.

For you see, they took Geraldo. By mistake, of course. It was my fault. I shouldn't have sent him out to fetch me a mango. But it was just to the corner. I didn't even bother to put his sweater on. I hear his sandals flapping against the gravel. I follow him with my eyes, see him scratching his buttocks when the wind picks up swiftly, as it often does at such unstable times, and I have to close the door.

The darkness becomes a serpent's tongue, swallowing us whole. It is the night of La Llorona. The women come up from the depths of sorrow to search for their children. I join them, frantic, desperate, and our eyes become scrutinizers, our bodies opiated with the scent of their smiles. Descending from door to door, the wind whips our faces. I hear the wailing of the women and know it to be my own. Geraldo is nowhere to be found.

Dawn is not welcomed. It is a drunkard wavering between consciousness and sleep. My life is fleeing, moving south towards the sea. My tears are now hushed and faint. The boy, barely a few years older than Geraldo, lights a cigarette, rests it on the edge of his desk, next to all the other cigarette burns. The blinds are down to keep the room cool. Above him hangs a single bulb that shades and shadows his face in such a way as to mask his expressions. He is not to be trusted. He fills in the information, for I cannot write. Statements delivered, we discuss motives.

"Spies," says he, flicking a long burning ash from the cigarette onto the floor, then wolfing the smoke in as if his lungs had an unquenchable thirst for nicotine. "We arrest spies. Criminals." He says this with cigarette smoke spurting out from his nostrils like a nosebleed.

"Spies? Criminals?" My shawl falls to the ground. "He is only five and a half years old." I plead for logic with my hands. "What kind of crimes could a five-year-old commit?"

"Anyone who so willfully supports the contras in any form must be arrested and punished without delay." He knows the line by heart.

I think about moths and their stupidity. Always attracted by light, they fly into fires, or singe their wings with the heat of the single bulb and fall on his desk, writhing in pain. I don't understand why nature has been so cruel as to prevent them from feeling warmth. He dismisses them with a sweep of a hand. "This," he continues, "is what we plan to do with the contras, and those who aid them." He inhales again.

"But, Señor, he's just a baby."

"Contras are tricksters. They exploit the ignorance of people like you. Perhaps they convinced your son to circulate pamphlets. You should be talking to them, not us." The cigarette is down to his yellow fingertips, to where he can no longer continue to hold it without burning himself. He throws the stub on the floor, crushes it under his boot. "This," he says, screwing his boot into the ground, "is what the contras do to people like you."

"Señor. I am a washerwoman. You yourself see I cannot read or write. There is my X. Do you think my son can read?" How can I explain to this man that we are poor, that we live as best we can? "If such a thing has happened, perhaps he wanted to make a few centavos for his mamá. He's just a baby."

"So you are admitting his guilt?"

"So you are admitting he is here?" I promise, once I see him, hold him in my arms again, I will never, never scold him for wanting more than I can give. "You see, he needs his sweater . . ." The sweater lies limp on my lap.

"Your assumption is incorrect."

"May I check the detainers for myself?"

"In time."

"And what about my Geraldo?"

"In time." He dismisses me, placing the forms in a big envelope crinkled by the day's humidity.

"When?" I am wringing the sweater with my hands.

"Don't be foolish, woman. Now off with your nonsense. We will try to locate your Pedro."

"Geraldo."

"A Worn Path"
Eudora Welty

It was December—a bright frozen day in the early morning. Far out in the country there was an old Negro woman with her head tied in a red rag, coming along a path through the pinewoods. Her name was Phoenix Jackson. She was very old and small and she walked slowly in the dark pine shadows, moving a little from side to side in her steps, with the balanced heaviness and lightness of a pendulum in a grandfather clock. She carried a thin, small cane made from an umbrella, and with this she kept tapping the frozen earth in front of her. This made a grave and persistent noise in the air that seemed meditative like the chirping of a solitary little bird.

. . . Every time she took a step she might have fallen over her shoelaces, which dragged from her unlaced shoes. She looked straight ahead. Her eyes were blue with age. . . .

Now and then there was a quivering in the thicket. Old Phoenix said, "Out of my way, all you foxes, owls, beetles, jack rabbits, coons, and wild animals! . . . Keep out from under these feet. . . ."

The path ran up a hill. "Seems like there is chains about my feet, time I get this far," she said, in the voice of argument old people keep to use with themselves. "Something always take a hold of me on this hill— pleads I should stay."

Poetry Selections

"All There Is to Know About Adolph Eichmann"
Leonard Cohen

EYES: Medium

HAIR: Medium

WEIGHT: Medium

HEIGHT: Medium

DISTINGUISHING FEATURES: None

NUMBER OF FINGERS: Ten

NUMBER OF TOES: Ten

INTELLIGENCE: Medium

What did you expect?

Talons?

Oversize incisors?

Green saliva?

Madness?

from "War Is Kind and Other Lines"
Stephen Crane

Do not weep, maiden, for war is kind.

Because your lover threw wild hands toward the sky

And the affrighted steed ran on alone,

Do not weep.
War is kind.

    Hoarse, booming drums of the regiment,
    Little souls who thirst for fight,
    These men were born to drill and die.
    The unexplained glory flies above them,
    Great is the battle-god, great, and his kingdom—
    A field where a thousand corpses lie.

Do not weep, babe, for war is kind.
Because your father tumbled in the yellow trenches,
Raged at his breast, gulped and died,
Do not weep.
War is kind.

    Swift blazing flag of the regiment
    Eagle with crest of red and gold,
    These men were born to drill and die.
    Point for them the virtue of slaughter,
    Make plain to them the excellence of killing
    And a field where a thousand corpses lie.

Mother whose heart hung humble as a button
On the bright splendid shroud of your son,
Do not weep
War is kind.

"Dream Deferred"

Langston Hughes

What happens to a dream deferred?

Does it dry up
like a raisin in the sun?
Or fester like a sore—
And then run?
Does it stink like rotten meat?

Or crust and sugar over—
like a syrupy sweet?

Maybe it just sags
like a heavy load.

Or does it explode?

 "Mother to Son"
Langston Hughes

Well, son, I'll tell you:
Life for me ain't been no crystal stair.
It's had tacks in it,
And splinters,
And boards torn up,
And places with no carpets on the floor—
Bare.
But all the time
I'se been a-climbin' on,
And reachin' landin's,
And turnin' corners,
And sometimes goin' in the dark
Where there ain't been no light.
So, boy, don't you turn back.
Don't you set down on the steps
'Cause you finds it's kinder hard.
Don't you fall now—
For I'se still goin', honey,
I'se still climbin',
And life for me ain't been no crystal stair.

"Patterns"

Amy Lowell

I walk down the garden-paths,
And all the daffodils
Are blowing, and the bright blue squills.
I walk down the patterned garden-paths
In my stiff, brocaded gown.
With my powdered hair and jeweled fan,
I too am a rare
Pattern. As I wander down
The garden paths.

My dress is richly figured,
And the train
Makes a pink and silver stain
On the gravel, and the thrift
Of the borders.
Just a plate of current fashion,
Tripping by in high-heeled, ribboned shoes.
Not a softness anywhere about me,
Only whalebone and brocade.
And I sink on a seat in the shade
Of a lime tree. For my passion
Wars against the stiff brocade.
The daffodils and squills
Flutter in the breeze
As they please.
And I weep;
For the lime-tree is in blossom
And one small flower has dropped upon my bosom.

And the plashing of waterdrops
In the marble fountain
Comes down the garden-paths.
The dripping never stops.

Underneath my stiffened gown
Is the softness of a woman bathing in a marble basin,
A basin in the midst of hedges grown
So thick, she cannot see her lover hiding,
But she guesses he is near,
And the sliding of the water
Seems the stroking of a dear
Hand upon her.
What is Summer in a fine brocaded gown!
I should like to see it lying in a heap upon the ground.
All the pink and silver crumpled up on the ground.

I would be the pink and silver as I ran along the paths,
And he would stumble after,
Bewildered by my laughter.
I should see the sun flashing from his sword-hilt and the buckles
on his shoes.
I would choose
To lead him in a maze along the patterned paths,
A bright and laughing maze for my heavy-booted lover.
Till he caught me in the shade,
And the buttons of his waistcoat bruised my body
as he clasped me,
Aching, melting, unafraid.
With the shadows of the leaves and the sundrops,
With the plopping of the waterdrops,
All about us in the open afternoon—
I am very like to swoon
With the weight of this brocade,
For the sun sifts through the shade.

Underneath the fallen blossom
In my bosom,
Is a letter I have hid.
It was brought to me this morning by a rider from the Duke.
"Madam, we regret to inform you that Lord Hartwell

Died in action Thursday se'nnight."
As I read it in the white, morning sunlight,
The letters squirmed like snakes.
"Any answer, Madam?" said my footman.
"No," I told him.
"See that the messenger takes some refreshment.
No, no answer."
And I walked into the garden,
Up and down the patterned paths,
In my stiff, correct brocade.
The blue and yellow flowers stood up proudly in the sun,
Each one.
I stood upright too,
Held rigid to the pattern
By the stiffness of my gown.
Up and down I walked,
Up and down.
In a month he would have been my husband.
In a month, here, underneath this lime,
We would have broke the pattern;
He for me, and I for him,
He as Colonel, I as Lady,
On this shady seat.
He had a whim
That sunlight carried blessing.
And I answered, "It shall be as you have said."
Now he is dead.

In Summer and in Winter I shall walk
Up and down
The patterned garden-paths
In my stiff, brocaded gown.
The squills and daffodils
Will give place to pillared roses, and to asters, and to snow.
I shall go

Up and down,
In my gown.
Gorgeously arrayed,
Boned and stayed.
And the softness of my body will be guarded from embrace
By each button, hook, and lace.
For the man who should loose me is dead,
Fighting with the Duke in Flanders,
In a pattern called a war.
Christ! What are patterns for?

ACKNOWLEDGMENTS

Acosta, Teresa Palomo. "My Mother Pieces Quilts" by Teresa Palomo Acosta. Reprinted by permission of the author.

Albee, Edward. From *The Sandbox* by Edward Albee. Copyright ©1959 by Edward Albee. All rights reserved. Reprinted by permission of William Morris Agency, Inc. on behalf of the Author. *Caution:* Professionals and amateurs are hereby warned that *The Sandbox* is subject to a royalty. It is fully protected under the copyright laws of the United States of America and of all countries covered by the International Copyright Union (including the Dominion of Canada and the rest of the British Commonwealth), the Berne Convention, the Pan-American Copyright Convention and the Universal Copyright Convention as well as all countries in which the United States has reciprocal copyright relations. All rights, including professional/amateur stage rights, motion picture, recitation, lecturing, public reading, radio broadcasting, television, video or sound recording, all other forms of mechanical or electronic reproduction, such as CD-ROM, CD-I, information storage and retrieval systems and photocopying, and the rights of translation into foreign languages, are strictly reserved. Particular emphasis is laid upon the matter of readings, permission for which must be secured from the Author's agent in writing. Inquiries should be addressed to William Morris Agency, Inc. 1325 Avenue of the Americas, New York, NY 10019, Attn: Owen Laster.

Anderson, Sherwood. Excerpt from "Death in the Woods" reprinted by permission of Harold Ober Associates Incorporated. Copyright ©1926 by Sherwood Anderson. Copyright renewed 1953 by Eleanor Copenhaver Anderson.

Auden, W. H. "The Unknown Citizen," copyright ©1940 and renewed 1968 by W. H. Auden, "O What Is That Sound," copyright ©1937 and renewed 1965 by W. H. Auden, from *W. H. Auden: Collected Poems* by W. H. Auden. Used by permission of Random House, Inc.

Azredo, Ronaldo. "velocidade" by Ronaldo Azredo, from *Concrete Poetry: A World View,* edited by Mary Ellen Solt. Reprinted by permission.

Baker, Russell. "Growing Up" and "An Analysis of Miss Muffett" from *Growing Up,* by Russell Baker. Copyright ©1982 by Russell Baker. Reprinted by permission of Don Congdon Associates, Inc.

Baraka, Amiri. "Preface to a Twenty Volume Suicide Note" reprinted by permission of Sterling Lord Literistic, Inc. Copyright by Amiri Baraka.

Becquer, Gustavo Adolfo. "They Closed Her Eyes" by Gustavo Adolfo Becquer, translated by John Masefield. Reprinted by permission of The Society of Authors as the Literary Representative of the Estate of John Masefield.

Benchley, Robert. "Family Life in America" as taken from *The Benchley Roundup, A Selection, by Nathaniel Benchley of his Favorites and Drawings* by Gluyas Williams. Copyright ©1954 by Nathaniel Benchley, renewed ©1982 by Marjorie B. Benchley. Copyright ©1921, 1922, 1925, 1927, 1928 by Harper & Brothers. Copyright ©1930, 1932, 1934, 1936 and 1938 by Robert C. Benchley. Copyright ©1949, 1950, 1953 by Gertrude D. Benchley. Copyright ©1929, 1930 by Chicago Tribune-New York News Syndicate, Inc. Copyright ©1929 by Bookman Publishing Company, Inc. Copyright ©1930 by Liberty Magazine, Inc. Copyright ©1930 by D.A.C. News, Inc. Copyright ©1933 by The Hearst Corporation, New York Mirror Division. Reprinted by permission of HarperCollins Publishers, Inc.

Bruni, Frank. "Death of Innocence" by Frank Bruni (March 8, 1992). Reprinted by permission of Tribune Media Services.

Byham, William C. From *Zapp! The Lightening of Empowerment* by William C. Byham, Ph.D., copyright ©1988 by Development Dimensions International. Used by permission of Harmony Books, a division of Random House, Inc.

Chaya, Prem. "On My Short-Sightedness." From *Twentieth Century Chinese Poetry* by Kai-yu Hsu, translated by Kai-yu Hsu, copyright ©1963 by Kai-yu Hsu. Used by permission of Doubleday, a division of Random House, Inc.

Chekhov, Anton. "A Wicked Boy" by Anton Chekhov, from *75 Short Masterpieces* by Roger B. Goodman, copyright ©1961 by Bantam Books. Used by permission of Bantam Books, a division of Random House, Inc.

Ch'ing, Ai. "To Hiroshima." From *Twentieth Century Chinese Poetry* by Kai-yu Hsu, translated by Kai-yu Hsu, copyright ©1963 by Kai-yu Hsu. Used by permission of Doubleday, a division of Random House, Inc.

Clifton, Lucille. Lucille Clifton, "miss rosie" from *Good Woman: Poems and a Memoir 1969-1980*. Copyright ©1987 by Lucille Clifton. Reprinted with the permission of BOA Editions, Ltd.

Cohen, Leonard. "All There Is to Know about Adolph Eichmann" by Leonard Cohen. ©1964 by Leonard Cohen.

Colette. "The Other Wife" from *The Collected Stories of Colette*, edited by Robert Phelps, translated by Matthew Ward. Translation copyright ©1983 by Farrar, Straus & Giroux, Inc. Reprinted by permission of Farrar, Straus & Giroux, LLC.

Cornford, Frances. "Childhood" and "The Guitarist Tunes Up" from *Collected Poems* by Frances Cornford, published by Cresset. Used by permission of The Random House Group Limited.

Cullen, Countee. "Incident" by Countee Cullen. Copyright held by the Amistad Research Center, adminstered by Thompson and Thompson, New York, NY.

Cummings, E. E. "next to of course God america I" by e. e. cummings. Copyright ©1963, 1991 by the Trustees for the E. E. Cummings Trust, from *Complete Poems: 1904-1962* by E. E. Cummings. Edited by George Frimage. Reprinted by permission of Liveright Publishing Corp.

de la Mare, Walter. "Silver" by Walter de la Mare, reprinted by permission of The Literary Trustees of Walter de la Mare and the Society of Authors as their representative.

Dickinson, Emily. "After great pain a formal feeling comes." By permission of the publishers and the Trustees of Amherst College, from *The Poems of Emily Dickinson*, Thomas H. Johnson, ed., Cambridge, Mass: The Belknap Press of Harvard University Press, copyright ©1951, 1955, 1979, 1983 by the President and Trustees of Harvard College.

Eliot, T. S. "Macavity: The Mystery Cat" from *Old Possum's Book of Practical Cats*, copyright ©1939 by T. S. Eliot and renewed 1967 by Esme Valerie Eliot, reprinted by permission of Harcourt, Inc.

Evans, Marie. "Status Symbol" from *I Am a Black Woman*, by Mari Evans (HarperCollins, 1970).

Faulkner, William. "Upon Receiving the Nobel Prize for Literature" from *Essays, Speeches and Public Letters by William Faulkner*, by William Faulkner, edited by James B. Meriwether. Copyright ©1950 by William Faulkner. Reprinted by permission of Random House, Inc.

Ferlinghetti, Lawrence. "Constantly Risking Absurdity" by Lawrence Ferlinghetti, from *A Coney Island of the Mind*, copyright ©1958 by Lawrence Ferlinghetti. Reprinted by permission of New Directions Publishing Corp.

Ford, Corey. "Snake Dance" by Corey Ford. Reprinted by permission of Steve Smith.

Frank, Anne. From *The Diary of a Young Girl: The Definitive Edition* by Anne Frank. Otto H. Frank & Mirjam Pressler, editors, translated by Sussan Massotty, copyright ©1995 by Doubleday, a division of Random House, Inc. Used by permission of Doubleday, a division of Random House, Inc.

Geiger, Don. "Consoling Meditation on the great Majority: Fathers" by Don Geiger. Reprinted by permission.

Gesner, Clark. From *You're A Good Man, Charlie Brown* by Clark Gesner, copyright ©1967 by Clark Gesner. Copyright ©1965, 1966, 1967 by Jeremy Music, Inc. Used by permission of Random House, Inc.

Gibbs, Angelica. "The Test" by Angelica Gibbs. Reprinted by permission.

Giovanni, Nikki. "Knoxville, Tennessee" from *Black Feeling, Black Talk, Black Judgment* by Nikki Giovanni. Copyright ©1968, 1970 by Nikki Giovanni. Reprinted by permission of HarperCollins Publishers, Inc.

Gomringer, Eugene. "ping pong," "silencio" and "wind" by Eugene Gomringer from *Concrete Poetry: A World View*, edited by Mary Ellen Solt. Reprinted by permission.

Gustafson, Ingemar. "Locked In" by Ingemar Gustafson, translated by May Swenson. Reprinted by permission.

Haley, Alex. From *Roots* by Alex Haley, copyright ©1976 by Alex Haley. Used by permission of Doubleday, a division of Random House, Inc.

Hansberry, Lorraine. From *A Raisin in the Sun* by Lorraine Hansberry, copyright ©1958 by Robert Nemiroff, as an unpublished work. Copyright ©1959, 1966, 1984 by Robert Nemiroff. Used by permission of Random House, Inc.

Hemingway, Ernest. Reprinted with permission of Scribner, a Division of Simon & Schuster, Inc., from *The Old Man and the Sea* by Ernest Hemingway. Copyright 1952 by Ernest Hemingway. Copyright renewed ©1980 by Mary Hemingway. From "Hills Like White Elephants." Reprinted with permission of Scribner, a Division of Simon & Schuster, Inc., from *The Short Stories of Ernest Hemingway*. Copyright 1927 by Charles Scribner's Sons. Copyright renewed ©1955 by Ernest Hemingway.

Henderson, Harold G. "Eight Haiku" from *An Introduction to Haiku* by Harold G. Henderson, copyright ©1958 by Harold G. Henderson. Used by permission of Doubleday, a division of Random House, Inc.

Highet, Gilbert. "The Old Gentleman" from *The Gilbert Highet Program* by Gilbert Highet, copyright 1952 by Oxford University Press, Inc. Renewed 1980 by Helen McInnes Highet. Used by permission of Oxford University Press, Inc.

Hsiang, Chu. "The Pawnshop." From *Twentieth Century Chinese Poetry* by Kai-yu Hsu, translated by Kai-yu Hsu, copyright ©1963 by Kai-yu Hsu. Used by permission of Doubleday, a division of Random House, Inc.

Hsu, Chih-Mo. "Serves You Right, Beggar." From *Twentieth Century Chinese Poetry* by Kai-yu Hsu, translated by Kai-yu Hsu, copyright ©1963 by Kai-yu Hsu. Used by permission of Doubleday, a division of Random House, Inc.

Hsu, Kai-yu. From *Twentieth Century Chinese Poetry* by Kai-yu Hsu, translated by Kai-yu Hsu, copyright ©1963 by Kai-yu Hsu. Used by permission of Doubleday, a division of Random House, Inc.

Hughes, Langston. "Dream Boogie," "Dream Deferred" and "Mother to Son" from *The Collected Poems of Langston Hughes* by Langston Hughes, copyright ©1994 by The Estate of Langston Hughes. Used by permission of Alfred A. Knopf, a division of Random House, Inc.

Iman, Yusef. "Love Your Enemy" by Yusef Iman.

Jarrell, Randall. "The Death of the Ball Turret Gunner" from *The Complete Poems* by Randall Jarrell. Copyright ©1969, renewed 1997 by Mary von S. Jarrell. Reprinted by permission of Farrar, Straus & Giroux, LLC.

Kees, Weldon. "Lines for an Album" reprinted from *The Collected Poems of Weldon Kees*, edited by Donald Justice, by permission of the University of Nebraska Press. Copyright 1975, by the University of Nebraska Press.

Kesey, Ken. Excerpt from *One Flew Over the Cuckoo's Nest* by Ken Kesey, copyright ©1962, 1990 by Ken Kesey. Used by permission of Viking Penguin, a division of Penguin Putnam, Inc.

King, Martin Luther, Jr. From "I Have a Dream" reprinted by arrangement with the Estate of Martin Luther King Jr., c/o Writers House as agent for the proprietor. Copyright Martin Luther King 1963, copyright renewed 1991 Coretta Scott King.

La Guma, Alex. "Out of Darkness" by Alex La Guma, from *Quartet: New Voices from South Africa*, edited by Richard Rive, copyright ©1963 by Crown Publishers, Inc. Used by permission of Crown Publishers, a division of Random House, Inc.

Lane, Mark. *Plausible Denial: Was the CIA Involved in the Assassination of JFK?* by Mark Lane. Reprinted by permission.

Larson, Cecile. "'Monument' at Wounded Knee" by Cecile Larson, from Michael and Suzanne Osborne, *Public Speaking,* Second Edition. Copyright ©1991 by Houghton Mifflin Company. Used with permission.

Laurence, William L. From "Atomic Bombing of Nagaski" by William L. Laurence. Copyright ©1945, New York Times Company. Reprinted by permission.

Lawrence, D. H. "To Women, As Far As I'm Concerned" by D. H. Lawrence, from *The Complete Poems of D. H. Lawrence* by D. H. Lawrence, edited by V. deSola Pinto & F.W. Roberts, copyright ©1964, 1971 by Angelo Ravagli and C. M. Weekley, Executors of the Estate of Frieda Lawrence Ravagli. Used by permission of Viking Penguin, a division of Penguin Putnam, Inc.

Lowell, Amy. "Patterns" from *The Complete Poetical Works of Amy Lowell,* by Amy Lowell. Copyright ©1955 by Houghton Mifflin Company. Copyright ©1983 renewed by Houghton Mifflin Company, Brinton P. Roberts, Esquire and G. D'Andelot Belin, Esquire. Reprinted by permission of Houghton Mifflin Company.

Lurie, Tobie. "Trio" from Mirror Images, by Tobie Lurie (Celestial Arts Press).

Malamud, Bernard. "My Son the Murderer" from *Rembrandt's Hat* by Bernard Malamud. Copyright ©1968, 1972, 1973 by Bernard Malamud. Reprinted by permission of Farrar, Straus & Giroux, LLC.

Manchester, William. Excerpt from *The Death of a President* by William Manchester. Copyright ©1967 by William Manchester. Copyright renewed 1995 by William Manchester. Reprinted by permission of HarperCollins Publishers, Inc.

Mansfield, Katherine. "Miss Brill" from *The Short Stories of Katherine Mansfield* by Katherine Mansfield, copyright 1923 by Alfred A. Knopf, a division of Random House, Inc. and renewed 1951 by John Middleton Murray. Used by permission of Alfred A. Knopf, a division of Random House, Inc.

Maugham, W. S. From "Rain" (*Miss Thompson*) from *The Complete Short Stories of W. Somerset Maugham.* Reprinted by permission of A. P. Watt Ltd., on behalf of the Royal Literary Fund.

Miller, Arthur. from *Death of a Salesman* by Arthur Miller. Copyright ©1949 renewed ©1977 by Arthur Miller. Used by permsision of Penguin Putnam, Inc.

Miller, Merle. from *Plain Speaking* by Merle Miller. Copyright ©1973, 1974 by Merle Miller. Reprinted by permission of Penguin Putnam, Inc.

Mora, Pat. "Gentle Communion" by Pat Mora is reprinted with permission from the publisher of *Communion* (Houston: Arte Publico Press—University of Houston, 1991). "Immigrants" by Pat Mora is reprinted with permission from the publisher of *Borders* (Houston: Arte Publico Press—University of Houston, 1986).

Mori, Toshio. "Abalone, Abalone, Abalone" by Toshio Mori. Reprinted by permission of the University of California, Los Angeles.

Murrow, Edward R. Excerpt from *In Search of Light* by Edward R. Murrow, edited by E. Bliss, Jr., copyright ©1967 by The Estate of Edward R. Murrow. Used by permission of Alfred A. Knopf, a division of Random House, Inc.

New York Times. From "Life at 'Jeff'" copyright ©1992, The New York Times Company. Reprinted by permission.

Norman, Marsha. From *'Night Mother* by Marsha Norman. Reprinted by permission of The Gersh Agency.

Oates, Joyce Carol. Excerpt from "Heat" by Joyce Carol Oates. Copyright ©1991 by Ontario Review, Inc. Reprinted by permission of John Hawkins & Associates, Inc.

Parker, Dorothy. "The Waltz" copyright 1933, renewed ©1961 by Dorothy Parker, from *The Portable Dorothy Parker* by Dorothy Parker. Used by permsision of Viking Penguin, a division of Penguin Putnam Inc.

Pastan, Linda. "To a Daughter Leaving Home" from *The Imperfect Paradise* by Linda Pastan. Copyright ©1988 by Linda Pastan. Used by permission of W.W. Norton & Company, Inc.

Piercy, Marge. "What's that smell in the kitchen?" from *Circles on the Water* by Marge Piercy, copyright ©1982 by Marge Piercy. Used by permission of Alfred A. Knopf, a division of Random House, Inc.

Plath, Sylvia. "Mirror" from *Crossing the Water* by Sylvia Plath. Copyright ©1963 by Ted Hughes. Originally appeared in the *New Yorker*. Reprinted by permission of HarperCollins Publishers, Inc.

Plautus. "The Ghost," from *The Rope and Other Plays* by Plautus, translated by E.F. Watling (Penguin Classics, 1964) copyright ©1964 by E. F. Watling. Reprinted by permission of The Penguin Group.

Podolny, Roman. From "Invasion" by Roman Podolny in *The Ultimate Threshold*, edited and translated from the Russian by Mirra Ginsburg. Copyright ©1970 by Mirra Ginsburg.

Robinson, Roxana. "Instant Intimacy" by Roxana Robinson. Copyright ©1999, The New York Times Company. Reprinted by permission.

Roethke, Theodore. "Child on Top of a Greenhouse," copyright ©1946 by Editorial Publications, Inc., from *The Collected Poems of Theodore Roethke* by Theodore Roethke. Used by permission of Doubleday, a division of Random House, Inc.

Romero, José Alejandro. "Sumpul" by José Alejandro Rowe. Originally appeared in *American Music*.

de Saint-Exupéry, Antoine. Excerpts from *The Little Prince* by Antoine de Saint-Exupéry, copyright 1941 and renewed 1971 by Harcourt, Inc., reprinted by permission of the publisher.

Salter, Mary Jo. "Welcome to Hiroshima" from *Henry Purcell in Japan* by Mary Jo Salter, copyright ©1984 by Mary Jo Salter. Used by permission of Alfred A. Knopf, a division of Random House, Inc.

Shaw, George Bernard. From *Pygmalion*, by George Bernard Shaw, reprinted by permission of The Society of Authors on behalf of the Bernard Shaw Estate.

Silverstein, Shel. "Sick" from *Where the Sidewalk Ends* by Shel Silverstein. Copyright ©1974 by Evil Eye Music, Inc. Used by permission of HarperCollins Publishers.

Simon, Neil. From *The Odd Couple* by Neil Simon. Copyright ©1966 by Nancy Enterprises. Reprinted by permission.

Smith, Lucy. "Face of Poverty" by Lucy Smith.

Sophocles. From "Antigone" from *Sophocles, the Oedipus Cycle: An English Version* by Dudley Fitts and Robert Fitzgerald, copyright ©1939 by Harcourt Brace & Company and renewed 1967 by Dudley Fitts and Robert Fitzgerald, reprinted by permission of the publisher. Caution: All rights, including professional, amateur, motion picture, recitation, lecturing, performance, public reading, radio broadcasts, and television are strictly reserved. Inquiries on all rights should be addressed to Harcourt Inc., Permissions Department, Orlando, FL 32887-6777.

Soyinka, Wole. "Telephone Conversation" by Wole Soyinka. Reprinted by permission.

Steinbeck, John. "Flight" from *The Long Valley* by John Steinbeck. Copyright 1938, renewed ©1966 by John Steinbeck. Used by permission of Viking Penguin, a division of Penguin Putnam, Inc. From *The Grapes of Wrath* by John Steinbeck. Copyright 1939, renewed ©1967 by John Steinbeck. Used by permission of Viking Penguin, a division of Penguin Putnam, Inc.

Steinem, Gloria. From *Revolution from Within: A Book of Self-Esteem* by Gloria Steinem. Copyright ©1992 by Gloria Steinem. Reprinted by permission of Little, Brown and Company (Inc.).

Tablada, Juan. "Images" ("Dragonfly" "Monkeys" "Toads" and "Tortoise") by Juan Tablada. From *Anthology of Mexican Poetry*. Reprinted by permission of Indiana University Press.

Teague, Bob. "Letters to a Black Boy" by Bob Teague.

Thomas, Piri. From *Down These Mean Streets*. Reprinted by permission of the author.

Thurber, James. "The Owl Who Was God" from *Fables for Our Time*, copyright ©1940 by James Thurber. Copyright renewed ©1968 by Helen Thurber and Rosemary A. Thurber. Reprinted by arrangement with Rosemary A. Thurber and The Barbara Hogenson Agency. All rights reserved.

Uris, Leon. From *Exodus* by Leon Uris, copyright ©1958 by Leon M. Uris. Used by permission of Doubleday, a division of Random House, Inc.

Viramontes, Helena Maria. "The Cariboo Café" by Helena Maria Viramontes is reprinted with permission from the publisher of *The Moths and Other Stories* (Houston: Arte Publico Press—University of Houston, 1985).

Wagoner, David. "My Father's Garden" from *Traveling Light: Collected and New Poems,* by David Wagoner (University of Illinois Press, 1999). Reprinted by permission of the author.

Walker, Margaret. "For My People" from *This Is My Century: New and Collected Poems* by Margaret Walker Alexander. Copyright ©1989 by Margaret Walker Alexander. Reprinted by permission of The University of Georgia Press.

Wasserman, Dale. "One Flew Over the Cuckoo's Nest" based on the novel by Ken Kesey. Unauthorized use is strictly prohibited. Reprinted by permission of Samuel French, Inc. All rights reserved.

Weidman, Jerome. "Slipping Beauty" from *The Horse That Could Whistle Dixie and Other Stories* by Jerome Weidman. Copyright ©1939 by Jerome Weidman. Copyright ©1951, 1952 by Avon Publishing Co., Inc. Reprinted by permission of Brandt & Hochman Literary Agents, Inc.

Welty, Eudora. Excerpts from "A Visit of Charity" in *A Curtain of Green and Other Stories,* copyright ©1941 and renewed ©1969 by Eudora Welty, reprinted by permission of Harcourt, Inc. Excerpts from "A Worn Path" in *A Curtain of Green and Other Stories,* copyright ©1941 and renewed ©1969 by Eudora Welty, reprinted by permission of Harcourt, Inc.

Williams, William Carlos. "This is Just to Say" by William Carlos Williams, from *Collected Poems: 1909-1939, Volume I,* copyright ©1938 by New Directions Publishing Corp. Reprinted by permission of New Directions Publishing Corp.

Wright, James. "Mutterings Over the Crib of a Deaf Child" by James Wright, from *Above the River,* copyright ©1990 by Anne Wright. Reprinted by permission of Wesleyan University Press.

Yamada, Mitsuye. "Marriage Was a Foreign Country" by Mitsuye Yamada, from *Camp Notes and Other Poems,* copyright ©1992 by Mitsuye Yamada.

Yevtushenko, Yevgency. "Babii Yar" by Yevgency Yevtushenko, from *20th Century Russian Poetry* by Yevgency Yevtushenko, copyright ©1993 by Doubleday, a division of Random House, Inc. Used by permission of Doubleday, a division of Random House, Inc.

Yezierska, Anzia. "Soap and Water" from *How I Found America: Collected Stories of Anzia Yezierska.* Copyright ©1991 by Louise Levitas Henriksen. Reprinted by permission of Persea Books, Inc. (New York)

Yu, Han. "A Withered Tree." From *Twentieth Century Chinese Poetry* by Kai-yu Hsu, translated by Kai-yu Hsu, copyright ©1963 by Kai-yu Hsu. Used by permission of Doubleday, a division of Random House, Inc.

The publisher has made every effort to contact copyright holders. Any omissions or errors will be corrected upon written notification.

Cool words, 43
Cornford, Frances
    "Childhood," 37–38
    "Guitarist Tunes Up, The,"
       191
Counterpoint, 384–89
Cox, Jeff, 360–61
Crane, Stephen
    counterpoint program,
      384–89
    "In the Desert," 65
    The Red Badge of Courage,
      85
    "War is Kind and Other
      Lines," 402–3
Crisis, 141
Crudity, portraying, 48
Cullen, Countee, 54
Cultural literature, 259–81
Cummings, E. E., 221

D

Dactylic meter, 204
de la Mare, Walter, 40
"Dead Wife, The," 398–99
"Death in the Woods," 95–96
Death of a President, The,
    310–11
Death of a Salesman, 178–79
"Death of Innocence," 320–21
"Death of the Ball Turret
    Gunner, The," 225
"Death Snips Proud Men," 369
Denotation, 183
Description, 70, 77, 90
Descriptive prose, 77–91
    character and setting, 80–81
    imagery, 83–84
    internalizing, 90
"Destruction of Sennacherib,
    The," 204
Dialog, 100, 112, 133
Diaries, 313–16
Dickens, Charles, 81–82
Dickinson, Emily, 213
Dignity, portraying, 48
Dimeter, 201
Dinesen, Isak, 83
Documentary materials, 283–331
    biography and autobiography,
      302–13
    diaries and letters, 313–16
    essays, 295–302
    oral histories, 316–17
    public speeches, 283–94
Doll's House, A, 168–70
Down These Mean Streets, 303
Drama, 132–79
    characters, 141–55
    Elizabethan period, 165–68
    Greek period, 156–59
    Medieval period, 162–65
    plot, 137–41
    realism style, 168–71
    Roman period, 160–62
    stage directions, 146–47, 155
    theater of the absurd,
      171–73

Dramatic economy, 156–57
Dramatic poetry, 211
"Dream Boogie," 207
"Dream Deferred," 403–4
Duerrenmatt, Friedrich, 143–44
Dynamic characters, 103

E

Ecclesiastes 3:1–3:8, 349–50
Editing a text, 90
Elegies, 210
Eliot, T. S., 255–56
Elizabethan drama, 165–68
Emotion, as key to meaning, 77
Emotional content
    and colors, 66–67
    developing empathy, 7,
      19–20, 89
    internalizing, 239
    nonverbal expression, 9–11
    vocal expression, 31–37, 39,
      40–52
    and word choice, 185
Emotional temperature, 43
Empathy
    and character portrayal,
      142, 154
    creating audience, 19–20, 239
    internalizing, 19–20, 89,
      260–61
"Emperor's New Clothes, The,"
    251–54
Emphasis, vocal, 40, 41–42, 43
End rhyme, 198, 199
Energy and performance, 6
Ensemble interpretation, 332–69
    chamber theater, 356–61
    children's literature, 366
    choral speaking, 341–55
    counterpoint, 384–89
    focus techniques, 335–37
    movement and positioning,
      338–40
    multimedia presentation,
      340
    readers theater, 361–66
    trios, 344–48
    working together, 334, 367
Enunciation, 34
Essays, 295–302
Evangeline, 204
Evans, Mari, 220–21
Everyman, 163–65
Exaggeration
    avoiding, 10, 204–5
    using, 193–94, 239
Excitement, portraying, 39
Exits, indicating, 338
Exodus, 78–80
Exposition, 138–40
Expository essay, 295
Expressiveness, vocal, 35, 45
Exterior setting, 103
External actions, 103
Externalizing, 15–16, 57, 60
Eyes, using
    expressiveness, 11–12

eye contact, 5, 335
focal points, 115–17,
    154–55, 335–37

F

Fables, 101–3, 256–58
"Face of Poverty," 186–88
Face-work, 11–12
Facial expression, 5, 11–12, 239,
    340
Family Life in America, 393–94
Faulkner, William, 326–27
Fear, portraying, 11, 39, 48
"Feeling into," 19
"Feeling-tones," 13
Feelings. *See* emotional content
Feet, poetic, 201
Ferlinghetti, Lawrence, 13–14
Figures of speech, 7–8, 190–96
First-person point of view, 104–5
Flavor values, 40, 64
"Flight," 17
Focal point and multiple
    characters, 115–17, 154–55
Focus, in ensemble interpretation,
    335–37, 356, 362
"For My People," 22–24
Force, vocal, 43–44
Ford, Corey, 121–23
"Fox and Swan," 82
Frank, Anne, 315–16
Frequency level, vocal, 45

G

Geiger, Don, 213–15
Gender
    in children's literature, 230,
      234–35
    of narrator, 111
"Gentle Communion," 218–19
Gesner, Clark, 362–63
Gesture, 5, 9–10
"Gettysburg Address, The," 326
Ghost, The, 160–62
Gibbs, Angelica, 124–26
Giovanni, Nikki, 44–45
"Goblin Market," 197–98
"God-Seeker, The," 112
Gomringer, Eugen, 355
Good Woman of Setzuan, The,
    337
Grapes of Wrath, The, 24–25
Greek drama, 156–59
Grimm, Brothers
    "Bremen Town Musicians,
      The," 247–49
    *Cat and the Mouse
      Together, The,* 357–60
Gromyko, Anatolii Andreievich,
    308–10
Group interpretation. *See*
    ensemble interpretation
Growing Up, 130–31
"Guitarist Tunes Up, The," 191
Gustafson, Ingemar, 281
Gustatory sense, 63–64, 84

ensemble interpretation, 341–55
   figures of speech, 190–96
   hyperbole, 193–94
   imagery, 188–89
   irony, 195
   metaphor, 191–92
   paradox and oxymoron, 194–95
   personification, 192–93
   rhyme, 198–99
   rhythm, 200–210
   simile, 190
   sound tools, 197–200
   types, 210–15
Point of view
   in biography and autobiography, 306
   choosing, 107–8
   first-person, 104–5
   objective *versus* subjective, 106
   shifting, 108–10
   third-person, 105–8
Posture, 5, 10–11
Power, portraying, 48
Preconceptions, avoiding, 57, 308
"Preface to a Twenty Volume Suicide Note," 222
"Premature Burial, The," 18
Present tense, 133
Presentational staging, 334
Primary sense appeals, 86, 190
Programs, organizing, 371–89
   choosing materials, 372–73
   ensemble programs, 384–89
   introductions, 372–73
   solo programs, 371–83
   transitions, 382–83
Projection
   emotional, 15–16, 19
   vocal, 313
Projectors, incorporating, 340, 383
Protagonist, 141
Public speeches, 283–94
Pulse, poetic, 39, 205
Punctuation, oral, 42
Pygmalion, 142–43

R

Raisin in the Sun, A, 144–46
Rap music, 201
"Rat's Daughter, The," 256–58
"Raven, The," 203
Readers theater, 361–66
Reading rate, 36
Reagan, Ronald, 291–93
Realism style in drama, 168–71
Red Badge of Courage, The, 85
Red Jacket (Sagoyewatha), 290–91
Relationship level of meaning, 31
Remembered action, 147
Remoteness, portraying, 48

Report level of meaning, 31
Resolution, dramatic, 141
Respecting the text
   avoiding exaggeration, 204–5
   avoiding preconceptions, 57, 308
   in gesture, 10
   in voice, 52
Revolution from Within, 327–28
Rhyme, 198–99
Rhythm, 200–206
"Rich Man and the Poor Man, The," 249–51
"Richard Cory," 222–23
Riders to the Sea, 138–39
Rivals, The, 364–66
Robinson, Edwin Arlington, 222–23
Robinson, Roxana, 321–23
Roethke, Theodore, 54
Roman drama, 160–62
Romero, José Alejandro, 27–29
Roots, 73
Rossetti, Christina, 197–98
Roughness, portraying, 48

S

Sadness, portraying, 39
Sagoyewatha (Red Jacket), 290–91
Saint-Exupéry, Antoine de, 236–38
Salter, Mary Jo, 223–24
Sandbox, The, 171–72
Sandburg, Carl
   "Buffalo Dusk," 350–51
   "Cool Tombs," 369
   "Death Snips Proud Men," 369
   "Jazz Fantasia," 46
Scene, portraying, 112
Secondary sense appeals, 86, 190
Secret Garden, The, 234–47
Seduction, portraying, 48
Sense memory, 16, 57–70
Senses
   appeals to, 77, 190
   hearing, 57–59
   and imagery, 83–84, 86, 188–89
   importance in performance, 57, 71
   interrelationship of, 63, 86
   kinesthetic, 67–69, 84
   sight, 60–61, 66–67
   smell, 61–62, 84
   taste, 63–64, 84
   touch, 65–66, 84
Sensory showing, 15–16
Sentient center, 105, 108
Sequential speaking, 348–50
Serenity, portraying, 39
Seriousness, portraying, 39
"Serves You Right, Beggar," 274
Setting
   description, 80–81, 82–83

in drama, 155
in narrative prose, 103
Shakespeare, William
   Hamlet, 166
   King Lear, 41
   Macbeth, 49–50, 167
   Midsummer Night's Dream, A, 176–77
   Sonnet 27, 184–85
   Sonnet 73, 202
Shaw, George Bernard, 142–43
Shelley, Percy Bysshe, 185–86
Sheridan, Richard Brinsley, 364–66
Shifting point of view, 108–10
"Shiloh," 15
"Sick," 245–46
Sight, sense of, 60–61, 66–67, 84
Silence, using, 41–42, 206
"Silver," 40
Silverstein, Shel, 245–46
Simile, 190
Simon, Neil, 152–54
Slides, incorporating, 340, 383
"Slipping Beauty," 114
"Slow but Sure," 105
Smell, sense of, 61–62, 84
Smith, Lucy, 186–88
"Snake Dance," 121–23
"Sniper, The," 127–30
"Soap and Water," 113
Soliloquies, 165
Solo programs, 371–83
Sonnet 27, 184–85
Sonnet 73, 202
Sonnet form, 202, 210
"Sorrow-Acre," 83
Sound, sense of, 57–59
Sounds
   duration, 40
   experiencing, 57–59
   poetic uses of, 197–200
   recorded, incorporating, 340
   tempo, 206–10
   vocal, 31–36
Soyinka, Wole, 267–68
Speaking tempo, 36, 39
Speech intelligibility, 34
Speeches, public, 283–94
"Splendor Falls, The," 199–200
"Spring and Fall: To a Young Child," 219–20
Stage directions, 146–47, 155
Staging
   multimedia, 340, 383
   positioning, 338–40, 348
Stance, 5
"Status Symbol," 220–21
Steinbeck, John
   "Flight," 17
   Grapes of Wrath, The, 24–25
Steinem, Gloria, 327–28
Strength, portraying, 10
Stress, portraying, 10
Strindberg, August, 148–52
Stronger, The, 148–52
Stupidity, portraying, 48